❧ Analysing Historical Narratives ☙

MAKING SENSE OF HISTORY
Studies in Historical Cultures
General Editor: Stefan Berger
Founding Editor: Jörn Rüsen

Bridging the gap between historical theory and the study of historical memory, this series crosses the boundaries between both academic disciplines and cultural, social, political and historical contexts. In an age of rapid globalization, which tends to manifest itself on an economic and political level, locating the cultural practices involved in generating its underlying historical sense is an increasingly urgent task.

Recent volumes:

Volume 40
Analysing Historical Narratives: On Academic, Popular and Educational Framings of the Past
    Edited by Stefan Berger, Nicola Brauch and Chris Lorenz

Volume 39
Postwar Soldiers: Historical Controversies and West German Democratization, 1945–1955
    Jörg Echternkamp

Volume 38
Constructing Industrial Pasts: Heritage, Historical Culture and Identity in Regions Undergoing Structural Economic Transformation
    Edited by Stefan Berger

Volume 37
The Engaged Historian: Perspectives on the Intersections of Politics, Activism and the Historical Profession
    Edited by Stefan Berger

Volume 36
Contemplating Historical Consciousness: Notes from the Field
    Edited by Anna Clark and Carla L. Peck

Volume 35
Empathy and History: Historical Understanding in Re-enactment, Hermeneutics and Education
    Tyson Retz

Volume 34
The Ethos of History: Time and Responsibility
    Edited by Stefan Helgesson and Jayne Svenungsson

Volume 33
History and Belonging: Representations of the Past in Contemporary European Politics
    Edited by Stefan Berger and Caner Tekin

Volume 32
Making Nordic Historiography: Connections, Tensions and Methodology, 1850–1970
    Edited by Pertti Haapala, Marja Jalava and Simon Larsson

Volume 31
Contesting Deregulation: Debates, Practices and Developments in the West since the 1970s
    Edited by Knud Andresen and Stefan Müller

For a full volume listing, please see the series page on our website:
http://www.berghahnbooks.com/series/making-sense-of-history

Analysing Historical Narratives

On Academic, Popular and Educational Framings of the Past

Edited by Stefan Berger, Nicola Brauch and Chris Lorenz

berghahn
NEW YORK • OXFORD
www.berghahnbooks.com

First published in 2021 by
Berghahn Books
www.berghahnbooks.com

© 2021, 2025 Stefan Berger, Nicola Brauch and Chris Lorenz
First paperback edition published in 2025

All rights reserved. Except for the quotation of short passages
for the purposes of criticism and review, no part of this book
may be reproduced in any form or by any means, electronic or
mechanical, including photocopying, recording, or any information
storage and retrieval system now known or to be invented,
without written permission of the publisher.

Library of Congress Cataloging-in-Publication Data

Names: Berger, Stefan, editor. | Brauch, Nicola, editor. | Lorenz, Chris, 1950- editor.
Title: Analysing historical narratives : on academic, popular and educational framings of the past / edited by Stefan Berger, Nicola Brauch and Chris Lorenz.
Other titles: On academic, popular and educational framings of the past
Description: New York : Berghahn Books, 2021. | Series: Making sense of history; 40 | Includes bibliographical references and index.
Identifiers: LCCN 2020052239 (print) | LCCN 2020052240 (ebook) | ISBN 9781800730465 (hardback) | ISBN 9781800730472 (ebook)
Subjects: LCSH: Historiography. | History--Methodology.
Classification: LCC D13 .A6325 2021 (print) | LCC D13 (ebook) | DDC 907.2--dc23
LC record available at https://lccn.loc.gov/2020052239
LC ebook record available at https://lccn.loc.gov/2020052240

British Library Cataloguing in Publication Data
A catalogue record for this book is available from the British Library

ISBN 978-1-80073-046-5 hardback
ISBN 978-1-80539-738-0 paperback
ISBN 978-1-80539-918-6 epub
ISBN 978-1-80073-047-2 web pdf

https://doi.org/10.3167/9781800730465

Contents

List of Illustrations	vii
Acknowledgements	ix
Narrativity and Historical Writing: Introductory Remarks *Chris Lorenz, Stefan Berger and Nicola Brauch*	1

Part I. Professional History Writing

Chapter 1. Thucydides' History of the Vanquished: Death, Narrative Gazes and Historical Time — 29
Alexandra Lianeri

Chapter 2. History beyond Narration: The Shifting Terrain of *Bloodlands* — 51
Wulf Kansteiner

Chapter 3. Secularization Narratives in 1950s Europe: Sources, Characteristics and Effects — 83
Herman Paul

Chapter 4. Narratives of Global History: Expounding Global Interconnections — 99
Gabriele Lingelbach

Part II. School Textbooks in History

Chapter 5. More Than Just Barbarians: The Two-Faced Narrative of Ancient Persia in German Textbooks since 1900 — 117
Björn Onken

Chapter 6. Historicizing Present-Day European Societies by
Telling Medieval (Hi)Story in Schoolbooks   131
Daniel Wimmer

Chapter 7. Narrative Structure of High School World History
Textbooks in Postwar Japan   147
Naoki Odanaka

Chapter 8. Historical Maps as Narratives: Anchoring the Nation in
History Textbooks   164
Everardo Perez-Manjarrez and Mario Carretero

Part III. Histories in Various Media

Chapter 9. Social Media and Multimodal Historical
Representation: Depicting Auschwitz on Instagram   191
Robbert-Jan Adriaansen

Chapter 10. The Civil Rights Movement (Re)Narrated   209
Kenan Van de Mieroop

Chapter 11. Media Narratives of 1970s Left-Wing Terrorism   223
Jörg Requate

Chapter 12. Time Travel as Running around in Circles: The
Popular Historical Novel and the Sense of Historicity in Today's
Society   240
Daniel Fulda

Part IV. National Histories

Chapter 13. National Narratives in Chinese Global History Writing   259
Xupeng Zhang

Chapter 14. Narratives of Brazilian History: From Liberal to
Politically Incorrect   282
Valdei Araujo

Chapter 15. Changing LUK: Nation and Narration in the First and
the Third Editions of *Life in the United Kingdom*   304
Arthur Chapman

Analysing Historical Narratives: Concluding Remarks   327
Stefan Berger and Chris Lorenz

Index   347

Illustrations

Figures

Figure 8.1a–c	Historical maps of Mexico sketched under contemporary demarcation: (a) The three cultural areas of 'Ancient Mexico', (b) Areas of Mesoamerica and (c) Main Indigenous and African rebellions in the New Spain.	172
Figure 10.1	'Dream', 2017.	211
Figure 12.1	'Continuation of Reality by Other Means'. Picture taken from the front page of the *Frankfurter Allgemeine Zeitung* (3 November 2009).	249
Figure 14.1	Main sources of historical narratives.	284
Figure 14.2	The feudal to commercial master narrative.	288
Figure 14.3	The conflict between govern and liberty master narrative.	292
Figure 14.4	The providential master narrative.	295
Figure 15.1	The first and the third editions' history chapters compared: distribution of content between time periods, stated in percentages.	310
Figure 15.2	The first and the third editions' history chapters compared: differences in the incidence of participants in the roles of 'Actor' and 'Acted-upon', and their location before and after verbs in the two the narratives, stated as percentage differences.	314
Figure 15.3	The first and the third editions' history chapters compared: differences in the incidence of processes	

	by process type (e.g. mental, material) in the two narratives, stated as percentage differences.	316
Figure 15.4	The first and the third editions' history chapters compared: differences in the incidence of circumstances by circumstance type (e.g. temporal, spatial) in the two narratives, stated as percentage differences.	318

Tables

Table 2.1	Numbering Nazi and Soviet victims in the bloodlands.	70
Table 2.2	Chronological sequence of crimes in the bloodlands.	71
Table 8.1	Historical maps distribution by frequency, topic and temporality.	175
Table 9.1	Frequency count of top ten Instagram filters posted to the location tag 'Auschwitz Memorial / Muzeum Auschwitz'.	197
Table 9.2	Top ten used hashtags according to frequency (case insensitive).	200
Table 9.3	Hashtag communities based on modularity, minimum degree of 156. Top ten nodes per community, sorted by eigenvector centrality.	201
Table 15.1	The first and the third editions' history chapters compared: chapter titles, and the distribution of content by word count.	309
Table 15.2	The first and the third editions' history chapters compared: the incidence of subsection headings coded under content categories.	311
Table 15.3	Narrative Types prevalent in the history chapters of the first and third editions of *LUK*.	319

Acknowledgements

This volume is a result of the long-standing engagement of the three editors with historical narratives. Nicola Brauch has dealt with the narrative structure of texts produced within the field of historical didactics, whereas Chris Lorenz has reflected on the debate on narrative in historical theory. He and Stefan Berger have a long-standing cooperation in examining historical narratives produced within national historiographies that go back to the research programme 'National Histories in Modern Europe', which was funded by the European Science Foundation between 2003 and 2008. They co-edited three collected volumes in this project. Nicola Brauch and Stefan Berger have intensified their cooperation since 2010, when both found themselves direct colleagues at Ruhr-University Bochum. In Bochum they were joined by Chris Lorenz, who came as a Marie-Curie / Gerda Henkel Fellow in 2014–15, and after became an international research fellow at the Institute for Social Movements (ISB).

The foundation of this volume was built at the conference 'Analysing Historical Narratives', which took place in Bochum in 2016. We would like to thank the Fritz Thyssen Foundation for funding the conference. We would also like to thank our authors for working with us during the following five years to create the present volume. We hope that this volume will be of interest to all who are reflecting on historical narratives in teaching, research, historical theory and the history of historiography. It is in no way meant as a comprehensive treatment of the subject area. Rather we present a range of case studies in the hope that they might inspire others to analyse the ways in which the narrative framings of history actually work.

The Editors
Bochum, March 2021

Narrativity and Historical Writing
Introductory Remarks

Chris Lorenz, Stefan Berger and Nicola Brauch

Historical Theory and the Issue of Narrative

Although many historians since the eighteenth century have occasionally asked and answered the question whether history can or should be called a 'science' or whether it belongs to the arts or to literature, 'the question of narrative' or 'narrativity' as such was only put explicitly on the table as a philosophical issue concerning history in 1965, with the publication of Arthur Danto's path-breaking *Analytical Philosophy of History*. This observation is not meant to deny or to relativize the *Methodenstreit* that has accompanied history as a discipline since its institutional origins, in which one side had emphatically claimed the autonomy of the *Geisteswissenschaften* vis-à-vis the natural sciences – and since the second half of the nineteenth century also vis-à-vis the social sciences.[1] Until the 1960s, however, the 'autonomy of historical understanding' (Louis Mink) had not been claimed in the name of its 'narrative' character.[2] Between then and now the discussion about 'the narrative character of history' has branched out exponentially – especially since the publication of Hayden White's modern classic *Metahistory* in 1973. As the debate about narrative simultaneously spread to many other disciplines – in particular to departments of (comparative) literature and later also to history didactics[3] – the result has been that although the word

Notes for this section begin on page 18.

'narrative' has remained the same over the years, the concepts of narrative have not.[4] As Paul Roth remarked in 2017, 'Although historians and others unapologetically use narratives to explain, as a category narrative explanations exist in a philosophical limbo'.[5]

Luckily, narrative has kept a core meaning that has remained stable through all the changes in time, that is 'the representation of a set of chronologically and logically connected events' ... 'Although there is discussion as to the boundaries of the phenomenon referred to as "narrative", the combination of a "set of events" (what can loosely be called plot) and "representation" (the use of some medium) seems to be common to all definitions'.[6] The term 'narrative' came to be used as 'the umbrella term to talk about representations of connected events in a way that was specific neither to particular genres (for example, journalism, novels, history) nor to particular media (the spoken and the written word, film, drama) and that was in principle indifferent to ontological status'.[7] In short, whether the events were real or fictional was irrelevant for the notion of narrative as such, although this difference is – obviously – constitutive for history as a scholarly discipline. As a consequence, *historical* narratives did not show up as a subspecies of narrative in the handbooks of what came to be known as 'narratology'.[8]

The famous exemption to this rule was Roland Barthes, who published his fundamental essay 'The Discourse of History' in 1967 as an application of semiotic analysis to historical writing. Barthes noted that normal historical discourse suppresses the voice of the narrator completely and thus claims 'objectivity'. Historical writing thus presupposes the all-knowing narrator, just like the realist novel. White later acknowledged his debt to Barthes.[9]

The emergence of the term 'narratology' is directly connected to the rise of a new interdisciplinary subject of the same name within cultural studies. The discussions on narrative among historians have 'intersected at points with those in narratology or "narrative theory" as it later was known. But by and large, debates among historians have taken place independently and been shaped by specifically disciplinary concerns'.[10] While narratologists overwhelmingly focused on questions of narrative strategies unrelated to the issue of truth, historical theorists mainly focused on the epistemological status of narrative as a form of explanation.[11]

Given this background, a lot of ink – if not most of it – has been spilt by historians and historical theorists in debating the borderlines between fact and fiction in history, and the connected question in what way(s) historical narratives can be said to explain the past that they describe – an issue that has regained a new and more general urgency ever since Donald Trump launched his pet word 'fake-news'.[12] This discursive constellation was a consequence of the circumstance that Hayden White played a major role in the debate from the 1970s and that he routinely liked to provoke historians by telling them that they, just like novelists, were 'fictionalizing' events when they configured them in the form of plots in narratives, thus intentionally blurring the borderline between fiction and fact. The fundamental point that events do not dictate how they are represented by historians allowed historians to emplot them and explain them as they liked, White argued.[13] So just like the *enfant terrible* of the philosophy of science in the 1970s, Paul Feyerabend, White's message was that, also in history, almost 'anything goes'.[14] The historian's choice for one narrative type of plot (comedy or romance, for instance) over another (tragedy or satire, for instance) is guided by her *aesthetic* and/or *political* preferences and not by epistemological criteria, as most historians were inclined to think. The same goes for the ways in which historians explain events by other means than by emplotment: whether they adduce causes and laws ('mechanicism' in White's terminology) or relate events to bigger wholes ('organicism' and 'contextualism' in White's terminology) in order to make them comprehensible, is also purely a matter of individual choice according to White.

The basic argument of White's provocative 'wake-up call' addressed to the historical profession was as fundamental as it was simple: when historians leave their archives and compose their factual, research-based findings into narratives (their 'representation'), they inevitably 'emplot' them – that is, they establish their meaning by constructing their 'plot', which always implies a beginning, a middle and an ending. But these 'plots', with their implied beginnings, middles and endings, cannot be found in reality, nor in what is left of the history in the archives. Therefore, the 'plotted' narratives of historians are never based on historical facts. History, as Louis Mink had already argued before White, is not an 'untold story' waiting to be 'retold' by historians. Therefore, narrativity is not a property of historical events themselves, but only of the way historians represent them.[15] And because – and as far as – narrating is 'plotting', according to White's famous phrasing, writing history is a fundamental 'poetic' activity: it is only regulated by the rules and conventions of literature and not held in check by any 'historical method'. So much for White's basic argument concerning the inescapable 'narrativity' of history and 'the fiction of factual representation'.[16]

White's narrativist arguments were neither welcomed by 'traditional' political and diplomatic historians in the 1970s and 1980s – for the obvious reason that they were under attack – nor by their challengers from social history, who from the 1960s drew their inspiration from the French Annales school. In this school, 'narrative' history was identified with the old-fashioned 'Great Men' and 'wars and battles' type of history, in which historians presented the events in their presumed chronological order. Instead of the 'superficial' *l'histoire evenementielle* the Annales school propagated and practised *l'histoire structurelle*, which aimed at discovering and reconstructing the 'deeper' (socio-economic, demographic and geographic) structures hidden behind the 'surface' of (political) events. In order to uncover and analyse these structures, historians needed to use the quantitative methods and the theoretical tools of the social sciences. In fact, in order to gain *any* scientific credentials, history needed to leave its traditional narrative forms of representation behind and transform itself into a social science according to the new gospel that was spreading from Paris over the rest of the world.[17]

The arguments of White, and later of like-minded historical theorists like Frank Ankersmit and Keith Jenkins, were squarely directed against all claims that history should become a 'social science'.[18] The major question in the debates of historical theory therefore became the following: if narrative indeed means 'plotting' and in this literary sense means 'fictionalizing', how can narrative history then be seen as a proper and autonomous form of knowledge? How can the constitutive claim of history since antiquity that historical narrative is 'true' and 'objective/unpartisan' in some meaningful sense – in contrast to all fictional narrative genres – be philosophically elucidated and vindicated? It was this direct connection between the question of narrative in history and the epistemological status of history as a discipline – that is, history's claim to some notion of truth and objectivity – that explains why the question of narrative came with high stakes in history and in historical theory.[19] It also explains why White's plea to abandon epistemology and to embrace epistemological anarchism with a good conscience, as Feyerabend was doing in the philosophy of science, was not initially applauded by most historians and historical theorists.[20] Even when many historians may have supported White's central message that writing narratives in history bears significant – formal – similarities to writing fictional narratives both in terms of constructing beginnings, middles and endings and in terms of constructing a plot, they simultaneously emphasized that writing history implied a claim to truth and objectivity that fictional narratives did not. As long as the question regarding history was phrased in terms of 'fiction or fact?' (alias 'narrative or knowledge?') most chose the latter horn of the dilemma. One may even hypothesize that the absence of an elucidation of the 'reality claim' of history in White's work has blinded most historians for a long time concerning the innovative narratological potential of White's approach to historical texts – as this volume hopefully exemplifies.

However this may be, the fundamental provocation of White's work has forced his many critics to reflect on and to formulate the criteria that distinguish historical from fictional narratives. In this discussion it soon became apparent that cherishing disciplinary hunches concerning the 'reality claim' of history is one thing, but transforming these hunches into clear criteria is another. This leads us to recent developments in narrative theory of history, but before that we will first summarize what could be called 'the realist position' that emerged out of the various critiques of White that has emerged since the 1980s.[21]

The basic realist critique of White's version of narrativism pertains to the irreducible argumentative and social character of historical discussion – in contrast to literary fiction. No matter how rich rhetorical and literary *aspects* of historical narratives may be, historical scholarship cannot be *reduced* to that, as Paul Ricoeur, Jörn Rüsen and Lionel Gossman, among others, have emphasized when they underlined the rational and empirical character of writing history. Thus, Gossman argued:

> The way historians communicate with each other and criticize each other's work suggests that they indeed expect their colleagues to be able to recognize the force of contrary arguments and narratives to adjust their own accordingly – either by developing answers to these arguments or by revising their own. . . . Historians do apparently believe that there are procedures of verification and criteria for judging between different hypotheses and narratives.[22]

In the same vein, Jörn Rüsen in his long career has always argued that history, in contrast to fiction, must always meet controllable standards of 'empirical plausibility'.[23] Alan Megill and Deirdre McCloskey summarized this realistic line of critique as follows: 'Historians are not in the business of producing literary artefacts that stand isolated from the world. They do produce literary artefacts, but in doing so they also produce arguments intended to persuade particular audiences of the truth of particular statements'.[24]

This means that historical narratives tend to exist in argumentative contexts that prevent historians from just telling their own narrative of, for instance, the Renaissance, the French Revolution or the Holocaust, as if each one of them were alone in the world. Contrary to the narrativism of Ankersmit and White, there are three fundamental ways in which historical narrative is – intersubjectively – 'open', in theory at least. The Belgian historian Bart Verschaffel has argued why this 'openness' makes history writing a rational undertaking, meaning that historical argument is open to questions aimed at obtaining clarification and to criticism:

> First of all the subject is public. . . . An argument can never be the only possible or the only relevant argument about a subject. Other texts are possible on the same subject matter by definition. Different studies are not therefore only linked intertextually (through borrowings, citations, echoes or nods). They are also connected in their *object*. Second, the relevant evidence is public [in principle, at least].[25]

So – importantly – it is not for the individual author to determine what material is relevant to his or her subject: this is established by the community of researchers through public discussion.

Finally, the methodical nature of the argument means that it is subject to rules that the argument does not determine for itself. Members of the disciplinary community, in complete contrast with novelists or critics, basically have access to the process in which the ideas are developed. They can evaluate how terms are defined, how assertions are crystallized and how descriptions are pulled together into wholes.[26]

There are, of course, cases where evidence is available to some historians exclusively – as was the case with the historical commission that wrote the official Dutch history of the Srebrenica mass murder, for example – but this is clearly frowned upon by the wider academic community of historians, as it goes against the basic premises of the profession, as outlined by Verschaffel.[27]

It is in the rationality of historical scholarship based on this tripartite – intersubjective controllable – 'openness' that the fundamental limitations of narrativism as the philosophical elucidation of the discipline are exposed. While it is true that narrativism has done historians and historical theorists a great service in the rediscovery of the literary and rhetorical aspects of the discipline, following almost two centuries in which they were repressed and pushed aside as 'unscientific', the problem with White's and Ankersmit's formulations is that these components have tendentially been taken for the whole – as Paul Ricoeur also argued in his critique of White.[28] The task of historical theory, however, is to avoid the devilish dilemma of 'narrative *or* knowledge' – a dilemma that was a consequence of the usual yet inaccurate identification of narrative and fiction – and to elucidate in which ways epistemological criteria are working in historical practice and discussion. Therefore, it is no wonder that the recent further development of narrativism by Matti-Jouni Kuukkanen, who emphasizes the essentially open and argumentative character of history writing, is taking place under the label of '*post*-narrativism'.[29]

Postnarrativism and the Issue of Narrative in Historical Theory

Postnarrativism has broken with the commonsensical idea that historical narratives can somehow *re*present 'historical reality' – as White and Ankersmit still do – because 'historical reality' is only constructed by historical arguments. Therefore postnarrativism is a variety of *non*-representationalism, which has broken with the idea that historians are striving to develop texts (or other media) that somehow *re*present a past that existed *outside* their research-based arguments: 'historical' reality in the non-representationalist view only enters a – discursive – existence when historians retrospectively 'label' a complex of heterogeneous events in the past – as, for example, 'Class Struggle in Antiquity', 'The Rise of the Gentry', 'The Thirty Years War', 'America's Century' or 'Bloodlands'. The historical past thus never existed as a present for its contemporaries (just as the future as imagined now will never be a present for its contemporaries in the future) and therefore 'the past' cannot be *re*-presented). Eugen Zelenak has aptly characterized the distinction between representationalism and non-representationalism as follows: 'It is possible to distinguish two general views of historical works within the philosophy of history. Proponents of representationalism maintain that historical works are primarily representations. Advocates of non-representationalism argue that historical works are not representations but rather the outcomes of specific practices'.[30] According to Kuukkanen and other non-representationalists like Paul Roth, what historians do in practice is present arguments that are evidence-based and that bolster a point of view that claims (1) to be explaining the evidence in a rhetorical way *ex post* (like White suggested with his four modes of emplotment), and (2) to be epistemologically superior to other points of view concerning a topic and a body of evidence at a particular moment (as White had explicitly denied by stating that the historians' choice for a point of view is of an aesthetic and/or a political character).

In short, according to postnarrativism, history writing essentially consists of 'colligating' heterogeneous events into complex holes (which was the main point of White's and Ankersmit's narrativism against the previous analytical approaches in philosophy of history, which focused on the 'atomic' level of singular statements in historical narratives, like in Danto's *Analytical Philosophy of History*). At the same time, however, postnarrativism rejects the narrativist claim that colligation is *not* guided by epistemic criteria (epistemic rationality) and that every sentence in a narrative is an essential part of it (which is 'narrative holism', as defended by Ankersmit).[31] Instead, according to postnarrativism, historical arguments are always directed at other historical arguments and are therefore located in a particular discussion and relative to a particular moment in time. Every historical argument is thus connected to a specific present, and therefore the only way to judge historical arguments is 'presentist'.[32]

Allan Megill and Deirdre McCloskey had reached similar conclusions earlier on when they argued: 'The need is not to abandon epistemological standards. These too are part of the discipline and of its conversation. They mark out a successful attempt to make history, like science, cumulative. Yet at the same time they create an obstacle. History that tries to do without rhetoric loses its contact with the wider conversation of mankind'.[33] This conclusion leads to two recent proposals of historical theorists – Kalle Philainen and Marek Tamm – how to solve the problem that White had put squarely on the historians table: how to conceive of historical representations as both knowledge – so based on the regulative ideas of truth and objectivity – and narrative.

This does not imply the claim that historical representation is necessarily narrative, because especially in the domain of digital history non-narrative forms of representation are increasingly being used, as Rigney observes. As a consequence of the rise of the new media there has been

> a shift away from plot as a key feature of narratives to that of immersivity (digitisation having provided new technologies for evoking virtual worlds) and interactivity (digitisation having afforded new agency to users). Add to this the fact that the hypertextual organisation of information and the availability of visual materials are generating new forms of semantic organisation, and new possibilities for producers and users to link events in ways that seem quite far removed from the core definition of narrativity given earlier.[34]

These changes have as yet hardly been reflected philosophically in narrative theory, but the contribution of Adriaansen in this volume is dealing with them empirically and is taking us to the borders of narrativity. But truth be told, 'in the world of new media, the word narrative is often used . . . to cover up the fact that we have not yet developed a language to describe these strange new objects', as Lev Manovich remarks.[35]

The key to the solution that both Philainen and Tamm propose is derived from narratology because both suggest that the specificity of historical narratives can best be conceptualized as a 'factuality pact' – that is, a pact in terms of the relationship between historians and their public that allows readers to check that the events reported are real. The observation behind this proposal is that it has turned out to be impossible to define the claims to truth and objectivity of historical narratives explicitly in terms of 'text-immanent' characteristics – such as the 'correspondence' and the 'scope' of narrative in relationship to reality.[36]

In a number of publications Pihlainen has pointed out that although historical and fictional stories share the narrative form, just as White claimed, historical narratives are distinguished in principle by their claim to be true and their reference to a (past) reality *outside* the text – and Ricoeur, Megill and Rüsen have made the same point.[37] Because of this, the historian's 'communicative act' is fundamentally different from that of the novelist. Historians have a commitment to reality and are bound by conventions to reflect this.[38] They share this with their readers. Because of the commitment to reality, from a textual perspective the historical narrative is a fundamentally 'disturbed' narrative in comparison with fictional texts (see Daniel Fulda's contribution in this volume). It is not a pure 'literary artifact', which has no necessary 'external' relationships: 'In addition to intending at communication, the historical text also intends at reality, at *discovery* rather than simply creation'.[39]

This distinction also involves a different 'ontological commitment' of historical and fictional narratives, in their intertextual relations and in the relationship between the author and her readers. This is because there is an entirely different pact for the historical text than for the fictional text:

The pact between the reader and the author reserves certain literary devices as referring to extra-textual evidence. The most obvious of such devices is quotation. Dialogue that is presented directly in the text is marked as opening up on the extra-textual through a system of notations demonstrating its origin. Yet this is something that also happens in fiction where speech is attributed to particular characters. The difference here, then, is obviously not textual despite the divergence between the means for indicating origin.[40]

The difference is not effected directly in the text but by reference to sources, which represent the link with the reality outside the text: 'Historical narratives present references and evidence with an eye on the validation of the truth of the account they offer . . . Truth-creation in historical narratives is not a textual feature but is based on a shared understanding between the author and reader concerning the legitimacy of interpretation and the epistemological standing of acceptable evidence'.[41] The claim to truth and objectivity must, therefore, be localized in the communicative relationship between historians and their public, and not in the historical text itself, according to Pihlainen.

A similar line of argument has recently been advanced by Marek Tamm, who uses Searle's theory of *speech acts* to analyse the pragmatic 'truth pact' between historians and their readership.[42] Historical truth is conceived by Tamm as an *intentional* category that is based on a pragmatic and communicative pact between the historians and their readers:

> Every historian has to make a kind of 'truth pact' with his addressees, asserting, more often implicitly than explicitly, that it is his intention to tell the truth. Needless to say, this commitment rarely takes such an abrupt and total form; it is, rather, an implicit pact of honesty or a declaration of his intention to confine himself to the truth bound to the evidence and disciplinary practices, as well as an explicit indication of the field to which this oath applies. However, it is extremely important that this 'pact' be sincere and serious, not part of the game we can often witness in the case of fiction.[43]

Tamm points out that the 'truth pact' between historians and their readers is very similar to the class of *speech acts* that Searle analysed as 'illocutionary assertives': 'In order to explain an assertive illocutionary act, Searle writes: "The point or purpose of the members of the assertive class is to commit the speaker (in varying degrees) to something's being the case, to the truth of the expressed proposition"'.[44] Searle identified the following characteristics for this type of speech act:

1. The essential rule: the maker of an assertion commits himself to the truth of the expressed proposition.
2. The preparatory rules: the speaker must be in a position to provide evidence or reasons for the truth of the expressed proposition.

3. The expressed proposition must not be obviously true to both the speaker and the hearer in the context of utterance.
4. The sincerity rule: the speaker commits himself to a belief in the truth of the expressed proposition.[45]

These four rules only specify the necessary conditions, but not the sufficient conditions, to be able to speak of the historian's claim to historical truth and objectivity. In our fallible universe, something – or almost everything – may go wrong in practice.

Like Pihlainen, Tamm sees the presence of footnotes as an essential textual feature of historical narratives, through which their referentiality and claim to truth take shape.[46] In addition, Tamm mentions quotations, the bibliography, tables and illustrations as clear 'signals of factuality' in historical narratives – even though these 'signals' are only picked up by readers who know in advance that they are dealing with a historical text.[47]

Tamm then takes objectivity to mean the relative quality of the discussions in academic disciplines, such as can be established on the basis of the quality criteria specific to that discipline. The pragmatic view of objectivity can then be expressed as follows:

> While traditionally the truth of the historian's statements has been often linked to their correspondence to historical reality, the pragmatist viewpoint considers it impossible to check any such correspondence since it is only the historian's claim, not a provable fact. In pragmatist terms, the historian's truth intent is based not on its direct relation with reality but is mediated in various ways and based on a disciplinary consensus as to methods of inquiry, cognitive values and epistemic virtues. The 'truth pact' is made reliable and checkable primarily by what might be called the regulative ideal of objectivity.[48]

Finally, Tamm stresses that the epistemic virtues do not allow themselves to be moulded into formal rules but nevertheless are essential to each discipline (as they form a constituent part of it).[49]

That this is so becomes obvious in cases where authors try to bend fundamental rules of a discipline. Writers who write fake autobiographies, for instance – such as 'Binjamin Wilkomirski' alias Bruno Dössekker with his initially highly praised 'Holocaust Testimony' *Brüchstücke. Aus einer Kindheit 1939–1948* (1996) – or those who deny the Holocaust – such as David Irving in *Hitler's War* (1977) – break the 'factuality pact' between the historian and the reader. In so doing they are not producing 'literary fiction' but fake or bullshit history – and this represents a fundamental difference.[50] The circumstance that factual statements are also fallible and in principle amenable to revision does not make them superfluous or suspect.

So, while narrativism in the versions of White and Ankersmit mobilized all philosophical attention to the historical narrative as a text, postnarrativism in the versions of Kuukkanen, Philainen and Tamm has brought the reality outside the text into play again. All in all, we can conclude retrospectively that the arguments derived from narratology, that were first introduced in the historical debate by White in order to question the strict borderlines between history and fiction, are now being used by Philainen and Tamm in order to restore these borderlines again through their adoption of the narratological notion of 'factuality pact'. Seen this way, paradoxically, narratology turns out to be both part of the problem of 'narrative in history' as well as part of its solution.

The Structure of the Volume

Overall, then, we have witnessed a wide range of debates surrounding narratives and the narrative nature of history-writing in historical theory (see above) and in history didactics.[51] However, we rarely had scholars examining concrete historical narratives asking about how historians had used narrative strategies in order to arrive at historical interpretations that include truth claims. Some exceptions only seem to confirm the rule. Philip Carrard, for example, subjected the history writing of the Annales school – which earlier on had declared 'narrative history' to be 'unscientific' – to a 'poetic' analysis inspired by White and Michel de Certeau. He argued that the Annales type of history-writing consists of a mix of narrative and non-narrative elements, like the description, the synchronic cross-section and the analysis (compare Wulf Kansteiner's chapter).[52] Norbert Frei and Wulf Kansteiner edited a volume discussing diverse narrative strategies of scholarly accounts of the Holocaust, out of which emerged the strong proposition that Saul Friedländer's masterpiece *The Years of Extermination* could only be written because the author had consciously broken with the narrative strategies of the realist novel, and had adopted non-linear strategies of the modernist novel.[53] Ann Rigney's book on the narratives of the French Revolution, and Jacques Ranciere's book *The Names of History*, are further outstanding examples of applying narrative theory to historical writing.[54]

Others have examined the role of narrative in the transition to and the development of scientific history. Daniel Fulda, for example, has analysed how modern German history writing in the eighteenth and early nineteenth century emerged out of aesthetic, poetic and narrative considerations.[55] In the context of the 'Writing the Nation' project that examined the writing of national histories in modern European history, several authors have explored the narrative structures and their emplotment in national histories.[56] With regard to popular histories, examinations of those popular forms of history writing have also at times highlighted the narrative structure of popular histories.[57]

Whilst, in sum, there have then been several attempts to analyse the narrative structure of historical texts, the number of actual explorations of how narrative strategies work in a variety of historical texts – or, how the narrative form conditions its content, to speak with White – until now has remained fairly limited.[58] So the diagnosis that Jerzy Topolski made in 1994, namely that 'White's rhetoric proposals and his analyses resulting from the same inspirations have not had, at least for the time being, any marked practical importance for professional historians', still seems to be largely valid at present[59] – at least with regard to narrative analyses of historical texts and in contrast to the enormous amount of discussions and critiques that his work has generated in the theory of history.

The current volume is an attempt to redress this remarkable imbalance between narrative theory and narrative research in history by furthering the actual study of emplotments and narrativity in a wide range of forms of history writing.[60] We have chosen to start our examination with 'scientific' accounts of history-writing, for they are often regarded as the ones following most directly the claims to truth and objectivity referred to above. Taking examples from ancient history as well as the history of the twentieth century, readers will observe in this part how all those scientific histories are guided by moral-political concerns that derive from the contemporary world inhabited by the historians. Alexandra Lianeri (Chapter 1) examines Thucydides' narration 'The Peloponnesian War', seeking his specific perspective on the defeat of the Athenians. Central to her argument is the entanglement of narrative gaze and historical temporality. Her main interest is in examining how Thucydides relates the past with the future. Thucydides, she argues, involves his readers by means of internal focalization. This narratological method lets the historical moment become 'visible' for the reader, who is at the same time confronted with how the contemporaries could never be certain about how future events would unfold. In this sense, Thucydides is not telling a history that holds lessons for the reader, nor does he try to persuade his readers that the future can be planned if only the contemporaries would know their history. Instead, by narrating a history of the vanquished (Athenians in this case), he conceptualizes an unforeseeable future as a force that lies beyond human cognitive capacities.

From ancient history we move to the history of the twentieth century, with Wulf Kansteiner's exploration of Timothy Snyder's *Bloodlands* (Chapter 2). Kansteiner's is an example of the benefits of applying insights from the linguistic turn to works of historical scholarship. A close textual analysis leads us to what Kansteiner describes as the 'inner workings' of Snyder's text, and the conclusion that the narrative purpose of the book has primarily to do with restoring the victims of Communism to equal status with those of the Holocaust. Many reading Kansteiner's text will hopefully be stimulated to reflect on their own practice as historians, and it is precisely such reflection that the volume as a whole wishes to engender in its readers.

Herman Paul (Chapter 3) looks at secularization narratives arguing that secularization was not just a theory, but a narrative that also circulated inside and outside the academic realm, affecting the ways in which scholars and non-scholars alike perceived religion. He calls for an expansion of the conventional focus on great thinkers and influential books in order to arrive at the 'narrative template'[61] of secularization, which had a deep impact on politics, culture, society and the everyday lives of people, including their understanding of the present and their predictions for the future. This is exemplified in relation to two specific examples of historical narrativizations of secularization from the 1950s.

In the final contribution to this part, Gabriele Lingelbach (Chapter 4) compares the way in which Donald Wright's history of Niumi and Giorgio Riello's history of cotton narrate the history of global interconnectedness. She underlines how global history as such has no distinct narrative pattern or preferred narrative form. Global histories oscillate widely between very different narrativizations of the global. The focus of her comparison is how different ways of relating global processes of transfer and exchange to regional and local processes lead to very different ways of narrativizing those histories. Wright's history is one that systematically introduces global developments first before asking about their impact on regional and local developments. Riello's, by contrast, constantly changes the spatial perspective moving between the local, the regional and the global, making his narrative more complex but also less clear. The latter is a more analytical and interpretative but also more abstract approach, whilst the former can narrate more freely. Wright's more concrete narrative form is also capable of incorporating more of an individual agency perspective, but at the same time it cannot systematize and generalize to the same extent as Riello's narrativization of the interaction between global, regional and local can. Thus, the latter is far better in working out structures that are at play in the interconnection between the global, the regional and the local. Overall, Lingelbach's chapter draws attention to how the narrativization of global histories is directly relevant for diverse interpretative and cognitive frameworks for the understanding between the global, the regional and the local.

In the second thematic part of the book, examples from history didactics take centre stage. Ranging widely across time and space, they emphasize on the one hand the strong influence of politics and of contemporary intellectual predilections on history textbooks, and on the other hand they highlight the proximity of textbook production with national imaginaries, even when the topic of the textbooks is no longer national. Björn Onken (Chapter 5) analyses how German history school textbooks deal with Persian history, first in narratives from ancient Persia, secondly in narratives dealing with the Islamic expansion in the Middle Ages, and thirdly in narratives related to Persia in confrontation with nineteenth-century imperialism. He argues that textbooks convey ambivalent narratives of the Persians in ancient history, orientalizing Persia to a great extent. This is also the tendency with narratives of the Islamic expansion, which are accompanied by critical evaluations of the relationship between religion and lack of tolerance. The narrative is complicated, however, for they also emphasize Persia and the Near East as the cradle of Western civilization. Old colonial representations are still present in colonial and imperial narratives dealing with the nineteenth century, although there is also today a much greater willingness by authors of Western textbooks to problematize the exploitation of the colonies and the crimes committed by the colonizers.

Daniel Wimmer (Chapter 6) examines narrativizations of the Middle Ages in attempts to construct spatial identities in the twenty-first century. He traces the diverse ways in which the Middle Ages still capture the imagination of twenty-first-century politicians. Focusing on narrativization of cultural encounters between Muslims and Christians in medieval times in school textbooks that were published between the 1970s and the 2000s, he traces the narrative building blocks that still influence many people's imaginary of the Middle Ages. His analysis is testimony to the power of long-lasting narrative structures focusing on medieval history and its actualizations for social, cultural and political purposes in present-day societies.

Naoki Odanaka (Chapter 7) analyses two specific Japanese world history school textbooks in the context of their production and reception history. Against the backdrop of the Japanese government's insistence that school textbooks must be both neutral and objective, Odanaka looks at the selection of materials and methodological presuppositions in world history textbooks. He shows how their respective narrative styles correspond to temporal and spatial understandings of the past that endow that past with very different meanings. How this is done corresponds closely to the social and intellectual environments in which the textbooks have been produced. Odanaka distinguishes between modernization narratives that remained dominant in Japan until the 1970s. However, when Japan finally seemed to have achieved the key aim under modernization (i.e. catching up and even possibly overtaking the West), modernization narratives were replaced by postmodern narratives that were far more sceptical towards the modernization paradigms.

Mario Carretero and Everardo Perez-Manjarrez (Chapter 8) outline how maps in school history textbooks often emphasize an essentializing narrative of national territory and nation-ness. Taking their examples from many different countries in Europe and the Americas, the authors argue that these maps strengthen the belief of high-school students in homogeneous unified nations sharing a timeless national identity that can be narrativized through heroic, teleological and moral storylines celebrating the idea and practice of nation.

The third part of this volume focuses on historical narratives in a variety of mass media, from Instagram, to e-cards and more traditional media like newspapers and popular historical novels. Robbert-Jan Adriaansen (Chapter 9) analyses historical narratives on Instagram arguing that social media generate their own distinct forms of narrating the past. Using examples from genocide heritage, the author argues that Instagram is an important medium through which young people are engaging with the past in an increasingly global way – one that transcends regional and national boundaries. Whilst this is often entirely different from formal environments of historical learning, such as school settings, we ignore these new forms of historical learning at our peril, as the new digital forms of communication challenge traditional narrative analysis simply by being so different in terms of form and context. The author gives many examples illustrating those differences, such as the use of hashtags, hyperlinks and the typical combination of visual and textual representations on Instagram.

Kenan van de Mieroop (Chapter 10) examines narratives of civil rights' activism that come from different individuals and groups in the United States. The civil rights movement is one of the most widely discussed and controversial subjects of American history. Both in scholarship and in popular culture, for example in electronic greeting cards, it is evident that different groups present different 'narratives' of the events that are related to different political outlooks. The author examines the narrative meanings inherent in some of these narratives of the civil rights movement. His semiotic analysis across different kinds of media offers critical insights into the diverse ways in which meaning is constructed through history and disseminated in contemporary society.

Jörg Requate (Chapter 11) investigates the narrativizations of 1970s left-wing terrorism in several media. Terrorist attacks, he argues, pose a particular challenge for mediatization: few events receive as much attention in the media as terrorist-related ones, not least as they provide many pictures of death and destruction that are highly marketable in the media. However, such visual narratives, Requate argues, work against understanding terrorism as communication, as they only capture the end point of a story that is not really explained otherwise. Hence such visual narrativizations decontextualize events, and do not provide historical understanding. Furthermore, media representations often carry a bias towards narratives constructed by the police, the legal profession, high politics, and scientific scholarship, depending on which narratives appear to be the most coherent and plausible to the journalists mediatizing them. In fact, the media have become, according to Requate, a major battlefield for different narratives on terrorism, all relying on diverse constructions of the past.

Daniel Fulda (Chapter 12) asks how contemporary media systems impact on the form of the popular historical novel – a genre that has seen a massive increase of sales figures since the 1980s. There is a literary market that thrives on 'realistic' narrations of the histories of colourful underdogs in history. By focusing on this popular segment of the market rather than high-brow literary works, Fulda shows how the past becomes a quarry for contemporary concerns that change rapidly and suit diverse political interests in contemporary society. He not only analyses the production of popular historical texts but also their reception among university students. As there are very few reception studies when it comes to the impact of particular forms of narrativization, this chapter is making a powerful plea for more such reception studies – a plea that is in line with the earlier observation that new forms of digital history are endowing the reader/viewer/player with unprecedented forms of agency.

The fourth and final part of the volume analyses historical narratives that have been prominent in national history writing. It considers in particular the interrelationship between national and transnational narratives in former empires and ethnocentric multinational states, such as China, Portugal and Britain. Xupeng Zhang (Chapter 13) investigates the national narratives present in Chinese global history writing that has been thriving in the country since the 2000s. On the one hand, this new boom in global history writing is a direct reaction to the criticism levied against traditional forms of world history that narrativized the world as a compilation of national histories. The new global history seeks to avoid the Eurocentrism that was a core ingredient of the old world history. On the other hand, global history reintroduces a national grand narrative for Chinese historians after the decline of the materialist concept of history, which once was regarded as the only grand narrative in China's historical studies. This new grand narrative contextualizes the Chinese nation in diverse eras of globalization ending up with the present day, when it arguably is becoming a leading world power in the latest era of globalization. The emphasis on China in fact combines national narratives with global ones. Zhang uses the example of Yu Pei, the former director of the Institute of World History at the Chinese Academy of Social Sciences, who argued that global history should indeed be rooted in one nation's special historical memory of globalizing processes. Zhang therefore asks whether the Chinese narrativizations of global history amount to a global history with Chinese characteristics. These global narratives would then not so much transcend national histories but complement them. And they might be used to demarcate a Chinese global history from its Western counterparts. Global Sinocentrism may in that sense replace global Eurocentrism.

Valdei Araujo (Chapter 14) examines early Brazilian national master narratives and the ways in which they constructed the nation through a differentiation between Brazil, Portugal and Europe. Araujo shows how constructions of democratization, ideologization and temporalization were crucial to the emergence of modern national narratives. These narratives facilitated and were a reaction to the independence processes that accompanied them. He also provides a fine example of a twenty-first-century retelling of the national master narrative in a presentist mode befitting the political turn away from the Workers' Party and towards more pro-capitalist forces in Brazil.

Finally, Arthur Chapman (Chapter 15) asks to what extent citizenship tests in Britain are constructing a particular national narrative through primers such as the Home Office's publication *Life in the United Kingdom* (*LUK*), which has gone through three editions (2004, 2007 and 2013), all of which included a dedicated 'history' chapter that amounts to an official history of Britain. By contextualizing *LUK*, Chapman explores, through grammatical analysis and an analysis of 'transitivity', the differences in the narrative strategies adopted by *LUK*'s history chapters over time, focusing, in particular, on its 2004 and 2013 iterations. He points to basic continuities on the macrolevel of these narrativizations of a national past. Key elements, such as the strong parliamentary tradition and the growing together of the four nations, or the absence of references to the labour movement, remain the same. However, on a micro-level of analysis, Chapman also notes striking differences in the 'grammar of narration', which incorporates subtle shifts in meaning that do not affect the story as a whole but do affect the way it is narrated.

Overall, the fifteen case studies that have been assembled in this volume underline the benefits of investigating, in Fulda's terminology, 'historiographic narrations'. The conclusion to this volume seeks to draw out some of the results that emerge from those case studies and to formulate an agenda for the future study of historical narratives that will hopefully contribute to an even greater self-reflexivity about historical writing among both practitioners and consumers of such historical narratives. Furthermore, it discusses the empirical analyses of historical narratives, which themselves have implications for historical theory.

Chris Lorenz was professor of historical theory at Leiden University and professor of German historical culture at VU University Amsterdam. Since 2016 he has been an international research associate at the Ruhr-University

Bochum. He has widely published on historical theory, historiography and on higher education. His publications include *De Constructie van het Verleden* (Boom, 2008, 9th.rev.edn); (ed.), *'If you're so smart why aren't you rich? Universiteit, Markt & Management* (Boom, 2008); (with co-editor Berber Bevernage), *Breaking Up Time: Negotiating the Borders between Present, Past and Future,* (Vandenhoeck, 2013) and *Entre Filosofía e Historia. Volumen 1: Exploraciones en Filosofía de la Historia,* and *Volumen 2: Exploraciones en Historiografía* (Prometeo Libros, 2015).

Stefan Berger is professor of social history at Ruhr-University Bochum, where he also directs the Institute for Social Movements and is executive chair of the Foundation History of the Ruhr. He is also an honorary professor at Cardiff University in the UK. He has published widely in the comparative history of social movements and labour movements, the history of deindustrialization and industrial heritage, nationalism and national identity studies, the history of historiography and historical theory. Among his most recent publications are *The Making of the New History: Historiographical Developments since the 1980s* (Cambridge University Press, 2021); *Writing History: Theory and Practice*, co-edited with Heiko Feldner and Kevin Passmore (3rd rev. edn, Bloomsbury, 2020); and *The Engaged Historian: Perspectives on the Intersections of Politics, Activism and the Historical Profession* (Berghahn Books, 2019).

Nicola Brauch is Professor of History Didactics/History Education for the History Department at Ruhr University Bochum since 2014. She has published in the field of history didactics. Among her recent publications are: '"The Debate Almost Came to a Fight . . .": Results of a Cross-National Explorative Study Concerning History Teachers' Shared Beliefs about Teaching Historical Sensitive Issues', published in *Pedagogy, Culture and Society* (co-authored with G. Leone and M. Sarrica, 2019), 'Didactics in Flux from a Mediterranean Perspective: The Nile's Potential for Upper Secondary History Education', published in *Mediterranean Rivers in Global Perspective* (edited by J. Bernhardt, M. Koller and A. Lichtenberger; Schöningh, 2019) and 'Bridging the Gap – Comparing History Curricula in History Teacher Education in Western Countries', published in *Palgrave Handbook of Research in Historical Culture and Education* (edited by M. Carretero, S. Berger and M. Grever; Palgrave Macmillan, 2017).

Notes

1. For an overview, see: Lorenz, 'History and Theory', 13–35.
2. See Mink, 'Autonomy of Historical Understanding'. Of course occasionally individual historians and philosophers have formulated some ideas about history and narrative, starting with the German Johann-Gustav Droysen (1808–1864) in his *Historik*. Also the Dutch historian Johan Huizinga (1872–1945) came close to defending a narrativistic view in his 1941 address 'Over vormverandering der geschiedenis' [On the change of form of history], but he did not develop a philosophical argument of his own, and just referred to the German neo-Kantian philosophers Rickert and Windelband.
3. Seixas, *Theorizing Historical Consciousness*.
4. Rigney, 'History as Text'. For recent overviews, see also: Carrard, 'History and Narrative'; Munslow, *Narrative and History*.
5. Roth, 'Essentially Narrative Explanations', 42; Roth 2020.
6. Rigney, 'History as Text', 184.
7. Ibid.
8. In the *Einführung in die Erzähltheorie* by Martinez and Scheffel, one of the most widely used textbooks on the subject in Germany, historical narratives only make their appearance in the last section of the last chapter. Moreover, this section only contains an uncritical summary of White's idea of 'emplotment'. Symptomatically, in the first chapter the authors make a distinction between 'factual narrative' and 'fictional narrative' without making a connection to historical narrative. Compare now, however, Fulda, 'Historiographic Narration'.
9. See also: Curthoys and Docker, 'Boundaries of History and Fiction'; Ranciere, *Names of History*.
10. Rigney, 'History as Text', 185. Cf. Bal, 'Point of Narratology', 727–53, which emphasizes the great variety of approaches in narratology, as Martinez and Scheffel do, and suggests that in the meantime the most interesting applications of narratological analysis can be found in fields outside text-oriented narratology, like anthropology, rhetoric, feminist studies and visual analysis.
11. Ann Rigney, Philippe Carrard and Lionel Gossman are three of the few exceptions among literary scholars who have shown a systematic interest in the relationship between fictional and historical narratives.
12. For an analysis and overview, see: Lorenz, 'Narrativism, Positivism'; Roth, 'Essentially Narrative Explanations'.
13. White, following Northrop Frye, distinguishes four types of plot: the romance, the satire, the comedy and the tragedy. In the – epic – romance, the hero struggles against evil and overcomes it: good triumphs over evil, light over darkness, and self-deliverance is the result. The romance offers the opportunity for identification. A prime example of this type of narrative is Michelet's history of the French Revolution, in which the French people are given the role of romantic hero. Satire is the opposite of romance: 'evil is not conquered and mankind remains the prisoner of meaningless finiteness'. In comedy there is no question of good overcoming evil entirely: there is hope for peace and quiet, when conflict is resolved through reconciliation. Ranke's depiction of the history of the European states is modelled on comedy. The plots of tragedy show the inevitable demise of the hero. However, the future is not entirely hopeless, as it is with satire. The audience or readers of a tragedy gain insight into the hard realities of life from the horrors presented to them, and 'sadder and wiser' are then able to face up to them. See: White, 'Introduction: The Poetics of History', in *Metahistory*, 1–43; White, 'Interpretation in History', in *Tropics of Discourse*, 51–80. For a nuanced contextualization and assessment of White's ideas of plotting, see: Paul, *Hayden White*, 57–82.
14. See especially Feyerabend, *Against Method*.

15. Rigney, 'History as Text', 199.

16. As Rigney, 'History as Text', 193, points out, White's treatment of emplotment is exclusively based on the nineteenth-century realist novel and does not deal with the modern twentieth-century novel. She criticizes this reduction as a 'one-size-fits-all approach to storytelling'. Carrard also argues against the idea that all history writing is narrative by specifying non-narrative textual strategies. Therefore he is pleading for a 'poetics' of history. See: Carrard, 'History and Narrative', 181–86, and 'Historiographic Discourse and Narratology', 140: 'Poetics . . . takes over when narratology leaves off, that is, when the latter toolbox is no longer appropriate, because the texts to be accounted for follow models that do not have a narrative structure'.

17. The historiography on the Annales is legion. See, for example, Burke, *French Historical Revolution*.

18. For Ankersmit's important role, see the Tamm and Zelenak Special Issue: 'Frank Ankersmit's Philosophy of History'. For Jenkins, see his *Rethinking History*.

19. In history didactics, Jörn Rüsen's *Historik* was and is influential as the theoretical foundation of teaching and learning history in school and society. See Rüsen, *Historik* and Brauch, 'Bridging the Gap'. In history didactics, 'narrativity' is the core aim of teaching history, now implemented globally in the history curricula of most schools.

20. 'Epistemological anarchism' was coined by the Austrian-born physicist and philosopher of science Paul Feyerabend (1924–1994), and implies the position that there is not a set of methodological rules in science that guarantees or explains the progress of knowledge. It boils down to the most radical formulation of methodological pluralism. Therefore, Feyerabend in *Against Method* claims to be just that – 'against method': methods only limit the creativity of practising scientists, and 'methodical rules' are therefore constantly broken in scientific practice, as the history of science amply illustrates.

21. Now also see Mitrovic, *Materialist Philosophy of History*.

22. Gossman, 'Rationality of History', 309 and 313, emphasis in original. Also see Martin Jay, 'Of Plots, Witnesses, and Judgements', 105: 'Another consideration also militates against the unfettered freedom of historians to narrativize arbitrarily, and this concerns the community of others that reads and judges their work. . . . It is not so much the subjective *imposition* of meaning, but rather the intersubjective *judgement* of meanings that matters'.

23. Rüsen, 'Rhetoric and Aesthetics'; and Rüsen, *Evidence and Meaning*. See also: Rüsen, *Historische Vernunft*; Rüsen, *Rekonstruktion der Vergangenheit*; Rüsen, *Historik*. For the wide reception of Rüsen's notion of 'empirical plausibility' in history didactics, see Seixas *Theorizing Historical Consciousness* and 'Model of Historical Thinking'; and Seixas and Peck, 'Teaching Historical Thinking'.

24. Megill and McCloskey, 'Rhetoric of History', 228.

25. Verschaffel, 'Geschiedschrijving', 96. Also see Mitrovic, *Materialist Philosophy of History*.

26. Ibid., 96.

27. See Blom et al., *Srebrenica*. For critical analyses of the Srebrenica report, see: Erna Rijsdijk, 'Reconstituting the Dutch State'; and Eelco Runia, 'Forget About It'.

28. Ricoeur, 'Geschichte und Rhetorik', and Ricoeur, *Time and Narrative*; see also: Stückrath and Zbinden, *Metageschichte*. Also see: Partner, 'Historicity in an Age of Reality-Fictions', 26–31. Cf. Rüsen, 'Rhetorics and Aesthetics'.

29. See: Kuukkanen, *Postnarrativist Philosophy of Historiography*; Simon and Kuukkanen, 'Forum: After Narrativism', 153–234.

30. Zelenak, 'Non-representationalism'.

31. Kuukkanen, *Postnarrativist Philosophy*, 30–50. Famously, Ankersmit has claimed from his *Narrative Logic* onwards that each narrative is defined by *all* sentences that it contains, and that changing just one sentence already produces a new narrative.

32. Kuukkanen, *Postnarrativist Philosophy*; Roth, 'The Pasts'; Zelenak, 'Non-representationalism'. Compare Landwehr, *Die abwesende Anwesenheit der Vergangenheit*.

33. Megill and McCloskey, 'Rhetoric of History', 235.

34. Rigney, 'History as Text', 197.

35. Cited in Rigney, 'History as Text', 198.

36. For the general problem of truth in history see Tucker, 'Historical Truth'.

37. Pihlainen, 'Confines of the Form'; Pihlainen, 'History in the World'; Pihlainen, 'On History as Communication'. His most important articles have recently been reworked and collected in his *The Work of History*.

38. Pihlainen, 'On History as Communication', 75.

39. Ibid., 71.

40. Pihlainen, 'Confines of the Form', 61.

41. Ibid., 62.

42. Tamm, 'Truth, Objectivity and Evidence'.

43. Ibid., 274.

44. Quoted in: Tamm, 'Truth, Objectivity and Evidence', 272.

45. Searle, *Expression and Meaning*, 12–20.

46. In history didactics, Wineburg defined sourcing, contextualization and corroboration as the three heuristics that professional historians use to come to intersubjective communicable narratives. See e.g. Wineburg, 'Making Historical Sense'.

47. Tamm, 'Truth, Objectivity and Evidence', 275–76. See also: van den Akker, 'Mink's Riddle of Narrative Truth', 349.

48. Tamm, 'Truth, Objectivity and Evidence', 278. Cf. Kuukkanen, 'Why We Need to Move'.

49. This is in line with the recent so-called 'virtue epistemology' as formulated, among others, by Paul, 'Performing History'.

50. See Martinez, 'Ein Faktualitätspakt'; and Fulda, 'Historiographic Narration'.

51. For the debate on narrative in history didactics, see and Brauch, 'Bridging the Gap'.

52. Carrard, *Poetics of the New History*. See also: Carrard, *History as a Kind of Writing*; Carrard, 'History and Narrative'; Carrard, 'Historiographic Discourse'.

53. Frei and Kansteiner, *Den Holocaust erzählen*.

54. Rigney, *Rhetoric of Historical Representation*; Ranciere, *Names of History*.

55. Fulda, *Wissenschaft aus Kunst*.

56. Berger and Lorenz, *Contested Nation*; Berger and Lorenz, *Nationalizing the Past*; Berger with Conrad, *The Past as History*. For further historiographical analyses, see: Ostrowski, 'Metahistorical Analysis'; Bentivoglio and Prado Júnior, '1930s Generation'. For the general reception of White among historians, see: Vann, 'Reception of Hayden White'; Spiegel, 'Rhetorical Theory/Theoretical Rhetoric'; Carrard, 'Hayden White and/in France'; Weber, 'Hayden White in Deutschland'; Ankersmit, 'Hayden White's Appeal to the Historians'.

57. Berger, Lorenz and Melman, *Popularizing National Pasts*; Korte and Paletschek, *History Goes Pop*; Korte and Paletschek, *Popular History*.

58. White, *Content of the Form*. Cf. Brauch, 'Alles authentisch'.

59. Topolski, 'Non-postmodernist Analysis', 34.

60. For one theoretical model of how to do this, see: Fulda, 'Historiographic Narration'.

61. Wertsch, 'Specific Narratives'.

Bibliography

Ankersmit, Frank. 'Hayden White's Appeal to the Historians'. *History and Theory* 37(2) (1998), 182–93.
Bal, Mieke. 'The Point of Narratology'. *Poetics Today* 11(4) (Winter 1990), 727–53.
Barthes, Roland. 'The Discourse of History'. Translated by by Stephen Bann. *Comparative Criticism* 3 (1967), 7–20.
Bentivoglio, Julio, and Caio Prado Júnior. 'The 1930s Generation and the Brazilian Historical Imagination: Exercising Metahistory'. *Storia della Storiografia* 65(1) (2014), 89–101.
Berger, Stefan, with Christoph Conrad. *The Past as History: National Identity and Historical Consciousness in Modern Europe*. Basingstoke: Palgrave Macmillan, 2015.
Berger, Stefan, and Chris Lorenz (eds). *The Contested Nation: Ethnicity, Class, Religion and Gender in National Histories*. Basingstoke: Palgrave Macmillan, 2007.
——— (eds). *Nationalizing the Past: Historians as Nation-Builders in Modern Europe*. Basingstoke: Palgrave Macmillan, 2010.
Berger, Stefan, Chris Lorenz and Billie Melman (eds). *Popularizing National Pasts: 1800 to the Present*. London: Routledge, 2012.
Blom, Hans, et al. *'Srebrenica, een "veilig gebied": Reconstructie, achtergronden, gevolgen en analyses van de val van een Safe Area' (NIOD)*. Amsterdam: Boom, 2002.
Brauch, Nicola. '"Alles authentisch – alles fiktiv?" Populärhistorische Prägung von Geschichtsbewusstsein und historisches Lernen an Beispielen der Artustradition', in T. Buck and N. Brauch (eds), *Das Mittelalter zwischen Vorstellung und Wirklichkeit* (Münster: Waxmann, 2012), 255–69.
———. 'Bridging the Gap: Comparing History Curricula in History Teacher Education in Western Countries', in M. Carretero, S. Berger and M. Grever (eds), *Palgrave Handbook of Research in Historical Culture and Education* (Basingstoke: Palgrave Macmillan, 2017), 593–613.
Bunnenberg, Christian, and Nils Steffen (eds): *Geschichte auf YouTube. Neue Herausforderungen für Geschichtsvermittlung und historische Bildung*, Berlin and Boston: De Gruyter Oldenbourg, 2019.
Burke, Peter. *The French Historical Revolution: The Annales School, 1929–1989*. Stanford, CA: Stanford University Press, 1990.
Carrard, Philippe. 'Hayden White and/in France: Receptions, Translations, Questions'. *Rethinking History* 22(4) (2018), 1–17.
———. 'Historiographic Discourse and Narratology: A Footnote to Fludernik's Work on Factual Narrative', in Jan Alber and Greta Olson (eds), *How to Do Things with Narrative: Cognitive and Diachronic Perspectives* (Berlin: De Gruyter, 2018), 125–40.
———. 'History and Narrative: An Overview'. *Narrative Works* 5(1) (2015), 174–96.
———. *History as a Kind of Writing: Textual Strategies in Contemporary French Historiography*. Chicago: University of Chicago Press, 2017.
———. *Poetics of the New History: French Historical Writing from Braudel to Chartier*. Baltimore, MD: Johns Hopkins University Press, 1992.
Curthoys, Ann, and John Docker. 'The Boundaries of History and Fiction', in Nancy Partner and Sarah Foot (eds), *The SAGE Handbook of Historical Theory* (London: SAGE Publications, 2013), 202–20.
Danto, Arthur C. *Analytical Philosophy of History*. Cambridge: Cambridge University Press, 1965.
Droysen, Gustav. *Grundriss der Historik*. Leipzig: Veit, 1868.
Feyerabend, Paul. *Against Method: Outline of an Anarchistic Theory of Knowledge*. London: Verso, 1975.

Frei, Norbert, and Wulf Kansteiner (eds). *Den Holocaust erzählen: Historiographie zwischen wissenschaftlicher Empirie und narrativer Kreativität.* Göttingen: Wallstein, 2013.

Fulda, Daniel. 'Historiographic Narration', in Peter Hühn et al. (eds), *The Living Handbook of Narratology* (Hamburg: Hamburg University, 2014). URL: http://www.lhn.uni-hamburg.de/article/historiographic-narration [last accessed 27 May 2019].

———. *Wissenschaft aus Kunst: die Entstehung der modernen deutschen Geschichtsschreibung 1760–1860.* Berlin: de Gruyter, 1996.

Gossman, Lionel. 'The Rationality of History', in Lionel Gossman (ed.), *Between History and Literature* (Harvard: Harvard University Press, 1990), 285–324.

Huizinga, Johan. 'Over vormverandering der geschiedenis', in *Mededelingen der Nederlandsche Academie van Wetenschappen, Afdeling Letterkunde,* vol. IV(3) (Amsterdam, 1941), 79–97.

Irving, David. *Hitler's War.* New York: Viking Press, 1977.

Jay, Martin. 'Of Plots, Witnesses and Judgements', in Saul Friedländer (ed.), *Probing the Limits of Representation: Nazism and the 'Final Solution'* (Harvard: Harvard University Press, 1992), 97–107.

Jenkins, Keith. *Rethinking History.* London: Routledge, 1991.

Korte, Barbara, and Sylvia Paletschek (eds). *History Goes Pop: Zur Repräsentation von Geschichte in populären Medien and Genres.* Bielefeld: Transcript, 2009.

——— (eds). *Popular History Now and Then: International Perspectives.* Bielefeld: Transcript, 2012.

Kuukkanen, Jouni-Matti. *Postnarrativist Philosophy of Historiography.* Basingstoke: Palgrave, 2015.

———. 'Why We Need to Move from Truth-Functionality to Performativity in Historiography'. *History and Theory* 54(2) (2015), 226–43.

Landwehr, Achim. *Die anwesende Abwesenheit der Vergangenheit: Essay zur Geschichtstheorie.* Frankfurt am Main: Fischer, 2016.

Lorenz, Chris. 'History and Theory', in Daniel Woolf and Axel Schneider (eds), *The Oxford History of Historical Writing,* vol. 5 (Oxford: Oxford University Press, 2011), 13–25.

———. 'Narrativism, Positivism and the "Metaphorical Turn"'. *History and Theory* 37(3) (1998), 309–29.

Martinez, Matías. 'Ein Faktualitätspakt', in Norbert Frei and Wulf Kansteiner (eds), *Den Holocaust erzählen: Historiographie zwischen wissenschaftlicher Empirie und narrativer Kreativität* (Göttingen: Wallstein, 2013), 181–85.

Martinez, Matías, and Michael Scheffel (eds). *Einführung in die Erzähltheorie,* 10th edn. Munich: C.H. Beck, 2020.

Megill, Allan, and Deirdre McCloskey. 'The Rhetoric of History', in John Nelson, Allan Megill and Deirdre McCloskey (eds), *The Rhetoric of the Human Sciences: Language and Argument in Scholarship and Public Affairs* (Madison: University of Wisconsin Press, 1987), 221–38.

Mink, Louis. 'The Autonomy of Historical Understanding'. *History and Theory* 5(1) (1966), 24–47.

Mitrovic, Branko. *Materialist Philosophy of History: A Realist Antidote to Postmodernism.* New York: Rowman & Littlefield, 2020.

Munslow, Alun. *Narrative and History.* Bastingstoke: Palgrave Macmillan, 2007.

Ostrowski, Donald. 'A Metahistorical Analysis: Hayden White and Four Narratives of 'Russian' History'. *Clio* 19(3) (1990), 215–35.

Partner, Nancy. 'Historicity in an Age of Reality-Fictions', in Frank Ankersmit and Hans Kellner (eds), *A New Philosophy of History* (Chicago: University of Chicago Press, 1995), 21–40.

Paul, Herman. *Hayden White: The Historical Imagination.* Cambridge: Polity Press, 2011.

———. 'Performing History: How Historical Scholarship is Shaped by Epistemic Virtues'. *History and Theory* 50(1) (2011), 1–19.

Pihlainen, Kalle. 'The Confines of the Form: Historical Writing and the Desire that It Be what It Is Not', in Kuisma Korhonen (ed.), *Tropes for the Past: Hayden White and the History/ Literature Debate* (Amsterdam: Rodopi, 2006), 55–67.

———. 'History in the World: Hayden White and the Consumer of History'. *Rethinking History* 12(1) (2008), 23–39.

———. 'On History as Communication and Constraint'. *Ideas in History* 4(2) (2009), 63–90.

———. *The Work of History: Constructivism and a Politics of the Past*. New York: Routledge, 2017.

Ranciere, Jacques. *The Names of History: On the Poetics of Knowledge*. Minneapolis: University of Minnesota Press, 1994.

Ricoeur, Paul. *Time and Narrative*, 3 vol. Chicago: Chicago University Press, 1984–1990.

———. 'Geschichte und Rhetorik', in Herta Nagl-Docekal (ed.), *Der Sinn des Historischen: Geschichtsphilosophische Debatten* (Frankfurt am Main: Fischer, 1996), 107–26.

Rigney, Ann. 'History as Text: Narrative Theory and History', in Nancy Partner and Sarah Foot (eds), *The SAGE Handbook of Historical Theory* (London: SAGE Publications, 2013), 183–202.

Rigney, Ann. *The Rhetoric of Historical Representation: Three Narrative Histories of the French Revolution*. Cambridge: Cambridge University Press, 1990.

Rijsdijk, Erna. 'Reconstituting the Dutch State in the NIOD Srebrenica Report', in *The Palgrave Handbook of State-Sponsored History after 1945* (Houndmills: Palgrave, 2018), 713–25.

Roth, Paul A. 'Essentially Narrative Explanations'. *Studies in History and Philosophy of Science* 62 (2017), 42–50.

———. 'The Pasts'. *History and Theory* 51(3) (2012), 313–39.

———. *The Philosophical Structure of Historical Explanation*. Evanston: Northwestern University Press, 2020.

Runia, Eelco. '"Forget About It": Parallel Processing in the Srebrenica Report'. *History and Theory* 43(3) (2004), 295–320.

Rüsen, Jörn. *Historik: Theorie der Geschichtswissenschaft*. Cologne: Böhlau, 2013 [English translation: *Evidence and Meaning: A Theory of Historical Studies*. Oxford: Berghahn Books, 2017].

———. *Historische Vernunft: Die Grundlagen der Geschichtswissenschaft*. Göttingen: Vandenhoeck & Ruprecht, 1983.

———. *Rekonstruktion der Vergangenheit*. Göttingen: Vandenhoeck & Ruprecht, 1986.

———. 'Rhetoric and Aesthetics of History: Leopold von Ranke'. *History and Theory* 29 (1990), 190–204.

Searle, John. *Expression and Meaning: Studies in the Theory of Speech Acts*. Cambridge: Cambridge University Press, 1979.

Seixas, Peter. 'A Model of Historical Thinking'. *Educational Philosophy and Theory* 49(6) (2017), 593–605.

——— (ed.). *Theorizing Historical Consciousness*. Toronto: University of Toronto Press, 2006.

Seixas, Peter, and Carla Peck. 'Teaching Historical Thinking', in A. Sears and I. Wright (eds), *Challenges and Prospects for Canadian Social Studies* (Vancouver: Pacific Educational Press, 2004), 109–17.

Simon, Zoltan Bolidizsar, and Jouni-Matti Kuukkanen. 'Forum: After Narrativism'. *History and Theory* 54(2) (2015).

Spiegel, Gabrielle M. 'Rhetorical Theory/Theoretical Rhetoric: Some Ambiguities in the Reception of Hayden White's Work', in Robert Doran (ed.), *Philosophy of History after Hayden White* (London: Bloomsbury, 2013), 171–82.

Stückrath, Jörn, and Jürg Zbinden (eds). *Metageschichte: Hayden White und Paul Ricoeur*. Baden-Baden: Nomos, 1997.

Tamm, Marek. 'Truth, Objectivity and Evidence in History Writing'. *Journal of the Philosophy of History* 8(2) (2014), 265–90.

Tamm, Marek, and Eugen Zelenak (eds). *Journal of Philosophy of History* 12(3) (November 2018). Special Issue: 'Frank Ankersmit's Philosophy of History'.

Topolski, Jerzy. 'A Non-postmodernist Analysis of Historical Narratives', in Jerzy Topolski (ed.), *Historiography between Modernism and Postmodernism: Contributions to the Methodology of the Historical Research* (Amsterdam: Rodopi, 1994), 9–85.

Tucker, Aviezer. 'Historical Truth', in Vittorio Hösle (ed.), *Forms of Truth and the Unity of Knowledge* (Notre Dame: University of Notre Dame Press, 2014), 232–59.

van den Akker, Chiel. 'Mink's Riddle of Narrative Truth'. *Journal of the Philosophy of History* 7(3) (2013), 346–70.

Vann, Richard T. 'The Reception of Hayden White'. *History and Theory* 37(2) (1998), 143–61.

Verschaffel, Bart. 'Geschiedschrijving – een waar verhaal, of de waarheid over verhalen?', in Franklin R. Ankersmit et al. (eds), *Op verhaal komen: over narrativiteit in de mens- en cultuurwetenschappen* (Kampen: Kok Agora, 1990), 83–107.

Weber, Wolfgang. 'Hayden White in Deutschland'. *Storia della Storiografia* 25 (1994), 89–102.

Wertsch, James V. 'Specific Narratives and Schematic Narrative Templates', in Peter Seixas (ed.), *Theorizing Historical Consciousness* (Toronto: University of Toronto Press, 2004), 49–63.

White, Hayden. *The Content of the Form: Narrative Discourse and Historical Representation*. Baltimore, MD: Johns Hopkins University Press, 1987.

———. *Metahistory: The Historical Imagination in Nineteenth-Century Europe*. Baltimore, MD: Johns Hopkins University Press, 1973.

———. *Tropics of Discourse: Essays in Cultural Criticism*. Baltimore, MD: Johns Hopkins University Press, 1978.

Wilkomirski, Binjamin. *Bruchstücke: Aus einer Kindheit 1939–1948*. Frankfurt am Main: Jüdischer Verlag, 1995.

Wineburg, Sam. 'Making Historical Sense', in Peter N. Stearns and Sam Wineburg (eds), *Knowing, Teaching, and Learning History: National and International Perspectives* (New York: New York University Press, 2000), 306–25.

Zelenak, Eugen. 'Non-representationalism in Philosophy of History: A Case Study', in Krzystof Brzechczyn (ed.), *Towards a Revival of Analytical Philosophy of History: Around Paul A. Roth's Vision of Historical Sciences* (Leiden: Brill, 2018), 116–29.

Part I

PROFESSIONAL HISTORY WRITING

CHAPTER 1

Thucydides' History of the Vanquished

Death, Narrative Gazes and Historical Time

ALEXANDRA LIANERI

The historian is an Oedipus.

—Roland Barthes, *Michelet*

Narrative theory has recently prompted a paradigm shift in the study of Greek and Latin historiography.[1] This did not just consist in identifying narrative techniques and rhetorical schemes at work in historical texts, but rather in recognizing such traits as fundamental to ancient historiographical reflection and practice. In 1907, F.M. Cornford's *Thucydides Mythistoricus* famously dismissed Thucydides' tragic mode as mythographic, rather than historical: an index of 'a certain traditional mode of thought, characteristic of the Athenian mind' grounded in a 'mythological conception of world'.[2] Likewise, for the greatest part of the twentieth century, the narrativity of Thucydides' history has implied questioning his status as a historian.[3] For instance, Anthony Woodman's *Rhetoric in Classical Historiography* identified the use of rhetoric in ancient historiography as poetic rather than historical; as he wrote about Thucydides, 'Verbatim speeches and classical historiography are a contradiction in terms'.[4] It was only in the 1990s that Simon Hornblower introduced into the study of Greek historiography narratological concepts, such as anachronism and focalization,[5] while Tim Rood's seminal monograph argued that Thucydides' narrative choices cannot be identified as intrusive elements, but as constitutive of the historian's voice.[6]

Notes for this section begin on page 46.

Recent scholarship in historiography has fully endorsed the narratological postulate that the 'content of the form', in Hayden White's phrasing, underpins the project attempted by Greek and Roman historians.[7] Studies of Thucydides then have deployed narrativist perspectives to identify plural levels of historical meaning;[8] the interweaving of different explanatory schemes and temporalities;[9] the deployment of 'immediacy' as both a rhetorical device and a claim that history moves us directly to the scenes of the past;[10] the mingling of the historian's aim to write about contemporary events and his contention that his work should outlast the age in which he composed it;[11] as well as the tension between Thucydides' authoritative and teleological voice on the one side, and the experience of historical participants confronting an unknown future on the other.[12]

This chapter approaches Thucydides' narrative from a perspective that shifts our attention from the ways in which 'the structure of the narration is ... lent to or pressed on' the past[13] to the reflexive and self-referential characteristics of narrativity. My interest is in the way ancient historical narrative articulates concepts of history and historical time. I focus on Thucydides with a view to discussing this reflexive function of narrative in terms that will ultimately bear upon present concerns of historical theory, and especially the quest to rethink the modern concept of linear, progressive and homogeneous time.[14] A key question underneath my analysis of Thucydides is, then, what historical theory can learn from narrative articulations of time in the paradigm of ancient historiography.

My starting point is Allan Megill's concept of 'unresolving tensions' of historiography – that is, tensions of the sort that are fundamental to historical representation and that cannot be resolved within its limits, either in practice or in principle. According to Megill, the most fundamental of these tensions derives from the opposition between 'determinism' and 'contingency', which pertains to both ancient and modern historiography, while other tensions, as, for instance, between present and past, only characterize the modern historiographical project. 'The assumption that humans are both under the thrall of external forces and act on their own accord', Megill writes, 'is a condition of justification of the genre of history'.[15] One of the sites in which this tension is foregrounded in Thucydides is the focalized narrative shifting between the historical actors' confrontation with contingency and the historian's determinist reconfiguration of the past.[16] By the same token, I argue, the narrative articulation of this tension formulates a meta-historiographical discourse, which pluralizes Thucydides' notion of history and requires us to rethink the categories of historical time underpinning the opposition between *historia magistra vitae* and modern historical consciousness.

In this chapter, I trace this discourse in images of death confronted by Thucydides' historical actors, who are at the same time his co-citizens and contemporaries: the Athenians. I explore the narrative confrontation between the gaze of Athenians as historical actors facing death and the perspective of the historian seeking to set this image in past time, as a frame against which the limits of historical knowledge are defined. This confrontation foregrounds an ambiguous and polysemous notion of history. On the one side, the gaze of the Athenians is opposed to the perspective of the historian, as the latter claims to look at the events from a position that allows him to identify true causes and lines of action accounting for why things happened the way they did. On the other side, the two gazes are intertwined in a way that the positions of seer and seen, historian and historical actors become reversible in the sense that is conveyed by what Maurice Merleau-Ponty described as the 'enigma of visibility', the condition in which a subject that sees inevitably exposes itself as the object of vision: 'That which looks at all things can also look at itself and recognize, in what it sees, the "other side" of its power of looking. It sees itself seeing'. As a consequence, the one who looks at the world allows the world to look back and interrogate his vision.[17] The reversibility of the gaze implies that images of death confronted by the Athenians can be read as enabling a counter-gaze turned to the historian, a gaze that transforms the unresolving tension between historical determinism and contingency into a field for reflection on historical writing as such.

My use of the notion of the gaze here is to be distinguished from narratological analyses of perspectives or focalization, which deploy a problematic on visibility as one-directional and moving from perceivers and the factors that determine their viewpoint to that which is seen or perceived.[18] The term 'gaze' is rather meant to highlight how images of death confronted by the Athenians shape Thucydides' viewpoint as much as they are shaped by it. Originating in Lacan's theory (partly formulated in response to Merleau-Ponty's thesis), the notion of the gaze was introduced into narratology to denote the representation of an act of looking that acts in turn to frame its object.[19] In this sense, the term does not merely refer to the condition of viewing, to a perspective formulated from a position external to the events narrated, but to the constitution of the seen by the act of looking. As Lacan phrased it, 'what determines me, at the most profound level, in the visible, is the gaze that is outside. It is through the gaze that I enter light and it is from the gaze that I receive its effects'. By the same token, the gaze involves the 'double dihedral of vision' and a two-directional relationship between viewer and object: to see includes the possibility of being seen.[20]

This duality of vision suggests that the gaze of the Athenians facing death confronts and reframes the deterministic view of time attributed by the historian to the past as a field of retrospective sight. Studying the historical narrativization of this gaze would then allow us to accentuate how the narrative both affirms and interrupts the temporality of historical determinism by introducing into it what we will identify as meaningless time. The gaze directed back to the historian from the field of actors seeing death fits uneasily within what Gérard Genette described as the sequential, forward-looking narrative time of events and actions, the 'pseudo-time' of the narrative, which acts to hide the temporal reversal by means of which the narrator makes meaningful a web of events and actions by moving from effects to causes, from ends to means.[21] Images of death in Thucydides offer an alternative to the operation of reversing time, by way of intertwining subject and object of looking, historian and historical actors looking at death and attesting to their radical inability to attribute meaning to time.

I identify this gaze by using a concept suggested by Reinhart Koselleck as gaze of the 'vanquished',[22] and seek to account for its historiographical implications through a threefold structure. In the first section, I discuss the narrative representation of death in images encountered by the Athenians as a theoretical commentary, a meta-historiographical language that complexifies Thucydides' reflection on history writing and historical time. In particular, I explore how these images reformulate Thucydides' critique of autopsy and foreground the intertwining of the gaze of historical actors and the historian's deterministic vision. The second section focuses on Pericles' Funeral Oration, with a view to exploring how the image of death that is both expelled by the speech and frames it encapsulates an interconnection of vision and blindness, on which historical knowledge is predicated. I argue that the withdrawn gaze of the dead around which Thucydides configures Pericles' foresight temporalizes the sight of Athens and becomes a field wherein historiographical determinism is fractured. The third section reads the Athenians' fascination with the scene of death in the final battle of the Sicilian war in the harbour of Syracuse as an interruption of meaningful time – in other words, a break in the narrative flow of events, which operates as a critical limitation of the capacity of historians to associate time with meaning.

Death-Images as Reflexive Language

Death-images in Thucydides not only tell a story about the past, but also a reflexive story about history writing. In this respect, they constitute a meta-historiographical commentary – a language about the modes of knowing the past. Formulated within an intellectual and political context that contrived a close relationship between seeing and knowing, reflections of Greek historians privileged sight as a field for both configuring and contesting knowledge.[23] For instance, the concept of autopsy – the personal visual examination of events that figures prominently in methodological statements of both Thucydides and Herodotus – did not just convey the identification of knowledge with sight, but highlighted the process of contestation and critique entailed by the juxtaposition of gazes. As Thucydides explained, his story was founded on reports of eyewitnesses; yet he also stressed the interpretive difficulty inherent in *opsis*, sight, including his own autopsy.[24]

This difficulty underpins Thucydides' narrative, which is organized by contrasting different visual perspectives, including that of historical actors, the historian, and his readerships.[25] On this level, Thucydides' juxtaposition of visions has been interpreted as reflecting his critique of autopsy and the methodological principles that enabled him to see through the illusion of appearances, to search for the truth about the events, in opposition to historical actors, which are shown to direct their gaze towards the wrong things and in the wrong ways. For example, the Athenians, as Gregory Crane notes regarding Amphipolis, are presented as deluded by the rhetoric of image-making, and they 'let ill-founded hope blind their judgment'. By contrast, Thucydides searched for the truth through the new medium of writing, as he 'wrote for readerly observers, contemplating in their mind's eye the phenomena, "seeing", but with a sight that transcends physical appearance'.[26] As Dewald condenses this argument regarding the first part of the *History*, 'Thucydides sets up a fissured consciousness, split *absolutely* between the viewpoint of the analytical Thucydides-narrator, who understands the full range of factors involved in events', and those of the speakers and actors whose partial perspectives direct the focalization of their points.[27]

Yet, in a characteristically astute argument, Dewald also qualifies her appeal to this 'absolute' split by noting the complexity of the narrative juxtaposition of perspectives: for example, she observes how Pericles, as historical participant, is assigned 'the only focalized voice within the narrative that in force and scope resembles that of the Thucydides-narrator himself'.[28] Other studies further identify a nuanced relation between the gaze of actors and the perspective of Thucydides. Emily Greenwood links the 'sustained emphasis on viewing and sight throughout the *History*' to 'the prerogative of theatre to instruct through showing' – itself an element of the ideology of Athenian citizenship.[29] Jonas Grethlein studies the role of 'side-shadowing' devises in conveying experience and restoring 'presentness to the past', in opposition to the teleological temporality attributed to the historian's retrospective voice. As he puts it, the experience of historical agents is captured by Thucydides' language and remains in tension with the narrator's teleology – a juxtaposition that gives the narrative an 'existential' dimension: the look back offered by the historian 'permits us [readers] to master the contingencies to which we are subject in life, to replace vulnerability with sovereignty. Teleology can thus serve as a means of coping with temporality'.[30]

Building on these studies, I approach the narrative configuration of death-images faced by Thucydides' historical actors as a gaze that produces a reflexive meaning, since it is simultaneously directed towards an unknown future and towards the historian-narrator translating contingency into teleology. My interest is not in the tension between determinism and the experience of contingency – that is, the juxtaposition of historiographical narrative and the experiential dimension as 'a shift away from language', in Ankersmit's phrasing.[31] While this tension highlights what Grethlein aptly describes as the retrospective mastery of contingency,[32] my focus is on a certain narrative articulation of the Athenians' gaze that sets it beyond mastery. The gaze of the vanquished interrupts Thucydides' mastery and eschews the historian's determinism, not in the experiential field but by way of a narrative articulation of time's meaninglessness.

This interlinking of Thucydides' perspective with the gaze of historical actors is configured around an event that is not (yet) seen by his actors – the end of the Peloponnesian War with Athens' defeat in 404 BCE – but nonetheless enters their horizon throughout the narrative. Figures of death encountered by the Athenians allude to what was still invisible for them: the forthcoming end of their story and the viewpoint from which Thucydides shapes the line of causes and effects that structures his narrative.[33] However, this allusion does not only subject the gaze of participants to the historian's perspective on the past – to a temporality into which these participants move as they gradually become aware of their future – but death-images also become significant for the historiographical enterprise itself. Far from being only formulated as a transformation of what is visible by actors to a retrospectively defined meaning of time, the task of history-writing as such is also embedded in a schism characterizing vision in the field of action: a rift between meaning and time that we encounter through the gaze of historical actors.

Images of death encountered by the Athenians attest to this rift as a peculiar form of 'foresight'. Their narrative focus evokes a defeat that is not accounted in the narrative (Thucydides' text breaks off suddenly in 411 BCE, before we reach the story's end) but with which Thucydides engages throughout his text. This engagement is defined by a tension between narrative poles. On the one hand, the *History* tells a story of the failed handling of concepts that would have enabled the Athenians to foresee the development of the war as it unfolded. This narrative pole is exemplified, for instance, in the historian's praise of Pericles' foresight:

> Under him [Pericles] Athens reached the height of its greatness; and after the war broke out he then too showed himself a far-sighted judge (προγνοὺς) of the city's strengths ... and after he died his foresight about the war became still more fully recognised. (2.65.5–6)[34]

This power of foresight, Thucydides says, allowed the city to survive the contingency of the plague, and even the disastrous defeat in the Sicilian expedition.

So, had they not made the mistakes cited in 2.65 according to this argument, the Athenians would have won:

> He [Pericles] told them that if they held back, looked after their navy, did not try to extend their empire during the war and did not expose the city to risk, then they would prevail. But they did just the opposite of this in every way, and in other respects apparently unconnected with the war they were led by private ambition and personal greed to pursue policies that proved harmful both to themselves and to their allies. (2.65.7, 1.144.1 and 2.13.2)

As Harvey Yunis claims, 'given Thucydides' unqualified admiration for Pericles and his leadership of the demos, we have no basis for inferring that Thucydides had any reservations about Pericles at all'.[35] This identification with Pericles is further highlighted in Thucydides' comments on the expedition to Sicily as an example of the gap between foresight and political practice. The disaster, we are told, was *not* the outcome of the absence of concepts through which to interpret the events, but of the Athenians' failure to link these concepts to action (2.65.11). By relating these concepts not only to the benefit of hindsight but also to Pericles' ability to interpret the events as they took place, Thucydides implicitly states that the war could have been planned and possibly gone otherwise.[36] So the counterfactual future implied by the narrative suggests that 'for Thucydides', as Richard Winton phrases it, 'the Peloponnesian War was lost by Athens, not won by Sparta'.[37]

The second narrative pole arises from the 'unavoidable awkwardness and irony of praising Pericles' foresight of victory in a war that was, in fact, lost'.[38] Narrative deployments of vision, and death-images in particular, register precisely this irony by reinforcing Thucydides' account of the war as *paralogos* – a concept denoting the radical unpredictability of the war, not merely in the sense of its contingent outcome but also as attesting to the irreducible gap between logos and historical reality. In book 1, Thucydides uses the concept *paralogos* as the Athenians warn the Spartans about the risks of imminent war: 'Think in advance how unpredictable (παράλογος) war can be before you find yourselves involved in one' (1.78.1–2). As H.P. Stahl pointedly asks: 'Do the Athenians realize how much this warning applies also to the powerful? The ambiguity and irony of this passage are surely the conscious intention of Thucydides'.[39] The concept does not merely make a claim that forthcoming events are naturally impossible to predict. *Paralogos* does not define the future as unforeseen by the actors. Rather, it makes the more radical claim that this future was unforeseeable, it stood out vertically on the conceptual horizon of the present, as there existed no logos through which to account for its meaningful relation to this present.[40] Does

Thucydides realize the extent to which his historiographical logos is also embedded in this vertical relation with the future? If, as Rood aptly warns us, it is 'dangerous to read Thucydides' analysis at 2.65 as his final thoughts on Athens' defeat',[41] then the gaze of the Athenians glimpsing the story's end offers an alternative to the historian's all-inclusive retrospective horizon — a reflection on temporal verticality and the unforeseeable.

The gaze alluding to the end of the Peloponnesian War is then a gaze interrupting the realm of historical meaning, a gaze suggesting not the failure of participants' interpretive and political intelligence, to use Chester Starr's term,[42] but rather the inadequacy of concepts deployed to interpret time, and, indeed, the very failure of languages that attribute meaning to time. Rather than allowing an interpretation of events leading to the defeat, this gaze points to a temporality that we may grasp through Jan Patočka's notion of meaning's point zero: a condition indicating not only the historian's inadequacy, his inability to grasp and understand a final meaning of events, but rather the possibility that all historical meaning may be effaced and lost, implying nothing less than 'the problematic nature of all meaningfulness' and a quest for the reconfiguration of meaning that arises from this loss.[43] Thucydides' narrative, then, unfolds in this borderline, in the breaking point between meaning's point zero and the historian's reconstruction of meaningful time that begins with this loss. The state of loss — the Athenians' gazing at the interruption of meaningfulness and the verticality of the future — becomes a condition of the possibility of historicizing time by the same move that it ceaselessly questions this enterprise.

The Withdrawn Gaze: Blindness and History Writing in the Funeral Oration

The interweaving of determinism and contingency is accentuated in images of death evoking the impending collapse of Athenian power. As time progresses in the narrative, each of these images gradually contributes to a growing state of knowledge acquired by historical actors of the forthcoming end of their story. Each new image then would be expected to build on the antithesis between a state of blindness associated with contingency and the deterministic perspective informed by knowledge of the story's end. For instance, the imagery of death in the narrative of the plague, which is set immediately after the Funeral Oration, challenges the glorifying image of the city forged by Pericles. Thucydides' vivid description of the plague transforms the very concepts through which Pericles invites the Athenians to gaze the city, or at least reveals a dual image through which Thucydides 'corrects the Funeral Oration' and proves this gaze to be 'illusory'.[44]

Witnessing the plague is a step towards knowing the story's end point, a movement towards the course of events leading to defeat. At the same time, Thucydides remarkably associates this step, first of all, with an affliction of the eyes, the loss of vision. The disease, he tells us, begins with vision, with a 'redness and inflammation of the eyes', and many of those who survived it 'escaped . . . with the loss of their eyes'. While the disease was a natural phenomenon, one may discern here a link between metaphorical and literal blindness – a device also deployed in other Greek works such as the *Oedipus Tyrannus*.

The same relationship is configured by Thucydides' depiction of death in the narrative of the Funeral Oration. Leo Strauss notes the paradoxical absence of verbal references to death in Pericles' speech, which peculiarly 'avoid[s] the words 'death', 'dying', or 'dead bodies'', in opposition to the narrative of the plague, which 'abounds with mentions of death, dead, dying, and corpses'.[45] Still, the removal of all talk of death is strikingly compensated by images. Indeed, the Oration is framed by images of death. It begins with Thucydides' introduction depicting the funeral ceremony and the public display of the bones of the deceased in Athens before the procession (2.34), and ends with Pericles' future image of the vanquished city, whose present power will be preserved for ever, yet only in the memory of the generations that come after: '[Athens] has acquired the greatest power that has ever existed, whose memory will live on forever . . . posterity will always recall that we were the Greeks to rule over most fellow Greeks' (2.64.3).

These images are intertwined with the vision of present contingency constructed by Pericles. The text accentuates this link by means of two unconventional shifts in the speech. First, Pericles refrains from the traditional practice of praising the deeds of the dead. While he suggests that these deeds were significant, he does not engage with them directly, but invites the Athenians to see them in relation to the glorious image of the city. The second shift issues directly from the first, and consists in a movement from the account of the deeds of dead soldiers to a theoretical problematic about representation. In 2.35, Pericles points to the distance between historical reality and representation, which is attesting to the distance between seeing and knowing: 'It is difficult to speak in due measure when even the impression [δόκησις, sense-perception, appearance] of truth can only be established with great difficulty'.[46] In this remarkable passage, the relation between sight and logos does not consist in a straightforward movement from *opsis* to knowledge. Rather the image of the dead requires the inscription of blindness into logos, an obscured gaze, the inability to see clearly: Thucydides' only aspiration is the *impression* of truth, rather than its establishment – and even this impression, we are told, is reached with the greatest difficulty.

These shifts sustain the intertwining of the image of dead soldiers and the narrative image of the city configured by Pericles. Virginia Hunter notes 'the almost architectonic quality of [Thucydides'] mind, which grasped in a single vision not just the war that he claimed to record but all of human history, as it were'.[47] The narrative scope suggested here is stricter: Thucydides includes in a single frame the story of the dead and Pericles' account of Athens as elements of one and the same snapshot, the same moment in time. In other words, the text does not simply link the praise of individual soldiers to Pericles' view of how Athens became a great power. The two stories become one image, and thus the city invited to gaze at itself is then torn between two positions of being in time: the position of the dead and that of historical participants facing an unknown future. As a consequence, the dead soldiers are not only the object of the Athenians' and Thucydides' gaze, but also a gaze itself, spectacle and spectator gazing back – indeed the spectator that qualifies Pericles' subsequent narrative of Athenian history. The construction of this narrative as a sight of the city that the Athenians are invited to gaze upon[48] is then configured as a self-reflecting vision, a gaze that makes a double movement: it does not proceed directly from the object (the city of Athens) but through the indirect route of the dead, which mediates the positioning of this object in time.

At the most immediate level, the Oration's focus on the gaze of Athenians upon the city's glory suppresses the presence of death in their horizon. Pericles explicitly refrains from talking about the dead until the greatest part of the eulogy of the city has been completed, and further invites the configuration of their deeds in terms that echo present glory: 'My main points are already made: the qualities I praised in the city were the ones these men and others like them enhanced by their virtues, and there are few other Greeks whose reputation would be found equalled by their deeds, as would theirs' (2.42.2). He goes on to affirm the effacement of all deeds of the dead in the light of their final sacrifice in the name of the city: 'Even those with other failings deserve to be first of all remembered for their manly courage in war in the service of their country' (2.42.3). He turns his gaze away from their tombs by replacing them with the boundless fame they ensured for themselves and Athens, stating that 'they ... gained for themselves an enduring tribute and the finest tomb, not the one in which they lie but that in which their fame survives in eternal memory' (2.43.2–3). Finally, Pericles even asks relatives 'to *forget* those whom they lost' (2.43.3). If, as Gerald M. Mara writes, what moves Athens in the Oration 'is the pursuit of reputation or distinction that defeats death',[49] then this movement is performed through a paradoxical erasure of the position in time associated with the dead. Yet on a different level, the gaze of the dead enters the narrative as a sign of interruption and temporal doubling. It becomes a broken mirror-image of the polis, to use a metaphor that Pierre Vidal-Naquet deployed in relation to tragedy, a gaze that produces cracks in the self-definition of the polis and its past.[50]

The figure of the dead challenges the principles according to which Pericles' Athens, with its evoked strengths – its political stability, its historical continuity, the conjunction of public good and private interest, its material self-sufficiency and its sense of commitment to common affairs – should be able to prevail over its opponents. It does so first by setting the impeding defeat within the sight that supposedly attests to the city's power to subjugate time. While Pericles forgets death, and his only mention of it describes it as unfelt (*anaisthetos*) calling upon the Athenians 'to avert their glance from it',[51] the narrative highlights the ineffaceable presence of death in the scene: from the introduction that sets both Pericles and his audience in a scene surrounded by death to the ending with the quest addressed to this audience to finish their lamentations (2.46.2). Set in the margins of narrative focus, these traces evoke at once past time – the time of the dead soldiers – and the future.

Moreover, unlike other parts of the narrative, where signs of the future are associated with Thucydides' historiographical authority and its reflection onto Pericles' voice, in the scene of the Oration these signs come from those who can no longer see: the dead. They are not predictions of events, but a certain opening to the city's temporality, a gaze that peculiarly associates time with blindness, with the withdrawal from the world of seeing. The gaze of the dead temporalizes Pericles' image of Athens by disrupting the relationship between sight and events as observable objects. Hence this gaze cannot be identified from a retrospective view of events, but is set in the divide between withdrawal and being, in a past that survives by means of interrupting the languages of the present. This is a negative gesture advancing not from seeing the past, but rather from the trace marking the collapse of the relation between seeing and understanding, from the self-reflecting gaze mediated by blindness. In this respect, the image of the dead becomes the field wherein the priority of retrospective vision is challenged and the linearity of time is fractured, while the historian becomes an Oedipus, in Roland Barthes's sense: a narrator whose blindness is key to the ability to solve the riddles of past time.

The Fascinated Gaze: Meaningless Time in the Harbour of Syracuse

Thucydides own reticence as to the end of the Peloponnesian War was analogous to his deployment of images prefiguring this end. Among them the image that evoked the defeat of Athens more perhaps than any other was the depiction of the destruction of the Athenian fleet in the harbour of Syracuse, an event that marked the end of the Athenian invasion of Sicily (415–413 BCE). The debate as to the narrative role of this defeat has many aspects that cannot be addressed here – among which is the question of whether Thucydides narrates the events in Sicily as part of a single war story (a war within a war) or as two different ones.[52] Yet, an aspect of this debate is important to my argument: unlike the narrative of the Peloponnesian War, which remains incomplete, books 6 and 7 narrate a war that concludes with the defeat of the Athenians, while the Peloponnesian War continues (2.65.11). In this respect, the defeat in Sicily serves to highlight Thucydides' attempt to reconstruct 'the dynamic and changeable nature of the war as it unfolded', as Greenwood aptly phrases it.[53]

This narrative function creates a tension on the historiographical level between Thucydides' attempt to interpret the defeat as a critique of the Athenians' poor foresight and planning, on the one side, and his emphasis on the unforeseeable dynamics of the war, on the other. The former intention is served in the Sicilian narrative by the text's focus on the distance between appearance and knowledge, the quest for critical interpretation of *opsis*. The latter is signalled by visual narrative: an image of death that confronts both readers and the Athenians with the collapse of languages attributing meaning to time.

The Sicilian expedition begins with the striking image of the fleet's departure. In 6.31.1–2 Thucydides describes the perception of a spectacular expeditionary force. So while the sight of the fleet brought to the minds of Athenians the impending dangers, nonetheless the spectacle of the grandeur of the expedition filled them with courage 'at the evidence before them of their present strength, the sheer quantity of every kind of resource *they could see with their own eyes*'. The image, the text explains, became for foreigners and the rest of the crowd an 'extraordinary spectacle' as they found 'the whole conception of the thing quite remarkable and incredible'; and the first armada was 'the most expensive and the most magnificent display of Greek power ever to be launched from any single city up to that time' (6.31.1). Scholarly discussions of the passage stress the opposition between Thucydides' knowledge and the ignorance of participants. Historical actors are presented as systematically 'misreading the signs', since they were 'impressed by the *opsis* more than the *dunamis* [power]', while they themselves sought this visual display.[54] Josiah Ober describes the passage as an 'example of the masses' false confidence resulting from seeing', demonstrating 'that . . . visual perception can be just as misleading as verbal persuasion'.[55] The parallel between *opsis* and manipulation is accentuated by the use of visual metaphors focusing on the false gaze of the masses – for instance in the debate of Nicias and Alcibiades in front of the assembly that decided on the expedition;[56] or, during the course of the expedition, in Nicias' deployment of what Greenwood translates as 'visible speech' (*emphanes logos*) in 7.48.3 in order to hide from the Athenian force his actual thoughts about withdrawal.[57]

The image in 7.71 depicting the fleet's destruction seems at first to separate the perspective of Athenians from that of Thucydides and readers. The use of identical vocabulary focused on seeing in the two passages encourages readers to think the story backwards, to inflect the flow of time looking at the gaze of the Athenians with a view to assessing it in relation to the end of the expedition.[58] At the same time, the scene of the defeat introduces into the narrative temporal verticality and the unforeseeable for both readers and actors. In 7.55.1 Thucydides uses the notion of *paralogos* to account for a previous naval battle lost by the Athenians. After Demosthenes and the reinforcements from Athens failed in their surprise attack on Syracuse, the Athenian navy was itself attacked by the Syracusan coalition and lost a critical battle. So Thucydides writes:

> Now that the Syracusans had won this brilliant naval victory too, despite their earlier apprehensions about the further fleet that had arrived with Demosthenes, the Athenians were completely demoralised. There was great surprise at this unexpected outcome (παράλογος), and even greater regret (μετάμελος) about having made the expedition itself. (7.55.1)

The unforeseeable outcome contrasts with the Athenian optimism, and leads them to doubt their original decision.[59]

The notion of *paralogos* assumes a different formulation in the context of the final battle, wherein the narrative creates no discursive space for self-reflection. The passage in question is imbued with a curious paradox. Despite the tremendous importance of this battle for the development of the war narrative, Thucydides presents it in terms that effectively suspend narrative advancement and compel readers to step momentarily outside time. The text invites this movement by withholding all comments on the course of the battle. Thucydides emphasizes the great confusion that dominates the scene in the harbour, but stops before offering the outcome. Moreover, this gap in authorial discourse is not compensated by the words of historical actors, even though this is a technique employed elsewhere in the *History* (speeches). Thucydides deploys internal focalization in order to engage us with the viewpoints of Athenian soldiers witnessing the event from ashore. Yet, unlike his critical treatment of sight, which is meant to distinguish the truth of events from how they appear, here the text foregrounds the very relationship between the gaze and logos. The description of conflicting sights engenders an event whose account continues to remain, at least for a while, outside narrative language and time. Rather than informing readers about what happened, the object of the Athenians' gaze gestures towards the paradoxical nature of this encounter, signalling at once a relation of attraction and separation, a state of fascination in the sense that the term derives from the Latin *fascinare*, to bewitch or enchant.

As the Athenian soldiers are watching, Thucydides writes, the battle takes the form of partially overlapping images, since they are unable to make sense of what happens, to move from sight to (historical) knowledge. Their experience of viewing holds narrative and temporal developments still. Reporting on this sight, Thucydides writes:

> Since the spectacle they were witnessing was close to the shore they were not all looking at the same thing at the same time. If one group saw their comrades coming out on top anywhere their spirits rose, and they fell to invoking the gods not to dash their hopes of a safe return; while those who were watching some reverse uttered loud cries of lamentation and were more crushed at the sight of what was going on than were those in the thick of the action; and yet others, who had their eyes fixed on some part of the battle where the outcome was undecided lived through agonies of suspense as the conflict continued inconclusively, even swaying their bodies in the extremity of their terror in sympathy with the movement of their opinions, as at any one moment they were either on the point of salvation or on the point of destruction. (7.71.1–3)

This is a forceful description, and was cited by Plutarch and others as exemplary of Thucydides' *enargeia*, the wording that transformed readers into spectators by bringing before their eyes the events and actions narrated.[60] But the narrative does more than simply invite readers to eyewitness the events of the past, as if they were present. In these final moments for the Athenian fleet, Thucydides reflects on the participants' conditions of viewing. In doing so he transforms the passage into an indirect comment on the writing of history. Thucydides' spectacle, as Walker notes, thematizes the difficulties of the historian who is himself enmeshed in the events and struggles to attain a '"complete vision" of contemporary history' wherein 'spectators, too close to the action to properly "see", provide conflicting accounts of what transpired'.[61]

The task of adjudicating when confronted with various testimonies of eyewitnesses was addressed by Thucydides in the theoretical statements of 1.22.3 as a problem of the historian's critical assessment. Here narrative suspense attests to the difficulty of reaching this assessment and Thucydides' quest for metahistorical reflection. But what kind of metahistorical comment is conveyed by this image? The focus on the gaze of Athenians means that narrative advancement of the course of the battle is absent, while internal focalization engages us only with the gazes of internal observers. The absence of the historian's discourse implies a certain withdrawal of his authority over his object. The unanticipated future engenders a past that, at least for a moment, remains outside narrative discourse and time. If the proliferation of discourses, as we learned from Michel Foucault, acts as a vehicle of power by confining our modes of understanding to stable frames of scientific account of objects,[62] then the complete absence of speaking in this passage eschews the assertion of the power of logos over the past.

By suspending the authority of retrospective vision, but also the power of logos as such, this image serves to highlight the *paralogos polemos*, the unforeseeability of the events narrated. In doing so, it compels reflection on the historian's relationship to what stands beyond his horizon of anticipation – his relation to the event not merely as unforeseen, but as radically unforeseeable, confronting the present as an interruption of the established meaningfulness of time. It is in this sense that the scene may be understood as a story of loss, reflecting Patočka's meaning's point zero: an event interrupting the operation of bestowing meaning to time, and thus entailing that this bestowal falls momentarily silent and that the world manifests a nothingness of meaning.[63] Such an interruption has a metahistoriographical function in so far as it implies that events have no stable meaning in time that is to be unveiled by the historian, but rather their meaning and relations require that someone has a sense for them – in Patočka's terms.[64] In other words, it implies that temporal meaningfulness is not lodged in what is, but in the process of understanding, in the movement, which begins anew when modes of meaningfulness collapse.

This collapse is conveyed in the narrative in the form of fascination with the image of death. For Maurice Blanchot, 'fascination' involves a relation in which what is ungraspable is also inescapable, and in which one can never cease reaching what, paradoxically, cannot be reached. Focusing on aesthetics, Blanchot speaks of a relation that forces us to abandon our 'sensory nature' by drawing us back from the world, by transforming the cognitive relation into one of fascination implying that the object of experience 'no longer reveals itself to us', yet at the same time 'it affirms itself in a presence foreign to the temporal present and to presence in space'. Fascination in this sense involves 'an indecisive moment', denoting the time of 'time's absence', a rupture in the continuous time of perception, that is not a purely negative mode, but is, on the contrary, a time without negation and without decision, when the cognitive processes defining what is present are suspended, and yet subjects are intensely engaged in the sight that confronts them.[65]

The speechless observers, whose bodies are drawn closer to the image of the fleet's destruction, while standing outside it, unable to grasp or understand that which draws them close, denotes a state of fascination, rather than cognition. As Blanchot puts it, 'whoever is fascinated does not see, properly speaking, what he sees. Rather, it touches him in an immediate proximity; it seizes and ceaselessly draws him close, even though it leaves him absolutely at a distance'.[66] Yet, this state of fascination, the desire to get closer to something that remains at a distance, is also the state of Thucydides' enterprise – formulated here as a metahistorical reflection on the links between historiography's determinism, which he sets against with the experience of radical contingency and lost historical meaning.

Thucydides' History of the Vanquished and Tensions of Historical Time

The tensions of historical time inscribed in Thucydides' engagement with the Athenians' gaze towards death can be grasped through Koselleck's concept of the history of the vanquished: the kind of history articulating the primary experience of defeat felt by a political or social class that has lost its domination and, for this very reason, is best equipped to interpret the distance between past and present reality brought about by this change. Significantly, Koselleck cites Thucydides' work among the great histories of the vanquished, reflecting both the historian's personal experience of defeat – as a commander in Amphipolis – and the collective defeat of Athens in the Peloponnesian War.[67] The history of victors, Koselleck argues, does not invite reflection on change, but 'is prone to interpret short-term success from the perspective of a continuous, long-term teleology ex post facto'. By contrast, the experience of the vanquished attests to the failure of concepts and temporalities through which historical actors used to make sense of their world. The vanquished face 'a greater burden of proof to explain why something happened in this and not the anticipated way'. As a consequence, 'a search for middle- or long-range reasons might be initiated to frame and perhaps explain the chance event of the unique surprise'. Hence, narratives of the vanquished contain an epistemological potential that transcends its cause: while history in the short run may be written by the victors, 'historical gains in knowledge stem in the long run from the vanquished'.[68]

One such gain was achieved by the uneasy conjunction of Thucydides' determinist historical perspective and the Athenians' confrontation with their unforeseeable loss. It involved the articulation of past time as necessarily obscure and sometimes meaningless. A contemporary of the Athenians facing death, as he stresses at the outset of his narrative, Thucydides' story of the vanquished registered the failure of language hitherto attributing sense to historical time. The historian's task was to address this failure through a retrospective doubling of time, the configuration of the reported events of the war in terms of a deterministic temporality: a narrative in which the Athenians were cast as negative examples who did not follow up on concepts that could have enabled them to correctly read the course of time, to reach the path from sight to knowledge. Yet on a different level, the Athenians' gazing at the city's loss, which is shared by Thucydides, registered a break in this retrospective story and a critical limitation of the historian's reconfiguration of the link between past time and meaning. In this respect, historical determinism is not merely confronted by contingency, but by the suspicion that no understanding of time, no matter how sophisticated, critical or comprehensive, would be sufficient to interpret the *paralogos* nature of (war) time, the relation of verticality that questions the concepts through which both historians and historical actors render time meaningful.

This latter dimension of the *History* then registers the probability of human failure to attribute meaning to time, and thereby the probability of a more radical articulation of the break between past, present and future, which Koselleck, among others, associated with modern historical consciousness.[69] Thucydides' intertwining of blindness and historical knowledge, and his narrative of fascination, configured a language of the unforeseeable, which, as Bernard Williams wrote in relation to tragedy, could perhaps be ascribed to the gods, *tychē*, or other non-human powers, but even if so, to powers that do not straightforwardly explain themselves or account for the consequences for humans of what they brought about.[70] The theoretical language entailed by death-images in the *History* constituted a reflection on this failure. As such, it contained a starker notion of historical time than those conveyed by modern temporalities.[71] The conception of time as a force that renders powerless human cognitive and constructive capacities may thus offer an alternative and limitation to the modern considerations of the past as foreign, but nonetheless as potentially mastered by narrative rendering both present and future largely controllable by human planning and action. The point of engaging with Thucydides' narrative tensions is then to deal with an aspect of time that cannot be understood as a thing or object, which cannot be mastered retrospectively or comprehended from outside, but which is present only in the seeking entailed by the loss of meaning and the unfolding of embryonic possibilities present in this shaking.[72] These include the possibility of a new form of writing about time that Thucydides pursued. But it needs to be recognized that such an engagement sprang from surrendering to the fascination with meaning's point zero – or, in Blanchot's terms, the fascination with time's absence.

Alexandra Lianeri is assistant professor in classics at the Aristotle University of Thessaloniki. Her research focuses on the modern history of *dēmokratia*, and the role of classics in modern intellectual history, as well as the history and theory of historiography. She is editor of *Knowing Future Time in and* through *Greek Historiography* (De Gruyter, 2016); *The Western Time of Ancient History: Historiographical Encounters with the Greek and Roman Pasts* (Cambridge University Press, 2011); and co-editor of *Translation and the Classic: Identity as Change in the History of Culture* (Oxford University Press, 2008).

Notes

I am grateful to Yorgos Avgoustis, Eftychia Bathrellou, Stefan Berger, Nicola Brauch, Chris Lorenz and Antonios Rengakos for their critical comments on previous drafts of this chapter and to Allan Megill for discussing the title.

1. Grethlein and Rengakos, *Narratology and Interpretation*; Grethlein, *The Greeks and their Past*; Grethlein, Huitink and Tagliabue, *Experience, Narrative and Criticism*.
2. Cornford, *Thucydides Mythistoricus*, ix.
3. Hesk, 'Thucydides'.
4. Woodman, *Rhetoric in Classical Historiography*, 13.
5. Hornblower, 'Narratology'.
6. Rood, *Thucydides: Narrative and Explanation*.
7. White, *Content of the Form*.
8. Grethlein and Rengakos, *Narratology and Interpretation*.
9. Rood, *Thucydides: Narrative and Explanation*; Rood, Atack and Philips, *Anachronism and Antiquity*.
10. Dewald, *Thucydides' War Narrative*; Tsakmakis and Tamiolaki, *Thucydides between History and Literature*.
11. Greenwood, *Thucydides and the Shaping of History*.
12. Grethlein, *The Greeks and their Past*; Grethlein, 'Experientiality'; Grethlein, *Experience and Teleology*.
13. Ankersmit, *Narrative Logic*, 1.
14. Lorenz and Bevernage, *Breaking up Time*.
15. Megill, 'History's Unresolving Tensions'.
16. Grethlein, *The Greeks and their Past*; Grethlein, 'Experientiality'.
17. Merleau-Ponty, *Basic Writings*, 294.
18. Ball, *Narratology*, 100–101.
19. Warhol, 'Gaze', 287.
20. Lacan, *The Four Fundamental*, 106.
21. Genette, 'Vraisemblance et motivation'; Genette, *Narrative Discourse*, 33–85.
22. Koselleck, *Transformations*, 76–83.
23. Goldhill, 'Seductions of the Gaze'; Blundell, Cairns and Rabinowitz, 'Vision and Viewing'; Kampakoglou and Novokhatko, *Gaze, Vision and Visuality*.
24. Thuc. 1.22; Marincola, *Authority and Tradition*, 68; Kallet, *Money*, 22.
25. Greenwood, *Thucydides and the Shaping of History*, 19–41.
26. Crane, *The Blinded Eye*, 227–28, 244.
27. Dewald, 'The Figured Stage', 243, my italics.
28. Ibid.
29. Greenwood, *Thucydides and the Shaping of History*, 20, 23.
30. Grethlein, *Experience and Teleology*, 51–52; Grethlein, *The Greeks and their Past*; Grethlein, 'Experientiality'.
31. Ankersmit, *Sublime Historical Experience*, 1.

32. Beyond the field of narratology, see disputes of this divide by Connor, 'Narrative Discourse'; Connor, *Thucydides*; Barker, *Entering the Agon*, 203–63; and Harman, 'Metahistory', 284–85.
33. Grethlein, *Experience and Teleology*, 29–52.
34. Unless otherwise noted, all translations of Thucydides are by Jeremy Mynott (2013).
35. Yunis, *Taming Democracy*, 69–70.
36. De Bakker, 'Authorial Comments', 252–53.
37. Winton, 'Thucydides', 116.
38. Taylor, *Thucydides, Pericles, and the Idea of Athens*, 83–84.
39. Stahl, *Thucydides*; Greenwood, 'Thucydides on the Sicilian Expedition'.
40. On the notion of verticality and the unforeseeable, see Derrida, 'My Chances', 6. On the (un)foreseeability of the future in Greek historiography, see Lianeri, *Knowing Future Time*.
41. Rood, *Thucydides*, 134; Rood, 'Thucydides, Sicily', 42.
42. Starr, *Political Intelligence*.
43. Patočka, *Heretical Essays*, 56–57.
44. Orwin, *Humanity of Thucydides*, 182–83; Taylor, *Thucydides, Pericles, and the Idea of Athens*, 66–69; Dewald, 'The Figured Stage', 97.
45. Strauss, *The City and Man*, 194–95.
46. I am indebted to Eftychia Bathrellou for her insightful comments on the translation of this phrase. Mynott's translation: 'It is difficult for a speaker to strike the right balance when there is not even any firm agreement between different perceptions of the truth'.
47. Hunter, *Thucydides the Artful Reporter*, 183.
48. *Theōmenous* 2.43.1; Crane, *The Blinded Eye*, 241 discusses the unusual for Thucydides deployent of the verb *theaōmai*, in opposition to the critical form of viewing conveyed by his use of the verb *skopein*.
49. Mara, *Civic Conversations*, 114.
50. Vidal-Naquet, *Le miroir brisé*.
51. Orwin, 'Beneath Politics', 119; Nichols, *Thucydides and the Pursuit of Freedom*, 36.
52. Greenwood, 'Thucydides on the Sicilian Expedition', 168–70.
53. Ibid., 169.
54. Kallet, *Money*, 57.
55. Ober, *Political Dissent*, 114. n. 14.
56. Greenwood, *Thucydides and the Shaping of History*, 38–39.
57. Ibid., 37.
58. Kallet, *Money*, 169.
59. Stahl, *Thucydides*, 185.
60. Walker, 'Enargeia'.
61. Ibid., 354.
62. Foucault, *History of Sexuality*.
63. Patočka, *Heretical Essays*, 56–57.
64. Ibid.
65. Blanchot, *Space of Literature*, 31–32.
66. Ibid., 33.
67. Koselleck, 'Transformations of Experience', 76.
68. Ibid.
69. Koselleck, 'Historia'.
70. Williams, *The Sense of the Past*, 58.
71. On the antagonism between ancient and modern temporalities see Lianeri 'Historia'.
72. Patočka, *Heretical Essays*, 77.

Bibliography

Ankersmit, Frank. *Narrative Logic: A Semantic Analysis of the Historian's Language*. Boston, MA: Martinus Nijhoff, 1983.
———. *Sublime Historical Experience*. Stanford, CA: Stanford University Press, 2005.
Ball, Mieke. *Narratology: Introduction to the Theory of Narrative*. Toronto: University of Toronto, 1985.
Balot, Ryan, Sara Forsdyke and Edith Foster (eds). *The Oxford Handbook to Thucydides*. Oxford: Oxford University Press, 2017.
Barker, Elton T.E. *Entering the Agon: Dissent and Authority in Homer, Historiography and Tragedy*. Oxford: Oxford University Press, 2009.
Blanchot, Maurice. *The Space of Literature*. Translated by Ann Smock. Lincoln: University of Nebraska Press, 1989.
Blundell, Sue, Douglas Cairns and Nancy Sorkin Rabinowitz (eds). 'Vision and Viewing in Ancient Greece'. *Helios* 40(1–2) (2013).
Connor, W. Robert. 'Narrative Discourse in Thucydides', in Michael Jameson (ed.), *The Greek Historians, Literature and History* (Stanford, CA: Anma Libro, 1985), 1–17.
———. *Thucydides*. Princeton, NJ: Princeton University Press, 1984.
Cornford, Francis Macdonald. *Thucydides Mythistoricus*. London: E. Arnold, 1907.
Crane, Gregory. *The Blinded Eye: Thucydides and the New Written Word*. Lanham, MD: Rowman & Littlefield, 1996.
De Bakker, Mathieu. 'Authorial Comments in Thucydides', in Ryan Balot, Sara Forsdyke and Edith Foster (eds), *The Oxford Handbook of Thucydides* (New York: Oxford University Press, 2017), 239–56.
Derrida, Jacques. 'My Chances/Mes Chances: A Rendezvous with Some Epicurean Stereophonies', in Joseph H. Smith and William Kerrigan (eds), *Taking Chances: Derrida, Psychoanalysis and Literature* (Baltimore, MD: Johns Hopkins University Press, 1984), 1–32.
Dewald, Carolyn. 'The Figured Stage: Focalizing the Initial Narratives of Herodotus and Thucydides', in Thomas M. Falkner, Nancy Felson and David Konstan (eds), *Contextualising Classics: Ideology, Performance, Dialogue* (Boston, MA: Rowman & Littlefield, 1999), 221–52.
———. *Thucydides' War Narrative: A Structural Study*. Berkeley: University of California Press, 2005.
Foucault, Michel. *The History of Sexuality. Volume 1: An Introduction*. Translated by Robert Hurley. New York: Vintage/Random House, 1978.
Genette, Gérard. *Narrative Discourse: An Essay in Method*. Translated by Jane E. Lewin. Ithaca, NY: Cornell University Press, 1980.
———. 'Vraisemblance et motivation', in Gerard Genette (ed.), *Figures II* (Paris: Èditions du Seuil, 1969), 71–99.
Goldhill, Simon. 'The Seductions of the Gaze: Socrates and his Girlfriends', in Paul Cartledge, Paul Millett and Sitta von Reden (eds), *Kosmos: Order, Individual and Community in Classical Athens* (Cambridge: Cambridge University Press, 1998), 105–24.
Greenwood, Emily. *Thucydides and the Shaping of History*. London: Bloomsbury, 2006.
———. 'Thucydides on the Sicilian Expedition', in Ryan Balot, Sara Forsdyke and Edith Foster (eds), *The Oxford Handbook to Thucydides* (Oxford: Oxford University Press, 2017), 161–78.
Grethlein, Jonas. *Experience and Teleology in Ancient Historiography*. Cambridge: Cambridge University Press, 2013.

———. 'Experientiality and "Narrative Reference" with Thanks to Thucydides'. *History and Theory* 49 (2010), 315–35.

———. *The Greeks and their Past: Poetry, Oratory and History in the Fifth-Century BCE*. Cambridge: Cambridge University Press, 2010.

Grethlein, Jonas, Luuk Huitink and Aldo C.F. Tagliabue (eds). *Experience, Narrative and Criticism in Ancient Greece: Under the Spell of Stories*. Oxford: Oxford University Press, 2020.

Grethlein, Jonas, and Antonis Rengakos (eds). *Narratology and Interpretation: The Content of Narrative Form in Ancient Literature*. Berlin: de Gruyter, 2009.

Harman, Rosie. 'Metahistory and the Visual in Herodotus and Thucydides', in Alexandros Kampakoglou and Anna Novokhatko (eds), *Gaze, Vision and Visuality in Ancient Greek Literature* (Berlin: De Gruyter, 2018), 271–88.

Hesk, Jon. 'Thucydides in the Twentieth and Twenty-First Centuries', in Christine Lee and Neville Morley (eds), *A Handbook to the Reception of Thucydides* (New Jersey: John Wiley & Sons, 2015), 218–37.

Hornblower, Simon. 'Narratology and Narrative Techniques in Thucydides', in Simon Hornblower (ed.), *Greek Historiography* (Oxford: Oxford University Press, 1994), 131–66.

Hunter, Virginia. *Thucydides the Artful Reporter*. Toronto: Toronto University Press, 1973.

Kallet, Lisa. *Money and the Corrosion of Power in Thucydides: The Sicilian Expedition and Its Aftermath*. Berkeley: University of California Press, 2001.

Kampakoglou, Aleaxandros, and Anna Novokhatko (eds). *Gaze, Vision and Visuality in Ancient Greek Literature*. Berlin: De Gruyter, 2018.

Koselleck, Reinhart. 'Historia Magistra Vitae: The Dissolution of a Topos into the Perspective of a Modernized Historical Process', in Reinhard Koselleck, *Futures Past: On the Semantics of Historical Time*. Translated by Keith Tribe (New York: Columbia University Press, 2004), 26–42.

———. 'Transformations of Experience and Methodological Change: A Historical-Anthropological Essay', in Reinhart Koselleck, *The Practice of Conceptual History: Timing History, Spacing Concepts*. Translated by Todd S. Presner (Stanford, CA: Stanford University Press, 2002), 45–83.

Lacan, Jacques. *The Four Fundamental Concepts of Psycho-Analysis*. London: Hogarth Press, 1977.

Lianeri, Alexandra (ed.) *Knowing Future Time in and Through Greek Historiography*. Berlin: De Gruyter, 2016.

———. 'Historia Magistra Vitae, Interrupting: Thucydides and the Agonistic Temporality of Antiquity and Modernity'. *History and Theory* 57(3) (September 2018), 327–48.

Lorenz, Chris, and Berber Bevernage (eds). *Breaking up Time: Negotiating the Borders between Present, Past and Future*. Göttingen: Vandenhoeck & Ruprecht, 2013.

Mara, Gerald M. *The Civic Conversations of Thucydides and Plato*. Albany, NY: SUNY Press, 2008.

Marincola, John. *Authority and Tradition in Ancient Historiography*. Cambridge: University Press, 1997.

Megill, Allan. 'History's Unresolving Tensions: Reality and Implications'. *Rethinking History* 23(3) (2019), 279–303.

Merleau-Ponty, Maurice. *Basic Writings*. Edited by Thomas Baldwin. London: Routledge, 2004.

Nichols, Mary P. *Thucydides and the Pursuit of Freedom*. Ithaca, NY: Cornell University Press, 2015.

Ober, Josiah. *Political Dissent in Democratic Athens: Intellectual Critics of Popular Rule*. Princeton, NJ: Princeton University Press, 1998.

Orwin, Clifford. 'Beneath Politics', in Christian. R. Thauer and Christian Wendt (eds), *Thucydides and Political Order: Concepts of Order and the History of the Peloponnesian War* (Basingstoke: Palgrave, 2016), 113–27.
———. *The Humanity of Thucydides*. Princeton, NJ: Princeton University Press, 1994.
Patočka, Jan. *Heretical Essays in the Philosophy of History*. Translated by Erazim Koh́ak. Chicago: Open Court, 1996.
Rood, Tim. *Thucydides: Narrative and Explanation*. Oxford: Oxford University Press, 1998.
———. 'Thucydides, Sicily, and the Defeat of Athens'. *KTÈMA Civilisations de l'Orient, de la Grèce et de Rome antiques* 42 (2017), 19–39.
Rood, Tim, Carol Atack and Tom Philips. *Anachronism and Antiquity*. New York: Bloomsbury, 2020.
Stahl, Hans-Peter. *Thucydides: Man's Place in History*. Swansea: Classical Press of Wales, 2003.
Starr, Chester G. *Political Intelligence in Classical Greece*. Leiden: Brill, 1974.
Strauss, Leo. *The City and Man*. Chicago: University of Chicago Press, 1964.Taylor, Martha C. *Thucydides, Pericles, and the Idea of Athens in the Peloponnesian War*. Cambridge: Cambridge University Press, 2010.
Thucydides. *The War of the Peloponnesians and the Athenians*. Edited and translated by Jeremy Mynott. Cambridge: Cambridge University Press, 2013.
Tsakmakis, Antonis, and Melina Tamiolaki (eds). *Thucydides between History and Literature*. Berlin: de Gruyter, 2013.
Vidal-Naquet, Pierre. *Le miroir brisé: tragédie athénienne et politique*. Paris: Les Belles Lettres, 2002.
Walker, Andrew. 'Enargeia and the Spectator in Greek Historiography'. *Transactions of the American Philological Association* 123 (1993), 353–77.
Warhol, Robyn. 'Gaze', in David Herman, Manfred Jahn and Marie-Laure Ryan (eds), *Routledge Encyclopedia of Narrative Theory* (London: Routledge, 2005).
White, Hayden. *The Content of the Form: Narrative Discourse and Historical Representation*. Baltimore, MD: Johns Hopkins University Press, 1987.
Williams, Bernard. *The Sense of the Past: Essays on the History of Philosophy*. Edited by Myles Burnyeat. Princeton, NJ: Princeton University Press, 2006.
Winton, R. 'Thucydides', in Christopher Rowe and Malcolm Shofield (eds), *The Cambridge History of Greek and Roman Political Thought* (Cambridge: Cambridge University Press, 2000), 111–21.
Woodman, Anthony J. *Rhetoric in Classical Historiography: Four Studies*. Portland, OR: Areopagitica Press, 1988.
Yunis, Harvey. *Taming Democracy: Models of Political Rhetoric in Classical Athens*. Ithaca, NY: Cornell University Press, 1996.

CHAPTER 2

History beyond Narration

The Shifting Terrain of Bloodlands

WULF KANSTEINER

People were perhaps alike in dying and in death, but each of them was different until that final moment, each had different preoccupations and presentiments until all was clear and then all was black. Some people died thinking about others rather than themselves, such as the mother of the beautiful fifteen-year-old Sara, who begged to be killed at the same time as her daughter. Here there was, even at the end, a thought and a care: that if she saw her daughter shot she would not see her raped . . . Only there in the ditch were these people reduced to nothing, or to their number, which was 33,761. Since the bodies were later exhumed and burned on pyres, and the bones that did not burn crushed and mixed with sand, the count is all that remains.

—Timothy Snyder, *Bloodlands*

This excerpt from *Bloodlands* captures some of the decisive qualities of the book. It is a carefully written text displaying an unflinching commitment to tangible portrayals of past violence, an almost spiritual belief in the solidity and redeeming power of numerical facts, and a deeply felt conviction in our ability to understand the history of mass murders like the Holocaust. Moreover, the paragraph reflects an interesting linguistic quality of the book. The language of *Bloodlands* often deals in descriptions, in generics and

---

Notes for this section begin on page 79.

generalities, in states of minds, and states of affairs that do not move time. Therefore, *Bloodlands* has a complicated relation to narration and argumentation. Less visible in the above quote is *Bloodlands*' concern with memory politics and historical reinterpretation.

The book invents a new region, appropriately called 'the bloodlands', which comprises Ukraine, Belarus, the Baltic states, Central Poland and Western Russia. In this territory, Soviets and Nazis killed 14 million civilians between 1933 and 1945 by means of intentional famines, political and ethnic cleansing, and genocide. The book seeks to establish the bloodlands as event, concept and memorial obligation.

The fields of historical theory, philosophy of history and history didactics suffer from a theoretical impasse that first developed in the 1970s. The linguistic turn in historical studies, initiated by historians like Hayden White and Dominick LaCapra, has resulted in a substantial body of work.[1] Generations of theorists have argued that the creative process of professional historical writing generates narrative texts that give voice to their authors' aesthetic, ideological and moral preferences.[2] The poststructuralist-inclined theorists have taken for granted that historians deal with true events and have not paid much attention to the research activities or epistemological underpinnings of historical scholarship. They have highlighted the essential narrative structures of historical writing, and rarely engaged in close readings of concrete historical texts.[3] That might explain why most historians have declined to engage with the narrativist challenge, and continue to adhere to conventional concepts of historical truth and historical narration.[4] The lack of curiosity on the part of many theorists about the empirical foundation and empirical ethics of historical writing has also met with determined criticism from more traditionally inclined philosophers of history and intellectual historians.[5]

With the present case study and similar analyses, I would like to relate the theoretical-methodological concerns of the linguistic turn to concrete texts of historical scholarship.[6] I want to expose the complicated inner workings of historical writings by identifying the texts' multiple layers, vectors and building blocks, and insert them into their scholarly contexts. The close encounters with historical writing are designed to provide new food for self-reflexive thought for theorists and historians alike. For that purpose, I apply a number of axiomatic principles and analytical strategies that have helped narratologists and linguists to unlock the secrets of narration and discourse, but have not as yet played a prominent role in the discussions about history in the wake of the linguistic turn.[7]

Text Types: Description, Argumentation and Narration

For narratologists and linguists, narratives are one of a handful of fundamental text types or discursive modes that cover the entirety of human text production. Some narratologists assume that the key text types are description, argumentation and narration.[8] Other experts embrace categories of classical rhetoric and add additional types such as exposition, explanation or instruction.[9] Of these text types, only narration has the primary function of depicting change over time. Therefore, narration plays a decisive role in historical writing and has become the primary concern of historical theorists.

My first methodological move consists of relativizing the focus on narration in a lot of recent historical theory. I suggest that historical writing consists of description, argumentation and narration, and that the task of blending the three text types is a characteristic of the work of historians. Put differently, almost all professional history texts seek to capture past reality (description), deliver a good story (narration) and make a compelling case about the nature of the past, the relation between past and present, and the mistakes of other historians (argument). Professional historical writing is thus a text hybrid; it utilizes all three text types.[10]

The three types can be clearly defined in distinction from each other, especially on the level of single sentences, but also with regard to longer text passages and possibly also with regard to whole books. Consider in this context the definition of discursive modes as suggested by text linguist Carlota Smith. She argues that fictional as well as non-fictional 'texts progress according to changes in location, temporal or spatial; or to changes in metaphorical location'.[11] Smith adds that narratives 'progress as time advances'.[12] In fact, for our purposes, narrative is the only mode that advances time.[13] Smith adds that 'descriptive passages progress spatially through a scene' and that in descriptions 'time is static or suspended'.[14] The classic example for descriptive writing is travel writing. Turning to our third discursive mode, Smith suggests that 'an argument passage brings something to the attention of the reader, makes a claim, comment, or argument, and supports it in some way'. She adds that 'passages in the argument mode are concerned with states of affairs, facts and propositions'.[15] Arguments do not advance time. Instead, they advance through what Smith calls 'motion through metaphorical space', or 'metaphorical progression'. This metaphorical progression is focused on a more or less abstract primary referent, for instance American democracy, digital technology, or, perhaps, bloodlands.[16] Finally, Smith differentiates between the foreground and the background levels of texts, which can reflect different modes of discourse. The decisive question to be posed about a given text regards its primary mode of progression – in other words, does the text progress temporally, spatially or metaphorically. Or, to rephrase the question, is the text trying to convince the reader about the accuracy of a specific assessment or explanation; is it trying to describe a specific setting; or is it trying to capture change over the time.

Smith's text-linguistic arguments permit us to see history in a new light. Perhaps there exist fundamentally different types of historical writing. All history features argumentative structures, narrative trajectories and descriptive passages. But the three text types' precise relationship to each other may differ substantially between different pieces of historical scholarship. There may exist primarily narrative-inclined texts supported by intellectual operations of description and argumentation; descriptively ambitious texts backed up by narrative and argumentative semantics; and argumentative texts aided along by description and narration. Hence it makes sense to assess the quality of a given text by what it is primarily aiming at. All history texts probably aspire to a measure of descriptive, narrative and argumentative success and integrity. But in a spirit of fair play the quality of a given text should probably be assessed in special consideration of its primary intellectual goal, be that descriptive, narrative, or argumentative objectives. It is likely all too easy – and tempting – to highlight the contradictions and logical dead ends in a text that is not primarily designed to deliver a well-thought-through argument but that rather seeks to shine as a narrative performance. That raises the important question of what kind of text *Bloodlands* wants to be?

From this axiom follow three important conclusions. First, since historical writings are linguistically overdetermined texts, one should refrain from reducing them to just one text type, whether that be description, argumentation or narration. Second, one should similarly desist from positing a priori a hierarchical relation between the three textual components of historical writing, and assume that one of them will always trump the other two. Therefore, I would want to suspend temporarily many historians' assumption that their scholarship serves primarily descriptive purposes (i.e. that it first and foremost reflects past reality), or, to put it in Smith's terms, that it primarily progresses spatially.[17] For the same reason, I would want to put on hold the belief of the advocates of the linguistic turn, who are convinced that professional history is always characterized by a primacy of narration, which is to say that its principal mode of progression is change over time.[18] Finally, I will also take leave of the supposition of some narratologists who have maintained that historical scholarship serves primarily argumentative goals, that means advances mostly metaphorically, and is therefore not even a legitimate object of analysis for the field of narratology.[19] As a third point, given the overdetermined nature of historical writing, one should realize that the very same text can be perceived and used from different textual vantage points. There can be legitimate disagreement about the intention, structure or function of a given text.[20] An author might be proud of having delivered a new argument about historical causality; a critic of the same text might be intrigued by the precise, life-like tableaus of past life; and a reader might immerse herself in the suspenseful storyline. Plus, the perception of the text might change substantially over time. The very same piece of scholarship might first be praised for its empirical veracity, later rejected because of its political polemics, and finally appreciated as a particularly compelling narrative world.[21]

The Texter

The narratological perspective offers additional useful analytical strategies. In my close reading of *Bloodlands* I want to differentiate between the real author, Timothy Snyder, on the one hand, and the figure of the texter that is permanently inscribed into a given piece of historical scholarship, on the other hand. The figure of the texter is an element of the text and defined in similar terms as the figure of the narrator in narrative-literary theory. For literary experts, the narrator is a key element of every literary fiction. It might be explicitly identified in the text and can even be involved in events under description, or it might never appear in person and look at events from a great distance. Either way, the narrator both observes and constitutes the story and thus serves as a communicative relay between author and reader. The narrator is the figure in the text that determines the selection and sequence of events, the choice of language and narrative tools, and the overall narrative trajectory of the text. Some narrators are quite judgemental; they offer detailed assessments of other actors and events. In this way, the text might directly or indirectly reveal a lot of information about the narrator, such as educational background, social status, political convictions, or general worldview.[22]

It makes a lot of analytical sense, and might help to overcome the impasse between narrativists and traditionalists in the field of historical theory, to posit the existence of a similar figure in non-fictional texts, including history texts.[23] Historians do not communicate directly with their readers. Like most producers of texts or images, they are not present at the moments of the consumption of their intellectual products which, to a larger or lesser extent, reflect their producers' intentions as well as the properties and limits of the chosen genre and medium. For the purpose of mediated communication, historians construct and permanently inscribe into their texts sets of events and actors, concepts of time and space, and models of causality and narrative cohesion. The concrete textual elements deployed for these purposes are coordinated from an overarching perspective by a text-immanent agent who, similar to the narrator, ensures the text's overall descriptive, argumentative and narrative coherence.[24] The agent is like a prism, positioned by the author inside the text to communicate with its readers. In light of above text-linguistic arguments, it would be misleading to call that agent a narrator because that terminological choice would imply a primacy of narrative construction and communication in the writing and reading of professional historical texts. To put it into the terms suggested by Carlota Smith: if we are dealing with a piece of professional historical writing that primarily (i.e. in the foreground of the text) advances through spatial progression, the text in question would be written in the mode of description and the text-immanent figure holding the reigns should be called a describer; if we are dealing with a text advancing primarily through metaphorical progression, the text-immanent figure should be called an arguer; and only if we are dealing with a history text that advances primarily through temporal progression would it make sense to call the text-immanent figure a narrator.

But in order to limit the extent of new terminology at this stage of our analysis, and while, however, assuming the existence of a great variety of historical prose texts, including texts reflecting primarily descriptive or argumentative modes of discourse and communicative purposes, we want to call the text-immanent figure a texter – all the while knowing full well that there exist at least three different types of texters: describers, arguers and narrators. Put differently, in sharp contrast to the narratological concept of the narrator, the texter is also responsible for coordinating and prioritizing the text's descriptive, argumentative and narrative components, and thus for deciding, through the act of prioritizing, if the text is a professional historical description, a professional historical argumentation, or a professional historical narrative.

In general, historical monographs consist of at least four different textual layers. The first and generally most voluminous layer is dedicated to the historical events under description. A second layer outlines the history and present configuration of relevant research fields, often referring critically or appreciatively to the work of other experts in the field and highlighting their descriptive, argumentative and narrative failures or accomplishments. A third, closely related layer presents the history of the present book by integrating it into its concrete historiographical context and presenting its specific research design and source material. The history of the book might feature other information – for instance, pertaining to the professional and private networks that have supported the project at hand. Finally, on a fourth textual layer, footnotes or endnotes offer references and running commentary. Most of these layers have significant narrative volition; the history of the present book is almost always a history of progress; the history of relevant research fields tends to be a history of qualified progress pointing at some decisive problems justifying the existence of the present book (see above characterization of the fields of historical theory, philosophy of history and history didactics); the history of the past can follow all kinds of narrative trajectories, depending on the taste and conviction of the texter. Readers will subject the various narrative trajectories to their expectations of narrative plausibility, assuming that actants either act in similar ways throughout the course of the text or that the texter is capable of attributing changes in behaviour to plausible causes. History texts, unlike for instance modernist novels, are generally subject to fairly rigorous standards of narrative non-contradiction, thereby enforcing a high degree of narrative coherence and homogeneity.

The narratives coexist, serve, or are supported by arguments running vertically and horizontally through the text, and seeking to convince readers of the plausibility of specific concepts, specific models of causality or specific interpretations of past events and present research environments.[25] These argumentative webs are subject to standards of proof and informal reasoning that might not be easily reconcilable with prevalent standards of narrative coherence. Readers might, for instance, expect a suspenseful, fully fleshed out course of action that the texter cannot deliver, given the scarcity or contradictory nature of available evidence.

It is the texter's job to handle such tensions between narration and argumentation by resolving, addressing or hiding them from readers.

On the microlevel of single statements, sentences or paragraphs, the differences between descriptive, narrative and argumentative discourse is clearly identifiable. But how should one aggregate a handful of close readings of a few paragraphs to amount to an accurate and fair assessment of a whole book? How does the relation between description, narration and argumentation unfold on the macrolevel of the entire text? Can the relation between microlevel and macrolevel ever be more than a metaphorical relationship? Given the plethora of textual elements, layers and vectors, any narratologically-linguistically informed analysis of historical writing only engages with a sliver of a given work of historical scholarship. The structuralist utopia of total text mapping is unattainable, and selection and purposeful arrangement of textual evidence abound – also in the present analysis. But the deconstructive detour through linguistic terrain might still be worthwhile – for example, if it manages to provide relevant new insights into well-known classical publications like *Bloodlands*.

The Limits of Narration

All narratives and arguments feature descriptive building blocks that, in principle, can be separated from their narrative and argumentative contexts.

In fact, the narrativist critique of historical writing, that feels wrong to many historians, raises an important question about the limits of narration in history. How much non-narrative information and non-temporal advancement does a book like *Bloodlands* include, and what role does this information play in the overall semantic efforts of the text? Is there in a degree zero of narration in historical writing, a kind of rock-bottom historical realism? Are there key and perhaps even extensive passages in historical texts that advance spatially in their description of past reality and whose factual accuracy are acknowledged by an overwhelming majority of historians as a result of compelling source material and source criticism?[26]

One could suggest, for example, that the sentence in *Bloodlands* 'Stalin was Georgian' (12) is a descriptive, non-narrative statement of fact that can be proven beyond reasonable doubt by way of a vertical argumentative link (i.e. a footnote). Having said that, one could also argue that the statement 'Stalin was Georgian' is not devoid of narration. The use of the past tense might indicate that the texter assumes a transformation has occurred – for instance, because Stalin is no longer Georgian or because he is dead. Both interpretations denote change over time. In addition, in textual practice, small-scale descriptive building blocks are closely intertwined with narrative and argumentative semantics. In *Bloodlands*, the statement 'Stalin was Georgian' is one of several stepping stones in the texter's argument that the multi-ethnic background of prominent Bolshevik leaders explains that they, for strategic reasons, 'were capable of subtle reasoning and tact on the national question'. This complex argument, crafting a wide-ranging narrative-causal link between personal experience and duplicitous political skills appears to elide proof beyond a reasonable doubt, the more so since the argument is delivered in an ironic key contrasting the Bolsheviks' alleged tact on the national question with Stalin's later murderous nationalistic paranoia. At the end of the swift ride from fact to irony we have left behind the field of gravity of historical facticity. There are no historical facts capable of demonstrating that they have to be expressed in the aesthetic mode of irony. But the question remains at what point precisely on that trip from fact to irony does epistemology retreat and aesthetics take over. Moreover, the possibility and actuality of proof plays an important role in historical practice, especially with regard to new research results and despite the fact that nearly every sentence in a professional work of history is narratively 'polluted'.

Assuming for a moment that the sentence 'Stalin was Georgian' is in fact a non-narrative statement, it should be analytically differentiated from sentences with obvious narrative depth – for example, the phrase 'Stalin's wife killed herself' (39). That is clearly a narrative statement expressing change over time and attributing agency – first she was alive, then she was dead, and she herself had brought about that course of events. Like our first example, however, Stalin's wife's death plays an important part in a larger narrative-argumentative line of reasoning that the texter conveys in a strange passive-aggressive mode indicating a considerable degree of argumentative disinterest or insecurity. The texter implies but does not explicitly argue that she committed suicide because she learned about the impending famine in Ukraine: 'As reports about failed requisitions were delivered to the Kremlin, Stalin's wife killed herself' (40). That tentative statement is in turn integrated into a narrative-argumentative scenario delivered with great narrative gusto and radical doubt at one and the same time. After her death, Stalin approached 'the problem of the famine with a new degree of malice' although what the suicide 'meant to Stalin, can never be entirely clear' (40). The texter suggests the existence of a direct causal chain reaching from news about the lack of food in Ukraine over Nadezhda Alliluyeva's death to the radicalization of Stalin's policies; but he does not want to fully commit himself. The texter seems to be very conscious of the fact that readers might point out that Stalin was similarly brutal before and after his wife's death and that she happened to suffer from mental illness. Therefore, the texter inserts a heavy dose of argumentative non-commitment in his text. Or, phrased differently, he wants to have his narrative-argumentative cake and eat it too! Consequently, in this case, the texter both embraces and deconstructs the fantasy of historical facticity by way of a rhetorical performance.

The close reading of the two text segments indicates that the two sentences have a similar epistemological status despite their different linguistic forms. On the one hand, it is important to differentiate between non-narrative and narrative sentences in historical prose, among other reasons because they are subject to different evidentiary requirements. Non-narrative facts like Stalin's ethnic background can often be more easily established as facts than narrative facts like Stalin's wife suicide or, a more appropriate example for narrative complexity, the reasons for Stalin's suicide. On the other hand, in textual historical practice, the two types of statements are generally treated in the same way, as non-controversial statements of fact. Neither sentence in *Bloodlands* is backed up by an explicit argumentative chain in the form of a footnote, and that is the rule in historical writing. Such proof is neither necessary nor practical because history books contain so many descriptive statements of facts that only a select few can be backed up by notes. In terms of proof economy, most non-narrative and small-scale narrative descriptions rely on performance and trust. Consequently, descriptive statements of no or little narrative complexity have a different epistemological status than large-scale narrative and argumentative trajectories. Furthermore, one should not forget that history texters pursue descriptive ambition on different scales. In addition to small-scale descriptive ambition put into practice in singular statements of fact – either well researched or posited as non-controversial – texters often seek to draw immersive, captivating large-scale pictures of events, settings or eras. These large-scale descriptive endeavours are inextricably intertwined with narrative and are beyond the reach of empirical proof that validates small-scale descriptive statements. Plus, as we will see below, even small-scale descriptive statements proven as fact are often carefully coordinated to align with a larger narrative-argumentative semantic pattern.

In the end, the characterization of a given text as primarily narratively, argumentatively or descriptively driven, depends on one's assessment of the relative ambition and accomplishments of the text with regard to these three registers of meaning production. The image of a texter hedging his bets by narratively insinuating a specific causal chain of events, but never coming forward with an explicitly developed argument, raises questions about his primary ambitions. In above text segment, he does not seem to like the role of an arguer. Therefore, checking the main arguments advanced in *Bloodlands* is an important analytical step in determining the text's preferred mode of discourse. As so often with books of history, explicit far-reaching arguments are found in the introduction and conclusion.

Argument I: History and Memory

In the conclusion of *Bloodlands* the texter relates his descriptive and narrative accomplishments to a set of explicitly developed arguments, one of which deals with the relation between history and memory. In terms of descriptive ambition, the texter claims to have produced the first comprehensive comparative history of the mass murder of civilians committed by the Nazi and the Soviet regimes between 1933 and 1945: 'Now [the] history of the bloodlands is complete' (380). His claim to accuracy is reflected in an exhaustive compilation of available victim figures. In fact, the book abounds with seemingly highly precise victim tallies forming an empirical bedrock of low narrative complexity. In the conclusion, this descriptive-empirical foundation plays a decisive role in advancing the texter's argument in favour of non-nationalistic memories of Soviet and Nazi mass murders.

The texter puts a premium on numerical accuracy because he seeks to counteract the political instrumentalization of inaccurate historical data in post-Second World War memory cultures. As the texter puts it somewhat clumsily: 'When history is removed, numbers go upward and memories go inward, to all of our peril' (405). What he is trying to say here is that a lack of historical accuracy (i.e. upward numbers) is a key factor in facilitating self-serving and morally and politically unsound nationalistic (i.e. inward) memories. He is rightly convinced that 'nationalists throughout the bloodlands (and beyond) have indulged in the quantitative exaggeration of victimhood, thereby claiming for themselves the mantle of innocence' (401). This argument is related to other, similarly compelling criticisms of contemporary memory culture. Identifying with victims of mass murder is indeed not much of an accomplishment while understanding perpetrators and bystanders constitutes a much more pressing moral challenge in today's world (399). Yet in his indictment of nationalistic memories based on inflated victim counts the texter might have committed an analytical error. He assumes that the reverse also holds true – namely, that insisting on accurate numbers goes a long way in advancing transnationally (i.e. outward) oriented memories of significant moral integrity.

In his efforts to integrate his descriptive and argumentative objectives, the texter assumes a direct correlation between history and memory – or, more precisely, between historical accuracy and memorial integrity. The texter argues that postwar societies in East and West never developed an accurate understanding of the Holocaust because they lacked knowledge of relevant facts: 'When an international collective memory of the Holocaust emerged in the 1970s and 1980s, it rested on the experiences of German and West European Jews, minor groups of victims, and on Auschwitz, where only about one in six of the total number of murdered Jews died' (376). In the conceptual world of *Bloodlands*, this moral failure appears to be directly related to the historical circumstances of the liberation of the Nazi death camps. American and British forces 'never saw the places where the Germans killed, meaning that understanding of Hitler's crimes has taken' until the end of the Cold War (xiv). Consequently, for many decades, the West lacked a true grasp of the nature and scope of Nazi genocide, largely because Western allies failed to liberate any of the Nazi death camps. They subsequently developed a faulty understanding of Nazi crimes on the basis of information gathered during the liberation of far less deadly concentration camps, such as Bergen-Belsen in northern Germany (457).

By contrast, Communist societies in Eastern Europe had access to accurate data because the Red Army liberated the major sites of Nazi atrocities (xiv). Unfortunately, however, Stalin immediately imposed an alternate, highly inaccurate set of facts on Soviet collective memory of the Second World War, a memory designed to make Jews disappear as a special victim category and foster a myth of Soviet suffering and Russian heroism. So according to the texter, the West embraced an erroneous memory with extraordinary enthusiasm due to a lack of authentic experiences, while the East got its memory wrong as a result of an authoritarian top-down campaign of deliberate forgetting. In the end, the Holocaust never found a home in European memory despite all the efforts and resources poured into the construction of Holocaust remembrance since the 1970s: 'Deprived of its Jewish distinctiveness in the East, and stripped of its geography in the West, the

Holocaust never quite became part of European history, even as Europeans and many others came to agree that all should remember the Holocaust' (378). Little wonder then that East and West failed even more spectacularly when it came to comprehending and remembering the Soviet crimes of the twentieth century. Soviet leadership and Soviet society had an excellent grasp of the geography of mass starvation, the great terror and the gulag concentration camp empire, but Soviet and later Russian leaders had simply no desire to advertise crimes that the Soviets had largely managed to commit in secrecy, and of which nobody in the West had any first-hand knowledge. As a result of this fourfold failure of Holocaust misremembrance and Holodomor and great terror forgetting, bloodlands memory has always betrayed bloodlands history, and harmed postwar societies in the process. Humanity has simply never recognized the complexity and extraordinary historical relevance of the bloodlands, and their exceptional potential as sites of memory. Equipped with the requisite self-confidence, the texter has now managed for the first time 'to introduce to European history its central event' (379).

The book's arguments about the correlation between history and memory are not systematically conceptualized, which is not surprisingly as we are dealing with a texter who maintains that 'Europe's epoch of mass killing is overtheorized and misunderstood' (383). Consequently, *Bloodlands*' argumentative infrastructure appears to be based on an implicit geographical-empirical reductionism. According to its logic, productive collective memories of a given event are more likely to evolve if a member of the memory collective in question was an eyewitness of the event to be memorialized, and can subsequently, under favourable cultural and political circumstances, imbue the memory of the event with a sense of authenticity and historical accuracy for the benefit of his/her in-group. Witnesses of different backgrounds or memory activists lacking first-hand experience do not seem to possess the memorial touch required for laying the foundation for a productive memory trajectory.

The history–memory link in *Bloodlands* can be assessed from a variety of vantage points, including perspectives that consider bloodlands a fact of history and a memorial imperative. However, since the texter explicitly invokes collective memory, it seems to be similarly reasonable to test his arguments from a memory studies' vantage point. From that perspective – historically, politically and morally relative as it is – the texter's arguments appear less reasonable. Few experts would currently assume a direct link between historical experience and memory politics. Collective memories are always mediated and socially constructed.[27] It is a long way from the experiences of soldiers of the Red Army, who liberated the death camps while passing in their rush to Berlin, and who might or might not have had an understanding of what had happened at these locations, to the formation of collective memories in important theatres of national and transnational memory. Such testimony would in any case have been subject to the creative forces of cultural tradition, including dominant narrative and iconographic templates, media genres and political exigency. The evolution of compelling sites of memory is simply not dependent on the factual presence of culturally-politically indigenous eyewitnesses but on the media construction of suitable stories and suitable eyewitness figures well adapted to changing standards of historical taste and memorial authenticity. In light of the high degree of institutionalization of Holocaust history and memory across Europe and beyond, it might be difficult to find any event that lives up to the texter's criteria of settled history and is permanently and unequivocally rooted in a given historical context, although he points to a worthy alternative candidate: the bloodlands.

Nor, the memory studies expert would continue, is there a direct link between the historical accuracy and the moral integrity of a given site of memory. European memory might inflate the relevance of the memory of the Holocaust and systematically forget gulag and Holodomor crimes, but Holocaust memory is probably still the best, most self-reflexive memory of genocide in existence. Especially in the early stages of Western Holocaust memory, carrier groups championed a problematic concept of Holocaust uniqueness, and occasionally operated with highly inflated victim counts, proclaiming that the Nazi perpetrators and their collaborators murdered over 4 million Jews in Auschwitz. Both problematic assertions seem to have helped rather than hindered the evolution of an exceptionally self-critical Holocaust memory in West Germany. Factual accuracy is neither a necessary nor a sufficient precondition for good memory politics. Memory, even under the best of circumstances and with the best possible outcomes, reflects ignorance, selectivity, myopia and questionable fantasies of coherence – not unlike history, I would suggest. The causal link between history and memory advanced in *Bloodlands* is never tested in light of readily available contradicting expert opinion. In argumentation theory that is one of the agreed upon signs of a poorly crafted argument.[28]

Argument II: Two Evil Dictators

A second key argument of *Bloodlands* is related to the texter's narrative ambition of wanting to bring different 'national histories together' (xix). At the outset he does not clarify what intellectual traditions and methodologies (comparative, transnational, global history, etc.) he hopes to bring to bear on the history of the bloodlands. Yet all of us are likely to agree with the texter when he argues that 'attention to any single persecuted group, no matter how well executed as history, will fail as an account of what happened in Europe between 1933 and 1945'. We are probably also in complete agreement when he adds that 'perfect knowledge of the Ukrainian past will not produce the causes of the famine', and that 'following the history of Poland is not the best way to understand why so many Poles were killed in the Great Terror' (xix).

One could respond to that argument with two critical remarks. First, writing national history does not entail directing one's analytical gaze exclusively at the history of the nation under description. In fact, most national history is written in a decidedly antagonistic key, pitching the fate of one's own nation against the history of enemies and competitors. The texters invented by Polish historians, for example, excel at chronicling the long history of Polish suffering, but they are similarly astute at offering detailed discussions about the motives and methods of the long list of foreign powers that have caused centuries of Polish misery.[29] Broadening one's horizon beyond a concern with one single nation is not enough. Writing non-national history entails abandoning a preconceived national moral point of view and adopting an analytical-conceptual lens that guarantees that the intellectual yield of the non-national or transnational analytical endeavour is clearly greater than the sum of its various national parts. The texter is aware of this expectation and therefore argues repeatedly that his history of the bloodlands highlights the dynamic interdependence between German and Soviet history. He maintains that the bloodlands have as yet not been properly understood as a historical phenomenon nor acknowledged as an important site of memory, because experts have failed to grasp the complex dynamic interaction between the Soviet and the Nazi political systems. The two systems must be compared 'to understand our times and ourselves' (379), because the victims – in this case the Soviet prisoners of war – 'died as a result of the *interaction* of the two systems' (380, texter's emphasis).

Yet a closer look at the narrative vectors of *Bloodlands* indicates that the texter has compiled a parallel not an integrated history of the Soviet and the Nazi systems of mass murder, and that might be a good thing. Time and again, the texter's scrupulous handling of the evidence demonstrates that responsibility for each atrocity in the long line of mass murders featured in *Bloodlands* can be clearly attributed to one or the other system of inhumanity. Consequently, either because of the nature of the crimes or the conventional narrative design of *Bloodlands*, the book rarely relates a history of interaction, but instead presents captivating stories of two evil dictators who happened to murder at approximately the same time and often in similar geographical locations. In pursuit of those narrative ends, the book presents a highly conventional cast of characters. The texter attributes agency to the villains

Stalin and Hitler and a few of their henchman. Occasionally, other actors appear on stage, for instance partisans, but the conventional narrative design is ill suited for the task of conveying an interactive history of two repressive systems, because said systems never assume the role of narrative actants.[30]

Let us focus on three specific narrative scenarios and contemplate them from a bloodlands-sceptical point of view using the texter's own data. Between 1931 and 1933, Stalin decided to have 5.5 million Soviet citizens, including 3.3 million Soviet citizens of Ukrainian ethnicity, starve to death by withholding from them essential food staples that these people had themselves produced. In the texter's version of events, the Nazis' concurrent rise to power and their rabid anti-Communism did not influence Stalin's decisions. The visible presence of the respective other as threat and rival helped Stalin and Hitler to solidify their power base, both nationally and internationally.

When Stalin later initiated a brutal campaign of political purges of the party – the army and the secret service in 1936, followed by a more extensive mass murder of peasants and various ethnic groups in 1937 and 1938 – the existence and objectives of Nazi Germany and Hitler did not play a role in Stalin's paranoid decision-making process. Moreover, the great terror went largely unnoticed in Western Europe (106). In 1939 and 1940, during the joint occupation of Poland, Stalin extended his time-tested campaigns of class warfare and political purges to the new territory, while Hitler's Einsatzgruppen for the first time tried their hand at racial warfare by successfully murdering and terrorizing Jewish and non-Jewish Polish citizens, despite the fact that they 'lacked the experience and the skills of the NKVD' (126). In the texter's coverage of events, the two similar campaigns of mass murder on either side of the Molotov–Ribbentrop line neither radicalized or jeopardized each other; both dictators simply committed their crimes as they saw fit, and they seemed to get along just fine.

When Nazi Germany invaded the Soviet Union in the summer of 1941 and immediately embarked on two murder campaigns – the execution of male civilians by the Einsatzgruppen and the systematic starvation of Soviet prisoners of war – Soviet policies indeed exacerbated the situation. Stalin's insistence that Red Army soldiers should not surrender prevented tactical withdrawals and pushed more men into German captivity than necessary: 'The policies of Hitler and Stalin conspired to turn Soviet soldiers into prisoners of war and then prisoners of war into non-people' (175). Nevertheless, the decision to murder these prisoners had nothing to do with Stalin's disdain for human life. It was Hitler and his generals who let them starve to death, unencumbered by any concerns about possible Soviet input or reaction. The two regimes were applying two substantially different concepts of 'non-people'.

In the narrative universe of *Bloodlands*, German and Soviet perpetrators keep operating largely independently of each other in their murder campaigns, despite their intense military entanglement. On occasion, the texter frankly concedes a significant degree of non-interaction, for instance regarding German genocide and ethnic cleansing: 'German policies of mass murder could affect the Soviet leadership only in the lands that were actually conquered: Ukraine, Belarus, the Baltic States and a very thin wedge of Russia. This was not very much of the Soviet Union, and the people in question were not of critical importance to the Soviet system' (181). In the fall of 1941, the Red Army forced Hitler and the SS to regroup and improvise, because the military attack of the Soviet Union turned out to be an 'utter fiasco' (184). However, as the texter explains compellingly, thanks to Himmler's ingenuity the perpetrators could re-prioritize Hitler's utopian fantasies and implement genocide before military victory: 'Himmler ignored what was impossible, pondered what was most glorious, and did what could be done: kill the Jews east of the Molotov–Ribbentrop line' (189). The Nazi decision and implementation of the 'Final Solution' partly resulted from military failure, although military defeat at the hands of a different army might have triggered similar radicalizations.

At this point in the narrative, the texter introduces an interesting counterfactual line of reasoning, pointing at inadvertent Nazi–Soviet cooperation in the persecution of Jews. 'One secret to Himmler's success', he argues was the fact that the Nazis 'were the war's second occupier' in the Baltic states, and could easily recruit collaborators for the Final Solution due to deeply resented recent Stalinist purges across Baltic territories (184). The Final Solution was indeed a shoestring operation that required substantial non-German personnel in addition to determined German leadership. But it is doubtful that the previous violent Soviet occupation was a necessary precondition for genocide. The Nazis had their own successful mechanism for enlisting collaborators – for instance, in the ranks of Soviet PoWs who preferred Trawniki-work to starvation (253, 256, 341–42), and among the members of the Jewish councils and the Jewish police faced with similar non-choices (258). Moreover, even without the recent Soviet crimes and the popularity of Bolshevik-Jewish prejudice, significant segments of East European societies were sufficiently antisemitically inclined to tolerate or support anti-Jewish violence. Finally, and perhaps decisively, the Nazis had no problems finding collaborators for their anti-Jewish campaigns in societies that had never been touched by Soviet violence, including France, Belgium, the Netherlands, Norway and Hungary. The double occupation 'made the experience of the inhabitants of these lands all the more complicated and dangerous', but it was not a precondition for the Final Solution (189). In the end, there are good arguments to assume that the 'psychic Nazification', as the texter calls it, was not 'much more difficult without the palpable evidence of Soviet atrocities' (195). Some pogroms might have been 'a joint production, a Nazi edition of a Soviet text', but not the Holocaust (195).

In summary, it is safe to conclude that key argumentative threads of *Bloodlands* are easily challenged because the book lacks the kind of conceptual ambition or narrative dexterity to support the arguments explicitly put forth in the introduction and conclusion. This is not an unusual phenomenon. A faulty coordination between explicitly identified analytical goals on the one hand, and narrative-descriptive performances on the other, happens often in historical scholarship. *Bloodlands* is simply not an argumentative book, which is all the more reason to take a close look at some concrete descriptive and narrative passages, and some larger descriptive and narrative semantic webs that play an important role in the text. Given the popularity of *Bloodlands*, the texter should have operated more successfully in this terrain.

Description I: Counting Victims

A close reading yields three unusual qualities of *Bloodlands* that are primarily descriptive, not narrative or argumentative exploits. First, the texter engages in a sustained and highly entertaining comparative and competitive coverage of the statistics of collective mass murder. Second, the texter covers new ground by offering intriguing, taboo-skirting tableaus of two types of violence that occurred frequently during the mass murder campaigns of the 1930s and 1940s, rape and cannibalism. The highly captivating scenes of violence raise questions as to their precise function in the overall comparative design of the book.

The texter is cognizant of the fact that his obsession with victim counts might raise moral concerns. Therefore, in his conclusion, he provides a series of prolepses, or better postlepses, discussing how victim numbers should be used responsibly. The following somewhat disjointed admonition is directed at the reader but probably also at the texter himself:

> Victims left behind mourners. Killers left behind numbers. To join in a large number after death is to be dissolved into a stream of anonymity. . . It is to be abandoned by history, which begins with the assumption that each person is irreducible. So even when we have the numbers right, we have to take care. The right number is not enough. Each record of death suggests, but cannot supply, a unique life. We must be able not only to reckon the number of deaths but to reckon with each victim as an individual' (406). And, more to the point: 'It is for us as humanists to turn the numbers back into people. If we cannot do that, then Hitler and Stalin have shaped not only our world, but our humanity. (408)

In an effort to turn numbers back into people, the texter includes in the book four epigrammatic vignettes of personal suffering. He presents the four individuals in question on the very first page of the book, on this occasion as nameless representatives of different victim groups: a starving boy in Ukraine in 1933; a young man to be executed in Katyn in 1940; a girl starving in Nazi-besieged Leningrad in 1941; and a Jewish girl swept up in the Holocaust in 1942 (vii, 49, 102; vii, 137, 379; vii, 175, 379; vii, 236, 379). All four individuals are briefly mentioned a second time, now identified by name in various chapters of the book. Finally, all four are featured one last time, again identified by name, on the first page of the conclusion. The four short vignettes and the brief mention of other non-prominent individuals represent the texter's attempt to return to the victims their humanity. Judging by the superficiality of these efforts and the extraordinary prominence of numbers in the book, the texter has not been able to escape the force field of Stalin's or Hitler's worlds.

Now that the history of the bloodlands has been written, the comparisons between Nazi and Soviet crimes may commence. In that spirit, the texter presents a seemingly endless string of comparisons – some predictable, some bizarre – and many concerned with numbers. Moreover, many of the comparisons reflect a clear agenda. The texter seems very eager to reduce the historical relevance of the Holocaust, or more specifically of Auschwitz, and to elevate the historical relevance of crimes committed by Nazis and Soviets against non-Jewish victims. That could be a laudable undertaking. Holocaust memory often, and professional Holocaust history on occasion, reflects questionable political priorities and a lack of rigorous self-criticism. But in my mind, the texter of *Bloodlands* sets up the comparisons and calibrates the numbers in a way that lacks political transparency. The very same texter who vigorously condemned inaccurate and self-serving victim counts and memory politics during the Cold War now presents a master-class in how to arrange accurate numbers and prima facie legitimate comparisons for partisan purposes. There is a duplicitousness and passive aggressiveness at work in the pages of *Bloodlands*, coupled with a gesture of empirical-descriptive impartiality, that turns the book into a disappointing ideological intellectual product. I do not mind the politics or the ideology but I resent them being advertised as superior history.

In the texter's opinion, we had a tough time understanding the scope and historical implication of the bloodlands because Auschwitz occluded our analytical gaze. Auschwitz has not only overshadowed 'German plans that envisioned even more killings', but our focus on Auschwitz has also prevented us from understanding that 'Germans murdered about as many Jews as non-Jews during the war' and that 'Stalin's own record of mass murder was almost as imposing as Hitler's' (x). In his efforts at accuracy and at cutting

Auschwitz down to size, the texter establishes a new numerical hierarchy of death in the bloodlands: it was starvation first, shooting thereafter, with gassing coming in third position. Plus, the gassing process was based on old technologies already well understood in ancient Greece and eighteenth-century Europe respectively (loc. 482). Following that line of thought, the texter sees no reason to condone all the hype about modernity and the Holocaust. For him, modernity can be measured in speed: Auschwitz 'was not the height of technology of death: the most efficient shooting squads killed faster, the starvation sites killed faster, and Treblinka killed faster' (382). Therefore, 'Auschwitz is the coda to the death fugue', a kind of afterword to the Holocaust (383). Consequently, when the texter announces the locations designating 'the worst crimes of Hitler', he settles on 'the ruins of Warsaw', 'the fields of Treblinka', 'the marshes of Belarus' and 'the pits of Babi Yar' (312). Auschwitz has been dropped from the competition. It was probably disqualified for memory doping.

Given the main intellectual currency of *Bloodlands*, the deconstruction of the Holocaust has to be accomplished in terms of statistics. The texter develops a strange habit in his treatment of numbers because he is convinced that 'somehow the remembrance of the dead is easier when the numbers are not round, when the final digit is not a zero' (406). There is no further elaboration of this axiom. I would suggest that 6 million is a very memorable number that has served the memory of some of the dead quite well. In *Bloodlands*, however, the desire to avoid round numbers results in a contradictory treatment of numerical evidence. Since the texter realizes that 'these large numbers can never be precise' (385), we time and again read statements like the following: 'In sum, *about* 780,863 people were killed at Treblinka' (273, my emphasis, also 408 without 'about') or 'the NKVD had executed *some* 386,798 citizens' (80, my emphasis). Obviously, the texter is not comfortable with his own figures. Should he round up or down or relate a number, gleaned from the documents of the perpetrators, that is likely to be false? The texter is also not a fan of the concept of the grey zone or 'other comforting clichés of the sociology of mass murder' (250). But with his hyper-empiricism and distaste for round numbers he has crafted a grey zone of his own that colonizes the space between 'about' and '780,863', and renders his numbers slightly suspect.

Bloodlands features a qualified acknowledgement of the extraordinary extent of Jewish suffering. As we have seen, the texter criticizes Soviet and Polish memory politics, which insisted on balancing the books of national sacrifice in such a way that the Holocaust could 'never become part of the Soviet history of the war'. Both countries failed to acknowledge that 'the Jews had suffered a very special fate' and 'were in a category of their own' (342). In essence, however, the texter engages in a similar numerical rebalancing act. Time and again hierarchies are constructed in such a way that Jewish suffering appears in the category of also-ran. It begins with a texter who is well versed in all matters memory but never once mentions the 6 million, not even in an effort to discredit that figure. Instead, he vacillates between 5.4 and 5.7 million victims of the Holocaust, depending on his inclination to include or discount the victims of Romanian anti-Jewish mass murder. The vacillation between these two figures is in and of itself already a strategy of forgetting. Perhaps victims are more easily remembered when their numbers do not end in a zero, but they are most certainly more easily remembered when their number has been clearly established and is consistently acknowledged as a known entity.

Initially, the texter announces clear accounting standards. He focuses on deliberate mass murders of civilians perpetrated by Nazis and Soviets within the geographical confines of the bloodlands. But in his bookkeeping practice, he often changes benchmarks both in terms of geographical scope and with regard to the categorization of the victims. For the most part, the texter counts by ethnicity. On other occasions, he counts citizens recognizing full well that the shift between ethnicity and citizenship has produced highly problematic results in East European memory politics (249). Either way, the numerical descriptive bedrock of the book refers to nation states and ethnicities, thus further complicating the objective of writing a transnational or anti-nationalistic history of the bloodlands.

Let us take a closer look at four prominent examples of victim counting in *Bloodlands*. In his tally of Barbarossa, the texter lists 10 million dead soldiers, 10 million civilians who died as a result of flight, bombs, hunger or disease, and 10 million civilians deliberately murdered by Germans, including more than 5 million Jews and more than 3 million PoWs (155). Jews appear here in the second to last category.

On another occasion, in a final calculation pitching Nazi vs. Soviet victims, he comes up with differently staggered results (383). He declares that in the bloodlands proper 10 million Nazi victims stand against 4 million Soviet victims. When including deliberate mass murders outside the bloodlands the tally rises to 11 and 6 million respectively. Finally, when all victims, including foreseeable civilian casualties through famines and warfare are

Table 2.1 Numbering Nazi and Soviet victims in the bloodlands.

	Bloodlands	Total, including areas outside bloodlands	Total, including foreseeable civilian deaths through warfare, famine, etc.
Nazi	10	11	12
Soviet	4	6	9

Table 2.2 Chronological sequence of crimes in the bloodlands.

Perpetrator	Period	Number
Soviet	1932–33	3.3 million civilians (mostly Ukrainians)
Soviet	1937–38	300,000 Soviet citizens (mostly Poles and Ukrainians)
Soviet and Nazi	1939–41	200,000 Polish citizens (mostly Poles)
Nazi	1941–44	4.2 million Soviet citizens (mostly Russians, Ukrainians, Belarussians)
Nazi	1941–44	5.4 million Jews (most of them Polish or Soviet citizens)
Nazi	1941–44	700,000 civilians shot as reprisals in Belarus and Warsaw
Soviet and Nazi Total	1932–44	14.1 million

considered, the numbers increase to 12 and 9 million. Shifting accounting standards in terms of geography and qualitative selection criteria (i.e. leaving aside the bloodlands) creates a more balanced statistic, and demonstrates in compelling fashion that 'Stalin's record was almost as imposing'. Jews do not appear in this calculation.

At the end of the book there is yet another settling of accounts, now focusing on what the texter wants to establish as the new iconic figure of 14 million. The tally is arranged in chronological sequence of the crimes. The victims of hunger, the great terror, the political decapitation of Poland, and the murder of Soviet PoWs and civilians precede the Final Solution, whose victims account for 38 per cent of the total. Exceptionality looks different.

The texter-referee is particularly mindful of the suffering of countries and ethnicities that have not figured prominently in popular histories of the Second World War. That inclination results in a rhetorical habit of attaching descriptive superlatives to national groups for the purpose of rectifying history and memory. A Jewish component does not figure prominently in these calculations. In fact, it seems that the texter tends to develop new categories of suffering as he traverses the different countries and nationalities that were part of the bloodlands in a strenuous effort of not having to talk about Jewish victims.

(1) Ukraine was at 'the centre of both Stalinist and Nazi killing policies' (403). The texter translates that into 3.5 million victims of Soviet policies, 3.5 million victims of German policies, and 3 million direct and indirect victims of combat.
(2) Another, subtly differently defined category, highlights suffering in Belarus. The country 'was at the centre of the Soviet–Nazi

confrontation' and 'no country endured more hardship under German occupation' (404, 249), amounting to an overall population loss of over 20 per cent.

(3) As the texter very well knows, the two acknowledgements he just expressed might disturb another nation that suffered in the bloodlands. Therefore, he quickly invents a number of additional categories of suffering, custom-made to fit Polish memory culture. 'Beyond Poland,' the texter claims 'the extent of Polish suffering is underappreciated.' The Soviet Poles suffered, for instance, more 'than any other national European minority in the 1930s' (404). That is a strange way of creating subcategories, but it gets even more peculiar, as the texter continues to pander to Polish memory. More Poles were killed in Warsaw in 1938 than Germans in Dresden in 1945; more Poles were killed during the Warsaw uprising than Japanese in Hiroshima and Nagasaki; and finally, the most bizarre comparison of all, which brings us back to the task of deconstructing the icon 'Auschwitz and Jewish victimhood': 'More *non-Jewish Poles* died at Auschwitz than did Jews of any European country, with only two exceptions: Hungary and Poland itself' (406). The twisted logic of that sentence clearly reveals the texter as the kind of coach who quickly moves the goalposts before his team enters the arena.

There are other, minor competitions with similarly suspicious goalposts: 'No other European capital suffered such a fate' as Warsaw (308). That descriptive superlative could be questioned. Minsk, the capital of Belarus, and Leningrad might be worthy competitors, although the latter seems to have been elegantly disqualified from the competition because it was not a national capital at the time. Intriguingly, there are even consolation prizes in the form of superlatives for the perpetrators. Germany remained the most powerful European country after the First World War (8), the Wehrmacht remained the most effective fighting force after the winter of 1941, and more Germans lost their homes after the Second World War than any other group (331). Finally, again quickly exchanging ethnicity for citizenship, 'more Soviet citizens died than any people in any war in recorded history' (334). In the seemingly haphazard accounting jungle of numbers, superlatives, ethnicities and nations, 6 million Jews have all but disappeared. I am sure all the numbers in *Bloodlands* are carefully researched, have survived peer review, and reflect the state of the art. Nevertheless, the mosaic that the texter has designed with the help of these numerical 'facts' amounts to a descriptive ideological masterpiece.

Description II: Immersive Violence

Bloodlands begins with a fitting announcement highlighting that the Second World War brought 'mass violence of a sort never before seen in history' (loc. 385). The texter follows through on that announcement, first, as we have seen, by documenting the extraordinary scope of violence through detailed, reliable and ideologically twisted statistics. In addition, the book features a series of violent scenes, often described in graphic detail, that pertain to four historical campaigns of exceptional cruelty directed at Ukrainian peasants, Jews, Jewish women and German women respectively. These scenarios visualize violence, render it palpable for the reader, open up venues of empathy, and partake in an aesthetic of what I would call dark readership – the kind of aesthetic that has turned many sites of wartime violence into dark tourist attractions, and many publications and films about the Holocaust into bestsellers. Cosmopolitan memory could probably not function without a significant element of this kind of dark, voyeuristic appeal.

The first string of violent scenes in *Bloodlands* deals with the Ukrainian famine, and features a vivid, taboo-skirting description of Ukrainian cannibalism. The texter rightly points out that 'cannibalism is a taboo of literature as well as life', but then goes on to describe in intriguing, gruesome detail one cannibalistic scenario after another: children fishing a severed head from a pond, which might or might not have belonged to a victim of cannibalism; roving bands of cannibals chasing children; families eating their youngest members; parents eating their children; a father getting ready to slaughter his daughter; a family eating their daughter-in-law; children eating another child while it is still alive; a mother encouraging her children to eat her after her death – fascinating visual scenarios juxtaposing innocence with utter depravity and ultimate self-sacrifice (49–51). For readers who have previously not paid much attention to the Ukrainian famine, the scenes go a long way in establishing lasting, searing sites of memory of the event.

The scenes of concrete Holocaust violence included in the book are less captivating, first and foremost because the texter competes against an extraordinarily extensive cultural memory in which almost all stages and brutalities of the Nazi persecution of Jews have been depicted in horrific detail. Moreover, reading the passages about the four different groups of victims side by side makes the aesthetic design of the Holocaust scenes appear more restrained and subdued – with one important exception. The texter explores in some detail the onslaught of sexual violence committed by German soldiers against Jewish women. As, in a fourth tableau of violence, he also covers the sexual violence committed by Soviet soldiers against German women, yet another strange comparison, one possibly not consciously designed as such, unfolds in the pages of *Bloodlands*.[31] The texter compares the acts of sexual violence committed by German perpetrators to those committed by Soviet perpetrators with the latter emerging as the worse criminals.

Despite his penchant for numbers, the texter provides few statistical data about sexual violence, although estimates do exist, but instead indicates by his choice of words that Soviet sexual violence was more widespread than German sexual violence. Regarding the Jewish victims, the texter refers to 'some soldiers' and specific German units perpetrating rape while stipulating that 'the outburst of violence against German women was extraordinary' (316). Together with the graphic descriptions of cannibalism, the scenes of sexual violence represent the most disturbing and most captivating passages of the book. Moreover, in the emotional economy of *Bloodlands*, the violence of Soviet soldiers committed in Germany and the violent scenes of the Ukrainian famine caused by Soviet leaders both overshadow the description of the Holocaust, including the scenes of rapes. Numbers and vivid acts of violence point in the same cumulatively uncomfortable direction, attesting to a state of balance between Soviet and German crimes. And once again that effect is achieved by leaving the bloodlands behind; German women suffered in a different geographical setting.

Similar to the extensive numerical data included in *Bloodlands*, the vivid violent scenarios have very little large-scale narrative volition; that applies in particular to scenes of sexual violence. They certainly mark change over time – for the women involved it was a change that killed them or that they had to deal with for the rest of their lives. But in the book, the scenes of sexual violence serve as powerful images that do not decisively move time. They do not move the narrative along, not even in a cumulative sense. As terrible as its sounds, the violence of the cohort Dirlewanger or the rapes committed by Soviet soldiers do not make much of a difference in the history of the bloodlands, as sketched out by the texter. The scenes do not advance the explicit purpose of the book, which is to explain the murder of the 14 million. But the scenes play a decisive role in the less openly acknowledged purpose of the book – namely, to establish as much as possible a factual, symbolic and emotional equivalency between the crimes of the Nazi and the Soviet regimes, and between the suffering of Jewish and non-Jewish victims.

Conclusion: What about Narration?

Of course, there is plenty of narration in *Bloodlands*, on every page and in many sentences. But the texter is not interested in complicated, twisted storylines or casting new ideas about the causes of mass murder into narratives about villains and regimes and their complex motives and self-radicalizing tendencies. The texter simply takes the outcomes of the catastrophes and the evilness of its perpetrators for granted; for instance, he stipulates unequivocally that the Ukrainian famine amounted to 'premediated mass murder' (41) and attributes responsibility almost exclusively to Stalin. But the latter's precise motives remain elusive. The texter repeatedly invokes Stalin's malice, mentions his political objectives and twisted political logic, and gestures vaguely towards an effective administration implementing mass murder. But the texter is not interested in spinning a new dramatic tale about Stalin's or Hitler's decision-making processes.

Bloodlands' arguments in favour of comparative mass murder research are similarly disappointing – and for similar reasons. The texter provides a competent but conventionally structured summary of the foreign policy objectives and decisions of Stalin and Hitler. The bloodlands emerge not as the site of a series of concerted mass murders committed by two collaborative, co-dependent or otherwise cooperative regimes but as string of independently conceived and executed crimes that happened to occur in the same broad area because both regimes craved colonial possession of this swath of extraordinarily fertile and valuable territory in Eastern Europe (19).

The texter's arguments about the relation between history and memory fare even worse. He cannot deliver on his explicit argumentative ambition of demonstrating that a responsible memory culture can only be crafted by way of highly accurate factual historical research about victim counts. Good numbers are certainly preferable to bad numbers, but they are not an obligatory ingredient for good memory politics and do not represent the best available strategy for turning bad memory politics into better memory politics. A society concerned with its past history as a perpetrator collective should first and foremost establish a memory culture of rigorous self-reflexivity and self-criticism. Honestly acknowledging the facts and the scope of one's crimes has to be a part of that endeavour. However, pursuing the kind of number fetishism on display in *Bloodlands* is counterproductive in this context. Highly accurate numbers are at best icing on the self-critical cake and at worst a serious distraction. Let us consider some current examples. For a number of years, Australian and Canadian societies have grappled with the long-term violence caused by their colonial heritage. In this context it is sometimes crucial to determine the number of victims, especially if we are talking about victims who have died recently. Hence, the need in Canada to research scrupulously the number of First Nation and Inuit women and girls who have disappeared during the last decades. Even more important, however, is the need to understand how deeply past and present settler societies are implicated in the ongoing violence against minorities, and that mainstream society and every privileged white member of that society has a moral obligation to improve the living conditions of said minorities in the here and now. An understanding of the historical causes of the crises supports the search for solutions, while a detail-oriented inquiry into nineteenth-century victim tallies might easily turn into a distracting, counterproductive obsession.

The texter might not be an accomplished arguer or have considerable narrative ambition but he excels at the art of historical description. Compiling and analysing the extraordinary amount of numerical data in Bloodlands required a lot more time and effort from the author than the texter was able to document in the endnotes of a book directed at a general audience. The data give rise to an entertaining comparative overview: Who killed the most? – The Nazis, but the race remained undecided longer than expected. Who killed more effectively? – The Soviets, despite their use of less innovative technology. Who killed faster? – The Germans, but not because of Auschwitz. Who was better at deportation and maintaining secrecy? – Definitely the Soviets, who had more experience and superior administrative skills. Finally, the all-important question: Who suffered the most? – Here the texter hesitates for a while before committing himself to the statement that 'the Jews had suffered a very special fate' (342).

The texter characterizes the book as 'a study of the dying rather than the suffering', but I wonder if it does not often amount to a study of killing, having been written on the basis of the killers' documents and from their perspective. If one strips the book of its judgemental adjectives, of which there are not many (for instance 12 x 'evil', 16 x 'brutal'), the perpetrators might have appreciated the text and taken comfort in their success. They certainly shared the texter's fondness for counting the dead and might therefore have felt that their extraordinary skill in accounting for their victims supplied 'the rounding rhetorical flourish' to careers spent killing humans (387). I doubt that many victims would have felt that the book has succeeded in 'grasping their lives rather than grasping at their deaths' (400) or in turning 'the numbers back into people' (408), although we could of course never have asked them that question – a fact revealing once more the strange projective quality of Holocaust memory culture of which the texter is rightfully critical.

Bloodlands illustrates that large-scale descriptive webs tend to have a different epistemological status than descriptive statements of single facts. Historians are unlikely to engage in the laborious task of building up such large-scale webs if they do not pursue a bigger cause that precedes the project, or, more likely, that takes shape over the course of a long-term research project like *Bloodlands*. In the present case, the texter has definitely crafted his numerical web with a clear memory narrative and argumentative goal in mind, which might or might not be fully shared by the author. The texter is convinced that for many decades Auschwitz, the Holocaust and

Jewish suffering has overshadowed the suffering of other groups in Eastern Europe during the 1930s and 1940s. That morally and politically problematic imbalance in history and memory should be rectified. Therefore, the texter submits the present book including its skilfully, passive-aggressively arranged constellations of violent vignettes and numerical facts. In the end, argumentation and narration return through the back door in a tour de force of extraordinary, peculiar descriptive ambition.

The texter should not be faulted for being critical of Holocaust historiography and memory, or for presenting arguments in favour of new empirical foci of historical research and cultural memory. These issues should always be subject to scholarly and democratic debate. But the texter pursues his objectives by way of a problematic sleight of hand. He assumes the role of historical sceptic when discussing the complexities of Holocaust history and memory, and then proudly dons the mantle of historical empiricism when advocating for the factual integrity of the bloodlands, all the while pretending that the former cannot just as easily be deconstructed as the latter – and that is disingenuous.

In the end, the texter in *Bloodlands* emerges as an arguer composing a text that advances metaphorically and tries to convince the reader that Nazi and Soviet crimes have the same historical relevance and therefore deserve the same memorial attention. That entails three argumentative goals: establishing a new memory icon (i.e. the 14 million in the bloodlands); elevating the status of East European victims; and forgetting a part of the Holocaust, including its alleged exceptionality and modernity, and the number of 6 million. Possibly because he does not dare to state the last goal directly, the texter tries to attain those argumentative goals by pretending to be a describer who has put together a text that advances spatially and assembles an unproblematic mosaic of non-controversial facts – primarily numbers and scenes of brutality – for the purpose of objectively describing the bloodlands. In essence, *Bloodlands* pretends to be something like a (time-) travel account while amounting to a heartfelt memory political plea. Put differently, and using again Carlota Smith's terminology, the texter pushes a lot of spatial passages into the foreground, although the text really advances metaphorically. Through that act of disingenuous text construction many of the arguments of the narrativists are confirmed, but not in the way that they have argued. In *Bloodlands*, figuration returns with a vengeance, not through narrative figuration – change over time does not play an important role in the book – but through metaphorical (i.e. argumentative) figuration. And herein lies the theoretical relevance of close readings like the one presented above. In a historical research environment like Holocaust history, in which the conclusion of the story is a given, communication and competition is primarily conducted through descriptive and argumentative diversity and not through narrative diversity. In this regard, professional historical writing about the Holocaust differs from Holocaust memory, which features a great deal of narrative variety.

Consider in this context Raul Hilberg's opus magnum, *The Destruction of European Jews*. Hilberg's texter is not interested in time, he wants to answer the question of how the machinery of destruction functions.[32] Therefore his text advances spatially, although that did not prevent him from falling into some highly relevant metaphorical traps, especially with regard to the description of the Jewish leadership's entanglement in genocide. Or consider Saul Friedländer's magnum opus, *The Years of Extermination*. Friedländer's texter has narrative ambition, although one of his key objectives is decidedly anti-narrational. Among other goals, he wants to tell readers how the victims felt, and change over time is irrelevant in the respective passages of the book. For the texter, nothing has changed between 1941 and today concerning the feelings of the victims and survivors of the Holocaust.[33] In distinction to Snyder's texter, Hilberg's and Friedländer's texters are more forthcoming about their objectives. More important and more interesting from a theoretical point of view, all three texts prominently feature non-temporal modes of discursive advancement on the level of the textual foreground. It remains an intriguing task to determine if and possibly for whom the texts therefore amount to primarily descriptive or argumentative rather than primarily narrative works of history.

The examples encourage the field of historical theory to do a much better job at understanding the empirical and linguistic-figurative qualities of argumentation and description. Thanks to the linguistic turn we have made a quantum leap in our insights into the dynamics of historical narration. Now we have to accomplish the same with regard to the dynamics of historical description and argumentation, and their relation to narration.

Wulf Kansteiner is professor of memory studies and historical theory at Aarhus University in Denmark. Kansteiner's empirical work addresses the role of visual media (film, TV, gaming) in the formation of social memory. Many of his theoretical texts engage with key concepts in the field of memory studies (trauma, generation, postmemory, transnational memory, migration and memory). Kansteiner is also active in the field of historical theory. In this context, he is inspired by a cohort of postnarrativist theorists eager to reconcile the insights of the linguistic turn with historians' self-perception of their work and recent advances in narratology, linguistics and argumentation theory. His publications pertaining to the theory of history include: 'Success, Truth, and Modernism in Holocaust Historiography: Reading Saul Friedländer Thirty-Five Years after the Publication of

Metahistory', *History & Theory* 48(2) (2009), 25–53; 'Sense and Sensibility: The Complicated Holocaust Realism of Christopher Browning', in Claudio Fogu, Wulf Kansteiner and Todd Presner (eds), *Probing the Ethics of Holocaust Culture* (Cambridge, MA, 2016), 79–103; and 'Der Holocaust als Bild, Argument und Erzählung: Raul Hilbergs Vernichtungmaschine', *Beiträge zur Geschichte des Nationalsozialismus* 35 (2019), 183–202.

Notes

1. White, *Metahistory* all the way up to White, *Fiction of Narrative*, LaCapra, *History and Criticism*; LaCapra, *Representing the Holocaust*; and Ankersmit during the narrativist phase of his career as a philosopher of history, *Historical Representation*; on White, see also Paul, *Hayden White*; on the key axes of the debates since the 1970s, see Rigney, 'History as Text'.

2. Representative for the second generation of historical theorists: Jenkins, *Re-thinking History*, Jenkins, *At the Limits of History*; Munslow, *Narrative and History*; and Roth, 'The Pasts'; and on the third generation: Kuukkanen, *Postnarativist Philosophy of History*, Pihlainen, *The Work of History*; also Stone, 'Excommunicating the Past'.

3. Notable exceptions: Rigney, *Rhetoric of Historical Representation*, and especially Cohen, *Historical Culture*. On Cohen, see Jenkins, 'Sande Cohen'.

4. Representative for countless spirited responses to the linguistic turn by historians: Evans, *In Defense of History*; Spitzer, *Historical Truth*; Appleby, Hunt and Jacob, *Telling the Truth*.

5. Ruesen, *Evidence and Meaning*; Lorenz, *Konstruktion der Vergangenheit*; Megill, *Historical Knowledge, Historical Error*; McCullagh, *Truth of History*; less compelling, Ankersmit, *Sublime Historical Experience*.

6. Kansteiner, 'Truth, Success, and Modernism'; Kansteiner, 'Sense and Sensibility'; Kansteiner, 'Der Holocaust'; Kansteiner, 'Gefühlte Wahrheit'; Kansteiner, 'Argumentation'.

7. Schmid, *Narratology*; Fludernik, *Introduction to Narratology*; Huehn et al., *Handbook of Narratology*; Hogan, *Affective Narratology*; Smith, *Modes of Discourse*; Meier, Aristar-Dry and Destruel, *Text, Time, and Context*; Coffin, *Historical Discourse*.

8. Aumüller, 'Text Types'; Chatman, *Coming to Terms*, 6–21.

9. Genung, *Practical Elements of Rhetoric*; Reisigl, 'Argumentation Analysis', 72–73; Smith, *Modes of Discourse*, 22–48.

10. See, in this context, Smith's remarks about the shift between different discursive modes within single paragraphs and the relation between discursive mode, rhetorical mode and genre: Smith, *Modes of Discourse*, 34, 40–42; for other classificatory systems, see Coffin, *Historical Discourse*, 44–47, 168; Kuukkanen, *Postnarrativist Philosophy*, 155–58.

11. Smith, *Modes of Discourse*, 25.

12. Ibid., 27.

13. Smith counts the modes of narrative and report among the temporally advancing modes, but for sake of brevity and simplicity we will here focus on narrative as the only mode that advances through changes in time. Ibid., 25.

14. Ibid., 28.

15. Ibid., 33.

16. Ibid., 31.

17. For Evans that means, for instance, that 'the truth about patterns and linkages of facts in history is in the end discovered not invented'; Evans, *In Defense of History*, 252.

18. To cite White: 'I treat the historical work at what it most manifestly is: a verbal structure in the form of a narrative prose discourse'; White, *Metahistory*, ix.

19. Fludernik has argued along these lines: 'It is clear that academic history is not narrative but argumentative, since it puts together arguments using existing sources and does not depict human experience'; Fludernik, *Introduction to Narratology*, 59–60.

20. On overlap, ambivalence and competition between different text types, see: Herman, *Basic Elements*; Ryan, 'Toward a Definition of Narrative'.

21. This applies to many classical texts of historical scholarship that have a long reception history; see, for example, the reception history of the single most important work of Holocaust history, Hilberg, *Destruction of the European Jews*; Bortz, *'I wanted to know'*, 175–219.

22. Schmid, *Narratology*, 57–78; Fludernik, *Introduction to Narratology*, 21–31; Lothe, *Narrative in Fiction and Film*, 20–27; Bal, *Narratology*, 18–31.

23. Fulda, 'Historiographic Narration'.

24. On the relation between narration and argumentation in non-fiction texts: Olmos, *Narration as Argument*; Hyland and Guinda, *Stance and Voice*; Bondi, 'Writing Economic History'.

25. van Boxtel and van Drie, 'Historical Reasoning'; the authors argue that 'there is no agreed-upon definition of historical reasoning' (142). Consequently, history is an 'ill-structured' discipline, 'lacking in established problem-solving procedures and a single correct solution'. Hence, 'generic reasoning heuristics and metacognitive understanding and skills are believed to play an important role' (143). Therefore, historical reasoning is best studied from the disciplinary point of view of argumentation theory and not logic, because 'argumentation theorists study the way in which people take up standpoints and defend these standpoints' in concrete social settings: van Eemeren et al., *Fundamentals of Argumentation Theory*, 6.

26. The question of the limits of narration is already raised in White, *The Content of the Form*, 5–10. Non-narrative sentences and non-narrative semantic webs can be descriptions of states and ongoing events that do not move time but might progress spatially. Non-narrative sentences or discursive structures can also reflect arguments that posit claims about states of affairs and facts, and often advance metaphorically; Smith, *Modes of Discourse*, 28–29, 33.

27. Erll, *Memory in Culture*.

28. Van Boxtel and van Drie, *Historical Reasoning*.

29. One of the best and most balanced recent accounts of Polish history during the Second World War, which clearly focused on the Polish state and Polish nation, comes to the very same conclusions as *Bloodlands* (i.e. that Polish suffering during the war is not sufficiently understood outside of Poland), and that account is Kochanski, *Eagle Unbowed*.

30. To seek inspiration about how to elevate an abstract entity like an administrative system into the role of a key actant of Holocaust history, the texter could have taken a look at Hilberg, *Destruction of European Jews*, or Kansteiner, *Der Holocaust als Bild*. Incidentally, despite claims to the contrary, the texter also largely fails to attribute narrative agency to the victims of Stalin and Hitler, as Friedländer does for instance in *Years of Destruction*, or Kansteiner in 'Truth, Success and Modernism'.

31. The texter might have had second thoughts about the ethics of covering the two types of sexual violence, as he includes a detailed discussion and explanation of the possible motives of the Soviet soldiers; *Bloodlands* contains no analysis of the motives of the German perpetrators.

32. Kansteiner, *Der Holocaust als Bild*.

33. Kansteiner, 'Truth, Success and Modernism'.

Bibliography

Ankersmit, Franklin Rudolf. *Historical Representation*. Stanford, CA: Stanford University Press, 2001.

———. *Sublime Historical Experience*. Stanford, CA: Stanford University Press, 2005.
Appleby, Joyce, Lynn Hunt and Margaret Jacob. *Telling the Truth about History*. New York: Norton, 1995.
Aumüller, Matthias. 'Text Types', in Peter Huehn et al. (eds), *Handbook of Narratology* (Berlin: Gruyter, 2009), 854–67.
Bal, Mieke. *Narratology: Introduction to the Theory of Narrative*. Toronto: University of Toronto Press, 2009.
Bondi, Marina. 'Writing Economic History: The Narrator and the Arguer', in Maurizio Gotti (ed.), *Communality and Individuality in Academic Discourse* (Bern: Peter Lang, 2009), 163–89.
Bortz, Olof. *'I Wanted to Know How this Deed Was Done': Raul Hilberg, The Holocaust and History*. Stockholm: Faethon, 2017.
Chatman, Seymour. *Coming to Terms: The Rhetoric of Narrative in Fiction and Film*. Ithaca, NY: Cornell University Press, 1990.
Coffin, Caroline. *Historical Discourse: The Language of Time, Cause and Evaluation*. London: Continuum, 2006.
Cohen, Sande. *Historical Culture: On the Recoding of an Academic Discipline*. Berkeley: University of California Press, 1988.
Erll, Astrid. *Memory in Culture*. Houndmills: Palgrave, 2011.
Evans, Richard. *In Defense of History*. London: Granta, 1997.
Fludernik, Monika. *An Introduction to Narratology*. London: Routledge, 2006.
Friedländer, Saul. *Nazi Germany and the Jews, 1933–1945: The Years of Destruction*. New York: Harper-Collins, 2007.
Fulda, Daniel. 'Historiographic Narration', in Peter Hühn et al. (eds), *The Living Handbook of Narratology* (Hamburg: Hamburg University, 2014). URL: http://www.lhn.uni-hamburg.de/article/historiographic-narration (last accessed 27 May 2019).
Genung, John. *The Practical Elements of Rhetoric*. Boston, MA: Ginn, 1887.
Herman, David. *Basic Elements of Narrative*. Malden, MA: Wiley, 2009.
Hilberg, Raul. *The Destruction of European Jews*. New Haven, CT: Yale University Press, (1963) 2003.
Hogan, Patrick. *Affective Narratology: The Emotional Structure of Stories*. Lincoln: University of Nebraska Press, 2011.
Huehn, Peter, et al. (eds). *Handbook of Narratology*. Berlin: De Gryuter, 2014.
Hyland, Ken, and Carmen Sancho Guinda (eds). *Stance and Voice in Written Academic Genres*. New York: Palgrave Macmillan, 2012.
Jenkins, Keith. *At the Limits of History*. London: Routledge, 2009.
———. *Re-thinking History*. London: Routledge, 1991.
———. 'Sande Cohen: On the Verge of Newness'. *Rethinking History* 12(4) (2008), 437–62.
Kansteiner, Wulf. 'Argumentation, Beschreibung und Erzaehlung in der wissenschaftlichen Historiographie', in Thomas Sandkuehler and Horst Walter Blanke (eds), *Historisierung der Historik: Joern Ruesen zum 80. Geburtstag* (Cologne: Boehlau, 2018), 151–68.
———. 'Gefühlte Wahrheit und ästhetischer Relativismus: Über die Annäherung von Holocaustgeschichtsschreibung und Geschichtstheorie', in Norbert Frei and Wulf Kansteiner (eds), *Den Holocaust erzählen: Historiographie zwischen wissenschaftlicher Empirie und narrativer Kreativität* (Göttingen: Wallstein, 2013), 12–50.
———. 'Der Holocaust als Bild, Argument und Erzählung: Hilbergs Vernichtungsmaschine'. *Beiträge zur Geschichte des Nationalsozialismus* 35 (2019), 183–202.
———. 'Sense and Sensibility: The Complicated Holocaust Realism of Christopher Browning', in Claudio Fogu, Wulf Kansteiner and Todd Presner (eds), *Probing the Ethics of Holocaust Culture* (Cambridge, MA: Harvard University Press, 2016), 97–103.

———. 'Truth, Success, and Modernism in Holocaust Historiography: Reading Saul Friedländer 35 Years after the Publication of Metahistory'. *History & Theory* 47 (2009), 25–53.

Kochanski, Halik. *Eagle Unbowed: Poland and the Poles in the Second World War*. Cambridge, MA: Harvard University Press, 2012.

Kuukkanen, Jouni-Matti. *Postnarativist Philosophy of History*. Houndsmill: Palgrave, 2015.

LaCapra, Dominick. *History and Criticism*. Ithaca, NY: Cornell University Press, 1985.

———. *Representing the Holocaust: History, Theory, Trauma*. Ithaca, NY: Cornell University Press, 1994.

Lorenz, Chris. *Konstruktion der Vergangenheit*. Cologne: Boehlau, 2017.

Lothe, Jakob. *Narrative in Fiction and Film*. Oxford: Oxford University Press, 2000.

McCullagh, Behan. *The Truth of History*. London: Routledge, 1997.

Megill, Allan. *Historical Knowledge, Historical Error: A Contemporary Guide to Practice*. Chicago, IL: University of Chicago Press, 2007.

Meier, Richard, Helen Aristar-Dry and Emilie Destruel (eds). *Text, Time, and Context: Selected Papers of Carlota S. Smith*. Dordrecht: Springer, 2009.

Munslow, Alun. *Narrative and History*. New York: Palgrave, 2007.

Olmos, Paula (ed.). *Narration as Argument*. Cham, Switzerland: Springer, 2017.

Paul, Herman. *Hayden White*. Oxford: Wiley, 2013.

Pihlainen, Kalle. *The Work of History: Constructivism and a Politics of the Past*. New York: Routledge, 2017.

Reisigl, Martin. 'Argumentation Analysis and the Discourse-Historical Approach: A Methodological Framework', in Christopher Hart and Piotr Cap (eds), *Contemporary Critical Discourse Studies* (London: Bloomsbury, 2014), 67–96.

Rigney, Ann. 'History as Text: Narrative Theory and History', in Nancy Partner and Sarah Foot (eds), *The Sage Handbook of Historical Theory* (London: Sage, 2013), 183–201.

———. *The Rhetoric of Historical Representation: Three Narrative Histories of the French Revolution*. Cambridge: Cambridge University Press, 1990.

Roth, Paul. 'The Pasts'. *History & Theory* 51(3) (2012), 313–39.

Ruesen, Joern. *Evidence and Meaning*. New York: Berghahn Books, 2017.

Ryan, Marie-Laure. 'Toward a Definition of Narrative', in David Herman (ed.), *The Cambridge Companion to Narrative* (Cambridge: Cambridge University Press, 2007), 22–35.

Schmid, Wolf. *Narratology*. Berlin: De Gruyter, 2010.

Smith, Carlota. *Modes of Discourse: The Local Structure of Texts*. Cambridge: Cambridge University Press, 2003.

Snyder, Timothy. *Bloodlands: Europe between Stalin and Hitler*. New York: Basic Books, 2010.

Spitzer, Alan. *Historical Truth and Lies about the Past*. Chapel Hill: University of North Carolina Press, 1996.

Stone, Dan. 'Excommunicating the Past: Narrativism and Rational Constructivism in the Historiography of the Holocaust'. *Rethinking History* 21(4) (2017), 549–66.

van Boxtel, Carla, and Jannet van Drie. 'Historical Reasoning: The Interplay of Domain-Specific and Domain-General Aspects', in Frank Fischer et al. (eds), *Scientific Reasoning and Argumentation* (New York: Routledge, 2018), 142–61.

van Eemeren, Franz, et al. (eds). *Fundamentals of Argumentation Theory*. Mahwah, NJ: Lawrence Erlbaum, 1996.

White, Hayden. *The Content of the Form*. Baltimore, MD: Johns Hopkins University Press, 1987.

———. *The Fiction of Narrative: Essay on History, Literature, and Theory 1957–2007*. Baltimore, MD: Johns Hopkins University Press, 2007.

———. *Metahistory: The Historical Imagination in Nineteenth-Century Europe*. Baltimore, MD: Johns Hopkins University Press, 1973.

CHAPTER 3

Secularization Narratives in 1950s Europe

Sources, Characteristics and Effects

HERMAN PAUL

Introduction

What secularization has in common with modernization and democratization is that it is increasingly referred to as a 'grand' or 'master narrative'.[1] The phrase is indicative for a notable change in attitude towards the once near-obvious claim that religion in modern societies is subject to decline. Whereas historians until recently used secularization as an analytical category – writing confidently about the 'secularization' of science, education, politics, and so forth – such interpretations are now increasingly becoming an object of study themselves. Secularization, in other words, no longer serves as a lens through which historians write the history of religion, but is subjected to historical analysis itself. Indeed, it is seen as deserving historical attention precisely because it once was a powerful, near-hegemonic way of thinking about the fate of religion in modern societies.

'Historicizing secularization' can take different forms, though. Some historians and sociologists focus specifically on secularization theory – that is, the body of sociological theories, models and hypotheses about organized religion in modernizing societies that has collectively become known as the 'secularization paradigm'. Secularization in this sense thus refers to the work of sociologists such as Bryan R. Wilson, David Martin and Karel

Notes for this section begin on page 94.

Dobbelaere, who during the 1970s successfully promoted the secularization paradigm among sociologists of religion.[2] Often, though not always, historicizing treatments of these sociologists' work is fuelled by scepticism about the plausibility of their secularization paradigm. In some cases, 'historicizing secularization' even openly serves the goal of relegating a once-powerful sociological paradigm to the realm of past theories and models.[3]

If 'historicizing secularization' in this first sense is of interest primarily to students of sociology and historians of the social sciences, social and cultural historians engaged in studying 'secularization narratives' usually cast their net much wider. Jeffrey Cox, for instance, argues that secularization was not just a sociological theory, but a word that was on everybody's lips, especially in the decades following the Second World War.[4] On closer analysis, 'secularization' such as used by politicians, opinion makers and church leaders in these decades often served as shorthand for a 'grand narrative' about the dwindling relevance of organized religion in the lives of Western people since the Renaissance, the Reformation, the Enlightenment and the Industrial Revolution. Its sweeping nature was what distinguished this popular secularization narrative from its sociological namesake, the 'secularization paradigm'. Indeed, when Wilson, Martin and Dobbelaere insisted on 'scientific' data collection and theoretical rigour, they did so precisely in order to dissociate themselves from sweeping, 'unscientific' generalizations about secularization.[5]

Yet 'unscientific' as secularization narratives may have been, they circulated as powerful templates for thinking about organized religion in media, parliaments, churches and trade union rooms throughout the Western world. Well before 'the religious crisis of the 1960s',[6] these narratives taught people how to think about religion in modernizing societies. By framing their perceptions, secularization narratives not only described a changing reality, but also contributed to religious change, as Sam Brewitt-Taylor argues in an essay on the emergence of 'secularization' in the British media.[7] For this reason, historians do not simply treat secularization narratives as 'popular' distillations of academic wisdom, or as markers of what Lutz Raphael calls a 'scientification of the social'.[8] Rather, they study these stories as narrative templates that influenced social relations, political decisions and cultural codes by shaping people's understandings of the past, their perceptions of the present and their expectations for the future.[9]

An important implication of this new research focus is that histories of secularization can no longer be confined to great thinkers and influential books.[10] Secularization narratives circulating outside of the academic realm, in political and civil society contexts such as churches, schools and parliaments, are then at least as interesting as academics talking about secularization. For if secularization narratives helped to shape reality by framing people's perception of it, then this likely happened especially in settings where declining membership rates called for action, in institutions that wanted, or were expected, to bring their ideological foundations, admission requirements and course curricula 'in tune with the time', and in organizations that felt they had to reinvent themselves in changing religious and political landscapes.[11] This is not to say, of course, that philosophers and sociologists are less interesting objects of study than schoolmasters, political executives or clergy members. It is to argue, however, that the impact of secularization narratives can best be traced in realms where religious privileges were being challenged (parliaments), government funding had to be secured (schools), or people had to prevented from filling out deregistration forms (churches).

Arguably, historians of secularization do not face particular methodological problems in shifting their attention from the academic to the public realm. Given the abundance of religious media in most European and North American countries, they do not have to fear a lack of source material. They do, however, face a challenge when it comes to understanding how secularization narratives could frame people's perceptions of reality, thereby simultaneously constructing and constraining what these people could think, say or do about religion. What features of those narratives contributed to this impact? If historians observe pastors in the 1950s talking about secularization and changing their worship style on Sunday mornings, how can they plausibly connect these observations or, more specifically, establish a causal connection between them? If secularization narratives prompted liturgical revision, how did they do that?

It is here that narrative analysis – the theme of this volume – comes in. Inspired by Hayden White's classic study of historical narratives in nineteenth-century Europe,[12] as well as Daniel Fulda's more recent 'historiographical narratology',[13] this chapter argues that historians interested in unpacking the 'discursive power' exerted by secularization narratives might want to consider four questions:

(1) What were the sources on which secularization narratives drew?
(2) What sort of ideological agendas did they serve?
(3) What effects did they achieve by narratively framing religious change in terms of secularization?
(4) What were their 'metahistorical presuppositions about the nature of the historical field',[14] or the assumptions about the nature of historical reality to which they were committed?

In what follows, I will clarify these questions, and illustrate their relevance by zooming in on two examples from 1950s Europe.[15]

Historicist Background

The first example comes from Leiden, the historic Dutch university town. Like many other churches in the country, the local Netherlands Reformed congregation – the mainstream Protestant domination, which included about a third of the local population among its members – had witnessed a marked increase in church attendance during the years of the Second World War.[16] By the late 1940s, however, it seemed that urgency had diminished: the pews became emptier again. Worried about the prospect of further decline, the church council began to count, and by 1952 concluded that on average no more than 10 to 15 per cent of its members attended services.[17] The council experienced these statistics as 'very alarming'.[18] It invited all elders and deacons to a meeting at which the local academy pastor, Klaus Oppenheimer, tried to shed light on the causes of 'secularization' – a phrase that by the 1950s had entered the periodical press as a synonym to 'church attendance decline'.

The lecture given by Oppenheimer, a theologian of German descent who had fled the Nazi regime in 1934, was typical of the genre. In the best tradition of conservative cultural criticism, it held the emergence of a 'mass society' in nineteenth-century Europe as well as the rise of 'materialist' philosophies of life responsible for a rapidly growing spiritual vacuum. Like many other early commentators on secularization, Oppenheimer believed that philosophers and scientists had played an influential role in marginalizing Christian religion. By studying the world 'as if God did not exist' (*etsi deus non daretur*), they had propagated worldviews that left God out of the picture. Finally, Oppenheimer also pointed to the church's neglect in responding effectively to external challenges: it had overall failed to recognize the social and intellectual needs of the present.[19] Presumably, this fourfold diagnosis did not fill the church council with hope. If Oppenheimer was right, most of the factors causing secularization were beyond its reach of influence. This may explain why the council felt it could do nothing more than distribute a leaflet among all registered church members in Leiden, summoning them in passionate prose not to be absent 'on the roll-call that is held every Sunday'.[20]

If Oppenheimer's story of increasing 'materialism', 'mass society' and 'unbelief' provides a classic example of a secularization narrative, what then were the sources from which Oppenheimer derived the template for his story? The author revealed his principal source in concluding that the four factors just mentioned had brought about 'a new type of human being that has no memories of the God who has revealed himself in Jesus Christ and lives in a world utterly different from ours'. Oppenheimer continued:

> This man has little knowledge, little memory, his mentality is materialistic. His intellect is poor. His ability for listening, attention, interest, contemplation, reflection is shrivelling . . . 'He no longer knows the depths of the spirit, of love, and of God's holiness'. . . . With an eye to this man, the German theologian Bonhoeffer has argued that we now enter a 'religionless age' (*religionsloses Zeitalter*) . . . With an eye to him, Prof. Hoekendijk argues in his recent article on mission . . . that we live in a post-age, in the age of the emergence of the 'fourth man', who is post-Christian, post-ecclesial, post-bourgeois, and post-personal . . . Here we find the real cause of non-attendance, the decline in church attendance also in our congregation.[21]

Apparently, it was Johan Christiaan Hoekendijk, the newly appointed professor of Biblical theology, missionary work and practical theology at Utrecht University, who had been Oppenheimer's guide. Just a few months earlier, Hoekendijk had created a minor stir among theologians with an article that had radicalized the genre of secularization narratives to a hitherto unprecedented degree. Its key protagonist was the 'fourth man', or the average postwar industrial worker in a large, anonymous city, who had little-to-no affinity with traditionally bourgeois-oriented religious institutions. In Hoekendijk's portrayal, this was not a man who read books, cared about his children being baptized, or thought about eternal joy or woe. The 'fourth man' rather cared about his pay slip, the latest movies and the hours still separating him from the weekend. The 'fourth man', in other words, was not a 'personality' in a middle-class sense of the word – which explains why he was called by a number instead of a name. If the church was going to have a future, Hoekendijk added, it would have to adjust itself to this new sort of human being by abandoning its middle-class language, practices and attitudes.[22]

Hoekendijk in turn had not himself invented the 'fourth man' image: he had borrowed it from Alfred Weber, the German sociologist cum philosopher of history who had depicted the history of humanity as divided in four evolutionary stages.[23] The details of Weber's periodization need concern us less than the historicist background of his argument. If historicism, in Friedrich Meinecke's classic definition, denotes a combination of 'development' and 'individuality' as key categories for conceptualizing change over time, then Weber's 'fourth man' was not only a typical product of conservative cultural criticism in Weimar Germany, but also a historicist construct.[24] More precisely, it was indebted to a historicist conception of history as a continuous course of development in which 'ages', characterized by distinct 'spirits' or 'ideas', could be distinguished.

Does this imply that Oppenheimer, the Leiden academy pastor, offered an analysis of secularization premised on historicist assumptions? This conclusion is less surprising than it may seem. Fuelled by experiences of war and postwar reconstruction, the 1950s was a decade that witnessed numerous attempts at historicizing the present. Economists, political theorists and theologians alike searched for concepts to grasp what was new and distinctive about their situation. Viewed with hindsight, it is striking how many of these 1950s thinkers drew on historicist repertoires in characterizing their 'age' or 'era' as a 'phrase' or 'stage' in a linear course of 'development'. This is particularly apparent from the popularity of 'post' prefixes, as in 'post-capitalism',[25] 'post-industrial'[26] and 'post-traditional'.[27] Christian thinkers, likewise, began to designate their era as 'post-Christian'.[28] Although not all 'post' prefixes presupposed such full-fledged philosophies of history as Weber's, their portrayal of societal change in terms of successive stages characterized by distinct ideas or mentalities illustrates the enduring influence of historicist categories of thought, even after the so-called 'crisis of historicism'.[29]

Ideological Implications

If Oppenheimer's example offers us a glimpse on the historicist background of secularization narratives in 1950s Europe (our first question), the ideological agendas underlying the genre as well as their impact on civil society agents (our questions two and three) can be illustrated with an example from 1950s Sheffield. Located in England's industrial north, Sheffield was home to a missionary initiative by the Church of England aimed at sharing the Gospel with steel industry workers who in large numbers had become alienated from the church. Known as the Sheffield Industrial Mission, this initiative was led by a chaplain who, not coincidentally, also became a founding father of secularization studies in the United Kingdom: Edward Ralph Wickham. As Hugh McLeod[30] and Callum Brown[31] have argued, Wickham's *Church and People in an Industrial City*[32] became a foundational text for an entire generation of historians and sociologists of religion, mainly because it offered a framework for historical analysis of religious affiliation that was as bold and sweeping as it was stimulating and thought-provoking.

Wickham's framework took the form of a narrative of decline: it described the history of Christianity in Great Britain between 1800 and 1950 in terms of 'general overall decline of church-going'.[33] This narrative framework was not especially new: declining religiosity, especially in urban contexts, had been a rhetorical commonplace among eighteenth-century revivalist preachers and nineteenth-century clergy alike. Arguably, this helps to explain the success of Wickham's book. It became a landmark study, not because its narrative organization was innovative, but because it corroborated stereotypical views of religious decline with quantitative data, largely derived from nineteenth-century church statistics. In Brown's summary description, Wickham's achievement was that he cemented 'the clerical myth of the unholy city, and of the irreligious working classes in particular', into modern scholarship.[34]

What Wickham himself considered more important, however, was that his study of ever-growing non-affiliation provided seemingly solid historical justification for the missionary programme that he was carrying out in Sheffield. Tellingly, *Church and People in an Industrial City* concluded with a lengthy chapter on 'The Mission of the Church in an Industrial Society', in which Wickham explained what lessons could be drawn from his story:

> [I]t suggests that the Church should be willing to submit herself to radical sociological self-examination, and take the conclusion into account for her own self-understanding and in the planning of her mission ... For if there are sociological and conditioning factors intimately related to the likelihood or otherwise of man's belief in the Gospel, if some environments make response more probable and others more improbable, then it follows as night follows day that the Church must be acutely concerned with those conditioning factors, from the point of view of her missionary task.[35]

Concretely, this meant that the church had to be present in factories and shops, and to support trade unions' fights for improvement of working conditions. It had to break down cultural barriers by exchanging the antiquated spaces of its classic church buildings for canteens and sports fields and by translating superannuated concepts like 'sin' into modern categories of 'guilt' and 'alienation' (key terms in the quasi-existentialist vocabulary of Wickham's liberal theological hero, Paul Tillich). On top of this, Wickham suggested that the church had to abandon its classic parochial structure in favour of more flexible networks, and to supplement traditional full-time clergy with lay preachers modelled on the French worker-priest (*prêtre ouvrier*) as well as with lay theologians, 'men of wisdom and good counsel who know the social temperature and have a finger on the social pulse'.[36]

Secularization narratives, in other words, were not without consequences. Even more explicitly than Oppenheimer, Wickham assumed the subject position of a medical specialist whose diagnosis and treatment plan were based at least in part on a patient's case history. For both men, indeed, secularization narratives served as medical histories culminating in diagnosis and concrete suggestions for medical treatment. As Wickham put it:

> [T]he disease is apparent; and only by understanding the history of the patient, how she got into this condition, and by a renewed understanding of her true function, can she be brought to health ... The history of the case from the beginnings of industrialization is not good, but sound analysis suggests some surgical operations that are desperately urgent, the mental outlook if the patient is to be whole and function aright, and the tough environment she must adapt herself to if she is to regain her youth and escape the peaceful obscurity of old age.[37]

In White's vocabulary, this is to say that secularization narratives were not only charged with 'ideological implications', but also (in some cases, at least) explicitly constructed with the aim of furthering reformist church-political agendas. Christian Smith is therefore right to draw attention to the political agendas implied in 'secularization' as an analytical category.[38] In mid-twentieth-century Europe, 'secularization' was a grand narrative told in answer to a question that was on the mind of growing numbers of church members: What can we do to counter church attendance decline? The felt urgency of this 'highly practical'[39] question explains why secularization narratives found a ready reception among clergy in 1950s Europe, and why both Protestant and Catholic churches at the time invested heavily in sociological analysis of the sort recommended by Wickham.[40]

There was no contradiction, then, between Wickham browsing through nineteenth-century clippings in the Local History Department of Sheffield City Library or spending a sabbatical at the University of Sheffield to write a historical monograph and this same Wickham visiting factory workers around lunchtime and eating sandwiches while talking informally about 'the basic questions of existence' (a Tillichian phrase again). The missionary practices that gained Wickham's Sheffield Industrial Mission a reputation well beyond England[41] grew out of, and were justified by, the secularization story told in *Church and People in an Industrial City*.[42]

Metahistorical Assumptions

Neither Wickham's secularization narrative nor its practical implications for missionary work in Sheffield went unchallenged. Oppenheimer's 'fourth man' narrative also elicited critical response from theologians in the Netherlands Reformed Church. Interestingly, this criticism did not focus exclusively on policy issues like the extent to which film was an effective tool for evangelism, but raised more fundamental questions pertaining to the sort of 'realism' propagated by secularization narratives. This is to say, in White's terminology, that critics did not merely challenge plots, modes of argument, and ideological implications, but also, at a more penetrating level, metahistorical 'conceptions of the historical process', or assumptions about what history essentially is (a story of progress or just 'one damn thing after another'?), what sort of 'facts' and 'actors' are involved in it (can angels or devils be attributed with historical agency?), and, by implication, what counts as appropriate historical reasoning.[43]

In the Netherlands, this type of criticism was voiced most strongly by the director of the Netherlands Reformed theological seminary, Hendrik Berkhof. Inspired by the dialectical theological movement that he had encountered as a visiting student in 1930s Berlin – theologians like Karl Barth criticizing the Lutheran Church for sacrificing Christian faithfulness to cultural relevance and political conformism – Berkhof was suspicious of what Barth, in the second edition of his *Römerbrief*,[44] had called the 'historicism' and 'psychologism' of modern liberal theology. These labels referred to historical and psychological modes of thinking about God that, in Barth's critical assessment, illustrated the all-too-human temptation to domesticate God into familiar categories of analysis.[45] If Berkhof, in response to Hoekendijk's 'fourth man', complained about a 'sociologism' or 'sociological myth' permeating the 1950s Netherlands Reformed Church, this Barthian background helps to elucidate the target of his criticism. Berkhof was not afraid of sociologists, but sceptical of colleagues whose assessment of the church's situation showed a greater faith in sociological analysis than in God, who cares for his church until the end of time. More specifically, Berkhof asked rhetorically how theologically sound was the worry about 'marginalization' of the church, which virtually all secularization narratives implied. Was there any reason for assuming that God preferred churches packed with name-Christians over small groups of people entrusting their lives to God? Consequently, was there any reason for looking back nostalgically to a supposedly golden age of faith in the sixteenth and seventeenth century, compared to which the present was inevitably found wanting?[46]

About a decade later, similar questions were raised by Michael J. Jackson, Wickham's successor as senior chaplain of the Sheffield Industrial Mission. Although Jackson had initially been a loyal disciple of Wickham, he underwent something like a theological conversion in the mid-1960s, which turned him into a sharp critic of the 'Pelagianism' that he detected in Wickham's missionary approach ('We are saved by our own efforts'). Not unlike Berkhof, Jackson questioned the metahistorical view underlying secularization narratives: 'a view of history which sees the Church as an institution failing and receding since the Industrial Revolution'. He objected that this failure was measured against a quantitative standard that the church would do better not to accept as its own. For what really matters, from a theological perspective, is faithfulness to God; numerical success is secondary at best. Using church attendance as a marker of church vitality therefore amounts to distorting the Gospel, which in turn runs a risk of producing 'a distorted Church or an organization where priorities are wrong or false purposes are served'.[47] Even more devastating was Jackson's judgement about Wickham's argument that 'God', 'sin' and 'resurrection' had to be translated into a modern idiom to be accessible to 'modern man'. Jackson called this 'dangerous nonsense': it would warrant relegating God as revealed in Jesus Christ to a prehistoric phase of modern religiosity. Would such a religion still qualify as Christian?[48]

Both critics, then, objected to what one might call the discursive power of secularization narratives. They did not care primarily about issues of historical accuracy – although Berkhof, a church historian by training, could not resist pointing out the danger of a presentist misreading of the historical record[49] – but about the genre's normative assumptions (what are the church's performance standards?) and the kinds of agency for which it allowed (was there any acknowledgment of God who cares for his church?). Their fear was that secularization narratives contributed to a 'sociological' understanding of the church, with the adjective serving as an equivalent to 'empirical', 'horizontal' or 'excluding God'. Consequently, in their perception, secularization narratives were themselves secularized: they offered secular history instead of theologically informed accounts of the church's pilgrimage through time.[50] This explains why the two critics were particularly worried about the influence that secularization narratives exerted in the church, and why both drew special attention to the spread of such narratives through widely read church periodicals and seemingly attractive missionary experiments.[51]

Conclusion

What does an historicization of secularization entail? Drawing on two examples from 1950s Europe, this chapter has argued that secularization was a narrative template that circulated not only among academics, but also among civil society agents who reflected with greater or lesser degrees of concern on the fate of religious institutions (churches, Christian schools, confessional parties) in cultural settings perceived as disadvantageous to their survival. The more historians trace the spread and use of secularization narratives outside the academic sphere in which such narratives have traditionally been studied, the more it becomes apparent that secularization stories were deeply embedded in contexts of religious and political disputes over the future of church and society.[52] They served as means for analysis, as frames of reference, and as guides to action for people who sought to understand the past in order to shape the future.

This is why, for historians, the ideological implications of secularization narratives are especially relevant. If 'secularization is not a zeitgeist but a process of conflict',[53] 'carried by some social actors and resisted by others',[54] then historians may commit themselves to what Philip Gorski calls a 'sociopolitical conflict model'[55] for understanding secularization. This model revolves around such questions as those raised by Christian Smith:

> How did the activists define and interpret the existence of a problem that demanded action and change to remedy? How did they diagnose the sources of

that problem and define a prognosis that promised to solve it? How did actors in the struggle work to legitimate their framing of reality and to undermine their opponents' framings?[56]

In addition, this chapter has proposed to focus research attention on the sources and effects of secularization narratives. In doing so, it has focused in particular on their metahistorical assumptions. These presuppositions regarding the nature of history turned out to be indebted to a historicist understanding of 'development' and 'individuality', especially in so far as secularization narratives depicted the present 'era' as a stage in a series of successive 'ages'. This historicist logic in turn allowed progressive pastors to argue that the church was 'out of tune' with the 'spirit of the age' and therefore needed radical reform. Also, it was this historicist account of history that most disturbed critics such as Berkhof and Jackson, with the effect that 1950s controversies over secularization were often inseparable from controversies over the 'nature' and 'meaning' of history. One might argue, therefore, that both the characteristics and the effects of secularization narratives in 1950s Europe were shaped by the historicist sources on which they drew.

This, finally, opens up a question that historians have not yet systematically pursued: How did historicist-inspired secularization narratives relate to other grand narratives with historicist underpinnings circulating in post-Second World War societies? Secularization belonged to a class of process terms that also included 'rationalization', 'individualization', 'bureaucratization' and, especially, 'modernization'.[57] Although it has been argued that historicism as defined in this chapter had disappeared by the end of the First World War,[58] many of these mutually dependent and mutually reinforcing categories actually drew on a historicist understanding of history as a linear and irreversible process of development that could be delineated into distinct stages.[59] This entanglement with other powerful process terms may help to explain the cultural power of secularization narratives, but also raises a follow-up question: Can modernization or individualization be analysed in the same way that this chapter has analysed secularization? And, if so, then to what extent did the sources, ideological agendas and metahistorical presuppositions of these grand narratives strengthen or modify each other? Perhaps the time has come for writing an entangled history of grand narratives circulating in post-Second World War Europe.

Herman Paul is professor of the history of the humanities at Leiden University, where he directs a research project on 'Scholarly Vices: A Longue Durée History'. The author of *Key Issues in Historical Theory* (Routledge, 2015) and *Hayden White: The Historical Imagination* (Polity Press, 2011), he is currently at work on a book-length study of historiographical virtues and vices, while editing a volume entitled *Writing the History of the Humanities*.

Notes

1. Cox, 'Secularization'; Cox, 'Master Narratives'; Nash, 'Reconnecting Religion'; Borutta, 'Genealogie der Säkularisierungstheorie'; Clark, 'Secularization and Modernization'.
2. Tschannen, *Les theories de la sécularisation*.
3. Borutta, 'Genealogie der Säkularisierungstheorie'.
4. Cox, 'Secularization'.
5. Paul, *Secularisatie*, 71–91.
6. McLeod, *Religious Crisis*.
7. Brewitt-Taylor, 'Invention'.
8. Raphael, 'Verwissenschaftlichung des Sozialen'.
9. Paul, *Secularisatie*; Harrison, 'Introduction'; Hunter, 'Process, Program, and Historiography'; Morris, 'Strange Death'; Morris, 'Secularization'.
10. As is still the case in Swatos and Olson, *Secularization Debate*; Taylor, *Secular Age*; and Weyns, *Gedoofde kaarsen*.
11. Paul, 'Erfenis van Wickham'; Smith, 'Introduction'.
12. White, *Metahistory*.
13. Fulda, 'Historiographic Narration'.
14. White, *Metahistory*, 13.
15. This chapter draws and expands on Paul, 'Erfenis van Wickham'; and Paul, 'Sociological Myth'.
16. Kloek, 'Kerkbezoek 1952'; Vossers, 'Uit de gemeente'.
17. Vossers, 'Uit de gemeente'.
18. N.N., 'Uit de gemeente'.
19. Oppenheimer, 'Oorzaken der onkerkelijkheid' [parts 1 and 2].
20. N.N., 'Hervormde lidmaten krijgen folder over kerkbezoek'.
21. Oppenheimer, 'Oorzaken der onkerkelijkheid' [part 2], 2.
22. Hoekendijk, 'Rondom het apostolaat'.
23. Weber, *Kulturgeschichte als Kultursoziologie*; Weber, *Dritte oder der vierte Mensch*.
24. Meinecke, *Entstehung des Historismus*.
25. Dahrendorf, *Soziale Klassen*.
26. Riesman, 'Leisure and Work'.
27. Rostow, *Stages of Economic Growth*.
28. Petras, *Post Christum*; Ehrenberg, 'Nazi Religion'; Ehrenberg, 'Totalitarian World Revolution'; Demant, 'Christianity and Civilization'; Toynbee, 'Christianity and Civilization'; Toynbee, 'World and the West'; Lewis, *De Descriptione Temporum*; Vahanian, 'Post-Christian Era'.
29. Hunter, 'Secularization: The Birth'; Paul, *Secularisatie*.
30. McLeod, *Religion and the Working Class*; McLeod, *Religion and Irreligion*.
31. Brown, *Death of Christian Britain*; Brown, *Religion and Society*.
32. Wickham, *Church and People*.
33. Ibid., 171.
34. Brown, *Death of Christian Britain*, 27.
35. Wickham, *Church and People*, 220.
36. Ibid., 261.
37. Ibid., 13.

38. Smith, 'Introduction', 1–96.
39. Wickham, *Church and People*, 7.
40. Ziemann, *Katholische Kirche*; Ziemann, 'Practical Sociologist'; Dols, *Fact Factory*; Dols, 'Of Religious Diseases'; Dols and Paul, *Pastoral Sociology*; Mittmann, 'Lasting Impact'; Morris, 'Enemy Within?'.
41. Bagshaw, *Church beyond the Church*; Mantle, *Working-Class Priests*; McFarland and Johnston, 'Faith in the Factory'.
42. Although *Church and People in an Industrial City* did not yet use the word 'secularization', Wickham would appropriate it as a key term in subsequent publications: Wickham, 'What Should Be the New Look'.
43. White, *Metahistory*, 2.
44. Barth, *Römerbrief*.
45. McCormack, *Karl Barth's Critically Realistic Dialectical Theology*, 248–49.
46. Berkhof, 'Tegen de bierkaai?'.
47. Jackson, 'No New Gospel', 543.
48. Ibid., 541, 543.
49. Berkhof, 'Tegen de bierkaai?', 38, 53–54.
50. Ibid., 71–72.
51. Jackson, *Sociology of Religion*, 176–202.
52. Hunter, 'Secularization'; Hunter, 'Secularisation'.
53. Collins, *Sociology of Philosophies*, 595.
54. Chaves, 'Secularization', 752.
55. Gorski, 'Historicizing the Secularization Debate', 115–19.
56. Smith, 'Introduction', 31.
57. Gilman, *Mandarins of the Future*; Engerman et al., *Staging Growth*.
58. Bevir, 'Historicism'.
59. Joas, 'Gefährliche Prozessbegriffe'; Krech, 'Über Sinn und Unsinn'.

Bibliography

Bagshaw, Paul. *The Church beyond the Church: Sheffield Industrial Mission, 1944–1994*. Sheffield: Industrial Mission in South Yorkshire, 1994.
Barth, Karl. *Der Römerbrief* (2nd edn). Munich: Chr. Kaiser, 1922.
Berkhof, Henk. 'Tegen de bierkaai?' *In de Waagschaal* 9 (1954), 37–39, 53–54, 71–72.
Bevir, Mark. 'Historicism and the Human Sciences in Victorian Britain', in Mark Bevir (ed.), *Historicism and the Human Sciences in Victorian Britain* (Cambridge: Cambridge University Press, 2017), 1–20.
Borutta, Manuel. 'Genealogie der Säkularisierungstheorie: Zur Historisierung einer großen Erzählung der Moderne'. *Geschichte und Gesellschaft* 36(3) (2010), 347–76.
Brewitt-Taylor, Sam. 'The Invention of a "Secular Society"? Christianity and the Sudden Appearance of Secularization Discourses in the British National Media, 1961–64'. *Twentieth-Century British History* 24(3) (September 2013), 327–50.
Brown, Callum G. *The Death of Christian Britain: Understanding Secularisation 1800–2000*. London: Routledge, 2001.
———. *Religion and Society in Twentieth-Century Britain*. Harlow: Pearson Longman, 2006.
Chaves, Mark. 'Secularization as Declining Religious Authority'. *Social Forces* 72(3) (March 1994), 749–75.
Clark, Jonathan. 'Secularization and Modernization: The Failure of a "Grand Narrative"'. *The Historical Journal* 55(1) (March 2012), 161–94.

Collins, Randall. *The Sociology of Philosophies: A Global Theory of Intellectual Change*. Cambridge, MA: Belknap Press, 1998.
Cox, Jeffrey. 'Master Narratives of Long-Term Religious Change', in Hugh McLeod and Werner Ustorf (eds), *The Decline of Christendom of Western Europe, 1750–2000* (Cambridge: Cambridge University Press, 2003), 201–17.
———. 'Secularization and Other Master Narratives of Religion in Modern Europe'. *Kirchliche Zeitgeschichte* 14(1) (2001), 24–35.
Dahrendorf, Ralf. *Soziale Klassen und Klassenkonflikt in der industriellen Gesellschaft*. Stuttgart: Ferdinand Enke Verlag, 1957.
Demant, Vigo Auguste. 'Christianity and Civilization', in Walter Robert Matthews (ed.), *The Christian Faith: Essays in Explanation and Defence* (London: Eyre and Spottiswoode, 1944), 191–204.
Dols, Chris. *Fact Factory: Sociological Expertise and Episcopal Decision Making in the Netherlands, 1946–1972*. Nijmegen: Valkhof, 2015.
———. 'Of Religious Diseases and Sociological Laboratories: Towards a Transnational Anatomy of Catholic Secularisation Narratives in Western Europe, 1940–1970'. *Journal of Religion in Europe* 9(2–3) (July 2016), 107–32.
Dols, Chris, and Herman Paul (eds). *Pastoral Sociology in Western Europe, 1940–1970*. Theme issue of the *Journal of Religion in Europe* 9(2–3) (July 2016).
Ehrenberg, Hans P. 'After the Totalitarian World Revolution: Some Thoughts on Church and State in the World Church after the War'. *International Review of Mission* 36(1) (January 1947), 81–87.
———. 'The Nazi Religion and the Christian Mission'. *International Review of Mission* 30(3) (July 1941), 363–73.
Engerman, David C., et al. (eds). *Staging Growth: Modernization, Development, and the Global Cold War*. Amherst: University of Massachusetts Press, 2003.
Fulda, Daniel. 'Historiographic Narration', in Peter Hühn et al. (eds), *The Living Handbook of Narratology* (Hamburg: Hamburg University, 2014). http://www.lhn.uni-hamburg.de/article/historiographic-narration (last accessed 10 November 2020).
Gilman, Nils. *Mandarins of the Future: Modernization Theory in Cold War America*. Baltimore, MD: Johns Hopkins University Press, 2003.
Gorski, Philip S. 'Historicizing the Secularization Debate: An Agenda for Research', in Michele Dillon (ed.), *Handbook of the Sociology of Religion* (Cambridge: Cambridge University Press, 2003), 110–22.
Harrison, Peter. 'Introduction: Narratives of Secularization'. *Intellectual History Review* 27(1) (January 2017), 1–6.
Hoekendijk, Johannes Christian. 'Rondom het apostolaat'. *Wending* 7 (1952), 547–66.
Hunter, Ian. 'Secularisation: Process, Program, and Historiography'. *Intellectual History Review* 27(1) (2017), 7–29.
———. 'Secularization: The Birth of a Modern Combat Concept'. *Modern Intellectual History* 12(1) (April 2015), 1–32.
Jackson, Michael. 'No New Gospel. Industrial Mission: 3'. *Theology* 69(558) (December 1966), 539–44.
———. *The Sociology of Religion: Theory and Practice*. London: B.T. Batsford, 1974.
Joas, Hans. 'Gefährliche Prozessbegriffe: Eine Warnung vor der Rede von Differenzierung, Rationalisierung und Modernisierung', in Karl Gabriel, Christel Gärtner and Detlef Pollack (eds), *Umstrittene Säkularisierung: Soziologische und historische Analysen zur Differenzierung von Religion und Politik* (Berlin: Berlin University Press, 2012), 603–22.
Kloek, P. 'Kerkbezoek 1952'. *Leids Hervormd Kerkblad* 13(18) (1953), 1.
Krech, Volkhard. 'Über Sinn und Unsinn religionsgeschichtlicher Prozessbegriffe', in Karl Gabriel, Christel Gärtner, and Detlef Pollack (eds), *Umstrittene Säkularisierung: Soziologische*

und historische Analysen zur Differenzierung von Religion und Politik (Berlin: Berlin University Press, 2012), 565–602.
Lewis, Clive Staples. *De Descriptione Temporum: An Inaugural Lecture*. Cambridge: Cambridge University Press, 1955.
Mantle, John. *Britain's First Working-Class Priests: Radical Ministry in a Post-War Setting*. London: SCM Press, 2000.
McCormack, Bruce L. *Karl Barth's Critically Realistic Dialectical Theology: Its Genesis and Development, 1909–1936*. Oxford: Clarendon Press, 1995.
McFarland, Elaine, and Ronnie Johnston. 'Faith in the Factory: The Church of Scotland's Industrial Mission, 1942–58'. *Historical Research* 83(221) (August 2010), 539–64.
McLeod, Hugh. *Religion and Irreligion in Victorian England: How Secular was the Working Class?* Bangor: Headstart, 1993.
———. *Religion and the Working Class in Nineteenth-Century Britain*. Basingstoke: Macmillan, 1984.
———. *The Religious Crisis of the 1960s*. Oxford: Oxford University Press, 2007.
Meinecke, Friedrich. *Die Entstehung des Historismus*. Munich: Oldenbourg, 1936.
Mittmann, Thomas. 'The Lasting Impact of the "Sociological Moment" on the Churches' Discourse of "Secularization" in West Germany'. *Journal of Religion in Europe* 9(2–3) (July 2016), 157–76.
Morris, Jeremy. 'Enemy Within? The Appeal of the Discipline of Sociology to Religious Professionals in Post-War Britain'. *Journal of Religion in Europe* 9(2–3) (2016), 177–200.
———. 'Secularization and Religious Experience: Arguments in the Historiography of Modern British Religion'. *The Historical Journal* 55(1) (March 2012), 195–219.
———. 'The Strange Death of Christian Britain: Another Look at the Secularization Debate'. *The Historical Journal* 46(4) (December 2003), 963–76.
Nash, David. 'Reconnecting Religion with Social and Cultural History: Secularization's Failure as a Master Narrative'. *Cultural and Social History* 1(3) (2003), 302–25.
N.N. 'Hervormde lidmaten krijgen folder over kerkbezoek'. *Nieuwe Leidsche Courant*, 11 December 1953.
N.N. 'Uit de gemeente'. *Leids Hervormd Kerkblad* 13(22) (1953), 1.
Oppenheimer, K.E.H. 'De oorzaken der onkerkelijkheid' [part 1]. *Leids Hervormd Kerkblad* 13(31) (1953), 1–2.
———. 'De oorzaken der onkerkelijkheid' [part 2]. *Leids Hervormd Kerkblad* 13(32) (1953), 1–2.
Paul, Herman. 'De erfenis van Wickham: naar een nieuwe fase in het secularisatieonderzoek'. *Tijdschrift voor Geschiedenis* 127(1) (2014), 107–27.
———. *Secularisatie: een kleine geschiedenis van een groot verhaal*. Amsterdam: Amsterdam University Press, 2017.
———. 'The Sociological Myth: A 1954 Controversy on Secularization Narratives'. *Journal of Religion in Europe* 9(2–3) (July 2016), 201–24.
Petras, Otto. *Post Christum: Streifzüge durch die geistige Wirklichkeit*. Berlin: Widerstands-Verlag, 1935.
Raphael, Lutz. 'Die Verwissenschaftlichung des Sozialen als methodische und konzeptionelle Herausforderung für eine Sozialgeschichte des 20. Jahrhunderts'. *Geschichte und Gesellschaft* 22(2) (April–June 1996), 165–93.
Riesman, David. 'Leisure and Work in Post-industrial Society', in Eric Larrabee and Rolf Meyersohn (eds), *Mass Leisure* (Glencoe: The Free Press, 1958), 363–85.
Rostow, Walt Whitman. *The Stages of Economic Growth: A Non-Communist Manifest*. Cambridge: Cambridge University Press, 1960.

Smith, Christian. 'Introduction: Rethinking the Secularization of American Public Life', in Christian Smith (ed.), *The Secular Revolution: Power, Interests, and Conflict in the Secularization of American Public Life* (Berkeley: University of California Press, 2003), 1–96.

Swatos Jr., William H., and Daniel V.A. Olson. *The Secularization Debate.* Lanham, MD: Rowman & Littlefield, 2000.

Taylor, Charley. *A Secular Age.* Cambridge: Belknap Press, 2007.

Toynbee, Arnold J. 'Christianity and Civilization', in Arnold J. Toynbee (ed.), *Civilization on Trial* (London: Oxford University Press, 1948), 225–52.

———. 'The World and the West: Russia'. *The Listener* 48(1238) (1952), 839–41.

Tschannen, Olivier. *Les theories de la sécularisation.* Geneva: Droz, 1992.

Vahanian, Gabriel. 'This Post-Christian Era'. *The Nation* 189(20) (1959), 438–41.

Vossers, D.J. 'Uit de gemeente'. *Leids Hervormd Kerkblad* 13(40) (1953), 1.

Weber, Alfred. *Der dritte oder der vierte Mensch: Vom Sinn des geschichtlichen Daseins.* Munich: R. Piper, 1953.

———. *Kulturgeschichte als Kultursoziologie* (2nd edn). Munich: R. Piper, 1950.

Weyns, Walter (ed.). *Gedoofde kaarsen en uitslaande vlammen: de secularisatie onder de loep.* Antwerp: Polis, 2015.

White, Hayden. *Metahistory: The Historical Imagination in Nineteenth-Century Europe.* Baltimore, MD: Johns Hopkins University Press, 1973.

Wickham, Edward Ralph. *Church and People in an Industrial City.* London: Lutterworth Press, 1957.

———. 'What Should Be the New Look?' in Leslie S. Hunter (ed.), *The English Church: A New Look* (Harmondsworth: Penguin Press, 1966), 144–67.

Ziemann, Benjamin. *Katholische Kirche und Sozialwissenschaften 1945–1975.* Göttingen: Vandenhoeck & Ruprecht, 2007.

———. 'The Practical Sociologist: Role and Performance of Pastoral Sociologists in the West German Catholic Church, 1945–1970'. *Journal of Religion in Europe* 9(2–3) (July 2016), 133–56.

CHAPTER 4

Narratives of Global History

Expounding Global Interconnections

Gabriele Lingelbach

Introduction

The global history approach has experienced a significant gain in popularity over the past years.[1] Many historians are using terms such as entanglement, transfer, connected history, *métissage, histoire croisée*; also history of the world, global history and history of globalization. In their empirical studies, an increasing number of historians examine trans- or intersocietal contacts and interactions that bridge certain geographical distances and connect individuals, groups or structures that differ from each other in political, social, economic or cultural aspects. Reciprocal perception, appropriations and delineations, connections and entanglements, and the generation of structures resulting from the same, are of core importance here. However, global history cannot claim to be a new paradigm in the study of history. It does not have a distinct set of methods, theories or concrete empirical questions to set it apart from other approaches, a set supported by consensus between all historians working in global history.

Furthermore, global historians are not united in preference for certain narrative structures or plots.[2] There are historians who structure their argument very systematically and analytically, as Jürgen Osterhammel has done in his *Transformation of the World*, in which he also employs a comparatistic

Notes for this section begin on page 112.

approach.³ But there are also historians who use a pointillist, or partly associative approach, such as Serge Gruzinski, who uses episodes or items to grasp transfers and highlight *métissages* in proving, for example, the presence of modified Christian motifs from Renaissance painting on sixteenth-century African ivory vessels.⁴ Here, his method is more descriptive and anecdotal than analytic. While several global historians, such as Janet L. Abu-Lughod, additionally assume a macro perspective and examine larger areas or many regions over a long period of time,⁵ and in doing so only seldomly address acting individuals or concrete locations, others concentrate on a microlevel instead, which allows them to also look at individual protagonists and to query their perception of global events or developments, how they interpreted, experienced or suffered them and how this affected their actions. Other historians, such as Angelika Epple, alternate between the macro- and microlevel. Epple uses the example of the chocolate manufacturer Stollwerck to look at both the enterprise's global acquisition of resources and structures of distribution, as well as its individual chocolate-vending-machine restaurants in different cities around the globe.⁶ Or Victoria de Grazia, who follows the thesis of twentieth-century Americanization of European patterns of consumption: she presents the tiredness of individual participants in a committee meeting of the International Chamber of Commerce on 26 June 1935 in conference hall 1 D at 28 Rue St Dominique in Paris, as well as the process of mechanization of European households after the war.⁷ Accordingly, the degree of vividness of global history texts can be extremely varied: narrating, concrete case studies sit side by side with analytical, abstract works that are often guided by theories; and so-called page-turners sit beside heavy volumes that make for rather cumbersome reading.

In short, there is no restricted selection of favourable narrative plots, or dramaturgical models and narrative constructions and devices that global historians could turn to when searching for principles of structure and presentation for their historiographical description. Rather, form follows content in so far as every global historian has to decide which narrative structure is best suited to doing justice to the presentation of their chosen topic and the corresponding research questions. Therefore, authors have to decide how they lend coherence, logic consistency, plausibility and, thereby, transparency to their presentation. Consequently, they can strictly trace a chronology in their presentations, or can employ analepsis (retrospection) or prolepsis (chronological anticipation). Depending on the chosen topic, they must decide at what point the 'story' sets in and when it ends. Furthermore, in most cases, the authors, in contrast to many other historians whose choices of topic often determine the areas to be examined, has to decide where to begin and end their narrative. Instead of a chronological examination of the subject matter, authors can also settle for a rather systematic one. Or they can combine chronological and systematic structural principles. This decision partly preconfigures the way in which cause and effect relationships are deduced. Authors can additionally sprinkle their narrative with digressions or relocate a significant amount of information to footnotes to give their text a certain three-dimensionality. Thus, the degree to which markers or signs of a scientific character (annotations, lists of sources and literature cited) are used varies greatly among many publications in global history. Furthermore, it is up to the authors to what extent they manifest as narrators, whether they apparently move into the background completely or whether they act as an omniscient narrator, or introduce different interpretations and raise questions to leave them partly unanswered. Global historians as authors can also assume a distant and analytical standpoint, and signal this by means of a corresponding characteristic linguistic style, or they can assume the role of plaintiff or defendant and fill this role through normative statements, emotional appeals, imploring formulas, and so on.

Authors of global history books also have to decide how they keep the reader's attention and how far they can cater to readers' expectations of being entertained. Accordingly, a choice between a more descriptive or more argumentative approach has to be made. They are furthermore free to choose if they want to include characteristic anecdotes to make abstract trains of thought concrete or to illustrate them. It is similarly up to them how strongly they rely on citations from sources to prove their own statements and to strengthen the reader's impression of authenticity. They may even decide to take recourse to fictional narrative elements, such as dialogues not documented by sources or to other means of paralipsis, that is an excess of information, such as protagonists' emotions, for which the author, strictly speaking, does not possess sufficiently documented evidence.

However, the decision for certain forms of presentation is not always taken completely consciously. Rather, it follows conventions that are, at least with historians from established university contexts, mostly preconfigured by the standards and traditions of their discipline, and which may in turn vary between countries. Since the latter are not only subject to permanent socially and discipline-dependent transformation, but vary depending on the type of publication (e.g. textbook, journal article or qualification work) or on the addressed readership (general public or peers), and may also differ according to the author's academic socialization, global historical presentation, like all historiography, follows certain benchmarks.

Given the great variety of global historiography, the following pages cannot offer a comprehensive overview of all narrative structures or modes of presentation that global historians have used in their work. Rather, two case studies will be presented to highlight the ways in which individual authors have tried to solve a core problem of global history on the narrative plane: Donald R. Wright's *History of Niumi*[8] and Giorgio Riello's *History of Cotton*.[9] These respective attempts will be analysed regarding how two global historians present the mediations and translations between, on the one hand, processes situated on the global scale and thereby on the macro-historical level, and on the other hand, those that take place rather in a regional or local realm, that is on a micro-level. The answer to the question, which has been identified by Roland Wenzlhuemer as the one central to global history – namely, how human action creates global connections and how these in turn feedback into human thinking, feeling and action – has been approached differently by the two authors introduced in the following, and has resulted in different forms of narrative presentation.[10]

Case Study 1: Donald R. Wright's *The World and a Very Small Place in Africa*

Donald R. Wright focuses on the Gambian Niumi region of approximately 400 square miles near the Atlantic estuary.[11] Wright's account starts at that point when at least moderately assured knowledge is available, meaning in approximately the year 1000, and guides the reader into the present. However, this is not a comprehensive, or 'total' history of a location, such as for example Hans Medick wrote on Laichingen[12] and Emmanuel Le Roy Ladurie wrote on Montaillou.[13] He rather focuses on the questions of which global developments had an impact on Niumi and which effects they produced on site. To present these processes on the macrolevel, Wright takes recourse to Wallerstein's world-systems theory and to the dependency theories connected to it.[14] For his examination of Niumi's development, by contrast, Wright uses own findings in sources, especially archival materials and transcripts of interviews with traditional storytellers, besides previous studies by other authors. Additionally, he conducted further interviews and longer field research trips on site.

Wright combines chronological and systematic principles in structuring the text. He begins with a personal introduction (see below) and, before moving into a chronological presentation, he explains broader outlines of the theoretical concept he uses – namely, the world-systems theory. The subsequent broad structure is chronological in so far as Wright treats four phases (before 1446, 1446–1816, 1816–1965 and 1965–2009) in one chapter each, while in turn dividing most of these into sub-chapters. Within the respective sub-chapters, Wright then uses a more systematic approach, and first describes the macrolevel and the changes happening on it; for example, the rise of the plantation complex (1446–1600) and the expansion of early Atlantic trade. Thus, a greater panorama is presented first, in a manner that reduces complexities. Only after that does he expound the consequences of transformations happening on the macrolevel for the regional structures and the inhabitants of Niumi.

The presentation is focused on the developments in global trade and their consequences for Niumi. Wright stresses how, before the mid-fifteenth century, it was above all transregional trade in salt and also slaves and fish that flourished, bringing prosperity to the inhabitants of Niumi, and high income and power to their regional leaders. After the arrival of the first Europeans, the population initially continued to profit from the establishment of the Atlantic plantation system and the slave trade. Among other things, the inhabitants of Niumi developed new markets for their products, and the assimilation of traders of Portuguese origin and their descendants is described positively. New crops, new products, new tools and even new 'foreign' manners all found their way into everyday life. However, the importation of European finished products now laid the foundations for later dependence on the world market. The path to an export economy for raw materials based on the world's division of labour for the import of consumer goods and non-productive items, as well as foodstuffs, especially grain – in Wright's interpretation, a disastrous path – began here.

After a phase of relative stability, between the early and mid-nineteenth century, Wright sees Niumi's economy as increasingly and acceleratingly being drawn into the capitalistic world system, with its new division of labour. From now, Niumi mainly just produced agricultural raw materials, especially peanuts, meant for export; but this happened to the detriment of subsistence agriculture and food self-sufficiency. Traders from the centres of the world system, mainly British citizens, simultaneously opened up African markets like Niumi for their manufactured products, such as textiles, thereby weakening the local rulers. With the establishment of colonial rule by Great Britain, there was also an expansion of infrastructure for the export of peanuts. An increasing proportion of the population thus became dependent on world market prices for peanuts on the one hand, and for the imported finished products or foodstuffs on the other, and the inhabitants of Niumi had no influence over these prices. Dependence on world market prices meant that in times of bad peanut harvests or high prices for imported goods, inhabitants of Niumi had to run into debt to be able to buy food – a debt spiral from which there was almost no escape. This did not change with Gambia's independence in 1965 'because political independence would not alter Niumi's position on the periphery of the world economy'.[15]

First of all, the narrative form chosen by Wright opens up analytical access to his topic. By leaning against the theoretical scaffolding of the world-systems theory, Wright is able not only to describe the developments of his chosen case study but also to explain them comprehensively. Here, the cause–effect mechanisms presented by Wright correlate with the perspective alternating between either macro or micro structures. Causes for change are usually situated on the macrolevel, whereas the effects of growing globalization and the emergence of centre–periphery constellations are presented on the microlevel: '[T]he influence of global events on local history, . . . how dealings with large economic complexes and, eventually, incorporation into an ever-growing world market, or . . . world system, had affected the way people lived for a long time in Niumi'.[16] Feedback from the numerous actions and reactions on the microlevel into the macrolevel, however, can hardly be presented by use of this narrative. Wright cannot explain how local agents' actions and adaptions in their turn stabilized structures on the macrolevel or contributed to their transformation. His mode of presentation similarly does not succeed in conducting exploration or in making general statements about the effects of globalization. As Niumi's representativeness cannot be documented, the presentation has to remain illustrative, and the generalizing statements speculative.

The degree to which Wright's presentation is inspired by Wallerstein's world-systems theory and its categorization of world regions into centres and peripheries is evident in that he characterizes the distribution of power within the web of relations – between the mostly anonymous structures of global trade, or the representatives of the centre, on the one hand, and the inhabitants of Niumi on the other – as increasingly asymmetrical. There was an exchange at the beginning of this development, in which Niumi elites could push through their interests and could act relatively autonomously; however, the inhabitants of the region, according to Wright, increasingly lost their agency and the elites of Niumi increasingly lost their sovereignty the more the region was integrated into the structures of divided labour caused by the export of local resources and the import of finished goods. Wright describes the beginning of trade relations between European traders and the inhabitants of Niumi as an interest-guided encounter that was still free of violence, and as a win–win situation: '[T]he vulnerability of the alien Europeans, who were outmanned and eternally dependent on local peoples for water, food, shelter, and cultural and commercial mediation, was palpable. Survival and success depended not on force of arms, but on finding a mutuality of interests, and then fostering these to the benefits of African states and foreign traders alike'.[17] However, by the end of the development, the balance of power had unilaterally shifted to the disadvantage of the inhabitants of Niumi, as they lost control over their living conditions: 'It was the classic pattern of colonial dependency, with the mother country at the distant core, in control of operations, and the colony on the periphery, its residents having little choice but to follow the only pattern laid out for their survival'.[18]

Wright's presentation shows similarities to what Hedwig and Ralf Richter termed the victim plot:[19] a story of suppression and incapacitation that hardly grants agency (in the sense of opportunity to take and implement decisions that are not entirely dictated by external conditions) to the subordinate as opposed to the hegemonial agents.[20] Wright's narrative plot therefore functions as a story of decline in which, apart from the loss of agency, a regrettable homogenization of patterns of behaviour and ways of life accompanied the globalization of economic relations. The third indicator of decline is economic weakness and its derivates – inadequate standards of living, poverty and hunger. Wright partially adapts his mode of presentation to this narrative of decline in arguing, normatively and accusingly, in relation to the interest-driven actions of both the centre and the indigenous elite, who get rich corruptly and recklessly at the expense of the 'simple' population, who are portrayed as passive and helpless. To underline the loss of the indigenous power to act, the processes on the macrolevel and their local consequences, are described in corresponding metaphors. The current wave of globalization, for example, 'came bearing down on The Gambia like the tidal surge of a tropical storm'.[21] Metaphors of 'overpowering' and 'nature' stress the helplessness and powerlessness of the inhabitants of Niumi.

This creates empathy in the reader, which is increased by Wright now and then inserting his own person into the text as a first-person narrator who recounts his subjective impressions from his trips to The Gambia. Thus, he commences the introduction to the new edition with the word 'I'. What follows is an introspection that is rather atypical for academic texts, as he proleptically describes, on the very first pages, how he came to Niumi for the first time in May 1974, how he circled above the region on the plane and what his first impressions on site were. He circumscribes the latter extremely negatively: the consequences of globalization are presented drastically to the reader, especially the deficient infrastructure, the omnipresence of 'Western' consumer goods, the raging poverty of the populace. From this diagnosis of the present, Wright draws his – normatively based – question: 'I recognized that something in that little place was awry. What was wrong in Niumi, I eventually came to understand, was the same thing that was wrong in a good part of the world'.[22] Furthermore, for the most part, Wright abstains from theoretical recourses and also from corresponding abstract terms, and his presentation remains vivid and concrete at all times. Quotes from conversations with the 'simple' populace and amateur photographs that are included in the book abet the impression of authenticity, as does the insertion of anecdotes. For instance, the detailed paraliptic account of a European trader's (the Portuguese Nuno Tristao, 1446, and his crew) first attempt at rowing upstream and the less than friendly welcome on the part of a well-organized formation of indigenous archers. When there is need to clarify terms, methods or theories, Wright provides these in graphically marked digressions – which may also be due to the text type of 'textbook' – or the insertion of longer and basic overviews, for instance relating to state structures in West Africa around 1600, or the development of transatlantic slave trade.

Paradigmatically, Wright's book can be seen as a Marxist-inspired variant of the so-called glocalization approach, which enquires into the connections between the manifold forms of globalization on the one hand, and their local or regional effects, the implementations of processes of globalization under local and regional conditions and specificities, on the other.[23] The glocalization approach stresses perception, reception and adaption of overarching transfers within the specific contexts of a given place. It also underlines the potency of logics and dynamics specific to a location. In this, it stands in opposition to the master narrative according to which globalization always entails homogenization and conformation of societies – for example, in the field of consumption patterns ('McDonaldization'). At the same time, the approach allows for a synthesis of global analyses and detailed micro studies. Beyond that, the book by Wright represents a currrent in global history, which also looks at developments in globalization from the perspective of 'simple people', who are portrayed as individuals, not as anonymous masses.

Case Study 2: Giorgio Riello's *Cotton: The Fabric That Made the Modern World*

Another way of looking at processes both on the macrolevel and on the microlevel is used by Giorgio Riello in his 2013 book.[24] At the centre of his presentation, there is no location, which per definition is confined to a specific place, but there is a mobile good instead: cotton. Riello follows his subject along the different stations of its 'biography': he visits the places of its production, as well as those of its processing and consumption. From cotton's point of view, so to speak, the reader perceives the change that has been caused in different places by cultivation and trade in, as well as consumption of, cotton and cotton products. Before their inner eye, the readers thereby also see the development of those global networks or transregional structures that are constituted by cotton and that in turn shape local and regional structures. In this fashion, Riello traces the gradual rise of cotton from a relatively insignificant plant, which at first was relevant for only a small portion of the global population, to what became the most frequently traded good worldwide – one that was a central factor in the lives of millions of people all over the world: 'The book narrates the success of cotton in becoming global'.[25]

At the same time, by concentrating on cotton and products made from it, Riello constructs the connection between the decline of certain regions of the world and the rise of others, thereby describing the process of growing global inequality. He therefore takes part in the intensive debate in global history regarding the so-called Great Divergence. The question that has been posed by Kenneth Pomeranz and others is why, over the course of the modern period, some regions in Europe have developed into rich, economically and politically leading regions, while others, above all in Asia, became impoverished and marginalized.[26] While some researchers stress that Europe became the leading region in the world due to its favourable climate, as well as geographical, ecological, political and social preconditions, Riello highlights that the rise of Europe could also be explained as being a consequence of interaction with (above all) Asia, and that the decline of Asia was partly caused by contact with Europeans. Since Riello consequently examines the interconnections between these processes of rise and decline, he does not so much aim at a history of cotton in itself, but rather at an analysis of global market conditions with the help of cotton, as 'cotton can be used as a lens through which to read other global phenomena that cotton came to exemplify and possibly explain'.[27]

To conceptually grasp the blatant change in production, distribution and consumption of cotton, as well as the interactions between the agents dispersed all over the globe, Riello, similar to Wright, decided in favour of a chronological structure, dividing his book into three chapters that comprise three phases of cotton trade: 1000–1500, 1500–1750 and 1750–2000. In a certain sense, these phases correspond to a focus on respective regions: for the early phase, India moves into focus; for the second phase, Riello mainly turns to Europe; and in the third phase, he first looks at North America and, moving across Europe, has a final look at his point of departure, Asia.

Riello begins his presentation in Asia, and especially with India, where, between approximately the eleventh and sixteenth centuries, multiple regional centres grew that were partly specializing in certain kinds of product. Their production complemented the persistent local, household-centered form of textile production, for example in India but also in Africa, without displacing it. According to Riello, textiles of varying quality were traded along the Indian Ocean from the different production sites. Intermediaries of different ethnic backgrounds at different locations distributed Indian products via land and sea routes – they bought, bartered and sold them on. In short, Asian agents defined a global system of commercial relations, and their products influenced the lifeworlds of consumers across a wide geographical area. Riello calls this system 'centrifugal', because it functioned via the diffusion of raw materials, technologies, knowledge and the splitting of profit between many agents. The different agents were largely independent in determining their own mode of cultivation of raw cotton and its processing into textiles. Hugh regional differences persisted, just as a multitude of commercial intermediaries, who interceded between spinners and weavers and the traders, who were active further away. Therefore, this was a network that connected different regions of the world; it was not defined by hierarchical relations but rather by relatively fluid relationships between equal agents.

The second part of the book, the period from 1500 to 1750, looks at the Europeans' growing role in cotton trade. For more than two hundred years, the European trade, according to Riello, was still based on techniques, materials and goods from other parts of the world. European agents especially learned from Asian producers, for instance regarding the techniques of dyeing and printing textiles: 'Europe acted like a sponge, absorbing technological and commercial knowledge, acquiring materials and translating and transforming products'.[28] At the same time, however, European traders also began to enter the market system of the Indian Ocean and to modify it according to their interests. They increasingly succeeded at making the spinners, weavers and textile printers dependent on them. Simultaneously, they gathered knowledge regarding the processes of production, which subsequently enabled them to implement import substitution. First, core stages of production, such as dyeing and printing, were relocated to Europe and, increasingly, complete textiles could be manufactured there from the raw materials that still had to be imported. In this chapter, Riello also treats the change in Europe that was triggered by the import of textiles from Asia – for instance, an increasing consumption of cotton clothes. The author again makes a point of the creative adaption of the Indian goods on the European agents' part, for example in relation to fashionable clothing: 'The overall result was often a hybrid that included original Indian influences, established canons in European textile design and some innovation introduced by the experienced eye of servants of the East India companies. Indian products were "Europeanised"'.[29] In the long run, however, these European products weakened the Asian producers.

In the third and final part of the book, Riello first turns towards the Americas, and explains that Europeans began cultivating cotton there that they so urgently needed for further processing in Europe. The slaves needed for the cultivation of cotton, in turn, were bought by European traders in Africa, partially bartered for textiles from Asian and increasingly from their own production. Only now did the geographically diversified division of labour and a commodity chain develop on a global scale, in which cultivation and processing, as well as recruitment of the labour force, each took place on different continents. Europe, however, was now at the centre, where the decisions were made. The final ascent of Europe is mainly explained by Riello through the competition with Asian production, which had to be superseded in terms of quality and quantity. This was achieved through geographical concentration of production, which did not have any equivalent in Asia.

The global system of cotton production and consumption constructed by European agents is called centripetal by Riello: it was no longer characterized by cooperation and symbiosis, but 'a system of trade, exchange and power in the service of a "core" that exploited resources, that made and controlled new technologies and that dominated markets to the detriment of Asian merchandise'.[30] Europe grew rich, while the distance between the West and 'the rest' grew. This global shift of power in Europe's favour is explained by Riello not so much through internal European developments, but by the very interconnections between Europe, especially Great Britain, and other parts of the world:

> Europe's divergence cannot be solely understood by looking within the borders of Europe, or by attributing it to Europe's peculiar culture, institutions, scientific and mechanical knowledge or natural endowments. This book has shown instead that divergence is a process based on a changing interaction between different areas of the world. . . . The possible rise of the West was founded . . . on the reframing of the workings and logic of power and exchange around the globe.[31]

So much for the plot of Riello's book. Riello's matter-of-fact style of presentation differs from Wright's. Among other things, Riello mostly abstains from subjective and/or normatively connoted statements. He does not judge history but retains a characteristic analytical style. Besides, graphicness or vividness is not Riello's primary goal, which is why he largely abstains from illustrating anecdotes. Individual agents are looked at only rarely. Although his analysis is very much centred on the microlevel, he mainly covers groups of agents, meaning collectives, not individual protagonists. Thus, in his description of the consequences of the intrusion of European traders into the hitherto existent networks in Asia, he descends onto the microlevel but refrains from evoking empathy or even pity or indignation in the reader through personalization. The emotionalizing quotes from interviews found with Wright do not have an equivalent in Riello. Although he mostly refrains from using quotes that illustrate agents' experiences, Riello does not abstain from reproducing sources that claim authenticity: the book contains numerous photos of textiles, as well as reproductions of paintings that depict the production, trade and forms of use of textiles. The reproductions of images partially take on the function of quotes from sources, in so far as they seem to reproduce the lifeworlds of producers or consumers of cotton. Especially in the case of poorer producers, slaves or textile workers, they only rarely left written source material that would allow for concrete conclusions to be drawn regarding their conditions of life. However, these images are used in an illustrating fashion rather than being sufficiently critically approached as sources. Furthermore, Riello makes strong use of reproduced maps, as the arrows and overlapping circles marked on them serve to visualize and make plausible those aspects of structures of entanglement that he seeks to strongly emphasize, while reducing complexity. And not least, Riello works with flow diagrams that are intended to visualize the point of the argument.

While Riello's style of presentation might be matter-of-fact, his narrative nonetheless has normative undertones, since he, just like Wright, is writing a story of decline. Riello also describes loss: the producers' loss of independence that accompanies the gravitational shift in textile production from Asia to Europe. He also sees the agents on the local plane being increasingly drawn into an anonymous process of globalization that deprives them of their agency and their self-determination. Furthermore, he describes the accumulation of power to European agents' advantage as negative, achieved as it was by violence and with a loss in diversity – the newly established system is even described by him as 'egocentric'.[32] The vocabulary used to compare the centrifugal system to the centripetal system implies valuation: 'The so-called "soft globalisation" of the early modern period based on encounters, discovery and trade gave way to a phase of "hard globalisation" measured by the integration of markets and price convergence. Polycentrism was replaced by Western power in economic and political affairs worldwide'.[33]

At the same time, with Riello, a direct connection between methodological approach and narrative structure is introduced, since he discloses his methodological approach in the introduction: for Riello, 'the global' is 'a lens through which problems – present and past – are analysed. It is a way to observe and consider phenomena and to pose questions'.[34] This 'lens' provides the author with criteria of relevance for inclusion in the narrative, but also for not mentioning certain aspects. The criterion of relevance in turn lends coherence to the presentation. Beyond that, this form of presentation is also capable of setting out the feedback effects of decisions and actions on the microlevel into the macrolevel, since, according to Riello, '[t]his book argues that what happened [for example] in Lancashire in the second half of the eighteenth century did have global causes as it had global consequences. The local and the global should be seen as part of one process'.[35] This approach affords the opportunity of gauging local agents' or intermediaries' options for action and their influence on macro structures more intensively than done by Wright. This global history perspective simultaneously allows for situating the cause for local, regional and national developments in the trans-societal entanglement itself, and to thereby enter into dialogue with other historians, who have mainly explained societal developments with endogenous causes. In many places in his book, Riello therefore also addresses established theses in research, and he disproves, expands or corrects them from the perspective of global history.

Conclusion

The two case studies presented here show two different options for presenting developments relevant to global history. Among other things, they differ in their degree of tangibility. Wright's descriptive mode allows for the construction of a relatively clearly structured narrative that is therefore easy to follow for the reader. It always presents the macrolevel first, to subsequently trace its consequences on the local level. Riello does not have this advantage, since he frequently changes the location under consideration, from where he tells his story; but above all it is also because, in his analytical, explaining approach, he has to write in a strongly abstracting manner, and in consideration of other opinions in research that explain the facts depicted differently from the way he does. The structure of the text, therefore, becomes much more complex and certainly more difficult to grasp for the reader. This is also true on the linguistic level, on which Riello has to work much more strongly with analytical terms than is the case with Wright. This is also due to the fact that both authors can stress the perspectives of individual agents to very different degrees, Wright much more so than Riello. Therefore, Wright can make offers of empathy to the reader, whereas Riello cannot.

Both works are especially different in their potential to not only describe developments, but to also explain them. Wright can elucidate with great precision about which causes were behind the changes to be observed on the microlevel. The developments in the global structures effecting the latter, however, remain a black box, whose operating modes he names through recourse to the world-systems theory, but whose occurrence he does not explain, because this would only be possible if the feedback effects from the micro- onto the macrolevel, from the local onto the global plane, were taken into consideration. But how the people in Niumi shaped those global connections that determined their lifeworlds largely remains in the dark. The constant switches between planes of presentation that Riello conducts can better grasp the mechanisms of transmission. He is able to identify groups of agents who shaped global connections that in their turn generated structures, which in their turn impacted the respective local lifeworlds. In this manner, relationality between the different levels is grasped, structures are simultaneously conceptualized as results of local actions and translocal movements, as well as their preconditions. Both narratological concepts of examinations in global history that are presented here therefore also ensure textual coherence in different ways, as they apply their own specific criteria of relevance to their subject matter: Wright by asking about the consequences of macro structural developments for changes in structures on the microlevel; and Riello through seeking out feedback effects between the micro- and macrolevels by identifying networks or groups of agents that act as intermediaries between both levels. The main story line, the 'red thread' that both create, however, is the same, with each of their presented plots being constructed as a story of decline. As a deep structure, it lends both continuity as well as meaning to the facts presented, and it simultaneously correlates with a postcolonial worldview that has made itself heard in academic historiography for several decades.[36]

Gabriele Lingelbach is professor of modern and contemporary history at Kiel University. She held fellowships of Harvard University, the Institute of Contemporary History (Institut für Zeitgeschichte) in Munich and the Institute for Advanced Studies Greifswald (Alfried Krupp Wissenschaftskolleg). She has published numerous monographs and articles on the history of historiography, as well as on historical theory and methodology. She has further research interests in the history of philanthropy and in disability history. Lately she has focused on global perspectives on German history. Among recent publications are 'Disability History' (edited special issue of *Geschichte in Wissenschaft und Unterricht*, 2019), 'Tourismusgeschichte' (special issue of *Geschichte in Wissenschaft und Unterricht*, co-edited with Moritz Glaser, 2018) and *Kontinuitäten, Zäsuren, Brüche? Lebenslagen von Menschen mit Behinderungen in der deutschen Zeitgeschichte*, co-edited with Anne Waldschmidt (Campus Verlag, 2016).

Notes

1. See introductions such as Berg, *Writing the History of the Global*; Conrad, *What is Global History?*; Middell and Naumann, 'Global History 2008–2010'; Sachsenmaier, *Global Perspectives*; Pernau, *Transnationale Geschichte*.
2. Wenzlhuemer, *Globalgeschichte schreiben*. A systematic analysis of plots outlined by global historians can be found in Crossley, *What Is Global History?*
3. Osterhammel, *Transformation of the World*.
4. Serge Gruzinski, *Les quatre parties du monde*, 298–302.
5. Abu-Lughod, *Before European Hegemony*.
6. Epple, *Das Unternehmen Stollwerck*.
7. Grazia, *Irresistible Empire*.
8. Wright, *The World*.
9. Riello, *Cotton*.
10. Wenzlhuemer, *Globalgeschichte schreiben*, 20.

11. Wright, *The World*. The following analysis is based on the third, greatly revised, edition from 2010. The first edition was published in 1997.
12. Medick, *Weben und Überleben in Laichingen*.
13. Le Roy Ladurie, *Montaillou*.
14 Wallerstein, *The Modern World System*.
15. Wright, *The World*, 183.
16. Ibid., 8.
17. Ibid., 57.
18. Ibid., 187.
19. Richter and Richter, 'Der Opfer-Plot'.
20. In the third edition of his book, however, Wright undertakes a reorientation. By complementing his book with a chapter on the latest developments in The Gambia since the military coup of 1994 and Yahya A.J.J. Jammeh's rise to all-dominant dictator, the local elite and especially the autocrat come to the fore, and are presented as causes of suffering. In the introduction to the third edition, Wright describes this reinterpretation as a partial emancipation from the axioms of the word-systems theory and the dependency theory. The all-domiant power of the macro structures is qualified by Wright (Wright, *The World*, 9, 212).
21. Wright, *The World*, 9.
22. Ibid., 7.
23. Robertson, 'Glocalization'; Epple, 'Lokalität und die Dimensionen des Globalen'.
24. Riello, *Cotton*.
25. Ibid., 1.
26. Pomeranz, *Great Divergence*.
27. Riello, *Cotton*, 2.
28. Ibid., 86.
29. Ibid., 133.
30. Ibid., 265.
31. Ibid., 293.
32. Ibid., 290.
33. Ibid., 282.
34. Ibid., 11.
35. Ibid., 152.
36. Text translated from German by Vivian Strotmann, Institute for Social Movements, Ruhr University Bochum.

Bibliography

Abu-Lughod, Janet. *Before European Hegemony: The World System AD 1250–1350*. New York: Oxford University Press, 1989.

Adamson, Glenn, and Giorgio Riello. 'Global Objects: Contention and Entanglement', in Maxine Berg (ed.), *Writing the History of the Global: Challenges for the 21st Century* (Oxford: Oxford University Press, 2013), 177–93.

Berg, Maxine (ed.). *Writing the History of the Global: Challenges for the 21st Century*. Oxford: Oxford University Press, 2013.

Conrad, Sebastian. *What Is Global History?* Princeton, NJ: Princeton University Press, 2016.

Crossley, Pamela Kyle. *What Is Global History?* Cambridge: Polity Press, 2008.

Epple, Angelika. 'Lokalität und die Dimensionen des Globalen: Eine Frage der Relationen'. *Historische Anthropologie* 21(1) (2013), 4–25.

———. *Das Unternehmen Stollwerck: Eine Mikrogeschichte der Globalisierung*. Frankfurt am Main: Campus, 2010.

Grazia, Victoria de. *Irresistible Empire: America's Advance through Twentieth-Century Europe*. Cambridge: Belknap Press of Harvard University Press, 2005.

Gruzinski, Serge. *Les quatre parties du monde: Histoire d'une mondalisation*. Paris: Édition de la Martinière, 2004.

Le Roy Ladurie, Emmanuel. *Montaillou, village occitan de 1294 à 1324*. Paris: Gallimard, 1975.

Medick, Hans. *Weben und Überleben in Laichingen 1650–1900: Lokalgeschichte als allgemeine Geschichte*. Göttingen: Vandenhoeck & Ruprecht, 1996.

Middell, Middell, and Katja Naumann. 'Global History 2008–2010: Empirische Erträge, konzeptionelle Debatten, neue Synthesen'. *Comparativ* 20(6) (2017), 93–133.

Osterhammel, Jürgen. *The Transformation of the World: A Global History of the Nineteenth Century*. Princeton, NJ: Princeton University Press, 2014.

Pernau, Margrit. *Transnationale Geschichte*. Göttingen: Vandenhoeck & Ruprecht, 2011.

Pomeranz, Kenneth. *The Great Divergence: China, Europe, and the Making of the Modern World Economy*. Princeton, NJ: Princeton University Press, 2000.

Richter, Hedwig, and Ralf Richter. 'Der Opfer-Plot: Probleme und neue Felder der deutschen Arbeitsmigrationsforschung'. *Vierteljahrshefte für Zeitgeschichte* 57(1) (2009), 61–97.

Riello, Giorgio. *Cotton: The Fabric That Made the Modern World*. Cambridge: Cambridge University Press, 2013.

Robertson, Roland. 'Glocalization: Time–Space and Homogeneity–Heterogeneity', in Mike Featherstone, Scott Lash and Roland Robertson (eds), *Global Modernities* (London: SAGE, 1995), 25–44.

Sachsenmaier, Dominic. *Global Perspectives on Global History: Theories and Approaches in a Connected World*. Cambridge: Cambridge University Press, 2011.

Wallerstein, Immanuel. *The Modern World System* (4 vols). New York: Academic, 1974–2012.

Wenzlhuemer, Roland. *Globalgeschichte schreiben: Eine Einführung in 6 Episoden*. Konstanz: UVK, 2017.

Wright, Donald R. *The World and a Very Small Place in Africa: A History of Globalization in Niumi, the Gambia*. New York: Routledge, 2010.

Part II

School Textbooks in History

CHAPTER 5

More Than Just Barbarians

The Two-Faced Narrative of Ancient Persia in German Textbooks since 1900

BJÖRN ONKEN

The ancient Persians are hardly mentioned in history lessons at school in modern Iran,[1] although they once ruled a powerful empire. Its origins are obscure, but around 550 BC their King Cyrus was able to subjugate the renowned civilization of Elam. This success was followed by a series of campaigns that led Cyrus to the capture of a vast territory including the western coast of Asia Minor and Babylon. The later kings Darius I (522–486 BC) and Xerxes (486–465 BC), however, failed in the beginning of the fifth century to overcome the Greek city states, because Greek forces defeated the invading Persians at Marathon in 490, Salamis 480 and Plataea 479 BC.

These battles seem to be a fundamental part of the European Tradition.[2] According to John Stuart Mill, the Greek victory at Marathon was even to British history more important than the Battle of Hastings.[3] In this narrative the Persians have to take the part of the Asian barbarians who attacked Greece and threatened the development of the European culture. The brave Greek soldiers defeated the invaders and saved Europe. The success of this narrative is connected to the ideology of orientalism, which claims a superiority of Europe over Asia in a general sense, and seems to determine the European picture of western Asia until the end of the twentieth century.[4] Postcolonial theories support this interpretation furthermore.[5] Since textbooks are supposed to be producers and reflections of the mainstream views on history in a society,[6] one expects to find the same tradition in textbooks. The review

Notes for this section begin on page 125.

of this hypothesis fits in well with recent trends in textbook research, which no longer tend to be concerned with comparing textbook representations with historiographical research in order to find factual inconsistencies or other errors. Rather, they aim to analyse the actual contents of textbooks and determine the reasons why such content-selections and structures were favoured.[7] The study presented here uses 'classical historical methodology', which is a common method for content-related textbook research.[8] In addition, elements of discourse analysis and narrative analysis are used.[9]

The starting point will be the description of the content and the analysis of the narrative structure of the parts dealing with the ancient Persians in the textbooks by Friedrich Neubauer, who was the Headmaster of the Lessing-Gymnasium in Frankfurt/Main.[10] Neubauer's 1912 textbook *Lehrbuch der Geschichte* for students in the 11th grade (age 16) serves as the main source because with more than 70,000 copies it was one of the most popular textbooks of the early twentieth century.[11] As European supremacy reached an unprecedented dimension in the beginning of the twentieth century, it should be the heyday of the ideology of orientalism. German textbooks from these years like the one of Neubauer, however, often presented the Persians not only as barbarians but with a quite different face as well. Usually the first Persian to be mentioned in a textbook is King Cyrus. He is often praised as a wise and successful ruler, and is sometimes even honoured with the title 'the Great'. In the 1912 *Lehrbuch der Geschichte* (history textbook) by Friedrich Neubauer, the following is said about Cyrus:

> He [Cyrus] was not only a famous commander-in-chief, but he was also known for his noble attitude towards those under subjugation and the gentle manner with which he treated them; the Greeks knew how to tell many tales about him, and Xenophon portrayed him in the novel-like Cyropädie as an exemplary good and wise ruler.[12]

But Cyrus is not the only Persian king who enjoyed high esteem. Because of its size, the administration of the empire was nearly as challenging as the conquest. Obviously, King Darius I (522–486 BC) managed to tackle this task and therefore received the admiration of Europeans, as Friedrich Neubauer's textbook shows:

> Then Darius became the organizer of the vast empire. . . . In addition to the organization of offices, finance and the army came, on the one hand, that of the law – the supreme judge was the king himself – and on the other hand that of commerce. It must have already been a great achievement if a state of peace was established in such a vast territory; this was encouraged by road construction, the completion of the Nile Canal begun by Necho, and especially by the fact that Dareios . . . established a single currency by way of introducing the Dareikos, a gold coin worth about 23 M. . . . The peoples of the Orient were united in a world empire that for the first time made the grand attempt to create a centralized government of the vast area.[13]

Neubauer describes the policies of Darius I and Cyrus in numerous positive terms such as 'famous', 'noble', 'wise', 'commerce', 'great', 'peace', 'road construction'. Terms like these were named by Klerides as characteristics of a benevolent representation.[14] Neubauer's view of the early Persian Empire is quite common in other contemporary German textbooks.[15] Some of them go even further in praising the Persians. In particular, religious tolerance is additionally mentioned as a quality of Persian rule.[16]

One must not, however, forget the 'dark side' of Persian history, which is also present in Neubauer's book. He blames the empire for its desire to subdue the Greeks, and considers the Greek victory as a great moment for world history: 'The Persian Empire soon stretched its hands also to Europe and to Hellas. The Greek ability to assert its national freedom and culture was of the greatest significance to the history of the world'.[17]

Although Neubauer is clearly a partisan of the Greeks here, he does not label the Persians as barbarians. One of the reasons the ancient Persians enjoyed a reasonable reputation in Europe in the early twentieth century was the linguistic connection between the Persian language and many European tongues. Because these languages belong to the Indo-European (Indo-Germanic) family of languages, scientists assumed that there must be a biological connection between the Persians and the Europeans, and Neubauer mentions this in his book, too:

> The fact that the Indo-Germanic peoples originally formed a unitary nation has been proven by comparative linguistic science, which has found a series of common linguistic roots ... It is not known where the original peoples had lived ... From their original place the Arians, who had later separated into Indians and Iranians, wandered towards the lowlands of the Indus and the Ganges. Other tribes [of the Indo-Germans], Greeks, Illyrians and Thracians turned to the Balkan Peninsula ... The Italians settled in the Apennine peninsula. The Celts, who for a long time also held large parts of present-day southern Germany, occupied Gaul, the Isles of Great Britain, a part of Spain and Upper Italy. The Germans occupied Lower Germany, Denmark and most of the Scandinavian areas. East of them lived Latvians and Slavs in the wide Eastern European lowlands. Everywhere these peoples met indigenous inhabitants whom they conquered and among whom they assimilated.[18]

The term 'Arier' was later misused by Adolf Hitler, but in the early twentieth century the term simply referred to the ancient Indians and Persians, as we see in Neubauer's text.[19] Neubauer is not, however, entirely unaffected by racist theories of his time as he wrote: 'The European Indo-Germans were called to produce the highest and richest culture of all peoples and to spread it throughout the world'.[20] Although Neubauer says that the European Indo-Germanic people had the vocation to produce the leading culture and thus shows racist thoughts, he does not despise the Persians as Barbarians.

The Persians were considered to be close relatives of the Europeans and obviously produced some successful kings. On the other hand, they attacked Greece – but this does not necessarily mean that the Persians are Barbarians. Persian Barbarians finally appear in Neubauer's book when Alexander destroys the Persian Empire.

> The Persian Empire, to which Darius I had formerly given his organization, had since then disintegrated under the Royal House, which, with few exceptions, was incapable and powerless, and was ruined by palace revolutions. Not even the outer structure of the empire could be preserved; Egypt, which was always unruly, had only recently been subjected again after about 60 years of independence; Persian satraps, and native princes founded principals, who had only a loose connection to the whole of the empire; The Persian kings paid tribute to a mountain peoples in order to travel securely from Persepolis to Susa. The internal development of the unity of the empire, especially for the army, was low. The army still lived from the contingencies of the subjugated peoples, which were occasionally imposed on them, without connection and organization; Greek mercenaries were recruited as the best troops. The then King Darius III Kodomannus was raised to the throne by an eunuch, whom he later got to be poisoned so as to save himself from him; He was a gentle ruler, but weak and without power to act. By contrast, when Alexander undertook his daring venture, he led into the field the genius and heroism of a unique personality; the lesser but well-ordered forces of his nation, a well-organized and well-trained army, whose core was his national troops; and, finally, the superiority that the education in Hellenism over that of barbarism gave him and his people.[21]

In this text Neubauer used serveral negative terms such as 'incapable', 'powerless', 'ruined' and 'weak' in his description of the Persians. The Persian Empire is in a state of decline and resembles the oriental societies of the nineteenth century as they appear in descriptions influenced by the ideology of Orientalism. We meet kings who lack the qualities of the earlier rulers. They are not even able to control the court, let alone the empire. They are subject to intrigues, and fail to recognize the necessity to care for the army. Finally, Neubauer uses the term 'barbarism' to describe the Persians in the days of Alexander.

Looking at Neubauer's book we find a narrative with two faces, which are shown in a chronological order. In the early days the Persians were praised for their achievements, but the later Persians were blamed for their weakness and indulgence. This shows that the bad image of the Persians in the days of Alexander is not connected to the ethnic origin of the Persians, who had highly esteemed ancestors. Neubauer's image of the Persians is therefore not a racist one, even though he uses parts of that ideology to describe the decay of the Persian Empire in its last days. The bad image of the Persians serves to explain how Alexander could defeat them although they still reigned a vast empire. Neubauer's point of view is therefore orientated towards success as he shows esteem for the victorious warlords Alexander and Cyrus, while on the other hand despising the defeated Persians. This resembles the values of the bourgeoisie and middle class in Imperial Germany, where individual success was an important element for social prestige.[22]

We must be aware of the fact that some other contemporary textbooks do not mention King Cyrus,[23] and some already connect the Persian Wars with a barbarian character of the Persians, and a bad image of the Persians prevailed among the public.[24] Although the majority of textbooks present the two-faced narrative like Neubauer, the well-informed teacher and author Fritz Friedrich complained in 1915 about the common mistake of seeing the Persians merely as barbarians.

> I would not like to dispense with an account of Iranian Mazda Religion. It is so clear and straightforward, and so easy to understand in all its essential features, that it would be possible to discuss it thoroughly in one hour. But it is by far the greatest intellectual product of a nation which, on the basis of the one-sided Greek accounts, we still tend to regard as barbaric. Its appraisal thus serves to correct a widespread historical error. Moreover, as I can assure from experience, even younger pupils are grateful to discuss it . . . In addition to this aspect of the Persian culture, the great administrative organization of Darius and the strict treatment of the law must, of course, be mentioned too, and the erroneous idea that the rule of the Grand King was an absolute despotism of arbitrariness.[25]

These conflicting views have their roots in ancient times. The high reputation of Cyrus is tied to the Greek author Xenophon (430–354 BC), who in his work 'The Education of Cyrus' praised the qualities of Cyrus.[26] Since, besides the good King Cyrus, negative assessments of later Persian kings were common in Greek literature the basic structure of the two-faced narrative is already recognizable in Greek antiquity.[27]

In the Middle Ages the Greek influence on European culture was limited, but the good King Cyrus was also known from the Bible.[28] The Persian attacks on the Greeks had not been forgotten, but Rome dominated the discourse on antiquity. In the early modern period the reputation of Cyrus and his empire was well established in Europe.[29] This changed in the eighteenth century, when some of the philosophers of the Enlightenment were more interested in the idea of freedom. With regard to ancient authors, the Greek city-states and especially Athens became examples of free societies in the past, while the Persians, on the other hand, became an example of a despotic and decadent regime. The Persian invasions of Greece were seen as indicators of the aggressive nature of Persian politics and the wars were glorified into a narrative of the collision of Europe and freedom with Asia and despotism, as Greek authors had already seen it.[30] Nevertheless, the good King Cyrus remained part of the discourse, as the high esteem of Cyrus in the works of Johann Gottfried Herder (1744–1803) shows.[31]

In addition to these narratives, the story of the succession of the four empires, which appears in pagan literature and in the Bible in the book of Daniel, influenced the European intellectuals. Already in antiquity, the Persians were seen as part of this series, following the Assyrians or Babylonians and being replaced by the Greeks who had to give way to the Romans in the end. In the early nineteenth century, the importance of this interpretation of history grew when Georg Friedrich Wilhelm Hegel took it up and made it a leitmotif of his view of history. According to Hegel, history represents the path of the spirit of the world through the four realms to their highest level in the European culture. Because the Persians succeeded in building an empire larger than any predecessor, Hegel had no reason to exclude them from his list of four empires and considered the Persians as an important stage in the history of humanity, but they had to give way to the superior Greeks in order to promote the progress of the world spirit.

Thus, according to Hegel, the Greek victories were important events in world history, for the spirit of the world had to profit from the development of Greek culture. Since Hegel was very popular in Germany in the nineteenth century, his thoughts strongly influenced German historical thinking.[32] Hegel's philosophy is certainly Eurocentric, but does not deny that European culture has its origins in the East. This concept is called 'ex oriente lux' and has a long tradition in European intellectual history since Jesus lived, died and resurrected in Judea in the East.[33] Even the German Emperor Wilhelm II (1888–1918) emphasized in his memoirs in 1922 the general importance of oriental roots in European culture.[34]

The thesis recently published by Gerdien Jonker that Europeans increasingly ignored the eastern roots of their civilization during the nineteenth century[35] is therefore not the whole story. There were certainly numerous voices which despised the Orient and Persia as a barbaric region.[36] One can also find those who supported imperialist politics.[37] But the academic discourses were dominated by attitudes that underlined the cultural achievements of Europe's eastern neighbours.[38] Last but not least, the great commitment to the construction of large museum departments for the presentation of artworks from ancient Mesopotamia including Persia[39] can hardly be reconciled with an idea of barbaric cultures.

In the German Empire the admiration of the first Persian kings made several contributions to national politics and the national narrative. First, it showed the advantage of uniting different states within an empire and harmonizing different standards as Darius did with the currency. Second, it presented Cyrus and Darius as successful rulers demonstrating the benefits of a monarchy as a political system. These lessons fitted well with the policy of the Hohenzollern ruling dynasty in Prussia, which 1871 united the formerly almost independent states in the German Empire and naturally favoured monarchy.[40] In particular, William II saw arguments for the legitimacy of his own rule in the history of the monarchies of ancient Mesopotamia.[41]

Additionally, as mentioned above, the two-faced narrative of the Persians fitted well into the value system of the bourgeoisie in the German Empire, where performance and individual success were important elements of social prestige. The victorious war heroes Cyrus and Alexander earned recognition in this value system, whereas the defeated Persians in the fourth century BC received contempt.

Looking at the history of the two-faced narrative the following question is obvious. How did the barbarian image of the Persians gained such headway as Fritz Friedrich reported 1915? It might be the result of a process Dieter Langewiesche described for narratives (according to him narratives tend to change to a simple story).[42] This could explain that a narrative with two faces narrowed to one of them. The bad image prevailed in this process because the dramatic stories of the wars and Alexander attracted much more attention than the earlier history of the Persians.

In the first half of the twentieth century the narrative of the ancient Persians in the textbooks changed little. During the Nazi era, the new curriculum in 1938 required the history of Persia to be portrayed as 'racial decline', but that did not prevail.[43] After the Second World War the West German state needed to find perspectives on history that were compatible with the views of the Western powers, but this did not have much influence on the representations of the Persians because the two-faced narrative was also common in other European countries.[44] German publishers could use several books that were printed before 1933 so that the new books were close to these.[45] As for many others narratives in these books, the story of the Persians changed little. One example is a book by Hans Erich Stier who was a professor of ancient history:

> Cyrus was the first important Indo-European ruler of world history. The Greeks described him in admirable terms. For Herodotus and Xenophon he was the image of a perfect ruler. In Isaiah 45:1, Cyrus, as the deliverer of Israel, sent by God, receives the title of kings, 'the appointed of the Lord'. . . .
>
> It seemed to be a question of time when Hellas would also be incorporated into the empire. But the development of Sparta and Athens had given rise to powerful states of considerable political and military strength. . . .
>
> The love of one's country and unselfish commitment to the cause of freedom and humanity had brought triumph over the imperialism of the great Oriental powers, which, despite what was anticipated at the time, ultimately secured the existence of a Western cultural world alongside the Oriental. . . .
>
> Despite internal unrest, the Persian Empire was still a world power in the fourth century. Artaxerxes III Ochos (358–338 BC) limited the power of the satraps. In 343 he conquered Egypt, which had been independent since 404/3. The Empire was superior to all other powers because of its manpower and extension. . . . From 336 a noble aristocrat occupied the throne of the Achaimenid Empire, Dareios III[46]

Apart from a much more friendly treatment of the Persians in the fourth century the text of Stier resembles very much the traditional narrative. By the end of the twentieth century, however, we see a different picture. During the decades of the second half of the twentieth century the presentation of the Persians in German textbooks grew smaller and smaller.[47] In the 1993 curriculum of the biggest German state, Nordrhein-Westfalen, we get a hint of the reasons for this development. The authors write that there is not enough time in the history lessons to cover Egypt and Mesopotamia (including Persia), and therefore the teachers should choose between the two topics.[48] Probably Egypt is the more popular topic, because Mesopotamia cannot compete with the magic of pyramids, mummies and hieroglyphs.[49] In most books after 1990 Mesopotamia is not mentioned at all and the Persians are reduced to being opponents of the Greeks in the Persian Wars, which does not provide a good basis for a balanced representation. From the originally two-faced narrative, only the later part with the bad image was still present.

For the books from 1990 to 2005 Katja Gorbahn observed a bias against the Persians,[50] and the study of books by Felix Hinz for Nordrhein-Westfalen from 2008 to 2010 produced a similar result.[51] But the claim of Gerdien Jonker that German textbooks of these years would see ancient Greece as the sole origin of the European civilization goes too far. He supports this claim with the observation that some German textbooks for senior high school students start with 'Democracy in Athens' as the first chapter.[52] He fails to mention, however, that all German students between the ages of 10 and 16 follow a chronological curriculum that starts with the Stone Age and includes Ancient Egypt. Jonker refers only to books for the senior high school students, who are older and study more intensively selected highlights, some of which may include Greek Democracy. Some German states like Nordrhein-Westfalen, however, issued curriculums for senior high school students even without Greek history.

Looking at most recent German textbooks it is evident that publishers of textbooks are currently trying to revise their perspective on Europe's relations with non-European cultures.[53] Part of this development are efforts to present the Persian Wars differently. One book even refers to old textbooks in order to correct them:

> The Persian Empire – a tyranny?
> In older history books the Persian Empire is often depicted as a tyranny, a despotism. Led by a king and ruled by bribable officials, the Persian Empire was considered to be the enemy of the Hellenes as well as every other civilized culture. This picture, however, only represented the views of the Greek witnesses; today's historians portray Persia differently.
> The Persian Empire was founded in the sixth century BC by Cyrus. His tomb is still in Iran today. He subdued many territories so that the Persian Empire

ranged from Europe to India. Persia was the transmitter of ancient civilizations, as can be seen today in the remains of roads, canal systems and trade routes. It was a great multifaceted empire, which usually allowed the subjugated to live out their cultures freely and limited itself to the collection of taxes.[54]

The attempts to renew the narrative have led to a spectrum of presentations that is wider than the usual differences between history textbooks in Germany. Several popular textbooks reduce the Persian Empire simply to the reign that was conquered by Alexander,[55] or even go without mentioning it at all.[56] The book *Mosaik* tries to present the Persian Empire as a 'bridge between East and West'.[57] Another book rejects the thesis 'A danger from Asia' with information about local self-government and religious freedom in the Persian Empire.[58] If the Persian Empire is described at all, these aspects are very often stressed. Some relicts of the bad image of the Persian invaders and the heroic Greek defenders do, however, still exist.[59] An entirely new perspective is provided by some books that discuss how Europeans in modern times have dealt with the story of the Persian Wars.[60] In this context, one book presents Frank Miller and Lynn Varley's *Comic 300*,[61] and asks the pupils to examine which image of Persians and Greeks is presented here.[62] This is certainly an interesting approach, and shows that the two-faced narrative of the Persian Wars is still relevant to modern Europe.

Björn Onken is a senior lecturer in history education at the University of Duisburg-Essen, and he also officially represents the vacant chair for history education and historical culture at the University of Münster. He has published in ancient history, classical tradition, history education and textbook research. Among his most recent publications are *Die Französische Revolution: Geschichtswissenschaft – Erinnerung – Unterricht*, co-edited with Ralf-Peter Fuchs (Wochenschau, 2020); *Orient? Jahresband der Zeitschrift für Geschichtsdidaktik 18* (Vandenhoeck & Ruprecht, 2019); and *Griechische Mythologie und Religion: Geschichtsunterricht praktisch* (Wochenschau 2019).

Notes

1. Kazemi, *Alte Mythen*, 107–12.
2. Cobet, 'Europa und Asien'; Holland, *Persian Fire*; Hinz, 'White Dwarves', 35f.
3. Mill, 'Early Grecian History', 283.
4. Said, *Orientalism*; Khawaja, 'Was will Edward Saids Orientalismus?'
5. Grewe, 'Geschichtsdidaktik postkolonial'; Sayyid, 'Empire, Islam and the Postcolonial', 129.
6. Repoussi and Tutiaux-Guillon, 'New Trends', 156; Lässig, 'Wer definiert relevantes Wissen?'.

7. Grever and Van der Vlies, 'Why National', 291.
8. Repoussi and Tutiaux-Guillon, 'New Trends', 163; Schönemann and Thünemann, *Schulbucharbeit*, 22f.
9. Klerides, 'Imaging the Textbook', 31–41.
10. Jacobmeyer, *Das deutsche Geschichtsschulbuch*, 1211.
11. Ibid.
12. Neubauer, *Lehrbuch der Geschichte für höhere Lehranstalten. III*, 18; Neubauer, *Lehrbuch der Geschichte für höhere Lehranstalten. A1*, 23.
13. Neubauer, *Lehrbuch der Geschichte für höhere Lehranstalten. III*, 17–19.
14. Klerides, 'Imaging the Textbook', 33.
15. Dahmen, *Leitfaden der Geschichte*, 14; Endemann and Andrä, *Grundriß der Geschichte, Erster Teil*, 23f; Endemann and Andrä, *Grundriß der Geschichte für höhere Schulen*, 13; Stich, *Lehrbuch der Geschichte*, 23f.
16. Schenk, *Lehrbuch der Geschichte für höhere Lehranstalten*, 47.
17. Neubauer, *Lehrbuch der Geschichte für höhere Lehranstalten. III*, 19.
18. Neubauer, *Lehrbuch der Geschichte für höhere Lehranstalten. III*, 15.
19. Wiesehöfer, 'Zur Geschichte der Begriffe Arier', 155.
20. Neubauer, *Lehrbuch der Geschichte für höhere Lehranstalten. III*, 15.
21. Ibid., 91f.
22. Flemming, 'Gesellschaft im Kaiserreich', 97.
23. Martens, *Lehrbuch für Geschichte für die oberen Klassen*; Jaenicke, *Die Geschichte der Griechen und Römer*.
24. Hinz, 'White Dwarves', 41–43.
25. Friedrich, *Stoffe und Probleme*, 74.
26. Morgan, *Greek Perspectives*, 294.
27. Wiesehöfer, *Das antike Persien*, 84; Morgan, *Greek Perspectives*, 293–297; Strootmann and Versluys, 'From Culture to Concept', 28.
28. Ambül, 'Kyros', 596.
29. Sancisi-Weerdenburg, 'Cyrus in Italy', Gehrke, 'Bild und Gegenbild', 89–91; Ambül, 'Kyros', 597–99.
30. Gehrke, 'Bild und Gegenbild', 94; Briant, 'History and Ideology', 192; Bichler, 'Der "Orient"'.
31. Hauser, '". . . die persische Herrschaft"', 289–93.
32. Wiesehöfer, '"Denn es sind welthistorische Siege"', 66; Meyer-Zwiffelhofer, 'Orientalismus', 591; Paniano, 'The "Persian Empire"'.
33. Cobet, 'Europa und Asien', 406.
34. Wilhelm I., *Ereignisse und Gestalten*, 168.
35. Jonker, 'Naming the West', 42.
36. Marchand, *German Orientalism*, 174–177; Berman, *German Literature*, 144–88; Gheiby, *Iran oder Persien?*, 191f.; Müller, 'Das Perserreich', 310f.
37. Marchand, 'German Archaeology', 22.
38. Marchand, *German Orientalism*, 497.
39. Wokoeck, '*German Orientalism*', 159–63.
40. Berger, 'Building the Nation, 251; Jacobmeyer and Thünemann, 'Einleitung', 9–12.
41. Mangold-Will, 'Die Orientreise Wilhelms II.', 62.
42. Langewiesche, 'Der historische Ort', 35.
43. Onken, 'Das antike Perserreich', 356–59.
44. Onken, 'Das antike Perserreich', 370.
45. Riemenschneider, 'Das Geschichtslehrbuch in der Bundesrepublik', 298.
46. Tenbrock and Stier, *Geschichtliches Unterrichtswerk*, 38a, 46a, 80a, 84a, 110.
47. Onken, 'Das antike Perserreich', 363–66.

48. Kultusministerium des Landes Nordrhein-Westfalen, *Richtlinien*, 56.
49. Cobet, 'Babylon, Jerusalem, Athen, Rom', 13 Fn. 48.
50. Gorbahn, 'Griechische Bürgerstaaten'.
51. Hinz, 'White Dwarves', 44–48.
52. Jonker, 'Naming the West', 45.
53. Grindel, 'Colonial and Postcolonial Contexts'.
54. Baumgärtner, *Horizonte 7/8*, 90; Baumgärtner, *Horizonte 6*, 92.
55. Fries, 'Alexander', 110.
56. Cornelissen, *Forum 1/2*.
57. Cornelissen, *Mosaik*, 112f.
58. Bernsen and Brückner, *Das waren Zeiten*, 82.
59. Hinz, 'White Dwarves', 44–48.
60. Hartmann and Ruhl, *Griechen und Perser*, 87–94.
61. Miller and Varley, *300*.
62. Brückmann, *Europa unsere Geschichte*.

Bibliography

Ambül, Annemarie. 'Kyros', in Peter von Möllendorff, Annette Simonis and Linda Simonis (eds), *Historische Gestalten der Antike: Rezeption in Literatur, Kunst und Musik. Der Neue Pauly, Supplemente 8* (Stuttgart and Weimar: Metzler, 2013), 595–602.

Baumgärtner, Ulrich (ed.). *Horizonte 6: Geschichte Gymnasium Baden-Württemberg*. Braunschweig: Westermann Verlag, 2004.

——— (ed.). *Horizonte 7/8: Geschichte Rheinland-Pfalz*. Braunschweig: Westermann Verlag, 2015.

Berger, Stefan. 'Building the Nation among Visions of Germany', in Stefan Berger and Alexei Miller (eds), *Nationalizing Empires* (Budapest: Central European University Press, 2015), 247–308.

Berman, Nina. *German Literature on the Middle East: Discourses and Practices 1000–1989*, Ann Arbor: University of Michigan Press, 2011.

Bernsen, Daniel, and Dieter Brückner. *Das waren Zeiten – Rheinland-Pfalz: Von den Anfängen bis zum 19. Jahrhundert Unterrichtswerk für Geschichte*. Bamberg: C.C. Buchner, 2016.

Bichler, Reinhold. '"Der Orient" im Wechselspiel von Imagination und Erfahrung: Zum Typus der "orientalischen Despotie"', in Andreas Luther, Robert Rollinger and Josef Wiesehöfer (eds), *Getrennte Wege? Kommunikation, Raum und Wahrnehmung in der alten Welt* (Frankfurt am Main: Verlag Antike, 2007), 475–500.

Briant, Pierre. 'History and Ideology: The Greeks and "Persian Decadence"', in Thomas Harrison (ed.), *Greeks and Barbarians* (Edinburgh: Edinburgh University Press, 2002), 193–210.

Brückmann, Asmut, et al. *Europa unsere Geschichte*, 1st edn. Wiesbaden: Eduversum Verlag, 2016.

Cobet, Justus. 'Babylon, Jerusalem, Athen, Rom. Vier Metropolen: Skizze eines europäischen Diskurses'. *Historische Zeitschrift* 293(1) (2011), 1–38.

———. 'Europa und Asien – Griechen und Barbaren – Osten und Westen'. *Geschichte in Wissenschaft und Unterricht* 47(7–8) (1996), 405–19.

Cornelissen, Hans-Joachim (ed.). *Forum 1/2*. Berlin: Cornelsen, 2015.

——— (ed.). *Mosaik*. Munich: Oldenbourg Verlag, 2011.

Dahmen, Joseph. *Leitfaden der Geschichte für höhere Mädchenschulen und Lehrerinnenseminare*. Leipzig: Ferdinand Hirt & Sohn, 1900.

Endemann, Karl, and J.C. Andrä. *Grundriß der Geschichte, Erster Teil: Alte Geschichte für die Quarta höherer Lehranstalten.* Leipzig: R. Voigtländer, 1902.

———. *Grundriß der Geschichte für höhere Schulen, Dritter Teil: Geschichte des Altertums für die Obersekunda höherer Lehranstalten.* Leipzig: R. Voigtländer, 1907.

Flemming, Jens. 'Gesellschaft im Kaiserreich', in Markus Bernhardt (ed.), *Das Deutsche Kaiserreich: Geschichte – Erinnerung – Unterricht* (Schwalbach: Wochenschau, 2017), 83–104.

Friedrich, Fritz. *Stoffe und Probleme des Geschichtsunterrichts.* Leipzig: B.G. Teubner, 1915.

Fries, Ursula. 'Alexander – wie gehen die Griechen mit fremden Kulturen um?' in Michael Sauer (ed.), *Geschichte und Geschehen 5/6* (Leipzig: Klett, 2015), 110f.

Gehrke, Hans-Joachim. 'Gegenbild und Selbstbild: Das europäische Iranbild zwischen Griechen und Mullahs', in Tonio Hölscher (ed.), *Gegenwelten zu den Kulturen Griechenlands und Rom in der Antike* (Munich: De Gruyter, 2000), 85–109.

Gheiby, Bijan. *Persien oder Iran? Die Deutschen entdecken das Land Zarathustras.* Mainz: Philipp von Zabern, 2012.

Gorbahn, Katja. 'Griechische Bürgerstaaten trotzen der persischen Weltmacht: Die Darstellung des persischen Reiches in Schulbüchern für die Sekundarstufe 1 seit 1990', in Saskia Handro and Bernd Schönemann (eds), *Geschichtsdidaktische Schulbuchforschung* (Berlin: Lit, 2006), 177–97.

Grindel, Susanne. 'Colonial and Postcolonial Contexts of History Textbooks', in Mario Carretero et al. (eds), *Palgrave Handbook of Research in Historical Culture and Education* (London: Palgrave Macmillan, 2017), 259–274.

Grever, Maria, and Tina van der Vlies. 'Why National Narratives Are Perpetuated: a Literature Review on New Insights of History Textbook Research'. *London Review of Education* 15(2) (2017), 286–301.

Grewe, Bernd-Stefan. 'Geschichtsdidaktik postkolonial – eine Herausforderung'. *Zeitschrift für Geschichtsdidaktik* 15(1) (2016), 5–30.Hartmann, Jörg, and Silke Ruhl. *Griechen und Perser – Konstruierte Geschichte?* Leipzig: Klett, 2005.

Hauser, Stefan. '". . . die persische Herrschaft war eigentlich die edelste und beste . . .": Die Achaimeniden in deutschen Diskursen im langen neunzehnten Jahrhundert', in Robert Rollinger, Kai Ruffing and Louisa Thomas (eds), *Das Weltreich der Perser: Rezeption – Aneignung – Verargumentierung* (Wiesbaden: Harrassowitz, 2019), 281–304.

Hinz, Felix. 'White Dwarves in the Firmament of historical Consciousness?' in Roland Bernhard et al. (eds), *Myths in German-Language Textbooks: Their Influence on Historical Accounts from the Battle of Marathon to the Élysée Treaty* (Brunswick: Eckert Dossiers 2019), 35–60.

Holland, Tom. *Persian Fire: The First World Empire and the Battle for the West.* London: Anchor, 2010.

Jacobmeyer, Wolfgang. *Das deutsche Geschichtsschulbuch 1700–1945: Die erste Epoche seiner Gattungsgeschichte im Spiegel der Vorworte.* Berlin: Lit, 2013.

Jacobmeyer, Wolfgang, and Holger Thünemann. 'Einleitung', in Wolfgang Jacobmeyer and Holger Thünemann (eds), *Grundlegung und Ausformung des deutschen Geschichtsunterrichts: schulische Diskurse zur Didaktik und Historik im 19. Jahrhundert* (Berlin: Lit, 2018), 5–23.

Jaenicke, Hermann. *Die Geschichte der Griechen und Römer für die Quarta und Untertertia höherer Lehranstalten.* Berlin: Weidmannsche Buchhandlung, 1904.

Jonker, Gerdien. 'Naming the West: Productions of Europe in and beyond Textbooks'. *Journal of Educational Media, Memory and Society* 1(2) (2009), 34–59.

Kazemi, Mohammad Reza. *Alte Mythen – neue Mythen: das iranische Geschichtsschulbuch von der späten Qadscharenzeit bis zur Islamischen Republik (ca. 1900–2003).* Hamburg: Dr. Kovacs, 2013.

Khawaja, Irfan. 'Was will Edward Saids Orientalismus? Eine Kritik'. *Zeitschrift für kritische Sozialtheorie und Phliosophie* 5(1) (2018), 146–176.

Klerides, Eleftherios. 'Imaging the Textbook: Textbooks as Discourse and Genre'. *Journal of Educational Media, Memory and Society* 2 (2010), 31–54.
Kultusministerium des Landes Nordrhein-Westfalen (ed.). *Richtlnien und Lehrpläne für das Gymnasium – Sekundarstufe 1*. Frechen: Ritterbach, 1993.
Langewiesche, Dieter. 'Der historische Ort des deutschen Kaiserreichs', in Bernd Heidenreich and Sönke Neitzel (eds), *Das deutsche Kaiserreich* (Paderborn: Schöningh, 2011), 23–35.
Lässig, Simone. 'Wer definiert relevantes Wissen? Schulbuchverlage und ihr gesellschaftlicher Kontext', in Eckhard Fuchs et al. (eds), *Schulbuch konkret: Kontexte – Produktion – Unterricht* (Bad Heilbrunn: Julius Klinkhardt, 2010), 199–218.
Mangold-Will, Sabine. 'Die Orientreise Wilhelms II.: Archäologie und die Legitimation einer hohenzollernschen Universalmonarchie zwischen Orient und Okzident', in Thorsten Beigel and Sabine Mangold-Will (eds), *Wilhelm II: Archäologie und Politik um 1900*, (Stuttgart: Franz Steiner, 2017), 53–66.
Marchand, Suzanne. *German Orientalism in the Age of Empire: Religion, Race and Scholarship*, Cambridge: Cambridge University Press, 2009.
———. 'German Archaeology in the Wilhelmine Era: An Overview', in Thorsten Beigel and Sabine Mangold-Will (eds), *Wilhelm II: Archäologie und Politik um 1900* (Stuttgart: Franz Steiner, 2017), 15–22.
Martens, Wilhelms. *Lehrbuch für Geschichte für die oberen Klassen höherer Lehranstalten, Erster Teil: Geschichte des Altertums*. Hannover: Verlag von Manz & Lange, 1901.
Meyer-Zwiffelhofer, Eckhard. 'Orientalismus? Die Rolle des Alten Orients in der deutschen Altertumswissenschaft und Altertumsgeschichte des 19. Jahrhunderts (ca. 1785–1910)', in Andreas Luther, Robert Rollinger and Josef Wiesehöfer (eds), *Getrennte Wege? Kommunikation, Raum und Wahrnehmung in der alten Welt* (Frankfurt am Main: Verlag Antike, 2007), 501–94.
Mill, John Stuart. 'Early Grecian History and Legend', in *Dissertations and Discussions*. 2nd Vol. reprint from 1973 of the 1859 edition. New York: Haskell House Publishers, 1859.
Miller, Frank, and Lynn Varley. *300*. Ludwigsburg: Cross-Cult, 2006.
Müller, Sabine. 'Das Perserreich in europäischen Lexika der Neuzeit', in Robert Rollinger, Kai Ruffing and Louisa Thomas (eds), *Das Weltreich der Perser: Rezeption – Aneignung-Verargumentierung* (Wiesbaden: Harrassowitz, 2019), 305–24.
Morgan, Janett. *Greek Perspectives on the Achaemenid Empire*. Edinburgh: Edinburgh University Press, 2016.
Neubauer, Friedrich. *Lehrbuch der Geschichte für höhere Lehranstalten. III. Teil Geschichte des Altertums für Obersekunda*. 19th edn. Halle an der Saale: Verlag der Buchhandlung des Waisenhauses in Halle, 1912.
———. *Lehrbuch der Geschichte für höhere Lehranstalten*. Ausgabe A 1. Teil, Geschichte des Altertums (Quarta), 23rd edn. Halle an der Saale: Verlag der Buchhandlung des Waisenhauses in Halle, 1915.
Onken, Björn. 'Das antike Perserreich zur Zeit der Achaimeniden in deutschen und italienischen Schulbüchern im 20/21. Jahrhundert', in Robert Rollinger, Kai Ruffing and Louisa Thomas (eds), *Das Weltreich der Perser: Rezeption – Aneignung – Verargumentierung* (Wiesbaden: Harrassowitz, 2019), 345–78.
Panaino, Antonio. 'The "Persian Empire" in Hegel's Vorlesungen über die Philosophie der Weltgeschichte', in Robert Rollinger, Kai Ruffing and Louisa Thomas (eds), *Das Weltreich der Perser: Rezeption – Aneignung – Verargumentierung* (Wiesbaden: Harrassowitz, 2019), 379–402.
Repoussi, Maria, and Nicole Tutiaux-Guillon. 'New Trends in History Textbook Research: Issues and Methodologies toward a School Historiography'. *Journal of Educational Media, Memory and Society* 2(1) (2010), 154–70.

Riemenschneider, Rainer. 'Das Geschichtslehrbuch in der Bundesrepublik: Seine Entwicklung seit 1945', in Klaus Bergmann and Gerhard Schneider (eds), *Gesellschaft – Staat – Geschichtsunterricht: Beiträge zu einer Geschichte der Geschichtsdidaktik und des Geschichtsunterrichts 1500–1980* (Düsseldorf: Cornelsen, 1982), 295–321.

Said, Edward W. *Orientalism*. New York: Pantheon, 1978.

Sancisi-Weerdenburg, Heleen. 'Cyrus in Italy: From Dante to Machiavelli. Some Explorations of the Reception of Xenophons Cyropedia', in Heleen Sancisi-Weerdenburg and Jan Willem Drijvers (eds), *Achaemenid History V. The Roots of the European Tradition. Proceedings of the 1987 Groningen Achaemenid History Workshop* (Leiden: Nederlands Instituut voor het Nabije Oosten, 1990), 31–52.

Sayyid, Salman. 'Empire, Islam and the Postcolonial', in Graham Huggan (ed.), *Oxford Handbook of Postcolonial Studies* (Oxford: Oxford University Press, 2013), 127–41.

Schenk, K. *Lehrbuch der Geschichte für höhere Lehranstalten. Ausgabe A, VII Teil. Lehraufgabe für die Obersekunda.* Leipzig: B.G. Teubner, 1898.

Schönemann, Bernd, and Holger Thünemann. *Schulbucharbeit: Das Geschichtslehrbuch in der Unterrichtspraxis.* Schwalbach/Ts: Wochenschau, 2010.

Stich, H. *Lehrbuch der Geschichte für die oberen Klassen der Gymnasien, 1. Teil. Das Altertum.* 6th edn. Bamberg: C.C. Buchner, 1910.

Strootmann, Rolf, and Miguel John Versluys. 'From Culture to Concept: The Reception and Appropriation of Persian in Antiquity', in Rolf Strootmann and Miguel John Versluys (eds), *Persianism in Antiquity* (Stuttgart: Franz Steiner, 2017), 9–33.

Tenbrock, Robert H., and Hans Erich Stier. *Geschichtliches Unterrichtswerk: Oberstufe I. Urzeit und Altertum bis zu den Karolingern.* 4th edn. Paderborn: Ferdinand Schöningh, 1956.

Wiesehöfer, Josef. *Das antike Persien*. Munich: Artemis, 1994.

———. '"Denn es sind welthistorische Siege . . ." Nineteenth- amd Twentieth-Century German Views of the Persian Wars'. *Culture & History* 11 (1992), 61–83.

———. 'Zur Geschichte der Begriffe Arier und arisch in der deutschen Spachwissenschaft und Althistorie des 19. und der ersten Hälfte des 20. Jahrhunderts', in Helen Sancisi-Weerdenburg and Jan Willem Drijvers (eds), *Achaemenid History V: The Roots of the European Tradition. Proceedings of the 1987 Groningen Achaemenid History Workshop* (Leiden: Nederlands Instituut voor het Nabije Oosten, 1990), 147–63.

Wokoeck, Ursula. *German Orientalism: The Study of the Middle East and Islam from 1800 to 1945*. London and New York: Routledge, 2009.

CHAPTER 6

Historicizing Present-Day European Societies by Telling Medieval (Hi)Story in Schoolbooks

Daniel Wimmer

This chapter focuses on the observation that narratives aiming at the legitimization, historicity and interconnection of societies are an inherent part of present-day portrayals of medieval history. This phenomenon could already be observed in the early nineteenth century, when the nation-states began to form in Europe. Currently, it can be noticed predominantly in media with a broad impact, such as schoolbooks, exhibitions, press products and historical novels.[1]

Schoolbooks that are used around the world to convey an officially approved perspective on history and society provide particularly good examples of narratives aiming at the legitimization, historicity and interconnection of societies, which may have an influence on the creation, strengthening and preservation of collective present-day identities.[2] This hypothesis will be discussed and substantiated by analysing schoolbooks published between the 1970s and the 2000s. The following are the main questions to be answered:

– In what way do schoolbook portrayals of medieval history address questions relating to the legitimization, historicity and interconnection of present-day societies?
– To which extent do these portrayals of medieval history reflect political and sociocultural changes?

Notes for this section begin on page 144.

- Another question to focus on, beyond the specific shape of the narratives, is:
  Why exactly do portrayals of cultural contact between Muslims and Christians in medieval times lend themselves to the conveyance of narratives aiming at the legitimization, historicity and interconnection of societies, which in turn can be indicative of the time-dependency of medieval narratives in schoolbooks?

However, this chapter will not explore actual present-day constructions of identity, either on an individual level or a collective one. It rather focuses on analysing 'offers of identity' (*Identitätsangebote*), meaningful narratives that historicize the (alleged) peculiarities of a society for the purpose of forming a collective identity in order to postulate a legitimization of the existing conditions. Thus, information on the constitution, the (approved) self-image of this society, can be obtained.[3]

Narratives Aiming at the Legitimization, Historicity and Interconnection of Societies in Portrayals of Medieval History

The existence of such narratives in schoolbook portrayals of medieval history relates to historiographys constitution as narration. Defined as a narrative act of evaluating past events, historiography is not able to show – to re-create – the reality of a past event in its entirety. Historiography means structuring, selecting and configuring contents to create a consistent and comprehensible portrayal of history in order to give a meaning to the past.[4] This emplotment always depends on the respective historiographer's present, as described by Swiss historian Valentin Groebner in *Das Mittelalter hört nicht auf* [The Middle Ages never end]:

> Portrayals of medieval history not only provide us with information on texts ... from the seventh, eleventh or fourteenth centuries, and on their authors ... These reconstructions of the medieval past provide us with just as much information on the medievalists themselves, on their readers and on collective desires and obsessions of the respective times they emerged in.[5]

Analysing historiographic narration (the way history is told) means also revealing the historiographers' intentions (the people who 'tell' history in the widest sense: scientific historians, schoolbook authors, novelists, curators of historical exhibitions, journalists, movie directors, even gamemasters of LARP).[6] A person's idea of how his or her community became what it is in the present is influenced by a multitude of narratives focusing on certain aspects of history. Only together do they form a meaningful and comprehensive narration of the past. Symptomatically, the contents of these narratives are dissociated from the historical contexts of past events they pretend to talk about, while simultaneously – according to the historiographers' intentions – referring to the characteristics of present-day societies.

Meanwhile, manifold research on these meaningful narrations aiming at historicizing contemporary communities can be found. Over the last decades, for instance, a variety of studies aspired to highlight the origins of the mythically overloaded national histories of the European nation-states. These studies agreed that, as a first step to forming a collective identity, most of these nation-states 'invented' their 'own' history in the nineteenth century by tracing back their roots to ancient or medieval times – using historicity to legitimize their own existence as territorially constituted states and to distance themselves from others. They also agreed that by defining the emplotment of this presumed 'national past', those comprehensive historicizing narrations influenced the idea of history in general. This influence has lasted for a long time (it still does in some European nation-states), mainly due to the ability of these narrations to regularly adapt to the changing political and social conditions of the 'nations' and nation-states they are referring to.[7]

Reflection of Social Changes in Portrayals of Medieval History?

The emergence of the European Union as a supranational actor and the effects of the different processes of globalization that European societies have increasingly experienced in the last twenty years, have made this nineteenth-century equation of territorial and normative identity constructions appear problematic – at least in Western Europe. Transnational and transcultural identities have emerged; previously clearly defined cultures now interweave.[8] Simultaneously, these new perspectives on the world[9] define new borders and new limits – new delineations have emerged while old ones persist.[10] In view of these profound political and sociocultural changes, the question arises of whether, and if so how, they are also reflected in the portrayals of medieval history, this once important medium used to endow the nation-state with a collective identity? And how does the modern world make them change their contents and structure?

Time-Dependency of Portrayals of Medieval History: 'Intercultural Diversity of Societies'

Focusing on the way the medieval encounter of Muslims and Christians is presented in history schoolbooks allows for an understanding of the adaptability of narratives aiming at the legitimization, historicity and interconnection of societies to the respective political and sociocultural conditions. Analysing the statements made between the 1970s and the 2000s in relation to the meaning of the medieval encounter between Muslims and Christians, it is possible to understand to what extent historiographical narration is time-dependent, and how it always refers to questions that present-day societies are attempting to answer.

One aspect of medieval history that refers predominantly to an 'encounter' between Muslims and Christians concerns the Crusades. Of course, there are other portrayals of cultural contact that can be found in history schoolbooks – also ones relating to medieval history.[11] Yet, due to its continuous presence in the analysed schoolbooks of the analysis period and the obviousness of the process of change the narratives aiming at the legitimization, historicity and interconnection of societies have been subject to over the course of time, the history of the Crusades lends itself to the discussion of the hypothesis.

To promote readability, the following analysis compares two schoolbooks with each other – *Geschichtliches Werden 2* (1974) and *Das waren Zeiten 2* (2003) – both of which are used in the same class level, the German *Mittelstufe*, and published by the same publishing company (*Buchner*).

Geschichtliches Werden 2 (1974) – the Crusades as an Expression of Truly Felt Readiness to Make Sacrifices for Christianity

The 1974 schoolbook *Geschichtliches Werden 2* dedicates three and a half pages to the history of the Crusades.[12] These pages are divided into two sections titled *Papst Urban II. ruft zum ersten Kreuzzug auf* [Pope Urban II calls for the First Crusade] and *Die Folgen der Kreuzzüge* [The aftermath of the Crusades]. The first section focuses on the historical events, whereas the second focuses on the political structures, economy and society.

The first section covers the period between 1095 and the end of the thirteenth century, from the Council of Clermont to the Fall of Acre in 1291, highlighting the putatively 'successful' early times of the Crusades in particular. In contrast, the history between the end of the First Crusade and 1291 is briefly resumed in a ten-line text.[13]

The introductory paragraph of *Geschichtliches Werden 2* focuses on the reasons for the outbreak of the Crusades. It is therefore a good example of the significance that the book ascribes to the history of the Crusades.

> Since the Turkish tribe of the Seljuqs had conquered Syria, Palestine and Asia Minor, beginning in the middle of the eleventh century, and even threatened Constantinople, rumours emerged in Europe that pilgrims had been attacked and robbed, and that the sacred places had been destroyed. These rumours, although untrue, created the atmosphere for the most adventurous endeavour of medieval Christianity: The Crusades.[14]

Regardless of the expression 'most adventurous endeavour of medieval Christianity' used to describe the Crusades having an obvious positive connotation, the Crusades themselves appear to be legitimate. Even though it is pointed out that the rumours were untrue, the state of knowledge of the medieval people on the presumed robbed pilgrims and the destroyed sacred places did not leave them any other choice but to become active. Along this line of reasoning, starting the Crusades is represented as a logical and legitimate reaction to hostile actions.

And, following the quoted sentences, another – responsible – person is named:

> 'It was the Eastern Roman emperor who felt threatened by the Turks and who asked Pope Urban II for support. Urban II used this request for help to call for the First Crusade to liberate the Holy Land from the 'pagan rule of the Turks'.[15]

In addition to the concerns for the pilgrims' safety in the Holy Land and for the integrity of the sacred places, a third reason, apparently, led to the call for the Crusade during the Council of Clermont: the pope's altruism in supporting the Eastern Roman emperor. Quotations of Urban II calling for the Crusade are even integrated into the text ('pagan rule of the Turks'), yet no explanation or historical context is given. The quotations rather seem to be a confirmation of the text's line of argumentation as to why the First Crusade started. The necessity and the legitimacy of the Crusades continue to appear obvious. The subchapter's last paragraph still emphasizes this effect: 'The assembly was deeply shocked. Shouting "It is the will of God", thousands had a cross made of red cloth, the Crusader's symbol, attached to their shoulders'.[16]

The following subchapter continues to describe the First Crusade as a legitimate and necessary 'adventurous' endeavour, now focusing on the Crusaders themselves. Interestingly, they do not appear as belligerent soldiers, but as 'normal' people empowered by the strength of their religious beliefs: 'In 1096, the first Crusaders left, most of them French and Norman knights, accompanied by soldiers and pilgrims, even by women and children'.[17]

Adding non-belligerent groups to the list of people who participated in the First Crusade mitigates its perception as a military campaign, as does the claim that the news that their sacred religious places had been captured was allegedly the only reason they were willing to sacrifice themselves. Participating in the Crusades is represented as a heroic effort, and proof of personal readiness to make sacrifices for their faith – a reasoning confirmed by the quotation of a historical source. In this text, 'a participant'[18] reports on the straining journey to the Holy Land:

> We persecuted (our enemies) across deserts and a dry and hostile land we just barely succeeded to leave. Hunger and thirst plagued us everywhere and there was barely anything left to eat other than thorn bushes, which we tore out and

ground in our hands; this was the food we meagrely lived off. The majority of our horses died there, prompting many of our knights to walk. Due to the lack of horses, our oxen served as war horses, and the goats, wethers and dogs had to carry our bags during this time of misery.[19]

By the end of this subchapter, the reader finds out that all these sacrifices for Christianity were ultimately rewarded: 'Finally, in the summer of 1099, the Crusaders arrived outside of the city of Jerusalem'.[20] And after several months of siege, Jerusalem had to surrender, and consequently 'a large part of its Muslim and Jewish population were killed mercilessly by the intruding victors'.[21]

It is obvious that the focal point of this portrayal of events until the surrender of Jerusalem is on the Crusaders as protagonists who ultimately accomplished their supposedly legitimate mission. Hence, the killing of Muslims and Jews in Jerusalem appears to also be part of this legitimizing context.

The second section observes the newly created political, social and economic structures in detail. Titled *Das Königreich Jerusalem* [The Kingdom of Jerusalem], the first subchapter highlights aspects of territorial organization, thus mentioning that Godfrey of Bouillon was declared king. But, the affirmative explanation 'due to his pious modesty, he only accepted the title of "Advocate of the Holy Sepulchre"'[22] also refers to the portrayal of the Crusades as a selfless endeavour in favour of Christianity: Godfrey of Bouillon only – humbly – 'protected' the places that were allegedly threatened, thus starting the First Crusade.

The events following the Conquest of Jerusalem are presented in this line of argumentation as well. It soon turned out that despite Godfrey of Bouillon's humble acceptance of his duty as Advocate of the Holy Sepulchre, and despite the Crusaders' will to sacrifice themselves for their faith, neither the security of the pilgrimage routes nor the protection of the sacred places could be guaranteed. And this was supposedly the reason why Bernard of Clairvaux called for a new Crusade: Christianity ought to be ready for more sacrifices to lead this endeavour to success.

According to the text, he succeeded: 'The sermon he preached in Speyer Cathedral on Christmas 1146 deeply touched the German King Konrad III; he decided to take the cross together with the French King'.[23] The text is not referring to the sermon's content, the result of Bernard of Clairvaux's preaching is the only thing that matters: there would be another Crusade. Furthermore, by only highlighting the French and German kings' emotional consternation, it is emphasized again that the Crusade is seen as a legitimate endeavour.

Looking at the political and social structures in the newly founded Crusader states, *Geschichtliches Werden 2* dedicates special attention to the Chivalric Orders, whose members almost appear as examples of true Christian charity: 'During the Crusades, Chivalric Orders were founded in the Holy Land. Not only did they secure the pilgrimage routes, they also cared for ill and distressed pilgrims'.[24] Those knights who entered the Holy Land during the Crusades seem to have taken on the roles of policemen and emergency aids rather than soldiers. This characterization focuses mainly on the positive connotation of those activities related to charity, just as the explanation of the knights' other tasks does: 'Like monks, their members committed themselves to a life of poverty, chastity and obedience, as well as to the fight against the infidels'.[25]

Aside from the legitimizing aspect of the Crusades, which was predominant in the first section, the aspect of altruism as the putative guiding motivation is the second important statement in relation to the history of the Crusades presented by *Geschichtliches Werden 2*. The focal point is noticeably put on activities that are perceived in a positive manner, while the negative (mostly violent) ones are barely mentioned when it comes to the portrayal of the attitudes or activities of protagonists who, consistently throughout the chapter, are exclusively European Christians.

Consequently, the last subchapter *Folgen der Kreuzzüge* [Aftermath of the Crusades] is also dedicated to this rather positivistic, Eurocentric perspective of the Crusades' history. It highlights both the (positive) impact that the Crusades had on the development of the (European) trade throughout the Mediterranean and the aspects of cultural contact, especially between Muslims and Christians. Muslim culture is presented as highly developed – which was apparently one reason why the Crusaders changed their attitude towards the Muslim population:

> Originally, the Crusaders considered the 'infidels' to be children of the devil who had to be wiped out mercilessly. But soon they learned how to respect people of a different faith, and became more tolerant. They were astonished when they learned of the superior knowledge of the Arabic savants.[26]

In this quotation, tolerating the Muslim population appears to be proof of favour. Of course, this situation can be described as a 'cultural encounter' between Muslims and Christians, but a clearly hierarchically defined one – a perspective that is also used in the following paragraph on the abundance of the Orient. Looting precious objects does not appear to have been seen as theft, but as a testimonial to the desirability of oriental products:

> In the Orient, the Crusaders got to experience a superior lifestyle. They saw the wealth of the imperial palaces in Constantinople, the colorful carpets and valuable arms in the houses of the Muslims. They vigorously tried to bring home booty. The Occident's treasuries were filled with products of decorative oriental arts, and the churches were filled with relics.[27]

Das Waren Zeiten 2: Delegitimizing the Crusades and Calling for Mutual Respect

The 2003 schoolbook *Das waren Zeiten 2* dedicates seven pages to the history of the Crusades.[28] In comparison to the 1974 schoolbook *Geschichtliches Werden 2*, the number of pages covering this topic doubled, an evolution that can be observed in all those German schoolbooks that have been analysed.

When it comes to the portrayal of the history of the Crusades though, significant changes to the quantity as well as the quality can be observed in German schoolbooks. Whereas the first section of the 1974 schoolbook was positivistically titled *Papst Urban II ruft zum ersten Kreuzzug auf* [Pope Urban II calls for the First Crusade], *Das waren Zeiten 2* raises a rhetorical question: *Kreuzzüge – Kriege um das Grab Christi?* [The Crusades – Wars over the Holy Sepulchre?]. Just by putting a question mark at the end of the sentence, the motivations behind the Crusades are problematized.[29]

The selection of contents also changed. The most notable events that *Geschichtliches Werden 2* had already presented are still part of the texts, of course: the reasons the Crusades happened, the Eastern Roman emperor's request for help, the Council of Clermont, the Conquest of Jerusalem and the Fall of Acre. Yet, other aspects are integrated into the subchapters as well, or even presented in the form of individual paragraphs.[30] The theory of the 'Just War' is explained and simultaneously questioned because of its use to legitimize the Crusades; the history of the Crusades is embedded in the context of the medieval persecution of heretics throughout Europe, led by the Roman Catholic Church.[31] And, the portrayal of the Crusades' aftermath – titled *Zwischen Abendland und Morgenland* [Between Occident and Orient] – is focused explicitly on aspects of intercultural exchange and transfer.

The integration of these additional aspects and their contextualization – delegitimizing the Crusades by questioning the theory of the Just War, showing the Church's violent history of persecuting people with other convictions to deny the singularity of the Crusades – prove the fundamental change of the emplotment, a change that also affects the ascriptions made to different events and structures. While in *Geschichtliches Werden 2* the allegedly legitimized Crusades seem to stem from the medieval people's rigidity of faith and the readiness to sacrifice their lives to liberate the Holy Land from the infidels, the impulses presented by *Das waren Zeiten 2* appear far less glorious:

> Religious zeal and the absolution of all sins promised by the Church, led the believers to follow the Crusaders. Love of adventure and economic reasons played a role, too: impoverished noblemen and later-born sons without claim to an inheritance expected rich booty or land.[32]

Using the word 'zeal' to describe a major motivation to become a Crusader devaluates the putatively once important religious dimension of this decision. Some Crusaders do not seem to have been led by their religious convictions but rather have been mislead by religious authorities – an impression confirmed by the portrayal of the multitude of Church-led persecutions in a separate paragraph. Indeed, none of the motivations appear very glorious, all being driven by selfishness: absolution of sins, love of adventure and the pursuit of wealth – they all refer to individual and not necessarily spiritual well-being.

Furthermore, warfare itself and its victims are highlighted in *Das waren Zeiten 2*: 'The Crusade had become a war of aggression against Muslims and Jews. . . . The death toll amassed on both sides during the seven Crusades is estimated to be between 10 and more than 22 million'.[33] Obviously, this text does not personalize every single victim to make the students feel empathy, but just by mentioning the enormous estimated number of victims, the text leaves the reader with an idea of the horror experienced by the participants of the Crusades, and (on a higher level) a rejection of violence in general – particularly because it is highlighted that the Crusades harmed Christians, Muslims and Jews alike. Still, the expression 'war of aggression' reinforces the perception of the Crusades as an illegitimate endeavour, as aggression could never be justifiable.

In relation to this attempt at showing that Christians, Muslims and Jews were equally struck by the violence of the Crusades, a separate, textually distinguished paragraph called *Lerntipp* (study tip) is integrated into the subchapter. Presenting two extracts from the *Gesta Francorum* and the opus of Arab historian Ibn al-Athir, it focuses on the Conquest of Jerusalem from multiple perspectives. As explained in the introductory sentences, this selection of historical sources aims to enable the students to examine history critically, and to deal with diverging perceptions and opinions in order to promote a sense of mutual understanding and consideration for people of another faith:

> We are presenting you with the description and evaluation of an event from two perspectives. Define the different perspectives. Examine both texts in terms of their credibility. List the facts mentioned by both reports in a table and compare them. Present in detail when and how both authors evaluate the event.[34]

Given that the Muslims certainly thought differently about the necessity to fight for the liberation of the sacred Christian places than the medieval Christians may have, the Christians' decision to undertake the Crusades appears questionable at the very least, if not illegitimate and incomprehensible. Yet, the portrayal of Pope Urban's call for the First Crusade in 1095 also pursues this didactical aim. The students are supposed to 'write an answer to M3 [M3 = the Pope's call, the historical source, D.W.] from a Muslim's point of view',[35] both to critically reflect on what they have read and to put themselves in the shoes of a person directly affected by the hostile acts depicted by the source.

In contrast to the remainder of the chapter, the concluding section *Zwischen Morgenland und Abendland* [Between Orient and Occident] focuses mainly on the portrayal of the transfer of knowledge and the cultural contact between the Muslim and the Christian worlds. This aspect of the Crusades' history is also presented from multiple perspectives, although, unlike the Conquest of Jerusalem, not by contrasting two sources but by presenting in detail the differences between Muslims and Christians by focusing on a Muslim source only. Referring to natural sciences, medicine and philosophy, this section explains how, and to what extent, the Christian Occident adopted the highly developed knowledge of the Muslim world ('Until the sixteenth century, European doctors depended on the medical knowledge of the Arabs').[36] Then, the following source – the Syrian Usama ibn Muniqid, who reports on the knowledge of twelfth-century European doctors in medicine – amends this reasoning:

> The Lord of Manaitira wrote to my uncle and asked him to send a doctor who would be able to cure his sick companions. My uncle sent him a Christian doctor named Tabit. After merely ten days, he returned, and we said to him: 'You cured the sick quickly', whereupon he told his story: 'They showed me a knight suffering from an abscess on his leg and a woman suffering from cachexia. I prepared an emollient patch for the knight, the abscess opened, and his condition improved; I put the woman on a diet and supplied her organism with some fluids. Then, a Frankish doctor came along and said: 'That one doesn't know how to treat them at all!', approached the knight and asked him: 'What do you prefer: living with one leg or dying with both legs?' The knight replied: 'I prefer living with one leg!' Then, the doctor said: 'Bring me a strong knight and a sharp axe!' The knight and the axe came, I stood next to them. The doctor put the leg on a block of wood and told the knight: 'Strike hard to cut off the leg'. In front of my eyes, he stroke once, and because the leg was not cut off yet, he stroke again: the marrow squirted, and the knight died immediately.[37]

Alas, the source also reports that the woman's treatment ended the same way as the knight's. At the end of the section, Tabit is quoted a last time when he reports sarcastically: 'I left after having learnt from their medical science what I didn't know before'.[38] The entire extract proves the inferiority of the Christian Occident to the Muslim Orient (although the oriental doctor was explicitly named Christian). Not only is the description of the treatment of both sick people testifying to the striking ignorance of the 'Franks' – in contrast to the refined medical knowledge of the Orient – but it also makes the European Christians appear as coarse, heartless and violent brutes.

Considering all previous sections dedicated to the history of the Crusades and their inherently negative portrayal of the Christians, the entire endeavour of the Crusades seems to be illegitimate, explicitly hostile towards other people's culture and knowledge, and overall a 'cultural encounter' forcibly provoked by the 'uncivilized' European Christians.

Historicizing Present-Day Societies by Telling Medieval History

After an in-depth analysis of these two history schoolbooks, *Geschichtliches Werden 2* and *Das waren Zeiten 2*, it has become evident that the presented portrayals of medieval history reflect society's views at the respective times of their origin.

In Which Way Were the Portrayals of the Crusades in Both Schoolbooks Subject to Narratives Aiming at the Legitimization, Historicity and Interconnection of Societies?

The underlying differences regarding the portrayal of the Crusades in both schoolbooks are obvious. In comparison, the history of the Crusades is not only presented more comprehensively in the 2003 schoolbook, but the emplotment – the meaning ascribed to the history of the Crusades – also changed fundamentally.

In *Geschichtliches Werden 2* (1974), the history of the Crusades is told focusing on the Christian Crusaders as protagonists. They were supposed to be on a legitimate mission, guided by their faith. Altruism, the will to assist people in need (the Eastern Roman emperor, the robbed or ill pilgrims), was another leading factor during the events. The narration is rather positive, its perspective Eurocentric. By contrast, *Das waren Zeiten 2* (2003) uses a multi-perspective approach, and tells a story about an illegitimate endeavour, highlighting the violent events and the brutality of the ignorant Crusaders while delegitimizing their motivations for participating in a Crusade.

There could not be a bigger contrast between the two narrations of the history of the Crusades. While there was no explicit ascription of meaning to the history of the Crusades in *Geschichtliches Werden 2* that exceeds the dimension of Christian-European self-reference – the act of fighting for the liberation of the sacred Christian places was important, not the opponent – a multitude of meanings was ascribed to the 'same' events in *Das waren Zeiten 2*. Knowing the 'other' well avoids conflicts, as violence is often provoked by powerful protagonists who misuse 'simple' people to achieve their goals; violence can never be tolerated, as a peaceful encounter across any type of border is more beneficial than violent conflicts – just to mention the most important meanings.

Initially, it can be observed that in *Geschichtliches Werden 2* the narrative aiming at the legitimization, historicity and interconnection of societies in connection with the portrayal of the history of the Crusades was not depicted in the same way that it was thirty years later in *Das waren Zeiten 2*. A look at the history of the Crusades shows the existence of a homogeneous society shaped by Christian-European values in a distant past, who, unlike others, had to hold its ground by means of confrontation.

The narrative in *Das waren Zeiten 2*, in contrast, is shaped in such a way that diversity, tolerance and the avoidance of conflict (by mistrusting authorities) appear as 'natural' elements in the history of every territorially defined community. The expansion of the perspective on history to also include sources that do not solely portray the Crusaders' point of view, leads to an increase in the number of people who can relate to the history of the Crusades as if it were 'their' story (students of Muslim faith, for example). Additionally, the history of the Crusades will be construed as morally bad by firmly rejecting these acts of violence and instead demanding empathy with the victims. Lastly, highlighting the benefits of peaceful cultural exchange – and its portrayal as natural – creates a positive example of an alternative concept.

Differences between Muslims and Christians are not hidden, of course, yet neither are they portrayed as 'irreconcilable' or as having to be handled in a confrontational manner. The 'others', especially the cooperation and the exchanges with them, are a part of the teleological narration that describes all those elements that have made societies what they are today.

To Which Extent Do These Portrayals of Medieval History Reflect Political and Sociocultural Changes?

An answer to this question can be found in the observation that portrayals of encounters and the mutual exchange of ideas and knowledge between Muslims and Christians cannot, or can only very rarely, be found in the schoolbooks of the 1970s and the 1980s, whereas these topics tend to play a more dominant role beginning in the 1990s. This change can also be observed in Spanish and French schoolbooks.[39] Since the emplotment of historiography always depends on the respective historiographer's present, there has obviously been an evolution of the important questions that Western and especially European societies are attempting to answer. In the 1970s and the 1980s, the topics of intercultural learning, multi-perspectival and mutual understanding were not perceived to be as important didactically as they became over the course of the 1990s.[40]

Yet, the use of this legitimizing, historicizing and interconnecting narrative on intercultural diversity is not limited to schoolbooks; the analysis of historical novels or exhibitions confirms that it has been used increasingly since the beginning of the 1990s. Even press articles frequently refer to an apparently peaceful, interreligious cooperation in medieval times.[41] Meanwhile the above-mentioned narrative on intercultural diversity and transcultural exchange has gradually become a less intense part of all present-day historicizing narrations of territorially defined communities.[42] This development happened simultaneously to the different processes of globalization, which ended with Europe's self-perception as a continent formed by homogeneous nation-states. Present-day Europe consists of a multitude of diverse, heterogeneous societies. The development of the emplotment used in these two analysed schoolbooks corresponds to this social evolution.

But Do the Portrayals of Cultural Contact between Muslims and Christians in the Middle Ages Actually Lend Themselves to the Promotion of Tolerance and Mutual Understanding?

Of course, the narrative on intercultural diversity conveys a concept of society that can surely be viewed as officially approved by the majority of the members of (West) European societies. It is helpful to build a meaningful and comprehensive narration of the past, which in turn legitimizes present-day social structures, thus promoting a sense of social unity.

Some continuities, however, are worth noticing: for example, the general choice that minorities defined by ethnicity or religion make when talking about the relationship of a majoritarian group with minoritarian 'others' in order to present the history of medieval diversity, and the specific choice of Jews and Muslims to play the role of these 'others'. Following the way Jews and Muslims are portrayed in those stories, the perception of them being different from the (Christian) majority of European societies is emphasized. And this is the exact opposite of what the stories about medieval history seem to intend.

Moreover, medieval Islam appears as a homogeneous block – unlike medieval Christian Europe. This continent is represented as states 'united in their diversity', another legitimizing, historicizing and interconnecting narrative that portrays the 'medieval roots' of present-day (EU) Europe. Naturally, the elaborated culture and civilization of medieval Islam is also portrayed in all present-day history schoolbooks, but the way this world is represented – ignoring its very diversity – leaves the impression that medieval Islam was a superior power block at the gates of the European continent, and one that reached from the Atlantic to the Indian Ocean. Present-day (right-wing) political discourses on an alleged threat to Western civilization by the Muslim world are often only deconstructed regarding their content, and not enough regarding their narrative structure.

The production of history books for schools can certainly not elude the time-dependency of historiography. As these books are a branch of historiography as well as the preferred 'tool' to disseminate the 'official' version of history and societal ideas, their analyses give insights into the societal changes necessary to understand past and present-day societies. Historicizing – the ascription of meaning by telling a comprehensive (hi)story of past events – also means legitimizing communities, a fundamental characteristic without which no community can persist. Therefore, historicizing present-day societies (in history schoolbooks) is nothing to worry about – however, a lack of awareness of historiography's constitution as structuring, selecting and configuring narration amongst its readers would be of concern.

Daniel Wimmer is assistant lecturer for European history and art history at the University of Applied Sciences Würzburg-Schweinfurt, where he is also the head of Internationalization. He was research assistant at the Chair of Medieval History at the University of Mannheim. His research interests are the reception of medieval history in the twentieth and twenty-first centuries, the history of the medieval Iberian Peninsula and the history of the Electorate Palatinate.

Notes

1. This case study is part of a PhD project realized at Mannheim University between 2009 and 2013 (Wimmer, *Mit dem Mittelalter die Gegenwart erzählen*).
2. Jacobmeyer, 'Konditionierung von Geschichtsbewusstsein'; Pingel, 'Geschichtsdeutung als Macht?'; Fuchs and Lässig, 'Europa im Schulbuch'; Apple and Christian-Smith, 'Politics of the Textbook'; Choppin, 'Le manuel scolaire'; Clauss and Seidenfuß, 'Für das Leben und die Schule . . .?'.
3. According to Irene Götz, the term 'offer of identity' implies a plural concept of identity. An identity is supposed to be created individually, combining a multitude of focalizations (Götz, *Deutsche Identitäten*, 206).
4. Fulda, 'Historiographic Narration'; Baberowski, *Der Sinn der Geschichte*, 11–30.
5. Groebner, *Das Mittelalter hört nicht auf*, 126.
6. LARPG is Live Action Role-Playing Game. 'LARPs can be viewed as forming a distinct category of RPG because of two unique features: (a) the players physically embody their characters, and (b) the game takes place in a physical frame' (Tychsen et al., 'Live Action Role-Playing Games', 255).
7. Hobsbawm, *Nationen und Nationalismus*; Hobsbawm and Ranger, *Invention of Tradition*; Anderson, *Die Erfindung der Nation*; Gellner, *Nationalismus und Moderne*.
8. Appadurai, 'Globale ethnische Räume'; Beck, Giddens and Lash, *Reflexive Modernisierung*.
9. Rogers Brubaker argues for an analysis of ethnically defined collectives as 'perspectives on the world' (Brubaker, *Ethnizität ohne Gruppen*, 31) to avoid the mistake of using a category of ethnological practices as a category of social analysis.

10. German ethnologist Irene Götz focuses on the 'territorial man' living in modern times as research object. She argues that the concentration of social and cultural studies focused on collective identity constructions on phenomena of transculturality and transnationality could lead to the 'territorial man', with the majority of the society and its perception of the world not being perceived (Götz, *Deutsche Identitäten*, 208; Götz, 'Nationale und regionale Identitäten').

11. Wimmer, *Mit dem Mittelalter die Gegenwart erzählen*, 505–50.
12. Neubig and Reichert, *Geschichtliches Werden Mittelstufe*, 24–27.
13. Ibid., 25–26.
14. Ibid., 24.
15. Ibid.
16. Ibid.
17. Ibid.
18. Ibid., 25.
19. Ibid.
20. Ibid.
21. Ibid.
22. Ibid.
23. Ibid., 26.
24. Ibid.
25. Ibid.
26. Ibid.
27. Ibid.
28. Brückner and Focke, *Das waren Zeiten 2*, 83–89.
29. Yet, *Das waren Zeiten 2* is not the only German schoolbook of the 2000s that uses a rhetorical question for the title of the chapter dedicated to the Crusades. Referring to the famous exclamation '*deus lo vult*' of the Council of Clermont, the equivalent chapter in *Geschichte Geschehen 2* was named *Ob Gott es wirklich wollte? – Der erste Kreuzzug* [The First Crusade – Was it really the will of God?] (Brückmann et al., *Geschichte Geschehen*, 144–52).
30. Brückner and Focke, *Das waren Zeiten 2*, 83–85.
31. Ibid., 84–85.
32. Ibid., 84.
33. Ibid., 84–85.
34. Ibid., 87.
35. Ibid., 86.
36. Ibid., 88.
37. Ibid., 89.
38. Ibid., 89.
39. Wimmer, *Mit dem Mittelalter die Gegenwart erzählen*, 505–50.
40. Onken, 'Die Kreuzzüge im Geschichtsunterricht'.
41. Ten historical novels were analysed, including novels written by Noah Gordon, Umberto Eco, Ken Follett and Ildefonso Falcones. In addition, eleven historical exhibitions were analysed. A list of all analysed sources can be found in Wimmer, *Mit dem Mittelalter die Gegenwart erzählen*, 653–78.
42. Ibid., 637–38.

Bibliography

Anderson, Benedict. *Die Erfindung der Nation: Zur Karriere eines folgenreichen Konzepts*. Frankfurt: Campus, 1996.

Appadurai, Arjun. 'Globale ethnische Räume: Bemerkungen und Fragen zur Entwicklung einer transnationalen Anthropologie', in Ulrich Beck (ed.), *Perspektiven der Weltgesellschaft* (Frankfurt: Suhrkamp, 1998), 11–40.

Apple, Michael, and Linda Christian-Smith. 'The Politics of the Textbook', in Michael Apple and Linda Christian-Smith (eds), *The Politics of the Textbook* (New York: Routledge, 1991), 1–21.

Baberowski, Jörg. *Der Sinn der Geschichte: Geschichtstheorien von Hegel bis Foucault*. Munich: Beck, 2005.

Beck, Ulrich, Anthony Giddens and Scott Lash. *Reflexive Modernisierung: Eine Kontroverse*. Frankfurt: Suhrkamp, 1996.

Brubaker, Rogers. *Ethnizität ohne Gruppen*. Hamburg: Hamburger Edition, 2007.

Brückmann, Asmut, et al. *Geschichte Geschehen. Sekundarstufe I, Band 2*. Leipzig: Klett, 2004.

Brückner, Dieter, and Harald Focke (eds). *Das waren Zeiten 2. Mittelalterliches Weltbild und modernes Denken. Ausgabe C*. Bamberg: Buchner, 2003.

Choppin, Alain. 'Le manuel scolaire – une fausse évidence historique'. *Histoire de l'Education* 1(117) (2008), 7–56.

Clauss, Martin, and Manfred Seidenfuß. 'Für das Leben und die Schule . . .? Eine Einführung', in Martin Clauss and M. Seidenfuß (eds), *Das Bild des Mittelalters in europäischen Schulbüchern* (Berlin: LIT, 2007), 7–17.

Fuchs, Eckhardt, and Simone Lässig. 'Europa im Schulbuch'. *Geschichte für heute* 1(2) (2009), 60–67.

Fulda, Daniel. 'Historiographic Narration', in Peter Hühn et al. (eds), *The Living Handbook of Narratology* (Hamburg: Hamburg University, 2014). URL: http://www.lhn.uni-hamburg.de/article/historiographic-narration (last accessed 27 May 2019).

Gellner, Ernest. *Nationalismus und Moderne*. Berlin: Rotbuch, 1991.

Götz, Irene. *Deutsche Identitäten: Die Wiederentdeckung des Nationalen nach 1989*. Cologne: Böhlau, 2011.

———. 'Nationale und regionale Identitäten: Zur Bedeutung von territorialen Verortungen in der Zweiten Moderne', in Manfred Seifert (ed.), *Zwischen Emotion und Kalkül. 'Heimat' als Argument im Prozess der Moderne* (Leipzig: Leipziger Universitätsverlag, 2010), 205–19.

Groebner, Valentin. *Das Mittelalter hört nicht auf: Über historisches Erzählen*. Munich: Beck, 2008.

Hobsbawm, Eric J. *Nationen und Nationalismus: Mythos und Realität seit 1780*. Frankfurt: Campus, 2005.

Hobsbawm, Eric J., and Terence Ranger (eds). *The Invention of Tradition*. Cambridge: Cambridge University Press, 1983.

Jacobmeyer, Wolfgang. 'Konditionierung von Geschichtsbewusstsein: Schulgeschichtsbücher als nationale Autobiographien'. *Gruppendynamik* 23(4) (1992), 375–88.

Neubig, Karl-Heinz, and Erhard Reichert. *Geschichtliches Werden Mittelstufe: Geschichte des Mittelalters und der Neuzeit bis 1789* (3rd edn). Bamberg: Buchner, 1974.

Onken, Björn. 'Die Kreuzzüge im Geschichtsunterricht – Praxiserfahrungen und Perspektiven', in Felix Hinz (ed.), *Kreuzzüge des Mittelalters und der Neuzeit. Realhistorie – Geschichtskultur – Didaktik* (Hildesheim: Georg Olms, 2016), 255–70.

Pingel, Falk. 'Geschichtsdeutung als Macht? Schulbuchforschung zwischen wissenschaftlicher Erkenntnis- und politischer Entscheidungslogik'. *Journal of Educational Media, Memory, and Society* 2(2) (2010), 93–112.

Tychsen, Anders, et al. 'Live Action Role-Playing Games: Control, Communication, Storytelling, and MMORPG Similarities'. *Games and Culture* 1 (July 2006), 252–75.

Wimmer, Daniel. *Mit dem Mittelalter die Gegenwart erzählen: Eine ferne Vergangenheit als Vermittlungsinstanz in Weltentwürfen des 20. und 21. Jahrhunderts*. Hamburg: Dr. Kovač, 2016.

CHAPTER 7

Narrative Structure of High School World History Textbooks in Postwar Japan

NAOKI ODANAKA

Introduction

This chapter aims to elucidate the structural principles of history – that is, narrative structure – which Japanese high school world history textbooks adopted after the Second World War. In this chapter, narrative structure means the shared modes of comprehension and explanation of a temporal structure, articulating the past, the present and the future, combined with a spatial structure that articulates areas or regions. As Hayden White says, historical text is a 'literary artifact', where historical events 'are rendered comprehensible by being subsumed under the categories of the plot structure in which they are encoded as a story of a particular kind'.[1] We comprehend, explain, narrate or descript history by dividing it into plural spatial–temporal units, and then reuniting these units after choosing a certain principle of history to be used.

We set this task to see how these textbooks reflect the social and intellectual conditions of postwar Japan – which is when and where they were written and read. As is well known, every text is political in a broad sense: it reflects and influences, intentionally or not, the real world surrounding it. Historical texts, including school textbooks, are no exception. According to White, politicization of historians, historical texts and historical interpretations happens as a rule.[2]

Notes for this section begin on page 161.

How then, and by what mechanism, does the real world influence world history textbooks? Our hypothesis is that narrative structure functions as a link between the condition of the real world and the contents of historical text. In our case, social and intellectual conditions determine which narrative structure is to be chosen, and this choice in turn influences the characteristics of world history textbooks.[3]

Japanese school textbooks after the Second World War are a good case for testing this hypothesis, because the authors had been asked by the government to be objective and neutral in their contents. Postwar Japan adopted the governmental check system for school textbooks (*kyokasho kentei seido*). Publishing houses, referring to the National Curriculum Standards (NCS, *gakushu shido yoryo*) issued by the government, edit textbook drafts (written mainly by university historians) and send them to the Ministry of Education. Then, ministry textbook examiners – trained as academic scholars but whose main task is to make authors and publishing houses for school textbooks follow the NCS – check the draft and request modifications if necessary. The NCS has been modified roughly every ten years since the end of the war (1951, 1960, 1970, 1978, 1989, 1999 and 2009), but always emphasizing that school textbooks must be objective and neutral at the political, social, economic and cultural levels.

We address this topic in the following five steps: we present the method and the materials of analysis; we comparatively analyse temporal structures adopted by the objects of analysis, namely two editions of a textbook; we analyse them at the spatial dimension; we comparatively clarify the Japanese social and intellectual conditions under which the two editions were written, and test our hypothesis by trying to link the contents of textbooks with the social and intellectual conditions of the space–time in which they were written; and finally, we briefly summarize our arguments and point out some questions that remain to be answered.

Method and Materials

Two concrete methods of analysis will be adopted. In the first, to analyse the temporal structure, we will clarify how history is periodized and how these periods are articulated. We carry out this task using the notion of 'regime of historicity' presented by the French historian, François Hartog.

According to Hartog, the regime of historicity is 'the modalities of self-consciousness that each and every society adopts in its constructions of time and its perceptions' or 'the way relations between the past, the present, and the future are configured'.[4] In greater detail, he states:

My focus is first and foremost on the categories that organize these experiences and allow them to be spoken; and more precisely, on the ways in which these universal categories or forms we call 'the past', 'the present' and 'the future' are articulated. How are these categories, which partake both of thought and action, actualized at different times, and in different places and societies, and how do they make possible and perceptible a particular order of time? What present are we dealing with in different places and at different times, and to what past and future is it linked?[5]

Hartog contends that there have been three regimes of historicity in Western historiography: pastism (*passéisme*), futurism (*futurisme*) and presentism (*présentisme*). The first, dominant until the eighteenth century, regards the past or history as a supplier of lessons and models. During the Renaissance, for example, ancient Greece was regarded as a model to be followed at the political, social and cultural levels. The second regime, emerging around the beginning of the nineteenth century and becoming dominant with the scientification of historical research in the Rankean manner in European countries, regards the past as the precondition of the future, and history as a teleological course of events towards the future as the goal. Historical materialist historians, for example, claimed to be scientific because they could predict the arrival of a socialist mode of production using their knowledge of the past and of historical laws. The third regime, blossoming in the 1970s and 1980s with the diffusion of postmodernisms (in plural form) and with the fall of the Berlin Wall, which hastened the current globalization, claims that the past changes according to our 'here and now', that is to say, the present. This very typical postmodernist stance can be found in many contemporary historical texts.

In our second method, to analyse the spatial structure, we will tackle the following questions: How is the world divided into subunits, that is to say, regions, areas, continents, and so on? How much is each region emphasized? Finally, how are these regions articulated? For this task, we judge that Hartog's argument is suggestive but insufficient. The notion of 'regime of historicity' seems to lack interest in or concern regarding the spatial dimension, which is an important component of history, especially when it covers a broad area of the world.

Suggestive for us, here, is the notion presented by French geographer Patrice Melé: the regime of reflexive territoriality. Heavily impressed by Hartog's notion of 'regime of historicity', he tries to extend it to the spatial dimension to enable it to function as a tool for the analysis of territory as a kind of space. He explains the regime of reflexive territoriality as follows:

> The notion of regime of reflexive territoriality is an analytical tool, a category making it possible to regroup different phenomena and situations according to some of their characteristics with which we could elucidate mutations of the

relation to the territory and the importance of certain contemporary processes of (re-)territorialization. To do so is to characterize the modalities of relation to the space and the ways to think about the territory.[6]

Although the application of Melé's invention is beyond the scope of this chapter, we share his opinion that the ways we have treated the concept of space are crucial in analysing the spatial phenomenon.

As our object of analysis, then, we have selected a textbook titled *Sekai no Rekishi* [World History], published by Yamakawa Shuppansha, a leading publishing house for high school history textbooks in Japan, whose market share is always over 50 per cent. *Sekai no Rekishi* was first published in 1973, with a second edition (renamed *Shin Sekai-Shi* [World History new edition]) in 1982, and a third (also named *Shin Sekai-Shi*) in 2014.[7] We will compare the 1973 and 2014 editions of this textbook. The former was edited by Shibata Michio (b. 1926) and Kanda Nobuo (b. 1921) and eight other contributors born between 1923 and 1935. The latter was edited by Kishimoto Mio (b. 1952), Haneda Masashi (b. 1953), Kubo Fumiaki (b. 1956), Minamikawa Takashi (b. 1955), and three other contributors born between 1963 and 1967. The contributors of both editions were all professional and academic historians.

We chose this textbook because its two editions were written by historians from different generations, influenced by different historiographical trends. Historians in postwar Japan can be classified into four generations: first, those who were born around the turn of the century and led historical research until the 1960s from various (for example, Marxist, progressivist, positivist) stances. Second are those who were born in the 1920s or early 1930s, and were heavily influenced by the first generation's stance on history. Third are those who were born in the 1940s, participated in the student revolts of 1968 as activists, and encountered and absorbed the new emerging trends in historical theory and methodology. Fourth were those born in or after the 1950s, who familiarized themselves with new trends in historical research from the very outset of their professional careers. The 1973 edition of the chosen textbook was written by second-generation historians, and the 2014 edition by fourth-generation ones. This generational difference could lead to variations in the book's historiographical position.

Temporal Structures: Towards De-monolinearization

In this section, we analyse the temporal structures of the two editions, focusing mainly on periodization and articulation. The main questions are as follows: What kind of periodization do they adopt? How does it function in the structuralization of the whole text by the articulation of periods?[8]

The 1973 edition comprises four main parts, containing one to three titled chapters, with a short introductory chapter concerning prehistory:

- Part 1: Chap. 1 – Ancient World
- Part 2: Chap. 2 – European World; Chap. 3 – Islamic World; Chap. 4 – East Asian World
- Part 3: Chap. 5 – Formation of Modern Europe; Chap. 6 – Development of Modern European and American Society; Chap. 7 – Changes in Asia
- Part 4: Chap. 8 – Beginning of Imperial Age and the First World War; Chap. 9 –Versailles System and the Second World War; Chap. 10 – Contemporary World.

Judging from the chapter titles, we may observe that Part 1 considers the ancient age, Part 2 the medieval one, Part 3 the modern one and Part 4 the contemporary one.[9] It means that this edition adopts a tetrameric periodization of world history.

We turn now to highlighting three characteristics of the 1973 edition. First, its authors claim in the preface that the purpose of learning history in high school is not to learn lessons or to predict the future but rather to instil in students a historical way of thinking. This edition, thus, does not refer to the future, claiming itself to be objective and neutral.

Second, Part 3 begins with the Age of Navigation.[10] The modern age began around the beginning of the sixteenth century. Therefore, the authors of the 1973 edition adopt, as the criteria of modernity, European (Western) values and ideologies that emerged around that time, such as Renaissance humanism, post-Westphalian state-consciousness and, to some degree, Protestant Christianity born from the Reformation.[11] According to the authors, these values and ideologies were exported to the rest of the world by European countries – a modernization process that created the contemporary world.

Third, the four parts are not just arranged chronologically. The authors state in the preface that they are logically connected in a monolinear way: the contemporary world is an entity (Part 4) that, created in line with the development of European modernity, modified certain economic and social characters in non-European regions (Part 3), which were set in place before European expansion (Part 2) on the basis of historical preconditions (Part 1). We find here a monolinear temporal structure, constructed by the authors at the logical level. Even though the authors do not discuss the future, we may observe that they follow a typical futurist regime in Hartog's sense, using a temporal structure which sets the *telos* of history: their present, in this case.

The 2014 edition comprises five main parts, each containing four or five titled chapters, with an introductory chapter concerning prehistory:

- Part 1, titled 'Ancient Age': Chap. 1 – The Orient and Ancient Greece; Chap. 2 – Ancient Rome and West Asia; Chap. 3 – South Asia, Southeast Asia and Oceania; Chap. 4 – East and Central Asia; Chap. 5 – Africa, North America and South America
- Part 2, titled 'Medieval Age': Chap. 6 – Trends in East and Central Asia; Chap. 7 – Trends in West Asia; Chap. 8 – Trends in South and Southeast Asia; and Chap. 9 – The Formation of Europe
- Part 3, titled 'Early Modern Age': Chap. 10 – Age of Exchange and Commerce; Chap. 11 – Trends in East and Southeast Asia; Chap. 12 – Trends in West and South Asia; Chap. 13 – The Growth of Europe
- Part 4, titled 'Modern Age': Chap. 14 – Europe and America in the Age of Revolution; Chap. 15 – Europe in the Age of Nationalism; Chap. 16 – State-Formation by Settlement and Migration;[12] Chap. 17 – Turmoil in Asia
- Part 5, titled 'Contemporary Age': Chap. 18 – Imperialism and the World; Chap. 19 – World Wars; Chap. 20 – The Cold War and the Independence of the Third World; Chap. 21 – Today's World.

Contrary to the 1973 edition, this one adopts a five-division periodization of world history, introducing the concept of the early modern period.

Here, we turn to highlighting the three characteristics of the 2014 edition and compare it with the 1973 edition. First, its authors claim in the general preface that we learn history in the high school classroom to acquire the capability to understand the present, as in the 1973 edition. Second, it adopts the concept of the 'early modern age'. The 1973 edition's modern age is divided into the early modern and modern ages. This leads us to the questions: What distinguishes the two ages in this edition? Moreover, what are the authors' criteria of modernity?

In the preface to Part 3, the authors answer these questions, stating that

- The modern age in the broad sense began around the beginning of the sixteenth century;
- However, we find many important events in the eighteenth century, such as the Industrial Revolution in England, American Independence and the French Revolution;
- These events had a huge impact on our everyday life by creating new technology, democracies, nation-states, and so on;
- We should, thus, distinguish the early modern and late modern ('modern' in this edition) ages to properly understand world history.

Taking into consideration their use of the term 'modern' to express 'late modern', we could say that the criteria of modernity in the 2014 edition are the values and ideologies created and diffused under the (late) modern age, rather than those of the early modern one.[13]

Third, the 2014 edition is constructed as a multilinear historical narrative: each period (ancient, medieval, early modern and modern) is directly connected to the contemporary age, and we are informed how it contributed to the development of today's world. The temporal structure adopted by the authors is clearly shown in the prefaces to each part:

- The ancient age gives us classical philosophy, a model of political unity (the Roman Empire), and so on;
- The medieval age is characterized by the growth of world religions, which still exercise centripetal power in all regions today;
- The early modern age is depicted as the starting point of contemporary globalization; and
- The modern age is dominated by the ideology of progress, which still captivates most of us today.

Here, we find a typically presentist regime, in Hartog's sense, in that the past is reconstructed and depicted from the contemporary point of view.

Comparing the two editions at the temporal level, we find both similarities and differences. Similarity is found in the absence of the future, consideration of which they both avoid. This may be the result of the authors' need to portray themselves as objective and neutral. Conversely, differences are found in the definition of the modern age and the linearity of the temporal structure.

Regarding the differences over how to define the modern age, the 1973 edition takes, as its criteria, humanism (Renaissance), state-consciousness (post-Westphalian system), and Protestantism (Reformation), whereas the 2014 edition prefers innovation (Industrial Revolution), democracy (American Independence and the French Revolution), and nation-states (French Revolution) as the keys to modernization.

Concerning the differences over linearity, the 1973 edition adopts a monolinear temporal structure of history, wherein ages are connected in a line, while the 2014 edition adopts a multilinear temporal structure, wherein each past era is directly connected to the present. We find, here, a tendency towards the de-monolinearization of narrative structure, meaning a shift from futurist to presentist regimes in Hartog's sense.

Spatial Structures: Towards De-Western Modernization

In this section, we analyse the spatial structure of the two editions, focusing on the division, the weight and the mode of articulation. The main questions are as follows: How is the world divided into subunits? What proportion of each of these books is devoted to describing them? How are they articulated?

To address the first question, the composition of parts, chapters and sections is suggestive. The 1973 edition's first chapter – the only chapter in Part 1 – is titled 'Ancient World' and is divided into seven sections: ancient Orient; *polis* (city-states) society in Greece; the Mediterranean empire of Rome; the prosperity of Iranian ethnical states; the rise and decline of ancient states in India; the formation of unified states in ancient China; and inland Asia. In contemporary terms, the ancient world is divided into five subunits: Europe (Greece and Rome), West Asia (Orient and Iran), South Asia (India), inland Asia and East Asia (China). In Part 2, covering the medieval age, they are then integrated into three, each of which receives the attention of one chapter: Europe, West Asia (Islamic world) and East Asia. In Part 3 arguing the modern age, these three subunits are reintegrated into two: Europe (plus the USA), which is assigned two chapters, and Asia, which is assigned one.[14]

The world is, thus, reduced from five subunits to three, and then to two, and this integration process always functions on non-European (Asian) subunits, that is to say: West Asia, inland Asia, South Asia and East Asia are gradually integrated into a single 'Asia' over time. Taking into consideration the fact that the United States is combined with Europe in Part 3, we can find here a tendency towards a dichotomy between the East and the West.

Shifting attention to the 2014 edition, we see the same tendency as that found in the 1973 edition. The ancient world is divided into ten subunits in Part 1: Europe (Greece and Rome), West Asia (Orient and West Asia), South Asia, Southeast Asia, Central Asia, East Asia, Oceania, Africa, North America and South America. The medieval world is then divided into six subunits in Part 2: East Asia, Southeast Asia, Central Asia, South Asia, West Asia and Europe. The early modern world is then divided into five subunits in Part 3: East Asia, Southeast Asia, South Asia, West Asia and Europe. Finally, the modern world is divided into five alternative subunits in Part 4: Europe, Asia, North America, South America and Oceania (Australia and New Zealand).

Thus, after first reducing the number of subunits from ten to six, they are then reduced to five, followed by the process of integrating the regions of Asia: West, South, Southeast, Central and East Asia are gradually merged into a single Asia.

For the second question, we will measure and compare the quantitative share of the East and the West in the two editions. Dividing East and West is, of course, always an arbitrary and artificial act. In Japan, however, Western and Eastern historical studies have been clearly divided in academia at the institutional and practical levels since the beginning of scientific and academic historical research after the Meiji Restoration (1868).[15] Thus, in the Japanese context, West and East are clearly distinguished from each other. The former means Europe, plus North America after the United States' independence. The latter means the rest of the world: Asia, Africa, and so on.[16]

The 1973 edition allocates 312 pages to its four parts, of which 133 (43 per cent) are allocated to the East and 179 (57 per cent) to the West. However, viewed periodically, that is:

- In Part 1 on the ancient age, 33 pages on the East and 16 on the West
- In Part 2 on the medieval age, 52 pages on the East and 28 on the West
- In Part 3 on the modern age, 24 pages on the East and 80 on the West
- In Part 4 on the contemporary age, 24 pages on the East and 55 on the West.

We may thus observe the following two characteristics of this 1973 edition. First, heavy emphasis is placed on the modern age in the West (80 pages, representing almost 25 per cent of the text). The Renaissance, Age of Navigation, Reformation, emergence of the Westphalian sovereign-state system, Industrial Revolution, American Independence, French Revolution, birth of nationalism/nation-states and so on, are regarded as the main line of world history that created the foundation of today's world. We could perceive the 1973 edition to be 'Westernization–modernization oriented'. An example of this point is the explanation of the French Revolution. In the 10 pages devoted to this topic, we find a very detailed description of the course of events, containing the names of Louis XVI, Marie-Antoinette, Lafayette, Mirabeau, Barnave, Robespierre, Danton, Babeuf, Napoleon and even Josephine, Napoleon's first wife.

Second, the East, which looms large in the ancient (67 per cent) and medieval (65 per cent) parts, diminishes greatly in the modern age (23 per cent) and contemporary age (30 per cent) parts. The Islamic and East Asian worlds, narrated and depicted in detail in Part 2, are reduced in parts 3 and 4 to a kind of appendix, or no more than a target and playfield of the Western powers. In brief, the 1973 edition implies that the East changed from an active historical actor to a passive one at around the beginning of the sixteenth century.

Turning to the 2014 edition, we find that it allocates 374 pages to five parts. Of them, 5 pages are used to explain the Age of Navigation from a global (that is, non-Western/Eastern) perspective, and five pages for today's globalization. Of the remaining 364 pages, 161 (44 per cent) are allocated to the East and 203 (56 per cent) to the West.

Periodically speaking, that is:

- In part 1 on the ancient age, 32 pages on the East and 25 on the West;
- In part 2 on the medieval age, 40 pages on the East and 36 on the West;
- In part 3 on the early modern age, 27 pages on the East and 40 on the West;
- In part 4 on the modern age, 20 pages on the East and 46 on the West; and
- In part 5 on the contemporary age, 42 pages on the East and 56 on the West.

We identify several impressive characteristics of the 2014 edition, of which we will now explain two. First, we find the emergence of a truly global perspective. The Age of Navigation is explained as a phenomenon wherein East and West came into contact, deepened trade and cultural transfer, and influenced each other as equal actors. Contemporary globalization is also covered from a global point of view. Second, although the total shares of East and West are almost the same as those in the 1973 edition, the 2014 edition does not show a sharp decline in the East's share in the modern and contemporary ages. While it is true that Part 4 of the 2014 edition allocates many more pages to the West, East and West are treated rather more evenly than in the 1973 edition. As for the pages assigned to the French Revolution, they mention only five names: Louis XVI, Turgot, Necker, Robespierre and Napoleon.

Regarding the third question, we find certain similarities and differences between the two editions. According to the 1973 edition, five plural subunits (regions, areas, civilizations, cultures and worlds) coexisted without strong interconnection in the ancient and medieval ages. This situation changed around the beginning of the sixteenth century, when European countries realized certain economic growth and entered into the Age of Navigation. Thereafter, the unification of the world began at the initiative of Europe, culminating in its supremacy over another subunit – namely, the East. At the beginning of Part 3 covering the modern age, the following is stated: 'In ancient and medieval ages, regions had developed their peculiar cultures, which, however, were "unified" into one unit, with their social structures transformed. This phenomenon owed heavily to the development of modern Europe'.[17]

The 1973 edition, thus, depicts world history as a space–time in which independent subunits were articulated by the economic power of Europe into a hierarchal unity, the top of which was occupied by Europe (and the USA).

The 2014 edition presents a slightly different picture. Like the 1973 edition, it bases the mainline of world history on the fact that plural subunits began to be articulated as a unified body under the supremacy of Europe at around the beginning of the sixteenth century, with the coming of the Age of Navigation. However, it identifies two reservations. First, even before the Age of Navigation, subunits had been articulated with one another in various ways, and more deeply than suggested by the 1973 edition. For example, the medieval age is characterized by a wide migration of population. Concretely, the 2014 edition states the following:

> Local societies, which were formed by the combination of religion and political power in the medieval Eurasian continent, did not exist independently of one another. They were closely interconnected economically and socially, influencing one another by the constant and wide-ranging long-distance trade. It was carried out by Sogds and Uyghurs in Central Eurasia; by Jews in the Mediterranean area, West Asia and South Asia; by Muslims and Hindus in the pan-Indian sea area; and by Chinese who moved to Japan and Southeast Asia. They played a really important role in inter-regional economic and cultural exchange.[18]

The second reservation was that European expansion after the Age of Navigation did not generate its supremacy in a short time, much less in an automatic manner. Europe was economically backward compared with East Asia, even in the eighteenth century. The Industrial Revolution, which began in England in the middle of that century, was the result of artisans' endeavours to catch up with the front runner, namely, East Asia. It was in the nineteenth century, when the Industrial Revolution was complete in England and spread to other Western countries, that the articulation of subunits became hierarchal.

Comparing the two editions at the spatial level – from the viewpoints of the division into subunits, of the share of each, and of the articulation among them – we detect a tendency towards de-Western modernization. The 1973 edition adopts a spatial structure that stresses the modern age in the West, claiming that the importance of the East decreased from the ancient and medieval ages to the modern and contemporary ones. The 2014 edition, meanwhile, adopts a spatial structure in which East and West are treated rather equally throughout the text.

Narrative Structure as a Link between the Real World and the Text?

We start this section by clarifying the social and intellectual conditions of the 1970s and 2010s in Japan. Regarding the social conditions, Japan had a watershed between the two decades. Japanese history from the middle of the nineteenth century to the 1970s could be summarized in a phrase:

modernization for catching up with the West.[19] Japan opened its doors to the world (*kaikoku*) in the 1850s, finding that many European and North American countries had achieved modernization and, through it, political and administrative institutionalization, social reforms and economic growth. Its political leaders, thinking that their country was far behind the West and that it could be colonized without efforts to modernize itself, set the primary target of all of their politics and policies – namely, economic development and military build-up (*fukoku kyohei*) to catch up with the West.

One of the best means of reaching the target was to imitate the front runners, which is what Japan did. As the front runner of modernization in the 19th century was the West, modernization meant Westernization in Japan. From the Meiji Restoration onward, Japanese leaders tried their best to introduce Western political, social, economic and cultural systems to Westernize their country so that they could catch up with Europe and North America.

To achieve modernization as soon as possible, Japanese leaders constructed a social system whereby they could mobilize all the national resources, including human ones. A Japanese economic historian, Yamanouchi Yasushi, called this the 'total war system'.[20] Yamanouchi argued that at the core of this system lay the mobilization, whose purpose did not have to be the conduct of war: it could also be economic development, economic and social recovery, Westernization, modernization, and so on. When we see Japanese history from *kaikoku* onward, we understand that it is nothing but a history of constructing a 'total war system'. The main target of Japanese leaders and people changed from Westernization, colonization, empire building, victory in the World Wars and economic recovery after 1945, to high economic growth – but the means was always the same: 'total war system'. Because Japan had to catch up with the West, its society had to be organized towards one target that all its members had to share.[21]

Things changed in 1980s, when Japan achieved its long-cherished desire, that is to say, the catching up with the West, especially in the economic dimension. Japan became the world's second biggest economic power, next to the United States, overtaking all the European countries. The 'total war system' thus became out of date. There was no longer a commonly shared target. A new age began in Japan when everyone had to search for their own individual target in life. This age continues today.

Regarding intellectual conditions, the 1970s and 2010s are very different from each other in the field of historical research. Historical research across the world was dominated by modernism – that is to say, scientific-progressive-national/nationalistic trends – from the mid-nineteenth century onward.[22] The same was true of Japan. Around the 1970s, however, we could see the emergence of an anti-, or at least a non-modernist historiography.[23] We could call this phenomenon the postmodernist (in a very broad sense) turn, which involved a renewal of social history (for example, labour history from below in England, the Annales School of historical anthropology in France, the Bielefeld School of *Sozialgeschichte* in Germany, and so on), the birth of gender history in the United States, and the introduction of Immanuel Wallerstein's world system theory into historical analysis. This tendency towards postmodernist historiography arrived in Japan immediately and resonated widely, especially among third-generation historians, who were about to start their academic careers, and the coming fourth generation. Moreover, the outputs of these new trends came into fashion in the 1980s under the name *shakaishi boom* (social history craze).[24]

The 1973 edition was written by the postwar second-generation, that is to say, modernist historians, and the 2014 one by the postwar fourth-generation, that is to say, postmodernist historians. We, thus, have a textbook and its revised edition that are products of different generations and stances.

We turn then to the main task of this section: trying to link the contents of the two editions and the social and intellectual conditions of the space–time in which they were written to test our hypothesis that narrative structure functions as the link. We will measure the consistency between the social and intellectual conditions on the one hand, and the narrative structure for each edition of the textbook on the other, to determine whether or not our hypothesis is supported. The two editions have almost the same contents because of the governmental requirement for objectivity and neutrality, even though they were written under different social and intellectual conditions from each other. We find here a gap between the similarity of the contents and the real-world differences. A certain buffer is thus necessary that could plug that gap by making it possible to narrate the same contents in different ways to reflect different real worlds. If the narrative structure of each edition is consistent with the social and intellectual conditions surrounding it, we could say that it functions as the buffer, that it links the contents and the real world, and that our hypothesis is supported.

As for the 1973 edition, 1973 was a year when Japan experienced an oil crisis that foreshadowed the end of the country's high economic growth and thus of the 'total war system'. Taking into consideration the time necessary for the preparation of that edition, we can say that the edition was written in the 'total war system' period, when almost everyone shared the same purpose: catching up with the West. The same must have been true of the authors of the edition. Japanese people were then living a history that was a single-tracked passing of time towards a common goal.

At the intellectual level, authors shared a belief in the linearity of time and history, and in the importance of the Western modern age (and the contemporary age, to some extent). This is typical of the modernist, that is to say, scientific-progressive-national/nationalistic history preponderant from the mid-nineteenth century to the 1960s. These social and intellectual conditions fit well with the narrative structure of the 1973 edition, which is composed of two elements: a monolinear temporal structure, and a spatial one characterized by the importance of the modern Western age.

Regarding the 2014 edition, 2014 was a year when Japan had already caught up with the West and had also passed its economic peak. The country was then in economic and demographic decline, leading to social anxiety. People could not find a unique and common end to pursue. Facing an aging society with a very low birth rate, the rise of neighbouring countries such as Korea and China, and a lingering economic slump for more than twenty years, the Japanese people could not share a common goal. Everyone was therefore forced to find their own individual goal if possible. Some found it, but others did not and were at a loss.

At the intellectual level, the 2014 edition was written by people who, after absorbing the new trends in history and its related disciplines – starting with cultural anthropology (Claude Lévy-Strauss), philosophy (Michel Foucault, Jacques Derrida) and linguistics (Ferdinand de Saussure) – came to doubt the linearity of time and history; they took for granted the importance of the modern and contemporary East and of globalization, and were sufficiently self-reflexive to find themselves still captured by Occidentalism (the Eastern counterpart of Saidian Orientalism), Westernization and modernity, a weakness that they needed to overcome.

These conditions also fit well into the narrative structure of the 2014 edition, which was composed of two elements: a multilinear temporal structure in which each 'past' was directly connected to the present, and a spatial one wherein East and West were fairly equally treated in every age. In both cases, the narrative structure is consistent with the social and intellectual conditions. We can thus say that our hypothesis is supported, because the narrative structure works as a link between the real world and the textbook's contents.

Conclusion

To conclude, we have found, on comparing two editions of one high school world history textbook in Japan, that the social and intellectual conditions prevalent at the time of writing were reflected through the choice of the narrative structure, even though they had been requested by the government and were regarded by most people as being objective and neutral.

There remain, however, many important questions concerning the narrative structure of Japanese world history textbooks. We will need to analyse other textbooks so that we can compare them with those discussed in this chapter (for example, those written by the postwar first-generation historians and those by the third-generation ones). We should try to find the characteristic of the temporal and spatial structures of the textbooks edited under other NCS than those that regulate the objects of our analysis. And at the theoretical level, we can and should pose certain questions, such as: Is there any relation between the temporal structure and spatial one adopted in each textbook? If so, what kind? How has the academic trend in historical research influenced the NCS and textbook description? These important questions await answers.

Naoki Odanaka is professor at the School of Economics, Tohoku University (Sendai, Japan). A specialist of modern and contemporary French history and of history-related sciences (historical theory, methodology of history, historiography, history education, and so on), he has written many books in Japanese, and several articles in English and French such as: 'From Responsibility to Compassion: Lessons from the Controversy over "Comfort Women" in Japan' (*Journal of Japanese Law* 31, 2011); 'Cinquante ans d'un quartier montpelliérain: le Petit Bard, 1960–2010' (*Bulletin Historique de la Ville de Montpellier* 38, 2016); 'Current Historians of the World, De-nationalhistoricize Ourselves!: Reading the *Writing the Nation* series in a Globalized Age' (*Asian Review of World Histories* 8(2), 2020), 'La Pergola: Un grand ensemble résidentiel à Montpellier (1960–2010): Evolution socio-spatiale et politique de la ville' (*Etudes Héraultaises* 54, 2020), and 'In Search of a Way to Form the Autonomous People: The Actuality, Social Influence, and Internationality of Historical Studies in the Second Half of Twentieth-Century Japan' (forthcoming).

Notes

This chapter is based on the research funded by JSPS KAKENHI 15K02925 and 19K01048. The chapter adopts the Japanese order of names when citing Japanese people: the family name appears first and then the first name.

    1. White, *Tropics of Discourse*, 86.
    2. White, 'Politics of Historical Interpretation'.
    3. We do not choose Japanese history but world history textbooks because, as Jie-Hyun Lim says, in the making of historical consciousness, world history precedes national history (Lim, 'Historicizing the World').
    4. Hartog, *Regimes of Historicity*, 9, 17.
    5. Ibid., 16–17.
    6. Melé, 'Identifier un régime de territorialité réflexive', 54.

7. Although it would be better to analyse all textbooks in the field, taking one textbook as an example should be sufficient because, under the governmental checking system, all the textbooks have to respect the government's guidelines (NCS) in order to be accepted by the Ministry of Education and be published.

8. Every NCS has contained the model of periodization to be followed. Its main modifications concern the beginning of the modern age. NCS 1951, 1960 and 1970 regarded the beginning of the sixteenth century as the starting point, emphasizing the impact of the Renaissance, the Reformation and the Age of Navigation (*Dai-Kokai Jidai*). Then, NCS 1978 and 1989 chose the mid-eighteenth century, positing that three revolutions (English Industrial, American Independence and French) made the modern world. Finally, NCS 1999 and 2009 readopted the first position. Regarding our objects of analysis, the 1973 edition follows NCS 1970, and the 2014 edition follows NCS 2009, thus adopting the same stance to the question 'When did the modern age begin?'

9. The titles of chapters comprising Part 2 do not use the word 'medieval', but Chap. 2 begins with a section titled 'Western Europe in the Early Medieval Age'. Chap. 3 starts with a section titled 'The Medieval Orient and Islamic Worlds'. Moreover, Part 3 begins with the phrase 'From the medieval age to the modern one'.

10. Age of Navigation has the same meaning as the 'Age of Discovery' or 'Age of Exploration', common in English-speaking academia. Japanese historians have avoided using these terms, because they seem Eurocentric.

11. Here, we could find the influence of Max Weber's argument that the ethic of Protestantism contributed to the birth of capitalism, leading to the modernization. His argument had a very strong impact on the first and second generations of Japanese postwar historians, who searched, through historical research, for the key to Japanese economic recovery and growth after 1945. See, for example, Otsuka, *Spirit of Capitalism*; Koschmann, *Revolution and Subjectivity*; Schwentker, 'Spirit of Modernity'.

12. Chapter 16 considers North and South America, Australia and New Zealand.

13. Here, we could see a certain distance between the 2014 edition and the NCS 2009, which the former should have adhered to, over the principal starting point of the modern age.

14. The last part, which is assigned to the contemporary age, is divided into chronological chapters in both editions, and so we can omit it from our analysis here.

15. Japanese historical academia has, thus, been divided into three fields: Japanese history, Western history and Eastern history. For the reasons behind this and the history of this tripartite system, see, for example, Lim, 'Historicizing the World', and Wang, 'Between Myth and History'.

16. This does not mean that there has been no debate over the arbitrariness of the East–West divide in Japanese historiography. 'Is Russia part of the West?' and 'How about South American history?' are examples of questions that have been raised. At the institutional level, however, Eastern and Western history are still clearly distinguished today. Almost all history departments at Japanese universities are divided into Japanese history, Eastern history and Western history sections.

17. Shibata and Kanda, *Sekai no Rekishi*, 160.

18. Kishimoto et al., *Shin Sekai-Shi*, 87.

19. See, for example, Goto-Jones, *Modern Japan*, which gives a concise and precise explanation of Japanese history from the middle of the nineteenth century, emphasizing the importance to Japan of the relation between modernization and Westernization, catching-up strategy, the 'total war system', and so on.

20. Yamanouchi, Koschmann and Narita, *Total War*.

21. Regarding the economic history of the 'total war system' in Yamanouchi's sense, see also Okazaki and Okuno, *Japanese Economic System*.

22. For the modernist tradition in Japanese historiography after the Meiji Restoration, see, for example, Kondo, 'Modernist Inheritance'.

23. In this chapter, we use the term 'postmodernist' in a very broad and loose sense, and avoid using the term 'postmodern' because it can have a narrow and particular meaning that does not fit our objects of analysis – namely, the 2014 edition, its authors and third- and fourth-generation Japanese historians.

24. As for the postmodernist shift in Japanese historiography, see, for example, Hasegawa, 'Challenges'.

Bibliography

Goto-Jones, Christopher. *Modern Japan*. Oxford: Oxford University Press, 2009.

Hartog, Francois. *Regimes of Historicity: Presentism and Experiences of Time*. Translated by Saskia Brown. New York: Columbia University Press, 2015.

Hasegawa, Mayuho. 'Challenges of "Social History" in Japan: New Perspectives in History'. *Oddyseus* 19 (2015), 49–65.

Kishimoto, Mio, et al. (eds). *Shin Sekai-Shi* [World History new edition]. Tokyo: Yamakawa Shuppansha, 2014.

Kondo, Kazuhiko. 'The Modernist Inheritance in Japanese Historical Studies: Fukuzawa, Marxists and Otsuka Hisao', in Gordon Daniels and Tsuzuki Chushichi (eds), *The History of Anglo-Japanese Relations 1600–2000*, Vol. 5 (London: Palgrave Macmillan, 2002), 173–88.

Koschmann, Julian Victor. *Revolution and Subjectivity in Postwar Japan*. Chicago: University of Chicago Press, 1996.

Lim, Jie-Hyun. 'Historicizing the World in Northeast Asia', in Douglas Northrop (ed.), *A Companion to World History* (Chichester: Wiley Blackwell, 2012), 418–32.

Melé, Patrice. 'Identifier un régime de territorialité réflexive', in Martin Vanier (ed.), *Territoire, territorialité, territorialisation* (Rennes: Presses Universitaires de Rennes, 2009), 45–55.

Okazaki, Tetsuji, and Okuno Masahiro (eds). *The Japanese Economic System and its Historical Origins*. Translated by Susan Herbert. Oxford: Clarendon Press, 1999.

Otsuka, Hisao. *The Spirit of Capitalism: The Max Weber Thesis in an Economic Historical Perspective*. Translated by Kondo Masaomi. Tokyo: Iwanami Shoten, 1982.

Schwentker, Wolfgang. 'The Spirit of Modernity: Max Weber's Protestant Ethic and Japanese Social Sciences'. *Journal of Classical Sociology* 5(1) (2005), 73–92.

Shibata, Michio, and Kanda Nobuo (eds). *Sekai no Rekishi* [World History]. Tokyo: Yamakawa Shuppansha, 1973.

Wang, Q. Edward. 'Between Myth and History', in Stefan Berger (ed.), *Writing the Nation: A Global Perspective* (Basingstoke: Palgrave Macmillan, 2012), 126–54.

White, Hayden. 'The Politics of Historical Interpretation'. *Critical Inquiry* 9(2) (1982), 113–38.

———. *Tropics of Discourse: Essays in Cultural Criticism*. Baltimore, MD: Johns Hopkins University Press, 1978.

Yamanouchi, Yasushi, Julian Victor Koschmann and Narita Ryuichi (eds). *Total War and 'Modernization'*. Ithaca, NY: Cornell University East Asia Program, 1999.

CHAPTER 8

Historical Maps as Narratives

Anchoring the Nation in History Textbooks

Everardo Perez-Manjarrez and Mario Carretero

In this chapter we analyse the relations between historical maps included in textbooks and the narrative constructions of the past. The historical map is a contemporary pedagogical device that depicts the configuration of territory through human action, but, most importantly, it explains historical phenomena led by connections of causality and historical context.[1] In this sense, this type of map provides a comprehensive historical account of key historical issues for a particular social context. This suggests that the historical map represents national territory while at the same time recreating national master narrative. This topic has been little studied in history education, which requires understanding of master narratives' structure and functioning. Thus, we present a case analysis of the subject based on Carretero's theoretical model of national master narratives in history education.[2]

Ultimately, we also aim to contribute to enhancing the knowledge of historical space as a key concept of history education. The spatial dimension is essential for historical thinking, and a cornerstone in people's explanation of history. Fixed spatial notions of where the events take place underpin the construction of historiographical knowledge and national historical narratives, as well as the personal storytelling of the past.[3] Training students and citizens to better understand historical maps may help them to develop a deeper and more nuanced understanding of history. Our contribution is based on research advances into the psychology of history education, but we firmly

---

Notes for this section begin on page 182.

defend the need for interdisciplinary collaboration to fully understand how people make sense of their surroundings by using representations of the past.[4]

Historical Narratives and How Societies Account for Their Pasts

The interest in narrative as an object and method of research is fairly recent.[5] Yet, narrative inquiry has become highly influential and is now a major point of reference for researchers in many disciplines.[6] Originally, the use and study of narratives was limited to the humanities and history, as an intellectual account of fiction and as an academic explanation of human historical development respectively.[7] However, late in the twentieth century, the situation changed and social sciences in general turned the attention towards narrative as a meaningful way to understand human development, human construction of knowledge and the mental processing of experience.[8] Today, narrative is recognized as one of the most effective mechanisms that societies use to account for their past, present and environment.[9]

Several scholars across disciplines agree that narrative 'permits a holistic approach ... that preserves context and particularity ... yields information that may not be available by other methods ... and provides access to subjective experience, providing insights into conceptions of self and identity, memory, language and thought, socialization and culture'.[10] In this sense, narrative research has enabled examination of social organization and cultural worldviews in general, as well as personal and social identity construction.[11] Temporality has been a central dimension in narrative studies. These have drawn special attention to the temporal relations in narrative construction, and have recently incorporated more dynamic approaches to time in narrative to provide broader understanding of social structures, interaction and self-identity construction.[12] Surprisingly, studies on the relation between temporal and spatial dimensions,[13] and the role of space in narrative in general, are scant, though it is relevant in social understanding and personal development.[14]

Psychological research has made significant contributions to narrative theory and methodology.[15] Psychologists in general acknowledge that narrative is a key instrument to understand personal and social cognitive development. It is defined as the primary human interface with reality, and is the most effective way for people to mediate their experiences with the environment.[16] Narrative allows people to successfully appropriate and make sense of social structures, and serves as a frame for self-understanding in the social world.[17] Ultimately, by using narratives, individuals experience a sense of agency in representing themselves and their surroundings.[18]

Correspondingly, sociocultural psychology studies have shown that narrative, as a cultural tool,[19] provides people with a global explanation of their social world by integrating their history, identity and culture. In this sense, a cultural master narrative condenses the vital events significant for a particular group, occurring in meaningful historical locations and driven by relevant historical characters.[20] In turn, it has also been found that the historical master narrative excels among different sociocultural accounts in enabling not only understanding but mutual recognition and belonging among people sharing a given territory.[21] National historical narratives are very successful in instilling the sense of national identity among people,[22] attached to idealized notions of national past and land where the so-called founding fathers and they grew up, sharing customs and traditions.

Likewise, social and political psychology research has pointed out that national master narratives are driven by a notion of identity grounded in essentialism and exceptionalism. This rests on a sense of common past and ethnicity that is unique and has supposedly lasted until current times.[23] In-group cohesion is also built upon shared value systems and a sense of otherness.[24] Representation of group identity is parallel to the construction of otherness, since this allows 'the peer group to gain its own identity *ex negative*'.[25] In historical narratives, the other tends to be positioned either as a colonialist invader, or an alien force inside the country.[26] National historical narrative is then elaborated under an 'us versus them' dichotomy.[27] It provides an identity account that determines who is within the limits of the collective and who forms part of the out-group.[28] Thus, this master narrative, functioning as a country's 'official history', delineates the identity frontiers of the nation. In this venue, this official history is not neutral. It meets the interests of a given group who define these frontiers and take their historical authenticity for granted.[29]

More recently, discursive psychology has cast light on the scope and functions of narratives for interaction within social space.[30] Recent studies have found two more narrative mechanisms concerning sociopolitical interaction and spatial issues: on the one hand, master narratives shape social spaces through the practices permitted in them – that is, they condition individuals' agency by stating what is allowed in common territory.[31] For instance, a patriotic master narrative would prioritize civic rights and freedom of movement for those born on national soil, but not for those who came from other territories.[32] On the other hand, these narratives also determine what practices maintain the idea of national territory. These practices include mandatory schooling, informal education in public spaces such as museums and historical sites, emphasis on regional customs and traditions, and reproduction of historical commemorations.[33] All of the above combine to form the idea of an everlasting national territory, preserved by the practices of those who supposedly have inhabited it forever.

Finally, we think that the case of the so-called 'Spanish Reconquest' of the territory from Muslims in the fifteenth century clearly exemplifies the above characteristics of historical master narratives, and sheds light on the importance of the representation of territory to historical understanding and identity construction. Previous studies have shown that there is a widespread social assumption that the territory in dispute during that historic period previously belonged to Spain,[34] even though historiography refutes that assumption. That territory could not be claimed as Spanish because Spain did not even exist when the Muslims arrived in what is currently part of the Spanish territory: Spain only became a nation-state in the nineteenth century.[35]

However, Spanish history curricula have been keen on stressing the opposite. Elsewhere our studies have shown that there are heavy identity and emotional factors influencing students' historical narratives about the 'Reconquest'.[36] Spanish students of different ages explain this issue in the third person plural – *we reconquered our territory* – in opposition to the others – *them, the Muslims* – and emphasizing the continuity of their assumed Spanish identity and Spanish territory from that time to the present day. Even further, in recent years the historical re-enactment of the 'Reconquest' has gained popularity in Spain, serving as a mechanism to strengthen national but also regional identity, and even providing fodder for the jingoism of conservative parties claiming to defend Spanish borders from undocumented immigrants.[37]

This example, and the above-mentioned advances in narrative research, show the important role of space in narrative analysis, and more specifically, of people's ideas of territory in understanding historical developments. As this line of research is still little explored, the present chapter is an effort to cast light on the subject.

Analysing Historical Narratives

By what mechanisms do historical narratives condition people's perceptions of the past and their environment? Historical narratives are present in a wide variety of sociocultural artefacts and institutions, such as history textbooks, museums, public commemorations and social media content. These have a strong influence on the historical framework that individuals use to navigate their everyday lives.[38] In order to understand these phenomena, we may pay attention to the interconnection between production and consumption of historical narratives.[39] The production process is related to how a society, state or group creates cultural products such as textbooks, films, traditions and mainstream media content, among other things. The consumption process takes place when people use those cultural products to interact with other people and make sense of social life.

Previously, Carretero and colleagues[40] have elaborated a theoretical model for historical narratives that helps to explain the interconnected nature of these processes by focusing on historical narratives' structure and functioning, and the ways these accounts impact students' historical understanding. This model is akin to the proposal of Penuel and Wertsch (2000) about the existence of a schematic narrative template common to numerous foundational narratives, and exemplified by the United States' foundational historical narrative, or the cases of Russia, Estonia and Georgia.[41] This theoretical model also has affinities with the aesthetic dramaturgical model delineated by Fulda, in which the narration of history is underpinned by fixed plots and characters' intentions. Therefore, the examination of historical narratives requires a closer look at the 'emplotment' and the multiple layers embedded in them.[42] The model we present aims to deepen the analysis of these mutual concerns, endowing a set of features key to the definition, operation and effectiveness of historical narratives. These features consider both patterns of sociocultural production and the reception of historical narratives, similar to what Fulda refers to as the approach to history based on cognitive macro-schema and sub-schemata.[43]

According to Carretero and colleagues' findings in extensive research conducted in Spanish-speaking countries,[44] historical narratives are structured on the basis of six core features: (a) a unifying main historical subject; (b) a monocausal and teleological historical plot; (c) an essentialist concept of the nation; (d) a heroic status of historical characters; (e) collective identification processes; and (f) a narrative moral anchoring. During the data processing of this study, we found that four of these six core features, (a) (b) (c) and (d), were suitable to analyse the history textbooks' historical maps. Thus, below we delve into the characteristics of these four features.

(a) A Unifying Main Historical Subject

In historical narratives, the nation is typically established as the main historical subject, pre-existent to and ubiquitous throughout history. It is contradictorily ahistorical, not seen as determined by any context or changes across time but rather by an omnipresent character, immune to historical transformation; for instance, in the above-mentioned example of the Reconquest, Spain is supposed to have always existed. Thus, the nation as a historical subject is essentialist, imagined as if its territorial boundaries have existed from the dawn of time until the present. The historical subject is also homogeneous. The nation means the 'people', the different social groups, ethnicities and minorities integrated as one single body. We have found these characteristics in previous studies. Historical narratives from students of different ages in Spain, Argentina and Chile mainly show that the nation takes centre stage as the main historical subject. Its existence is taken for granted and is represented as a homogeneous body integrating 'all' its inhabitants – for example, Argentina as all the Argentineans – instead of considering a diverse range of social and political groups shaping the country's identity.[45]

(b) A Monocausal and Teleological Historical Plot

Historical narratives are usually articulated by schematic narrative templates,[46] such as the search for freedom or defence of territory.[47] These types of plots are mostly straightforward and guided by monocausal explanations, opposite to multicausality as in the case of historiography. A teleological notion of history underlies monocausal plots. The existence of a natural territory eternally belonging to the nation is a pre-established outcome of the historical process, instead of considering the configuration of national territories as the result of complex political, social and historical processes. Needless to say, this historical territory is precisely the same as the present national territory. For example, we have found in our studies that when Spanish students were asked to make historical sketches of how the Iberian Peninsula was centuries back, they tend to draw the current national territories of Spain and Portugal as if these were the natural frontiers of two countries that simply did not exist at that time.[48]

(c) An Essentialist Concept of the Nation

As explained in the first feature, the concept of the nation in historical narratives is conveyed as an entity that predates any historical process, even those that led to its formation. Along with this feature is identity – a sense of belonging that is equally eternal and essentialist. Our empirical studies show that historical concepts (e.g. nation, revolution and independence) are expressed within the framework of the general structures provided by master narratives. Adolescents use a concept to construct a narrative and, at the same time, that narrative expresses the concept itself. Therefore, concepts play a double role in historical narratives. On one level of analysis, they are tools for building narratives, giving them meaning and direction. At the same time, the characteristics of the concepts are defined through the narratives, which contextualize and particularize them.[49] In other words, from a disciplinary point of view, historical concepts are abstract and open entities, but when they are part of master narratives they become concrete and essentialist.

(d) A Heroic Status of Historical Characters

Historical master narratives offer key events as well as role models for people to identify with.[50] Historical characters symbolically enable individuals to recognize themselves in a collective imaginary, the national identity, and to take up specific positions, and the set of values inherent to the actions and stances of those historical characters.[51] Characters are usually located in the storyline in terms of their agency, and are positioned with the attendant rights and values; some studies' results show how historical narratives position historical actors on the basis of their actions (i.e. making them those of victims, heroes or aggressors), and attribute to them the entitlements inherent to these positions.[52] National heroes tend to appear in history textbooks and students' narratives as individuals who had an a priori historical project, rather than as human beings in the context of complex social and political settings. Thus, historical figures such as Columbus and El Cid (circa 1048–1099) in Spain and José de San Martin (1778–1850) in Argentina are presented in history textbooks and represented by students as heroes having a far-reaching project, which really does not correspond with their actions.[53]

Historical Maps as Narratives: What Does the Map Say Per Se?

Prior studies demonstrate that history education, as any other subject in school, has implicit and explicit narratives to convey mainstream social and educational goals.[54] There is prescribed content presented to students in the classrooms, but there are tacit moral and ideological narratives that underlie this content and permeate youth learning. The textbook, as the main official learning resource in history education, exemplifies his. It successfully disseminates mandatory school history as well as the national master narrative and the implicit symbolism inherent to it that pertains to class, ethnicity and culture, to mention a few.[55] Supporting resources in history textbooks, such as timelines and maps, help students to better understand historical content, and pass on both explicit and implicit narratives. The role and value of these supporting resources have not gone unnoticed among history education scholars; there are interesting efforts analysing the advances of teaching history by using chronological friezes and images.[56] Yet, there is scant research to date, particularly on the subject of historical space learning.[57]

Our studies on this[58] suggest that historical maps play an important role in the configuration and development of students' historical understanding. The historical map is a spatial representation of the past, made in the present for educational purposes: it aims to provide a clear broad picture of history.[59]

Historical maps mainly indicate political ownership and distribution of territories, but more importantly, these types of maps give a sense of historical events by interlacing notions of space, time, change and continuity, as well as socio-economic and political factors relevant to fostering people's historical understanding.[60] The historical map embodies the country, its characteristics, history, identity and the prospects of the social groups inhabiting it. Even though in some countries historical maps in schoolbooks are very similar to atlases, historic maps or early world maps, there are important differences: atlas depictions focus on the nature and forms of territories, the general geographic landscape and its configuration by human action, whereas the historic map depicts events that reflect the geographic landscape at some specific time past, having significance to the time and place they portray; that is, while they served in their time, now they are historical sources by themselves.[61]

In our view, historical maps constitute narratives per se. They establish causality, elaborate specific themes, depict main historical characters and represent different historical temporalities to provide general historical explanations. By analysing the historical maps, we seek to show how they unfold the implicit historical master narrative within history textbooks. In this sense, as our previous studies suggest, we can hypothesize that this type of historical maps reproduce a historical narrative based on an essentialist notion of the nation.[62] In order to confirm this assumption, herein we present the case study of the historical maps in Mexican history textbooks. We analyse the narrative structure of historical maps, using the four characteristics of historical narratives presented above: (a) a unifying main historical subject; (b) a monocausal and teleological historical plot; (c) an essentialist concept of the nation; and (d) a heroic status of historical characters. This analysis allowed identification of the historical maps' types, characteristics and sequences that delineate per se a particular historical narrative. Also, this analysis shed light on the ways in which these maps transmit a master narrative of the nation through their own components.

The empirical data we use derives from an ongoing research on history textbooks and students' historical representations in Latin America. Herein we present the analysis of two Mexican history textbooks – the ones for the fourth and fifth grades – both designed and distributed in 2016[63] by the Mexican Public Education Secretary. They cover the full mandatory history course in Mexican primary school for students from 9 to 11 years old. Their design follows the official guidelines stipulated by the Mexican government regarding the historical content mandatory for all primary schools in the country. It is worth noting that the Mexican government provides these history textbooks free to primary school students and history teachers, and that their use is compulsory in public schools.[64] These textbooks offer a great number of historical maps in contrast to other textbooks we have analysed in previous comparative studies between Mexico and Spain.[65]

(a) Representation of Historical Maps and the Main Historical Subject

Historical maps in history textbooks are the graphic expression of the historical content presented throughout the manual. They depict the territory at every stage of a country's history. However, the historical evolution of territory is usually taken for granted. As can be seen in Mexican history textbooks, there is a recurrent mechanism by which historical perception of the territory remains static, as conditioned by the iterative emphasis of modern national territory. This is the recurrent overlapping of the present-day map of the country over the rest of the other époques' historical maps. For instance, as can be seen in Figure 8.1, three different historical maps accounting for different historical moments – The three cultural areas of 'Ancient Mexico', Areas of Mesoamerica and the Main Indigenous and African Rebellions in the New Spain during the New Spain Viceroyalty, 1523–1761 – are elaborated under the current political and territorial distribution of Mexico.

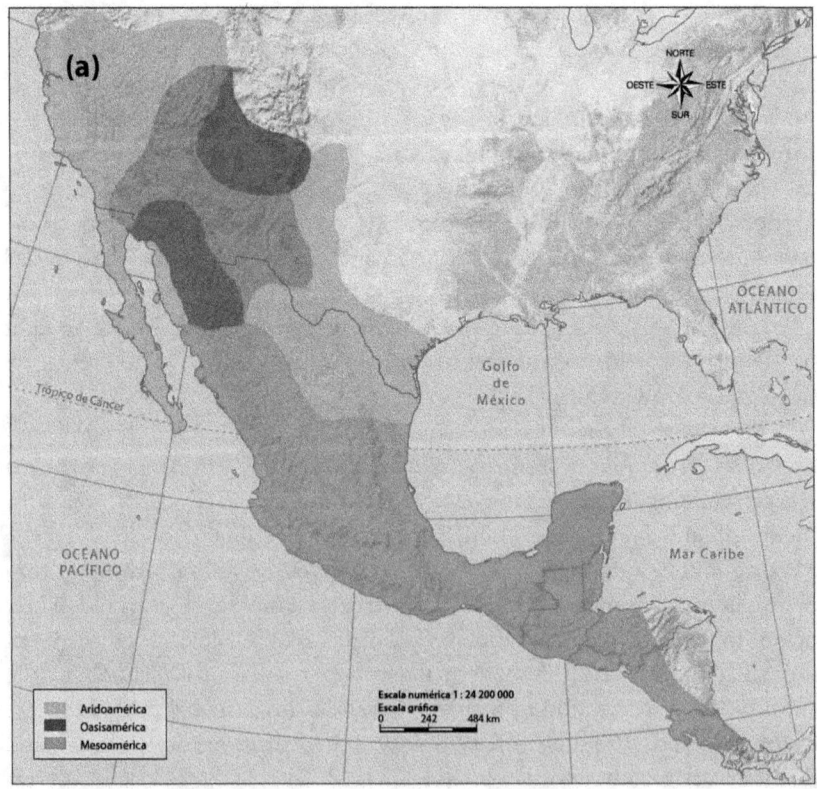

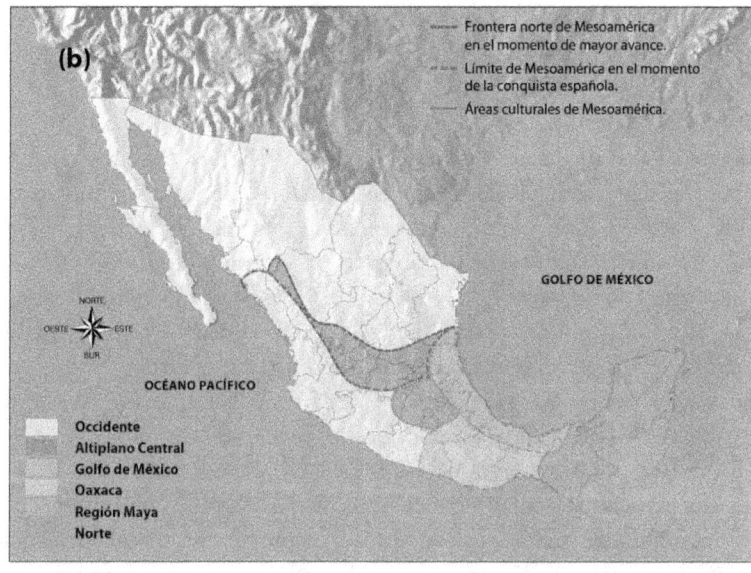

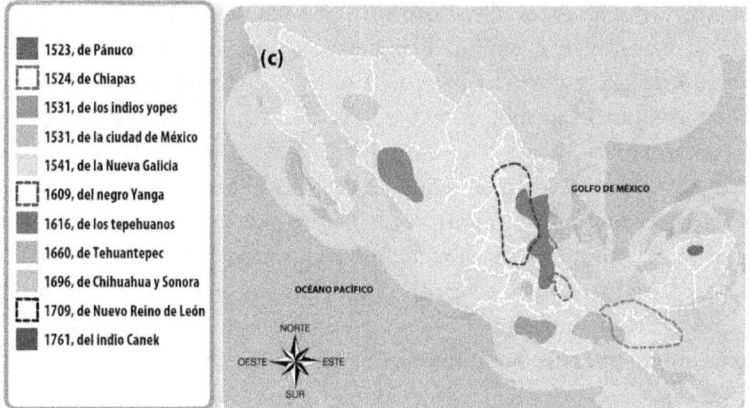

Figures 8.1a–c Historical maps of Mexico sketched under contemporary demarcation: (a) The three cultural areas of 'Ancient Mexico', (b) Areas of Mesoamerica and (c) Main Indigenous and African rebellions in the New Spain.

Figure 8.1b Legend bottom left: West; Central highlands; Gulf of Mexico; Oaxaca; Maya Region; North
Legend top right: 1. Northern border of Mesoamerica at the time of its greatest progress, 2. Limit of Mesoamerica at the time of the Spanish Conquest, 3. Cultural areas of Mesoamerica

Figure 8.1c Legend (the dates refer to rebellions): 1523, Pánuco rebellion; 1524, Chiapas rebellion; 1531, Yopes indian rebellion; 1531, Mexico City Rebellion; 1541, New Galicia rebellion; 1609, Yanga blacks rebellion; 1616, Tepehuanos Indian rebellion; 1660, Tehuantepec rebellion; 1696, Chihuahua and Sonora rebellions; 1709, New reign of Leon rebellion; 1761, Rebellion of the Indian Canek

This overlapping makes possible two interesting discursive mechanisms: the merging of past and present, and the continuity of an imagined historical subject. First, as seen in Figure 8.1, the description and distribution of millennia-old cultures' territory, such as the Mexicas or Mayans, relies on the external and internal boundaries of current Mexico. Similarly, description of the main indigenous and African revolts during the viceroyalty of the New Spain is elaborated under the demarcation of the current Mexican map. These maps' temporalities range from from 6,000 BC, 2,500 BC, and the sixteenth century to seventeenth century. However, as all these maps are grounded in the contemporary political division of Mexico, there is a sense of merging all these territorial temporalities into one as if there was a lack of distinction between past and present. It is worth noting that this overlapping is not explicitly indicated in the caption of the maps. Therefore, the students cannot distinguish how the historical map pretends to be a description of the past using present boundaries for didactic purposes at the same time.

Secondly, the juxtaposition of the maps of the so-called 'Ancient Mexico', Mesoamerica, New Spain and present-day Mexico foster a sense of ubiquity to the historical subject. In all the historical periods to which the historical maps refer, Mexico has not existed yet. However, the demarcation of present-day territory in those maps gives the sense of continuity of Mexico as a historical subject throughout all its history – ancient, colonial and contemporary. Mexico is embodied in the modern nation's frontiers, despite the fact that cultural boundaries have changed from 2,500 BC to the seventeenth century, along with demographic changes and dynamic flux of arrival and erosion of different civilizations. In sum, the Mexican nation appears as a constant historical subject, omnipresent, and the national territory is taken for granted as it is presented as a continuous space that, despite the interventions and transformations, it has historically remained in its essence.

(b) Military Control of the Territory as the Main Historical Plot of Historical Maps

As can be seen in Table 8.1, there are twenty-three historical maps altogether in the two history textbooks, covering the full history course for primary school in Mexico, from the settlements of the Americas to the beginning of the twenty-first century. It calls attention to the fact that the most commonly used historical maps are military and political, eight and seven respectively (see Table 8.1). Accordingly, the great majority of historical maps follow a specific narrative sequence of struggle for, colonization of, and control of the territory. They underscore the main historical events concerning the conquest and invasion of the 'Mexican territory' by foreign powers (either the Hispanic monarchy, the United States of America, or France), as well as the liberation battles from those external forces, and the internal struggles

Table 8.1 Historical maps distribution by frequency, topic and temporality.

Module	Historical Maps per Module	Title	Topic	Temporality (Century)
1. Settlement of the Americas and the Dawn of Agriculture	2	The Three Cultural Areas of Ancient Mexico	Culture	6000 BC – I
		Routes of Settlement of the Americas	Geography	6000 BC – I
2. Mesoamerica	2	The Areas of Mesoamerica	Geography	2500 BC –
		Main Mayan Ceremonial Sites	Culture	XV
3. The Encounter between America and Europe	5	The Four Voyages of Christopher Columbus to America	Trade	XVI
		Spanish Expeditions	Military	XVI
		Trade Routes from Asia to Europe and Main Trade Products	Trade	XVI
		Hernan Cortes' Routes to Tenochtitlan Capital City	Military	XVI
		Spanish Expansionism and Foundation of Cities (1519–1578)	Military	XVI
		New Spain's Territorial Division by Realms during the XVII Century	Politics	XVII
4. The Viceroyalty of New Spain	4	New Spain's Territorial Expansion between XVI and XIX Centuries	Politics	XVI–XIX
		Economic Regions, Main Commercial Ports and Merchandise Traded at the End of XVIII Century	Trade	XVIII
		Main Indigenous and African Rebellions in New Spain	Politics	XVI–XIX
5. The Path to Independence	2	Miguel Hidalgo's Route of Independence	Military	XIX
		Insurgent Campaigns (1810–1821)	Military	XIX

Table 8.1 (continued)

Module	Historical Maps per Module	Title	Topic	Temporality (Century)
6. The First Years of Independence	3	The First (Mexican) Empire (1823)	Politics	XIX
		First Political Territorial Administration of Independent Mexico (1824)	Politics	XIX
7. Reformism and Restored Republic	1	Mexico's Territory Losses (1846–1848)	Military	XIX
		Reform War (1858–1860)	Military	XIX
8. The Porfiriato Era and the Mexican Revolution	2	Mexican Revolution (1910–1920)	Military	XX
		Railway Network in 1910	Trade	XX
9. Warlords and the National Institutions (1920–1982)	1	Rural and Urban Populations in Mexico (1930–1980)	Politics	XX
10. Mexico at the Turn of the XX Century, and the Edge of the XXI Century	1	Migratory Flows Estimated by Regions (2010)	Politics	XXI

that configured the nation – nineteenth-century civil wars and the Mexican Revolution. This in turn delineates a characterization of the territory in terms of warfare: routes of siege, war campaigns, land colonization and control, liberation battles, and political and economic expansion networks.

The above characterization suggests two conclusions. Firstly, that territory is not historically conditioned by different sociocultural interplays, migration cycles, or any human interaction but primarily through war. The great majority of historical maps discursively present the national territory as a battleground – a space where conquest, colonization and liberation are at stake. Thus, historical maps' implicit plot is simplified to a monocausal sequence of battles unfolding in a teleological sense towards an anticipated end. Secondly, in the above respect, that within this war-oriented characterization of historical maps underlies an ongoing nation-building narrative. The sequence of historical maps speaks, implicitly or explicitly, of the Mexican nation's traumas, configuration and successes. In this sense, the historical maps are oriented towards one common narrative theme, the origins of the Mexican nation.

(c) Historical Maps' Temporality and the Essentialist Concept of the Nation

In history textbooks, promoting understanding of the interdependence between space and time is fundamental for young learners' historical understanding development. Throughout these Mexican manuals, historical maps are presented along with timelines that provide contextual support to make sense of the territory. What calls for attention is that, without the anchor that the timelines and historical contents provide, historical maps speak of a delimited temporality that in turn underlies a specific historical narrative. The two historical topics with the majority of historical maps are European colonialism and the independence of New Spain (current Mexico). As seen in Table 8.1, more than half of historical maps (fourteen out of twenty-three) are devoted to explaining these two topics. Nine historical maps illustrate the Conquistadors' arrival in and the colonization of Mesoamerica, while five are used to depict the origins of the Mexican nation-state.

The majority of historical maps in Mexican history textbooks emphasize two historical periods: the sixteenth to eighteenth centuries, and the nineteenth century (see Table 8.1). The maps describing the sixteenth to eighteenth centuries illustrate the expansionism of the Hispanic monarchy in the Americas, and subsequent colonialism. They mainly highlight the leading role and influence of 'Europe' in the configuration of current Mexican territory. The nineteenth-century historical maps refer to the birth of Mexico as an independent nation. They extol New Spain's military campaigns of independence from the Hispanic monarchy, and most importantly, the political and war configurations of the Mexican nation-state.

The emphasis given by the historical maps to these two periods suggests a specific intentionality: the reinforcement of the nation's origins by the depiction of the spatial construction of the national territory. These maps describe the foundational events of Mexico as a nation. Together they delineate a narrative of the European and liberal construction of the Mexican nation-state, based on the configuration of colonial territory that resulted from European colonization, which eventually represents the grounds of the subsequent land demarcation of Mexico as an emergent independent nation-state. It is not the sociocultural land delimitation of the indigenous peoples that is taken as a basis of the Mexican national territory, but the spatial demarcation resulting from the conquest and colonization of the Hispanic monarchy.

(d) The Historical Maps' Main Characters and the Status of National Historical Heroes

Although history textbooks and history education narratives do not expressly set it out, there is relevant research showing that the territory is mostly determined by people's interactions and culture development in a broad sense.[66] Over time, the territory changes or endures its frontiers as a result of collective and individual agency. Yet, in general, collective and individual agency is taken for granted in teaching historical maps, underestimated or even overestimated in its influence, as in the case of the actions of exceptional individuals over collective action. In regard to the above, the present analysis shows a very interesting finding: the implicit construction of the heroic and exemplary status of certain historical characters in historical maps. In Mexican history textbooks, the historical maps highlight the agency of individuals portrayed as 'discoverers', 'conquistadors' or 'founding fathers'. As seen in Table 8.1, there are maps of the voyages of Columbus to reach 'the Americas', the Spanish expeditions, the routes of Hernan Cortes to get to Tenochtitlan, the capital city of the Mexica (Aztec) hegemony, and the campaign for independence of Miguel Hidalgo (1753–1811), the so-called founding father of Mexico.

This depiction of people's agency gives the idea that the territory has been configured by the military and strategic prowess of 'heroes' – exceptional people with admirable and patriotic values who wanted to change the course of their country's history. However, we can call three aspects into question with regard to the relationship between historical maps and historical characters' agency. The characterization of these historical agents is based on labels assigned after their actions took place. Miguel Hidalgo did not design a 'Route of Independence', conceiving himself as a liberator or founding father of the Mexican nation; and nor did Christopher Columbus plan routes to reach 'America', actually perceiving himself more as an entrepreneur than a 'discoverer'. These are labels that traditional Western historiography has created to build a master narrative,[67] and they are transmitted implicitly in historical maps.

In the second place, there is the issue of the overstatement and misinterpretation of historical characters' intentionality. While it is true that the actions of these historical agents had a strong impact on Europe, the Americas, and particularly on Mexico, the intentionality of these historical characters cannot be assumed as self-evident. Historical maps appear as confirmation of these presumed deliberate intentions. For instance, the map entitled 'The Four Voyages of Christopher Columbus to America' illustrates facts as deliberated. In other words, the map is indicating that Columbus already knew where he was heading to and for what purposes. Yet, historiography has demonstrated that those routes, and that map, were post facto products, as Columbus did not have a route plan and was not even aware of the existence of the 'Americas'. As a matter of fact, the first map including part of the 'new continent's' lands and also using the name of America in honour of Americo Vespuccio was elaborated by the cartographer Martin Waldseemüller (1470–1520) in 1507, more than ten years later than Columbus's voyages. Mexican history textbooks indeed overlook this clarification, as indeed happens in many Latin American countries.[68]

Finally, the stress on these exceptional historical characters overshadows collective groups' agency. In opposition to the great figures, there are few references to collective groups and people's practices and customs, such as those related to the map about the main Mayan ceremonial sites, or even less about collective agency such as indigenous and African rebellions during the colonial era. History textbooks' maps give little description of the territory that indigenous peoples occupied before the arrival of Europeans, and without any reference to social organization. Actually, the inclusion of historical maps referring to indigenous religious practices and rebellions suggests the reinforcement of a particular representation of indigenous cultures characterized by a lack of agency and rationality. As we have found in previous studies,[69] narratives about indigenous peoples describe their passiveness and highlight their idolatry and savagery as evidence of backwardness and absence of reasoning, in opposition to the Europeans' technological progress and civility equated to agency, which is similar to the comparison between historical maps about Europeans and indigenous peoples.

Conclusions

This chapter has shown the narrative configuration of historical maps in history textbooks. Using four categories of Mario Carretero's theoretical model of historical narratives,[70] we have analysed the different components of the historical map that make it a narrative per se. Also, by these components, it has been demonstrated that historical maps anchor the master narrative of the nation in history textbooks. The findings show that the Mexican nation is presented as the main subject throughout the historical maps, constant and ahistorical, by the juxtaposition of all maps with the contemporary national territorial demarcation. This mechanism blends time, past and present, and gives a sense of everlasting presence to the Mexican nation. Furthermore, it is not a minor issue that the map labelling, such as 'Ancient Mexico' referring to a cultural distribution of indigenous peoples before the Conquistadors' arrival and the origin of Mexico, strengthens the idea of an essentialist nation. These types of labels also seem to be useful to foster identification and emotional attachment to a distant past; our findings cannot verify this, though it would be interesting to conduct research on this assumption.

The idea of an essentialist nation is also reinforced by the temporal sequence of historical maps, which progressively presents the foundational events that led to its origins. The depiction of historical maps and historical characters is also noteworthy in terms of how the territory is conveyed. The different references to the territory as a battleground, the boundaries and historical events sketched in terms of warfare, along with exceptional (military) actors winning battles and conquering territories, strengthen a monocausal plot of confrontations, whose resolution ultimately results with the conformation of the nation. This resolution is not incidental, as the historical characters, presented in historical maps as exceptional and visionary, had supposedly the intention to achieve specific goals. This has important implications for national identity construction, in the sense that the above reinforces belonging, collective imaginary, and the shared system of values represented in their actions.[71]

Thus, the full analysis showed that the historical map's narrative is grounded in warfare concepts and monocausal temporality, driven by exceptional characters and heroic national figures, which all together configurated the nation. It is worth highlighting that, implicitly, colonialism plays a significant role in the configuration of the nation and the national territory. As we observed in previous studies,[72] our findings have led us to think that there is a narrative construction of territory based on the overlap of two main concepts: colonialism and the nation. Mexico's history and territory begins with the discovery and control of native lands by Europeans, as sixteenth- to eighteenth-century maps evince. Further on, the so-called 'Mexicans' reclaimed these lands, and a patriotic sequence of events unfolds through maps: liberation, defence and consolidation of the national territory, and therefore the nation. In such a way, the emphasis of historical maps in these historical époques supports the narrative of the nation and implies that the origins of Mexico and its territory relies on the colonial boundaries. How do these two concepts coexist in the narrative construction of the national territory? This is a relevant question not only for the case of Mexico, but is also pertinent for historical narratives of former colonized countries.

A similar situation occurs with regard to the relationship between historical narratives and agency. It shows that any reference in maps to particular characters, such as heroes, that correspondingly omits other historical and social groups, implicitly relates to causality models and entitlements. How agency is ascribed through narratives, and in this case in historical maps, is an interesting question to explore in the future. Also, this situation is not neutral, but nor is it an exception. Representations of the territory involves silencing other voices and scenarios. As we found in previous studies,[73] indigenous people and other minorities are excluded from the nation-building narrative, as they are in this case from the demarcation of territories. Furthermore, as seen in analysis of conventional historical narratives,[74] social, cultural, anthropological and economic factors are left aside in the configuration of territory. All this might be a call to reflect: for example, do we still want to teach about historical space only as a sequence of battles, and pledges of allegiance to military prowess? Are we willing to keep teaching history in the prevailing language of warfare and nationalism? The teaching of historical space is key in the development of people's historical understanding, and it demands a more complex notion of territory and the past in general.

Ultimately, findings demonstrate that the representation of territory plays an essential role in consolidating the national master narrative: it is the concrete representation of its history, and the physical evidence of its historical configuration and evolution, as well as of the identity, culture and social organization of the collective. Nevertheless, the different ways that people construct the territory and territorial representations have not been much studied, let alone incorporated in education. In this sense, psychological studies could draw much benefit from a fruitful interaction with other social sciences, and with historiographical studies in particular. The seminal idea of Anderson about the nation as an imagined community[75] could be conceptually rephrased as the need to fully understand how this 'imagination' is really taking place in psychological and social terms.[76] Further research is needed on all these issues, and it is hoped that the present chapter will promote discussion around them.

Everardo Perez-Manjarrez is a visiting scholar at the Harvard Graduate School of Education, USA. He investigates the intersections between citizenship and history in adolescents' learning of social sciences. Some of his latest publications are 'Facing History: Positioning and Identity Negotiation in Adolescents' Narratives of Controversial History' (2019, *Qualitative Psychology*); '"Pragmatic, Complacent, Critical-Cynical or Empathetic?": Youth Social Scrutiny and Civic Engagement' (in press, *Teachers College Records*); and *Historical Re-enactment: New Ways of Experiencing History* (Berghahn Books, forthcoming, co-edited with M. Carretero and B. Wagoner).

Mario Carretero is professor at Autónoma University of Madrid, where he was dean of the Faculty of Psychology, and researcher at FLACSO (Argentina). He has carried out extensive research on history education. Some of his publications are *History Education and the Construction of National Identities* (2012, co-edited with M. Asensio and M. Rodriguez-Moneo); *Constructing Patriotism* (2011, funded by the Guggenheim Foundation); *Palgrave Handbook of Research in Historical Culture and Education* (2017, co-edited with S. Berger and M. Grever); and *Historical Re-enactment: New Ways of Experiencing History* (Berghahn Books, forthcoming, co-edited with B. Wagoner and E. Perez-Manjarrez).

Notes

This chapter was made possible by the contribution of Projects RTI-2018-096495-b-I00 (MINECO-FEDER) from Spain, PICT-2016-2341 from ANPCYT (Argentina) and a research grant from the National Council on Science and Technology of Mexico (CONACYT), Mexico, awarded to the first author.

 1. Carretero, 'How to Teach Trump's Wall?'; Dym and Offen, 'Maps'.
 2. Carretero, 'Teaching History Master Narratives'; Carretero and Bermúdez, 'Constructing Histories'.
 3. Berger, 'History Writing'; Carretero, 'How to Teach Trump's Wall?'
 4. Carretero, Berger and Grever, 'Introduction'.
 5. Brockmeier and Harré, 'Narrative'; De Fina and Georgakopoulou, *Handbook of Narrative Analysis*; Hammack and Pilecki, 'Methodological Approaches'.
 6. Bamberg, 'Narrative, Discourse and Identities'; Garro and Mattingly, 'Narrative as Construct'.
 7. Bamberg, 'Narrative Analysis'; Fulda, 'Historiographic Narration'.
 8. Smith, 'Content Analysis'.
 9. Bruner, 'Life as Narrative'; De Fina and Georgakopoulou, *Handbook of Narrative Analysis*.
 10. Smith, 'Content Analysis', 327–28.
 11. De Fina and Georgakopoulou, *Handbook of Narrative Analysis*.
 12. Zerubavel, *Time Maps*.
 13. Lucić and Bridges, 'Ecological Landscape'.
 14. Wright, 'Evaluating Place'.

15. Bamberg, 'Why Narrative'; Fulda, 'Historiographic Narration'.
16. Andrews, Squire and Tamboukou, *Doing Narrative Research*; Rudrum, 'From Narrative Constitution'.
17. Bamberg, 'Narrative Analysis'; Somers, 'Narrative Constitution of Identity'.
18. Somers and Gibson, 'Reclaiming the Epistemological Other'.
19. Wertsch, 'National Memory'.
20. Carretero and van Alphen, 'Do Master Narratives Change'.
21. Carretero, *Constructing Patriotism*.
22. Billig, *Banal Nationalism*; Wertsch, 'Narratives as Cultural Tools'.
23. Carretero, *Constructing Patriotism*; Liu et al., 'Social Representations'.
24. Hammack, *Narrative and the Politics of Identity*.
25. Deppermann, 'Using the Other', 273.
26. Perez-Manjarrez and González, 'Who is Entitled to Be Citizen?'.
27. Carretero and Bermúdez, 'Constructing Histories'.
28. Hilton and Liu, 'Culture and Intergroup Relations'.
29. Wertsch, *Voices of Collective Remembering*.
30. Abell, Stokoe and Billig, 'Narrative and the Discursive (Re)Construction'; Edwards, 'Discursive Psychology'; Potter and Edwards, 'Social Representations'.
31. Bamberg, 'Narrative, Discourse and Identities'; Haste, 'Culture, Tools and Subjectivity'; Hammack and Pilecki, 'Methodological Approaches'.
32. Hilton and Liu, 'How the Past Weighs on the Present'.
33. Carretero, Asensio and Rodríguez-Moneo, *History Education*; McCalman and Pickering, *Historical Re-enactment*.
34. Carretero, van Alphen and Parellada, 'National Identities'.
35. Álvarez-Junco, *Spanish Identity*.
36. Lopez, Carretero and Rodríguez-Moneo, 'Conquest or Reconquest?'
37. Carretero, 'Reconquest'.
38. Berger, Eriksonas and Mycock, *Narrating the Nation*.
39. Carretero and Lopez, 'Narrative Mediation'.
40. Carretero, 'Teaching History Master Narratives'; Carretero and Bermúdez, 'Constructing Histories'.
41. Sulviste and Wertsch, 'Official and Unofficial Histories'; Wertsch and Karumdze, 'Spinning the Past'; Wertsch, *Voices of Collective Remembering*.
42. Fulda, 'Historiographic Narration'.
43. Ibid.
44. Carretero, Asensio and Rodríguez-Moneo, *History Education*; Lopez, Carretero and Rodríguez-Moneo, 'Conquest or Reconquest?'
45. Carretero and van Alphen, 'Do Master Narratives Change'.
46. Wertsch, 'National Memory'.
47. Barton and Levstik, *Teaching History*.
48. Lopez, Carretero and Rodríguez-Moneo, 'Conquest or Reconquest?'; Carretero, van Alphen and Parellada, 'National Identities'.
49. Carretero and Lee, 'History Learning'.
50. Barton and Levstik, *Teaching History*.
51. Perez-Manjarrez, 'Facing History'.
52. Barton and Levstik, *Teaching History*; Carretero, *Constructing Patriotism*.
53. Carretero, Jacott and López-Manjón, 'Learning History'; Lopez, Carretero and Rodríguez-Moneo, 'Conquest or Reconquest?'; Carretero and van Alphen, 'Do Master Narratives Change'.
54. Banks and McGee Banks, *Multicultural Education*; Barton and Levstik, *Teaching History*.

55. Alridge, 'Limits of Master Narratives'; Epstein, *Interpreting National History*; Foster and Crawford, *What Shall We Tell the Children?*
56. Carretero and Lopez, 'Narrative Mediation'; Zerubavel, *Time Maps*.
57. Kosonen, 'Making Maps'.
58. Carretero, 'How to Teach Trump's Wall?'; Carretero, van Alphen and Parellada, 'National Identities'; Parellada, Carretero and Rodriguez-Moneo, 'Historical Borders'.
59. Dym and Offen, 'Maps'.
60. Carretero, 'How to Teach Trump's Wall?'
61. Dym and Offen, 'Maps'.
62. Carretero, van Alphen and Parellada, 'National Identities'.
63. It is available with an open-source license through https://historico.conaliteg.gob.mx.
64. See Carretero, *Constructing Patriotism*, Chapter 2, for an extensive analysis of Mexican history textbooks.
65. Carretero, Jacott and López-Manjón, 'Learning History'.
66. Levstik, 'Narrative Constructions'.
67. Zea, *América en la Conciencia*; O'Gorman, *Invention of America*.
68. Carretero, *Constructing Patriotism*.
69. Carretero and Kriger, 'Historical Representations'; Perez-Manjarrez and González, 'Who is Entitled to Be Citizen?'
70. Carretero, 'Teaching History Master Narratives'.
71. Barton and Levstik, *Teaching History*.
72. Carretero and Perez-Manjarrez, 'Historical Narratives', 7188.
73. Carretero and Kriger, 'Historical Representations'; Perez-Manjarrez and González, 'Who is Entitled to Be Citizen?'
74. Carretero, 'Teaching History Master Narratives'; Wertsch, 'National Memory'.
75. Anderson, *Imagined Communities*.
76. Carretero, 'Teaching History Master Narratives'.

Bibliography

Abell, Jackie, Elizabeth H. Stokoe and Michael Billig. 'Narrative and the Discursive (Re) Construction of Events', in Molly Andrews et al. (eds), *The Uses of Narratives: Explorations in Sociology, Psychology and Cultural Studies* (New Brunswick, NJ: Transaction Publishers, 2004), 180–92.

Anderson, B. *Imagined Communities: Reflections on the Origin and Spread of Nationalism* (revised version). London: Verso, 1983 (2006).

Alridge, Derrick P. 'The Limits of Master Narratives in History Textbooks: An Analysis of Representations of Martin Luther King, Jr'. *The Teachers College Record* 108(4) (2006), 662–86.

Álvarez-Junco, José. *Spanish Identity in the Age of Nations*. Manchester: Oxford University Press, 2011.

Andrews, Molly, Corinne Squire and Maria Tamboukou. *Doing Narrative Research*. London: Sage, 2013.

Bamberg, Michael. 'Narrative Analysis', in Harris Cooper (ed.), *APA Handbook of Research Methods in Psychology*, Vol. 2 (Washington, DC: American Psychological Association, 2012), 77–94.

———. 'Narrative, Discourse and Identities', in Jan Christoph Meister, Tom Kindt and Wilhelm Schernus (eds), *Narratology beyond Literary Criticism: Mediality, Disciplinarity* (Berlin: De Gruyter, 2005), 213–37.

——. 'Why Narrative?' *Narrative Inquiry* 22(1) (2012), 202–10.
Banks, James A., amd Cherry A. McGee Banks. *Multicultural Education: Issues and Perspectives*. Washington, DC: John Wiley & Sons, 2009.
Barton, Keith C., and Linda S. Levstik. *Teaching History for the Common Good*. Mahwah, NJ: Lawrence Erlbaum Associates Publishers, 2004.
Berger, Stefan. 'History Writing and the Constructions of National Space: The Long Dominance of the National in Modern European Historiographies', in Mario Carretero, Stefan Berger and Maria Grever (eds), *International Handbook of Research on Historical Culture and History Education* (New York: Palgrave Macmillan, 2017), 39–57.
Berger, Stefan, Lina Eriksonas and Andrew Mycock (eds). *Narrating the Nation: Representations in History, Media and the Arts*. New York: Berghahn Books, 2008.
Billig, Michael. *Banal Nationalism*. London: Sage, 1995.
Brockmeier, Jens, and Rom Harré. 'Narrative: Problems and Promises of an Alternative Paradigm', in Jens Brockmeier and Donal Carbaugh (eds), *Narrative and Identity: Studies in Autobiography, Self and Culture* (Amsterdam: John Benjamins Publishing Company, 2001), 39–58.
Bruner, Jerome. 'Life as Narrative'. *Social Research: An International Quarterly* 71(3) (2004), 691–710.
Carretero, Mario. *Constructing Patriotism: Teaching History and Memories in Global Worlds*. Charlotte, NC: Information Age Publishing, 2001.
Carretero, Mario. 'How to Teach Trump's Wall? Historical Consciousness and National Territories Representations', in Anna Clark and Carla L. Peck (eds), *Contemplating Historical Consciousness: Notes from the Field* (New York: Berghahn Books, 2019), 76–90.
Carretero, Mario. '"Reconquest" – Historical Narrative or Xenophobic View?' *Public History Weekly* 7(7) (2019): DOI: http://dx.doi.org/10.1515/phw-2019-13423.
Carretero, Mario. 'Teaching History Master Narratives: Fostering Imagi-Nations', in Mario Carretero, Stefan Berger and Maria Grever (eds), *Palgrave Handbook of Research in Historical Culture and Education* (London: Palgrave, 2017), 511–28.
Carretero, Mario, Mikel Asensio and María Rodríguez-Moneo. *History Education and the Construction of National Identities*. Charlotte, NC: Information Age Publishing, 2012.
Carretero, Mario, Stefan Berger and Maria Grever. 'Introduction: Historical Cultures and Education in Transition', in Mario Carretero, Stefan Berger and Maria Grever (eds), *International Handbook of Research on Historical Culture and History Education* (New York: Palgrave Macmillan, 2017), 1–35.
Carretero, Mario, and Angela Bermúdez. 'Constructing Histories', in Jaan Valsiner (ed.), *Oxford Handbook of Culture and Psychology* (Oxford: Oxford University Press, 2012), 625–48.
Carretero, Mario, Liliana Jacott and Asunción López-Manjón. 'Learning History through Textbooks: Are Mexican and Spanish Students Taught the Same Story?' *Learning and Instruction* 12(6) (2002), 651–55.
Carretero, Mario, and Miriam Kriger. 'Historical Representations and Conflicts about Indigenous People as National Identities'. *Culture & Psychology* 17(2) (2011), 177–95.
Carretero, Mario, and Peter Lee. 'History Learning', in Keith Sawyer (ed.), *The Cambridge Handbook of the Learning Sciences*, 2nd edn (Cambridge: Cambridge University Press, 2014), 587–604.
Carretero, Mario, and Cesar Lopez. 'The Narrative Mediation on Historical Remembering', in Sergio Salvatore et al. (eds), *Yearbook of Idiographic Science* (Rome: Firera & Liuzzo, 2011), 285–95.
Carretero, Mario, and Everardo Perez-Manjarrez. 'Historical Narratives and the Tensions between National Identities, Colonialism, and Citizenship', in Holger Thünemann, Meik

Zülsdorf-Kersting and Manuel Köster (eds), *Researching History Education: International Perspectives and Research Traditions*, 2nd edn. (Schwalbach, Germany: Wochenschau Verlag, 2019), 71–88.

Carretero, Mario, and Floor van Alphen. 'Do Master Narratives Change among High School Students? A Characterization of How National History Is Represented'. *Cognition & Instruction* 32 (2014), 1–23.

Carretero, Mario, Floor van Alphen and Cristian Parellada. 'National Identities in the Making and Alternative Pathways of History Education', in Alberto Rosa and Jaan Valsiner (eds), *The Cambridge Handbook of Sociocultural Psychology*, 2nd edn. (Cambridge: Cambridge University Press, 2018), 424–42.

De Fina, Anna, and Alexandra Georgakopoulou. *The Handbook of Narrative Analysis*. Malden, MA: John Willey & Sons, 2015.

Deppermann, Arnulf. 'Using the Other for Oneself: Conversational Practices of Representing Out-Group Members among Adolescents', in Michael Bamberg, Anna De Fina and Deborah Schiffrin (eds), *Selves and Identities in Narratives and Discourse*, 9th edn. (Amsterdam: John Benjamins Publishing Company, 2007), 273–302.

Dym, Jordana, and Karl Offen. 'Maps and the Teaching of Latin American History'. *Hispanic American Historical Review* 92(2) (2012), 213–44.

Edwards, Derek. 'Discursive Psychology', in Kristine L. Fitch and Robert E. Sanders (eds), *Handbook of Language and Social Interaction* (Mahwah, NJ: Lawrence Erlbaum Associates, 2005), 257–73.

Epstein, Terry. *Interpreting National History: Race, Identity and Pedagogy in Classrooms and Communities*. New York: Routledge, 2009.

Foster, Stuart J., and Keith A. Crawford (eds). *What Shall We Tell the Children? International Perspectives on School History Textbooks*. Greenwich, CT: Information Age Publishing, 2006.

Fulda, Daniel. 'Historiographic Narration', in Peter Hühn et al. (eds), *Handbook of Narratology* (Berlin: De Gruyter, 2014), 227–40.

Garro, Linda C., and Cheryl Mattingly. 'Narrative as Construct and Construction', in Cheryl Mattingly and Linda C. Garro (eds), *Narrative and the Cultural Construction of Illness and Healing* (Berkeley: University of California Press, 2000), 1–49.

Hammack, Philip L. *Narrative and the Politics of Identity: The Cultural Psychology of Israeli and Palestinian Youth*. New York: Oxford University Press, 2011.

Hammack, Philip L., and Andrew Pilecki. 'Methodological Approaches in Political Psychology: Discourse and Narrative', in Paul Nesbitt-Larking et al. (eds), *The Palgrave Handbook of Global Political Psychology* (New York: Palgrave Macmillan, 2014), 79–98.

Haste, Helen. 'Culture, Tools and Subjectivity: The (Re)construction of Self', in Thalia Magioglou (ed.), *Culture and Political Psychology: A Societal Perspective* (Charlotte, NC: Information Age Publishing, 2014), 27–48.

Hilton, Dennis J., and James H. Liu. 'Culture and Intergroup Relations: The Role of Social Representations of History', in Richard Sorrentino and Susuma Yamaguchi (eds), *Handbook of Motivation and Cognition across Cultures* (Amsterdam: Academic Press, 2008), 343–68.

———. 'How the Past Weighs on the Present: Social Representations of History and Their Role in Identity Politics'. *British Journal of Social Psychology* 44(4) (2005), 537–56.

Kosonen, Katariina. 'Making Maps and Mental Images: Finnish Press Cartography in Nation-Building, 1899–1942'. *National Identities* 10(1) (2008), 21–47.

Levstik, Linda S. 'Narrative Constructions: Cultural Frames for History'. *The Social Studies* 86(3) (1995), 113–16.

Liu, James H., et al. 'Social Representations of History in Malaysia and Singapore: On the Relationship between National and Ethnic Identity'. *Asian Journal of Social Psychology* 5(1) (2002), 3–20.

Lopez, Cesar, Mario Carretero and Maria Rodríguez-Moneo. 'Conquestor Reconquest? Students' Conceptions of Nation Embedded in a Historical Narrative'. *Journal of the Learning Sciences* 24(2) (2014), 252–85.

Lucić, Luca, and Elizabeth Bridges. 'Ecological Landscape in Narrative Thought'. *Narrative Inquiry* 28(2) (2018), 346–72.

McCalman, Ian, and Paul Pickering (eds). *Historical Re-enactment: From Realism to the Affective Turn*. New York: Palgrave Macmillan, 2010.

O'Gorman, Edmundo. *The Invention of America: An Inquiry into the Historical Nature of the New World and the Meaning of its History*. Mexico: FCE, 1976/2016.

Parellada, Cristian, Mario Carretero and Maria Rodriguez-Moneo. 'Historical Borders and Maps as Symbolic Supports to Master Narratives and History Education'. *Theory & Psychology. Special Issue on Borders* (2020), 1–17, DOI: pDs:O//dIo: i1.o0r.g1/107.171/0779/5093595345342302909662220.

Perez-Manjarrez, Everardo. 'Facing History: Positioning and Identity Negotiation in Adolescents' Narratives of Controversial History'. *Qualitative Psychology* 6(1) (2019), 61–77.

Perez-Manjarrez, Everardo, and Maria F. González. 'Who Is Entitled to Be Citizen? Agency and Historical Representations of Indigenous in Mexican and Argentinean Adolescents' Narratives', in Maria F. González and Alberto Rosa (eds), *Hacer(se) Ciudadanos: Una Psicología para la Democracia* (Buenos Aires: Miño y Davila, 2014), 287–326.

Penuel, W., and J. Wertsch. 'Historical Representation as Mediated Action: Official History as a Tool', in J.F. Voss and M. Carretero (eds), *Learning and Reasoning in History: International Review of History Education* (vol. 2). (New York: Routledge, 2000), 23–38.

Potter, Jonathan, and Derek Edwards. 'Social Representations and Discursive Psychology: From Cognition to Action'. *Culture & Psychology* 5(4) (1999), 447–58.

Rudrum, David. 'From Narrative Constitution to Narrative Use: Towards the Limits of Definition'. *Narrative Inquiry* 13(2) (2005), 195–204.

Smith, Charles P. 'Content Analysis and Narrative Analysis', in Harry T. Reis and Charles M. Judd (eds), *Handbook of Research Methods in Social and Personality Psychology* (New York: Cambridge University Press, 2000), 313–35.

Somers, Margarete R. 'The Narrative Constitution of Identity: A Relational and Network Approach'. *Theory and Society* 23(5) (1994), 605–49.

Somers, Margarete R., and Gloria D. Gibson. 'Reclaiming the Epistemological Other: Narrative and the Social Constitution of Identity'. CSST, Working Papers, University of Michigan, 1993.

Sulviste, Peeter, and James V. Wertsch. 'Official and Unofficial Histories: The Case of Estonia'. *Journal of Narrative & Life History* 4(4) (1994), 311–29.

Wertsch, James. V. 'Narratives as Cultural Tools in Sociocultural Analysis: Official History in Soviet and Post-Soviet Russia'. *Ethos* 28(4) (2000), 511–33.

———. 'National Memory and Where to Find It', in Brady Wagoner (ed.), *Handbook of Culture and Memory* (Oxford: Oxford University Press, 2018), 259–81.

———. *Voices of Collective Remembering*. Cambridge: Cambridge University Press, 2002.

Wertsch, James V., Zurab Karumdze. 'Spinning the Past: Russian and Georgian Accounts of the War of August 2008'. *Memory Studies* 2(3) (2009), 377–91.

Wright, Lyn. 'Evaluating Place in Orientations of Narratives of Internal Migration'. *Narrative Inquiry* 28(1) (2018), 198–214.

Zea, Leopoldo. *América en la Conciencia de Europa*. Mexico: Universidad Nacional Autónoma de México, 2015.

Zerubavel, Eviatar. *Time Maps: Collective Memory and the Social Shape of the Past*. Chicago: University of Chicago Press, 2012.

Part III

Histories in Various Media

CHAPTER 9

Social Media and Multimodal Historical Representation

Depicting Auschwitz on Instagram

ROBBERT-JAN ADRIAANSEN

As people increasingly spend more time online, social media have become one of the most important means of communication in contemporary society. Social media have transformed the ways people communicate, have created communities beyond traditional social networks, and have posed new challenges about the limits of understanding and the spread of disinformation. Social media have also become important platforms for communicating about the past. Heated debates about disputed memories ignite on Twitter; gamers live stream and discuss historical video games on Twitch; tourists review heritage sites and museums on TripAdvisor; students and pupils learn for exams by watching YouTube clips; history buffs create Wikipedia pages, answer questions on Quora and discuss content on Reddit – the list is endless. Yet, social media are underrepresented as a subject of study in historical culture.[1] This may partly be related to the relative novelty of the phenomenon, but also to the fact that the theories and models of understanding historical representation that scholars have at their disposal – most importantly narrative theories – are not unequivocally applicable to social media. Narrative theory harks back to the medium of the book and its embeddedness in literary conventions and modes of argument and emplotment. Social media mobilize a great array of signifiers, such as emojis and hashtags, and modes of signification, such as memes and snaps, which seem to elude the interpretive framework of narrativism. At

Notes for this section begin on page 205.

the same time, they open new possibilities for narration, as platforms allow the creation or sharing of narrative content in the form of, for example, live streams, edited videos, blog posts, podcasts, and forum discussions. While semioticians argue that social media indicate a 'broad move from the now centuries-long dominance of writing to the new dominance of the image', and 'the move from the dominance of the medium of the book to the dominance of the medium of the screen', we can at least ask ourselves whether narrative theory alone is sufficient to study the dynamics of historical representation on social media platforms.[2]

In this chapter I will present an exploratory analysis of digital representations of violent pasts by focusing on Instagram posts of the Auschwitz-Birkenau Memorial and Museum. Instagram is a relevant case, first because it is one of the world's most popular social media platforms, with over a billion monthly active accounts as of June 2018,[3] and second, because Instagram is a media-sharing social networking service that primarily focuses on photo sharing. It is, as one of the founders preferred to call it, a 'visual communications tool'.[4] On Instagram, the image is the main signifier, with text in the form of a caption, hashtag or comment only secondary to the image. This particular configuration of image and text raises the question of what the limits and possibilities of narrative theory are for the study of historical representation in new media. The answers will be sought by introducing the concept of multimodality – derived from social semiotics – to the study of historical representation. Pictures taken at the Auschwitz-Birkenau Memorial and Museum somehow compel visitors – and the people with whom they share these pictures – to relate to the historical events and to make them meaningful as they are confronted with historical traces of one of the most inhumane chapters of human history. Instagram is only one platform on which this process takes place, but because it explicitly enables its users to combine different modes – semiotic resources such as still image and text that materialize meaning – rather than text alone to represent the past, I will concentrate on this platform for my analysis. Studying the interplay of these modes without assuming the dominance of text may provide new insights into the discussion of the representation of the Holocaust, which has emphasized (the limits of) narrative representation since the 1990s.[5]

Narrative Theory and Multimodality

Over the past decade, historians, philosophers and linguists have increasingly questioned the relevance of narrative theory for digital (historical) representations. The criticism focuses on the non-linearity of hypertext, on the interactive nature of digital communication versus the static form of the text, on the fact that the variety of new communication forms – such as email, weblogs, video blogs, podcasts and tweets – mobilize different non-textual modes of communication – such as moving and still images – either with or without written text.[6] Moreover, the new communication possibilities that the internet and digital communication have opened up have added to what Frank Ankersmit called the 'postmodern privatization of the past' – the loss of value of 'official' historical narratives in the light of the postmodern deconstruction of the myth of historical objectivity.[7]

For two reasons, historical references on social media platforms pose a challenge to the idea that historical representation is mainly to be understood in narrative terms. In the first place, it is important to emphasize that social media posts are not static but interactive representations. Social media platforms are environments in which anyone can create, publish and absorb historical information. This calls into question the traditional idea of historians being the 'gatekeepers' of historical knowledge.[8] Narratologists have already been taking notice of these developments and have started to emphasize, for example, the fact that online meaning making is an interactive process where people post, comment, chat, repost, embed, like, tag and respond at fast and sometimes real-time rates. The interactive quality of meaning making on social media challenges the narrativist model of the single, autonomous author, with the internet understood as a space of 'dialogical production' of meaning rather than a marketplace of passive consumers.[9] This implies that we should let go of the (academic) monologue as both the normative model for historical representation and the analytical frame of reference for the analysis of digital historical representations.[10]

In the second place, written text is only one of many different modes – different semiotic resources that are available in communication forms to express oneself – that constitute social media posts.[11] On Instagram, written text is even subordinate to the still or moving image. Communication platforms can encourage or restrict the use of particular modes, depending on their purpose, and can also enable the use of multiple modes, such as written language, hashtags, static and moving images, and videos, in single posts. At the same time, posts can have restrictions, such as the allowed number of words, which create barriers to narrative emplotment. Yet, the fact that social media platforms allow for the simultaneous use of multiple modes supports the now popular position in semiotics that language is no longer the dominant medium of communication and that other modes of communication should not be studied in terms of language.[12] The approach that studies how multiple modes interact to create meaningful representations is called 'multimodal analysis'.

Multimodal analysis aims to 'use several semiotic modes ... together with the particular way in which these modes are combined'.[13] It promises an integrated approach to communication and semiotics, studying the various modes and their interaction in the production of meaning. This does not mean that it aims to replace theories of narrative representation, but it aims at reversing the logocentrism of semiotics, and stresses that these theories apply only to linguistic representation, with other modes being studies for their own dynamics. Yet, it does in a broader sense entail a critique of the logocentrism of modern Western society in general, which appears to be being overhauled by contemporary multimodal forms of communication – a situation that needs to be acknowledged by academia.[14]

Although multiple approaches have been developed in 'multimodal studies', all rely on four main assumptions: (1) communication is multimodal; (2) solely focussing analyses on language provides no adequate account for meaning; (3) different modes have different affordances with their own material and historical limitations; and (4) modes concur together, each with a special role, in meaning making.[15] It must, however, be stressed that multimodality is an approach and not a theory.[16] It still requires additional theories of how meaning is made in order to be useful for analysis. This is generally due to the fact that multimodal analysis stems from social semiotics. Because social semiotics studies the social organization of communication and the use of semiotic resources, and sees meaning as a social construction rather than an expression of thought, it is quite open to the study of modes other than written or spoken language. The downside is that social semiotics does not provide a theory of what signs stand for. Social semioticians define their aims in terms of systematically collecting, documenting and cataloguing semiotic resources; analysing the historical, cultural and institutional contexts of these resources; and discovering and developing new semiotic resources.[17] This means that when studying historical representation, social semiotics can be of help for cataloguing used modes, and studying historical variability of the use and interplay of these modes, but it does not account for meaning itself. Multimodal analysis can thus not replace this function of narrative theory, but it does provide a conceptual framework for mapping how other – generally overlooked – modes contribute to semiosis as well as written language. In this case I will discuss the use of different modes in meaning-making processes on Instagram posts of Auschwitz-Birkenau.

The Modes of Instagram

In cataloguing multimodality, numerous taxonomies of available communicative modalities have been proposed by authors such as Charles Forceville and Eduardo Urios-Aparisi, who included (1) written language; (2) spoken language; (3) static and moving images; (4) music; (5) non-verbal sound; and (6) gestures.[18] Although such taxonomies are ideal-typical and always prone to discussion, they are useful heuristic tools to identify the various modes at play in a multimodal representation. By design, Instagram employs a limited number of modalities.

The visual arrangement of the various modes of an Instagram post differ depending on whether one visits the platform through a browser or an app – but in any case, a post consists of three sections. The first section, the header in the app, contains metadata in written text, such as the username of the poster and an optional location tag (where the photo was taken), as well as the user's profile picture. The second section contains the content of the post. Traditionally this is a single still image on Instagram, although since 2017, users can upload up to ten images in a single post that can be swiped through by viewers, which enables users to create visual narratives – a feature previously reserved for advertisers only.[19] Also videos of three to sixty seconds can be posted. The last section, displayed as the footer in the app, contains icons to like (heart), comment (text balloon), chat and share (paper aeroplane) and bookmark (banner) the post. It shows – in written language – how many people have liked the post, and displays comments and the date of the post. If the poster has added a caption, it is displayed as a first comment, which is only visually distinguished from the regular comments by a horizontal rule. A caption can contain written language, including hashtags, and ideograms (emojis). Interestingly, hyperlinks can be posted but are not clickable in the comments. Users can only post a clickable hyperlink in their user profile text.

Although the interplay of all these various modes contributes to the representation of the past in Instagram posts, in this chapter I will focus on two modes in particular: the photographic image and the hashtag.

Images

The image – traditionally in the mode of a still photograph – stands at the heart of the platform, as Instagram was originally launched as a photo sharing app. Pictures can be posted instantly when taken via the app's camera function, or old pictures can be uploaded. Although images can be posted 'as is', a range of post-processing options are available. Besides a set of basic image-editing tools that enable the user to change variables such as lux, brightness, contrast, warmth and saturation, a set of forty-one predefined 'filters' can create a distinct 'mood' or 'atmosphere' in the image. Some filters particularly target land- and cityscape photography – such as Lark, which brightens the image and intensifies all colours except red, or Hudson which produces cooler colours – while many other deliberately create a range of vintage effects. Slumber, for example, achieves according to Instagram 'a retro look of subtle desaturation and hazing' – it is named

Slumber 'because the effect is dreamy. It does something especially retro to blacks and blues'.[20] Many filters appeal to different dimensions of nostalgia. X-Pro II uses vignettes in combination with saturated warmer colours to recreate the atmosphere of 8 mm film, and enables users to use the meaning potential associated with that atmosphere. The filter Willow combines vignetting with a grayscale post-processing of the image, and the filter 1977 mimics the look of photos from the 1970s by creating a brighter and faded look by increasing exposure.[21]

The nostalgic effects of Instagram filters are the result of deliberate design choices. Instagram was originally conceived to provide a combination between an instant camera photo and a telegram, hence the name. The founders imagined the snapshot itself to be the telegram, and accordingly prioritized the image over the text.[22] Both the platform's logo and the fact that Instagram crops pictures into a square format refer to the history of instant cameras. Instagram's self-positioning echoes the core message of twentieth-century Kodak advertising, which 'taught amateur photographers to apprehend their experiences and memories as objects of nostalgia, for the easy availability of snapshots allowed people for the first time in history to arrange their lives in such a way that painful or unpleasant aspects were systematically erased'.[23]

Theorists have argued that the popularity of 'faux-vintage' photography is characteristic for a broader trend in which 'social media increasingly force us to view our present as always a potential documented past',[24] or as 'a therapeutic response to an existential crisis of the self in postmodernism'.[25] It would indeed make sense to speculate about these trends as expressions of a presentist regime of history. It fits in with François Hartog's argument that, ever since the fall of the Berlin Wall, Western historical culture prioritizes present demands over the historical space of experience and future expectation, resulting in a situation in which the past is approached from contemporary questions, issues and memories. Faux-vintage filters on Instagram can be seen as an example of the tendency to view the present as already history. In contemporary society the present – in Hartog's words – turns its 'back on itself in order to anticipate how it will be regarded when it is completely past, as though it wanted to "foresee" the past, to turn itself into a past before it has even fully emerged as present'.[26] Faux-vintage Instagram snapshots have the same function. They 'create instant "good old days" upon which friends can reminisce and feel nostalgic, even if the event occurred just last night'.[27] The Instagram snapshot thus functions as an instant archive that wards off the void of oblivion by instantly historicizing live or recent events.[28]

It is clear that nostalgic filters can be used to historicize the present by invoking a nostalgic mood through filters. But when representing heritage sites, especially sites of mass violence and suffering, such as Auschwitz, which

Table 9.1 Frequency count of top ten Instagram filters posted to the location tag 'Auschwitz Memorial / Muzeum Auschwitz'.

	Filter	Frequency	Relative frequency	Total likes	Relative likes	Total comments	Relative comments
1	Clarendon	495	15.1%	14,779	9.6%	401	10.9%
2	Moon	331	10.1%	12,069	7.8%	316	8.6%
3	Inkwell	296	9.1%	12,835	8.3%	359	9.8%
4	Lark	273	8.3%	15,778	10.2%	369	10.0%
5	Gingham	250	7.6%	11,234	7.3%	231	6.3%
6	Juno	216	6.6%	10,537	6.8%	216	5.9%
7	Lo-fi	158	4.8%	5,484	3.5%	147	4.0%
8	Ludwig	145	4.4%	6,960	4.5%	213	5.8%
9	Willow	131	4.0%	4,643	3.0%	122	3.3%
10	Crema	92	2.8%	6,278	4.1%	103	2.8%

themselves already bear reference to the past, filters can be used to signify the history of the site, an experienced mood, or a combination of both.

A survey of 7,822 Instagram posts containing still-image content that were posted to the location tag 'Auschwitz Memorial / Muzeum Auschwitz', between 6 September 2016 and 6 August 2017 (the date of collection), indicates that filters were applied to 42 per cent of the posted images. This number only includes in-app filters; an additional number of images may have been edited with other apps. Noting that so many of the posted images of Auschwitz have been deliberately aestheticized is in itself an interesting find, and a closer look at the filters used can reveal aspects of the affective aspects of both the interpretation and representation of Auschwitz by Instagram users.

The popularity of Clarendon comes as no surprise, as Clarendon – a filter that brightens, highlights and intensifies shadows – is overall the most popular filter on Instagram.[29] This popularity can be explained by being an all-purpose filter and by being the first filter on the list from which to choose. Other generally popular filters such as Juno and Valencia do not stand out in this dataset. Interestingly, the three grayscale filters – Moon, Inkwell and Willow – make up almost a quarter of the used filters.

The use of black-and-white in visual representations of the Holocaust is not uncommon in popular culture. The most notable example might be Steven Spielberg's *Schindler's List*, the black-and-white cinematography of which has – according to Geoff Eley and Atina Grossman – a dual function. On the one hand, filming in monochrome added to Spielberg's striving for authenticity, and underlined his historical realism. On the other hand, to the audience, it both distances and reduces historical distance. It distances in the sense that it marks this past as essentially different from the present, and sets itself apart from contemporary popular culture that represents in colour, but it also reduces distance because the black and white 'resonates with this existing archive of representation' and places the movie in the mnemonic framework of historical photographs, newsreels and other sources we are so familiar with.[30] Yet, the 'reality effect' of *Schindler's List*, Miriam Bratu Hansen argued, does not stem from its colourless cinematography, or from Spielberg's use of authentic locations, but from the way in which the movie echoed familiar images and tropes from other Holocaust films.[31]

Similarly, Instagram users use black-and-white filters to turn their pictures into traces of a past that speak for themselves. These photos depict mostly buildings, barbed wire and the gate at Auschwitz I, or the railway tracks and entrance building at Auschwitz II-Birkenau.[32] Photos of this type of site predominantly depict no people, and many photographers must have gone to great lengths to avoid capturing fellow visitors in their shots. The historicizing tendencies of black and white filters are sometimes explicitly corroborated in the captions, when users refer, for example, to their visit in terms of 'time travelling'.[33] Others use black and white because it 'captures the mood', as one commenter put it.[34]

The use of these filters also compensates for a lack of genuinely experienced authenticity on behalf of the visitors. In his caption to a black-and-white photo of the famous Auschwitz gate, super_hans92 remarks: 'Eye opening experience. I was let down by how commercialized it was. Regardless, a lot of it was a touching memorabilia to the millions of people who died passing these gates'.[35] Even though, in his post, the black-and-white makes the 'Arbeit macht Frei' sign unreadable against the backdrop of a tree, and the photo lacks any particular aesthetic quality; the filter also renders the groups of tourists down the road nearly invisible to a quick glance, as they morph into the background of trees and buildings. Through this filter, super_hans92 was able to constitute an image of the camp that represented Auschwitz *as if* it had not become a carefully maintained and partly restored 'dark tourism' destination. The photo now captured the Auschwitz he had wanted to see.

Colourful filters render different effects. Whereas grayscale filters tend to flatten out the picture, the effects various filters have on the colours of the photograph open up different possibilities for meaning making. User mnnclaessens, for example, uses the filter Reyes on a photo of the Auschwitz gate on a rainy day, with people hiding underneath their umbrellas in the background. Reyes desaturates the images and brightens it a bit, which has a nostalgic effect, but also has a gleamy effect that confirms her caption 'a piece [of] sad history'.[36] Instagram user grit2106 uses the Amaro filter – which adds light to the centre of the image and darkens around the edges – on a photo of the railway tracks and the main entrance gate to Auschwitz II-Birkenau with a low-view camera angle.³⁷ As an effect, the sky behind the gate tower lightens up as a halo, with the railway tracks, going through the gate, implying a movement into the halo's bright core. Whether the choice of filter was an intended move to turn the gate into a symbol of passage into the afterlife, or whether the filter was chosen for purely aesthetic reasons remains unclear, as the caption 'Never forget! Learn from history! #auschwitz #history #sad #fcknzs #neveragain' does not explicitly refer to the contents of the image.

Hashtags

The second modality is written language, available for captions. The central position of the image is emphasized by limitations to the caption section. Although the caption has a word limit of 2,200, only the first three lines representing some 130 characters are visible in browsing mode, forcing readers to click 'more' to read the full caption in the individual post. Another restriction exists in the fact that the main element of hypertext, the hyperlink, cannot be used in captions or comments.

In a post there are only three resources that provide contextual meaning: hashtags, location and person tags. Contrary to hyperlinks – which are only allowed in the user's 150-word bio – hashtags are allowed, which turns Instagram into a self-referential system that provides contextual meaning by embedding the post in a network of other posts tagged with the same hashtags. Second, the optional location tag adds to this, as users can choose to tag the post with a predefined location or create a new location by themselves. Location tags range from toponymies and public places to businesses and institutions. As with the hashtags, location tags are prime ways to increase exposure as users can browse Instagram either via a list of suggested posts and users, or via a person, tag or location search. Third, the poster can tag Instagram users who are visible in the photo, resulting in the tagged person's username appearing in the picture as a link.

In particular, hashtags offer a rich resource for analysis, as they constitute the main way of finding posts on Instagram. Instagram does not have a full-text search, but lets users search by account name, location, or indeed hashtag. As such, hashtags make up what has been called a 'folksonomy': an index to the content which is provided through user-generated metadata.³⁸ This contrasts the taxonomy, which refers to a pre-established index created by the platform owners. At the same time, hashtags are a form of textual representation, which gives the hashtag an interesting dynamic.³⁹ In addition, it must be noted that, whereas on Twitter in-line hashtags are not uncommon, on Instagram hashtags tend to stand outside of narration, and are posted as a list in the caption of the post, sometimes accompanied by narrative, but often not. Because hashtags function both as an index to the image and as the semantic context of the image, they are used to provide narrative context to

Table 9.2 Top ten used hashtags according to frequency (case insensitive).

1	#auschwitz	2,797
2	#poland	1,925
3	#history	734
4	#holocaust	659
5	#travel	618
6	#concentrationcamp	588
7	#birkenau	524
8	#auschwitzbirkenau	513
9	#krakow	503
10	#memorial	417

the image and to appeal to audiences to whom the image might appeal for reasons other than narrative meaning.

In the same dataset, 52 per cent of the posts use hashtags in the caption. When we take a look at the most frequent hashtags used in our sample (see Table 9.2), it is clear that toponyms such as '#poland' and '#krakow', and references to the site and its history (or history in general) such as '#auschwitz', '#history', '#holocaust', '#memorial' and '#concentrationcamp', are the most used categories of hashtag. This may come as no surprise, as we are dealing with a historical site visited mostly by tourists, students and teachers.

Yet, a frequency count provides little insight into the relationships between the hashtags. It is through using hashtags together in posts that users create a semantic network in which they position their post. Therefore, an analysis of hashtag co-occurrences can provide more information about the semantic structure that hashtags constitute.

I created a co-occurrence matrix of the 6,340 hashtags used in the dataset, out of which I constructed a graph in which the hashtags are the nodes and the co-occurrences are the edges. Using the data visualization tool Gephi, I applied the Louvain Method for community detection, which establishes communities through machine learning based on a comparison of edge densities between communities.[40] Filtering nodes with a minimum of 156 edges or co-occurrences, I established four categories of hashtags. Table 9.3 shows the top ten hashtags per community, sorted by eigenvector centrality, which measures the relative importance of the nodes (hashtags) in the network by assigning a score relative to the frequency of connections to high scoring nodes. Eigenvector centrality thus prioritizes nodes that are connected to high-scoring nodes over isolated nodes with a higher frequency of occurrence.

The four communities can be named 'history, 'artistic photography', 'general photography' and 'travel'. It is important to note that these

Table 9.3 Hashtag communities based on modularity, minimum degree of 156. Top ten nodes per community, sorted by eigenvector centrality.

Community 1: History		Community 2: Artistic photography		Community 3: General photography		Community 4: Travel	
Hashtag	Eigenvector centrality	Hashtag	Eigenvector centrality	Hashtag	Eigenvector centrality	Hashtag	Eigenvector centrality
history	0.940212	auschwitz	1	pic of the day	0.813006	travel	0.969381
krakow	0.913503	poland	0.999108	photo of the day	0.788873	travelgram	0.864806
concentration camp	0.901951	igerspoland	0.561707	polonia	0.75852	instatravel	0.83442
holocaust	0.900557	Vsco	0.554045	insta good	0.739394	trip	0.820223
birkenau	0.876086	explore	0.54595	Photo	0.716562	travelling	0.77433
auschwitz birkenau	0.873949	vscocam	0.531302	photographer	0.60535	travel photography	0.726169
europe	0.84319	ig_europe	0.452346	instadaily	0.590837	travelling	0.661999
memorial	0.841276	visit poland	0.408199	like4like	0.577647	wanderlust	0.632004
photography	0.828532	ig_worldclub	0.407314	love	0.577107	traveller	0.605528
polska	0.818948	clouds	0.390002	sky	0.568505	traveller	0.582237

categories do not necessarily denote a particular interpretation of Auschwitz, but primarily embody what have been called 'latent' communities.[41] These are communities of users that share the same interests, and constitute and operate in a shared semantic field surrounding their topics of interest. They do not imagine themselves as communities; their members are primarily engaged with the shared topic of interest, and only through that topic with each other; therefore, they exist only latently and can also only be witnessed indirectly.

The first community relates Auschwitz-Birkenau to the past, and the understanding and experience thereof. Hashtags such as 'sad', 'horror', 'scary' and 'silence' indicate the hauntedness of the site, whereas hashtags such as 'tragedy' and 'suffering' indicate a specific narrative interpretation of the site's history. Hashtags such as 'memory', 'remembrance' and 'neverforget' convey a message of the importance of remembrance. The high eigenvector values indicate a dense and coherent semantic field, as the hashtags from the first community are also numerically most used, and used together. This community captures how the general audience indexes Auschwitz.

The second community is a more particular one, also indicated by the relative distance of the eigenvector values of the particular hashtags to the general hashtags #auschwitz and #poland, which have also been grouped in that category, but which could be grouped anywhere as they are the two central nodes in the entire network. This community applies specific hashtags that target an audience interested in artistic or aesthetic photography, with some hashtags connected to semi-formalized 'communities' of 'Instagramers'. #igerspoland, for example, refers to the Polish network group of instagramers.com, a web platform dedicated to bringing together Instagram fans, and fans of mobile photography. Using the hashtag #igerspoland can lead to the picture being reposted by the Instagram account with the same name, which may draw new viewers and followers to your account. The same accounts for hashtags such as #polandphotos, #ig_europe, #igerskrakow and #ig_worldclub. Some hashtags, like #vsco and #vscocam stem from another photo-sharing platform with even more extensive editing features than Instagram, and allows its users to share their content on Instagram as well. Usually, these photos have been edited with that app before being uploaded to Instagram, but the hashtag is used by anyone posting with more artistic quality, or at least by anyone aiming to spread their post among a community of people who are interested in posts with particular artistic features. The hashtags of this community show co-occurrence, but a relatively weak eigenvector (thus a relative isolation from the main nodes), which indicates that the semantic field this community constitute is not primarily concerned with the history, memory or geography of the visited site, but with the aesthetics of the posted photos.

The third community also uses hashtags that refer to photography, but on a more general level. The people constituting this community are less artsy, and apply these hashtags primarily to gain as many likes and as much exposure as possible by people browsing the hashtags. The co-occurrence of hashtags such as #like4like – which is used to indicate that a like of this picture will get a like back – and hashtags such as #sky, #landscape, #architecture – which refer to the specific contents of the picture – indicate that, compared to the previous community, these users care less about having the picture reposted on specific popular Instagram accounts, and aim at maximizing the reach by using hashtags that many people browse. Users who particularly aim at the largest possible exposure of their post often use long lists of hashtags to reach the widest possible audience. After all, Instagram is only searchable by hashtags, accounts or locations. The higher eigenvector also shows that this community is less isolated from the main nodes.

The last community uses various travel-related hashtags. Hashtags such as #travel and #travelgram are hugely popular hashtags, the use of which enlarges the chances of random visitors stumbling upon the post. Next to this element of exposure, this cluster of hashtags also indicates that the many travellers and tourists who visit Auschwitz use Instagram to document their trip as a visual travel blog. These travellers often make Instagram meaningful as a part of their larger itinerary, and reflect upon the site from the larger perspective of their trip. For example, soshetravelled commented upon her picture of the Auschwitz II-Birkenau entrance building as follows: 'When I travel to places affected by deeply traumatic events, I make it a priority to visit the museums preserving their memory. It's not always easy but my world perspective and respect for peace is increased and my understanding of events greatly fortified'.[42] It would be interesting to trace these itineraries from the perspective of historical culture – but that is beyond the explorative scope of this chapter.

Conclusion

Although the narrativist paradigm in the theory of history states that emplotment is the prime means for generating historical meaning, digital platforms such as Instagram have opened up new ways of representing the past and of historical meaning making. On Instagram, written text, and especially written narrative, is not the main mode on which historical representation relies. In my sample, 33 per cent of the posts did not contain a caption – hashtags excluded – and 45 per cent of the posts contained a caption of a single line (of which, in 20 per cent of the cases the caption consisted of a single word). As the image, and primarily the still image, is placed centrally, text does interact with the image in a multimodal way.[43] Hashtags create semantic contexts in which the image is embedded; these contexts extend beyond the particular representation as it places the post in a larger semantic network that can highlight historical aspects of the site, can emphasize the 'mood' of the site, or can underline the instant historization of faux-vintage photography.

Multimodal analysis cannot and does not aim to answer the particular theoretical or philosophical issues concerning historical representation, but it can index the various modes that are used in historical representations – modes that diverge from the traditional narrative mode of representation. Another added value is that social semiotics offers us the possibility to study historical meaning making in reference to the social communities that it – explicitly or tacitly – co-constructs. This I have shown in the discussion of the semantic networks of Instagram hashtags. However, this chapter has only partly explored the potential of multimodal analysis, in this case in relationship to the representation of Auschwitz on Instagram. At the same time, studying digital historical representations urges us to apply methods explored in the digital humanities and computational sciences. On Instagram, hashtags can be, but are generally not, used inline in sentences, and so do not provide meaning through their embeddedness in micronarratives, as is often the case on Twitter. They do, however, constitute semantic networks through their co-occurrence in posts, and through the fact that they are linked to other posts that use the same hashtag. These networks can be recognized as mnemonic communities, but not in an organized or a semi-organized sense. They rather constitute latent mnemonic communities recognizable only indirectly. Yet they are coherent communities, as through the hashtags they use they share an inventory of concepts that frame their posts in a specific way, and they target shared audiences that browse and show interest in these hashtags.

Given the fact that today social media platforms provide the daily means of communication for large and ever-growing numbers of people in our societies, particularly for the young, it is important to acknowledge this, and to study digital historical representation and its particular representational dynamics. Narration is an important part of that endeavour, but, as this chapter has shown, it is certainly not the only part.

Robbert-Jan Adriaansen is assistant professor in the theory of history and historical culture at Erasmus University Rotterdam (EUR). His research focuses on conceptions of time, historical understanding and historical consciousness. He is currently working on a research project on historical re-enactments financed by the EUR's Erasmus Initiative 'Vital Cities and Citizens', and studies the representation of the past on social media. Key publications include: 'Picturing Auschwitz: Multimodality and the Attribution of Historical Significance on Instagram', *Journal for the Study of Education and Development: Infancia y Aprendizaje* 43(3) (2020); 'Historical Consciousness: The Enigma of Different Paradigms' (co-authored with M. Grever), *Journal of Curriculum Studies* 51(6) (2019), 814–30; and *The Rhythm of Eternity: The German Youth Movement and the Experience of the Past 1900–1933* (Berghahn Books, 2015).

Notes

1. For the notion 'historical culture', see: Grever and Adriaansen, 'Historical Culture'.
2. Kress, *Literacy in the New Media Age*, 1.
3. Statista, 'Instagram: Active Users 2018'.
4. Honan, 'Inside Instagram'.
5. Friedländer, *Probing the Limits*; Huyssen, 'Monument and Memory'.
6. Waaldijk, 'Design of World Citizenship', 113.
7. Ankersmit, *Historical Representation*, 153–54.
8. Rigney, 'History as Text', 197.
9. Deumert, 'Performance of a Ludic Self', 25–26.
10. Van den Akker, 'History as Dialogue', 107; Rigney, 'When the Monograph', 108.
11. Hoffmann, 'Narrative Revisited', 9.
12. Kress, Leite-García and van Leeuwen, 'Discourse Semiotics', 257.
13. Kress and van Leeuwen, *Reading Images*, 177.
14. Lemke, 'Metamedia Literacy', 317.
15. Adami, 'Multimodality', 452.
16. Adami and Kress, 'Introduction', 234.
17. Van Leeuwen, *Introducing Social Semiotics*, 3–4.
18. Forceville and Urios-Aparisi, 'Introduction', 4.
19. Instagram Blog, 'Share Up to 10 Photos'.
20. 'Instagram Introduces Five New Filters'.
21. Poulsen, 'Becoming a Semiotic Technology', 11.
22. Zappavigna, 'Social Media Photography', 273.
23. West, *Kodak and the Lens of Nostalgia*, 1.
24. Jurgenson, 'Faux-Vintage Photo'; Chopra-Gant, 'Pictures or It Didn't Happen', 5.
25. Chopra-Gant, 'Pictures or It Didn't Happen', 12.
26. Hartog, *Regimes of Historicity*, 114.
27. Mendelson and Papacharissi, 'Look at Us', 268.
28. Bartholeyns, 'Instant Past', 67; Lizardi, *Nostalgic Generations*.
29. 'Study: The Most Popular Instagram Filters from around the World'.
30. Eley and Grossmann, 'Watching Schindler's List', 47.
31. Hansen, '"Schindler's List" Is Not "Shoah"', 299.
32. See also: Adriaansen, 'Picturing Auschwitz'.
33. '@flowerkong on Instagram: "Day 06 – time traveling – #history #memorial #auschwitz #silent #oswiecim #poland #sad #太沈重 ** 身邊任何人突然消失感覺真係不太好!"'.

34. '@waksolis on Instagram: "Depressing. Cold. Inhumane. Mad world. Stripped of all human dignity. More than 1 million lost their lives. A prayer for all the the lost . . ."'.
35. 'Jordan Davis on Instagram: "Eye opening experience. I was let down by how commercialised it was. Regardless, a lot of it was a touching memorabilia to the millions of . . ."'.
36. 'Manon on Instagram: "A piece sad history #auschwitz #arbeitmachtfrei #polen"'.
37. 'Grit on Instagram: "Never forget! Learn from history! #auschwitz #history #sad #fcknzs #neveragain"'.
38. Vander Wal, 'Folksonomy'.
39. Zappavigna, 'Searchable Talk', 228.
40. Blondel et al., 'Fast Unfolding'.
41. Yin et al., 'Latent Community'.
42. 'So She Travelled on Instagram: "When I travel to places affected by deeply traumatic events I make it a priority to visit the museums preserving their memory. It's not . . ."'.
43. I have further analysed image-caption pairs in: Adriaansen, 'Picturing Auschwitz'.

Bibliography

Adami, Elisabetta. 'Multimodality', in Ofelia García, Nelson Flores and Massimiliano Spotti (eds), *The Oxford Handbook of Language and Society* (Oxford: Oxford University Press, 2016), 452–73.

Adami, Elisabetta, and Gunther Kress. 'Introduction: Multimodality, Meaning Making, and the Issue of "Text"'. *Text & Talk* 34(3) (2014), 231–37. https://doi.org/10.1515/text-2014-0007.

Adriaansen, Robbert-Jan. 'Picturing Auschwitz: Multimodality and the Attribution of Historical Significance on Instagram'. *Journal for the Study of Education and Development: Infancia y Aprendizaje* 43(3) (2020), 652–81. https://doi.org/10.1080/02103702.2020.1771963.

Akker, Chiel van den. 'History as Dialogue: On Online Narrativity'. *BMGN – Low Countries Historical Review* 128(4) (2013), 103–17. https://doi.org/10.18352/bmgn-lchr.9354.

Ankersmit, Frank. *Historical Representation*. Stanford, CA: Stanford University Press, 2002.

Bartholeyns, Gil. 'The Instant Past: Nostalgia and Digital Retro Photography', in Katharina Niemeyer (ed.), *Media and Nostalgia*. Palgrave Macmillan Memory Studies (London: Palgrave Macmillan, 2014), 51–69. https://doi.org/10.1057/9781137375889_4.

Blondel, Vincent D., et al. 'Fast Unfolding of Communities in Large Networks'. *Journal of Statistical Mechanics: Theory and Experiment* 10 (2008), P10008. https://doi.org/10.1088/1742-5468/2008/10/P10008.

Chopra-Gant, Mike. 'Pictures or It Didn't Happen: Photo-Nostalgia, IPhoneography and the Representation of Everyday Life'. *Photography and Culture* 9(2) (2016), 121–33. https://doi.org/10.1080/17514517.2016.1203632.

Deumert, Ana. 'The Performance of a Ludic Self on Social Network(ing) Sites', in Philip Seargeant and Caroline Tagg (eds), *The Language of Social Media* (Basingstoke: Palgrave Macmillan, 2014), 23–45. https://doi.org/10.1057/9781137029317_2.

Eley, Geoff, and Atina Grossmann. 'Watching Schindler's List: Not the Last Word'. *New German Critique* 71 (1997), 41–62. https://doi.org/10.2307/488558.

@flowerkong on Instagram: 'Day 06 – time traveling – #history #memorial #auschwitz #silent #oswiecim #poland #sad #太沈重 ** 身邊任何人突然消失感覺真係不太好!'. Instagram. https://www.instagram.com/p/BUNSDFdl3os/ (last accessed 15 May 2018).

Forceville, Charles, and Eduardo Urios-Aparisi. 'Introduction', in Charles Forceville and Eduardo Urios-Aparisi (eds), *Multimodal Metaphor. Applications of Cognitive Linguistics 11* (New York: Mouton de Gruyter, 2009), 3–17.

Friedländer, Saul. *Probing the Limits of Representation: Nazism and the 'Final Solution'*. Cambridge, MA: Harvard University Press, 1992.

Grever, Maria, and Robbert-Jan Adriaansen. 'Historical Culture: A Concept Revisited', in Mario Carretero, Stefan Berger and Maria Grever (eds), *Palgrave Handbook of Research in Historical Culture and Education* (London: Palgrave Macmillan, 2017), 73–89. https://doi.org/10.1057/978-1-137-52908-4_4.

'Grit on Instagram: "Never forget! Learn from history! #auschwitz #history #sad #fcknzs #neveragain"'. Instagram. https://www.instagram.com/p/BXLphPKnAcz/ (last accessed 12 May 2018).

Hansen, Miriam Bratu. '"Schindler's List" Is Not "Shoah": The Second Commandment, Popular Modernism, and Public Memory'. *Critical Inquiry* 22(2) (1996), 292–312. https://doi.org/10.1086/448792.

Honan, Mat. 'Inside Instagram: How Slowing Its Roll Put the Little Startup in the Fast Lane'. Gizmodo. https://gizmodo.com/5878942/inside-instagram-how-slowing-its-roll-put-the-little-startup-in-the-fast-lane (last accessed 25 September 2017).

Hartog, François. *Regimes of Historicity: Presentism and Experiences of Time*. New York: Columbia University Press, 2015.

Highfill, Samantha. 'Instagram Introduces Five New Filters to Make Your Life Look Cooler'. *EW.Com*, 16 December 2014. http://ew.com/article/2014/12/16/instagram-new-filters/ (last accessed 12 May 2018).

Hoffmann, Christian R. 'Narrative Revisited: Telling a Story in the Age of New Media', in Christian R. Hoffmann (ed.), *Narrative Revisited: Telling a Story in the Age of New Media* (Amsterdam: John Benjamins Publishing, 2010), 1–18.

Huyssen, Andreas. 'Monument and Memory in a Postmodern Age'. *The Yale Journal of Criticism* 6(2) (1993), 249–61.

Instagram Blog. 'Share up to 10 Photos and Videos in One Post'. http://instagram.tumblr.com/post/157572774352/170222-multiple (last accessed 11 May 2018).

'Jordan Davis on Instagram: "Eye opening experience. I was let down by how commercialised it was. Regardless, a lot of it was a touching memorabilia to the millions of . . ."'. Instagram. https://www.instagram.com/p/BW40zIhBCyh/ (last accessed 12 May 2018).

Jurgenson, Nathan. 'The Faux-Vintage Photo Part I: Hipstamatic and Instagram'. *Cyborgology* (blog), 10 May 2011. https://thesocietypages.org/cyborgology/2011/05/10/the-faux-vintage-photo-part-i-hipstamatic-and-instagram/ (last accessed 12 May 2018).

Kress, Gunther. *Literacy in the New Media Age*. London: Routledge, 2003.

Kress, Gunther, Regina Leite-García and Theo van Leeuwen. 'Discourse Semiotics', in Teun A. van Dijk (ed.), *Discourse as Structure and Process* (London: Sage, 1997), 257–91.

Kress, Gunther, and Theo van Leeuwen. *Reading Images: The Grammar of Visual Design*. London: Psychology Press, 1996.

Leeuwen, Theo van. *Introducing Social Semiotics*. London: Psychology Press, 2005.

Lemke, Jay L. 'Metamedia Literacy: Transforming Meanings and Media', in David Reinking et al. (eds), *Handbook of Literacy and Technology: Transformations in a Post-typographic World* (Mahwah, NJ: L. Erlbaum Associates, 1998), 283–301.

Lizardi, Ryan. *Nostalgic Generations and Media: Perception of Time and Available Meaning*. Lanham, MD: Lexington Books, 2017.

'Manon on Instagram: "A piece sad history #auschwitz #arbeitmachtfrei #polen"'. Instagram. https://www.instagram.com/p/BW-HtNogzt3/ (last accessed 12 May 2018).

Mendelson, Andrew L., and Zizi A. Papacharissi. 'Look at Us: Collective Narcissism in College Student Facebook Photo Galleries', in Zizi A. Papacharissi (ed.), *The Networked*

Self: Identity, Community and Culture on Social Network Sites (London: Routledge, 2010), 251–73.

Poulsen, Søren Vigild. 'Becoming a Semiotic Technology: A Historical Study of Instagram's Tools for Making and Sharing Photos and Videos'. *Internet Histories* 2(1–2) (2018), 121–39. https://doi.org/10.1080/24701475.2018.1459350.

Rigney, Ann. 'History as Text: Narrative Theory and History', in Nancy Partner and Sarah Foot (eds), *History as Text: Narrative Theory and History* (London: Sage, 2013), 183–201.

———. 'When the Monograph Is No Longer the Medium: Historical Narrative in the Online Age'. *History and Theory* 49(4) (2010), 100–17. https://doi.org/10.1111/j.1468-2303.2010.00562.x.

'So She Travelled on Instagram: "When I travel to places affected by deeply traumatic events I make it a priority to visit the museums preserving their memory. It's not . . ."'. Instagram. https://www.instagram.com/p/BW4fj21h9CI/ (last accessed 17 May 2018).

Statista. 'Instagram: Active Users 2018'. Statista, 2019. https://www.statista.com/statistics/253577/number-of-monthly-active-instagram-users/ (last accessed 10 November 2020).

'Study: The Most Popular Instagram Filters from around the World'. Learn, 10 February 2016. https://www.canva.com/learn/popular-instagram-filters/ (Last accessed 16 May 2018).

Vander Wal, Thomas. 'Folksonomy: Vanderwal.Net'. http://www.vanderwal.net/folksonomy.html (last accessed 1 December 2017).

Waaldijk, Berteke. 'The Design of World Citizenship: A Historical Comparison between World Exhibitions and the Web', in Marianne van den Boomen et al. (eds), *Digital Material: Tracing New Media in Everyday Life and Technology* (Amsterdam: Amsterdam University Press, 2009), 107–20.

'@waksolis on Instagram: "Depressing. Cold. Inhumane. Mad world. Stripped of all human dignity. More than 1 million lost their lives. A prayer for all the the lost . . ."'. Instagram. https://www.instagram.com/p/BKhzUTjAFLi/ (last accessed 17 May 2018).

West, Nancy Martha. *Kodak and the Lens of Nostalgia*. Charlottesville: University Press of Virginia, 2000.

Yin, Zhijun, et al. 'Latent Community Topic Analysis: Integration of Community Discovery with Topic Modeling'. *ACM Transactions on Intelligent Systems and Technology* 3(4) (2012). https://doi.org/10.1145/2337542.2337548.

Zappavigna, Michele. 'Searchable Talk: The Linguistic Functions of Hashtags'. *Social Semiotics* 25(3) (2015), 274–91. https://doi.org/10.1080/10350330.2014.996948.

———. 'Social Media Photography: Construing Subjectivity in Instagram Images'. *Visual Communication* 15(3) (2016), 271–92. https://doi.org/10.1177/1470357216643220.

CHAPTER 10

The Civil Rights Movement (Re)Narrated

Kenan Van de Mieroop

'In the past twenty years, the Civil Rights Movement of the 1950s and 1960s has assumed a central place in American historical memory.'[1] That, at least, is the main claim of the 2006 book, *The Civil Rights Movement in American Memory*, and in the years following its publication, that centrality was to be cemented in place. The election and presidency of Barack Obama regularly brought the question of race to the forefront of media attention in the United States, and in this context, references to the African American struggle for civil rights became widespread. For the editors of that volume, Renee Romano and Leigh Raiford, it is important to point out that when the Civil Rights Movement is discussed in the contemporary United States, it is often spoken about through the frame of a particular narrative: they claim that there is a widely recognized, even standard, narrative of this important movement:

> There exists today what we might call a consensus memory, a dominant narrative of the movement's goals, practices, victories and, of course, its most lasting legacies. This consensus memory offers that the 'Civil Rights Movement' began in 1954 with the Supreme Court's Brown v. Board of Education decision to desegregate southern schools 'with deliberate speed', and ended in 1968 with the death of Martin Luther King Jr. and the rise of Black Power in the country's northern and western cities. Charismatic and eloquent leaders led a non-violent movement of African Americans and supportive whites in a struggle that sought to change legal and social rather than economic barriers to equality.[2]

Notes for this section begin on page 221.

The narrative of the Civil Rights Movement outlined above, is sometimes called the 'heroic' narrative, or the 'classical phase'. A 'myth', in Roland Barthes' sense of the term (1972), the account of the Civil Rights Movement seems to connote the central ethereal concepts of American political discourse all at once: the terms freedom, democracy and progress, the utterance of which is almost synonymous with America, are all exemplified in the story of the struggle of black people to obtain their civil rights.

As a romantic story of American triumph, the heroic narrative has indeed been widely disseminated and adopted. But it has also been adapted and challenged. Indeed, much has been written regarding the different ways that the Civil Rights Movement has been variously interpreted and represented, and the fact that different and often competing narratives of the Civil Rights Movement exist is something that historians are keen to point out.[3] Yet the question of how these narratives differ as narratives – that is, as formal discursive constructions that effect or frame meaning – is rarely discussed. In order to address this question, in this chapter I will examine some different narrative representations of the Civil Rights Movement formally, drawing on a multidisciplinary narratological approach, on semiotics and on transmedial critiques. Taking a diverse group of representations from different registers, I seek to understand how language and imagery are mobilized within them in order to figure forth (to borrow a phrase from Hayden White) different narrative meanings from the manifold figures, events and phenomena that are said to constitute 'the Civil Rights Movement'.

The Interpretation of Dreams

An electronic greeting card for the occasion of Black History Month bears a picture of a muscular, black, male body emerging from darkness, seen from the back. Above him, a single-word sentence reads: 'Dream' (Figure 10.1). A single word is not a narrative, as it does not fit the minimum definition of a narrative: it has no beginning, middle or end; no transformation or change of state; and no discernible plot. This e-card might, therefore, seem to be a strange place to begin a discussion of narratives of the Civil Rights Movement. Yet, I have chosen to discuss it at the beginning of this chapter because, in spite of its apparent simplicity, this e-card is remarkably efficient at conveying specific messages about contemporary problems of race and the history of the Civil Rights Movement. What is the latent power in such an image? It is here that concepts from semiotics and narratology can aid in revealing some of the word–image secrets used to convey these meanings.

The first secret is that a narrative is present within it after all. The heroic narrative of civil rights, the story outlined and summarized by Romano and

The Civil Rights Movement (Re)Narrated 211

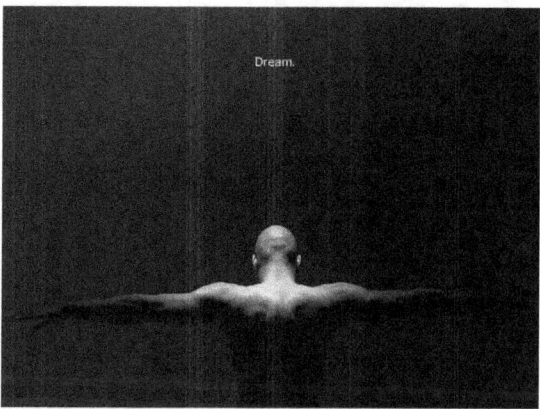

Figure 10.1 'Dream', 2017. Retrieved on 6 September 2017 from http://www.care2.com/send/card/6131, link no longer available.

Raiford at the beginning of this chapter, is here condensed even further, reduced to the signifier 'Dream'. The heroic narrative is present in this single word as its connotation. The effectiveness of the message contained in this e-card rests on a gamble – namely, that the recipient of the card will recognize the connotation first, instead of its denotation. For the card to be understood, the connotative content of the signifier must overpower the denotation, and come to the fore. The dream here referred to is not, after all, the dream that is the object of Freudian psychoanalysis; it is the romantic vision of the heroic leader of the Civil Rights Movement, Dr Martin Luther King Jr. and his 'I have a dream', the memorable refrain of his most iconic speech delivered on the Washington Mall in 1963. It is not only the culmination of King's speech that day, it is the climactic moment of the heroic narrative of the Civil Rights Movement. It is the moment of *peripeteia*, the term Aristotle used to name the turning point of a story. The hero and main character comes to the heart of the country and delivers a famous speech that moves a nation. In the years following the march on Washington, so the story goes, the Voting Rights Act and the Civil Rights Act are passed and the final heroic victory of the Civil Rights Movement is achieved.

Many historians have been critical of how King's most iconic speech has been remembered in American culture. For example, David Blight has noted that much of the rich imagery summoned by King in the so-called 'dream' speech, has been forgotten. For instance, the main point of the beginning part of King's speech was the claim that America had issued a 'bad check' to blacks, and he was very critical of the United States and the injustices that blacks had suffered. But there is also an interesting narratological point to be made about this speech – as a climactic and iconic moment, it has come to stand for the story as a whole.

Of course, the word 'dream' does not do all this work on its own. Were this to be the case, then simply mentioning the word in any context would call up images of the Civil Rights Movement; obviously, that is not the case. The card depends upon a word–image dialectic in which it is the black body that helps the aforementioned connotation to emerge.[4] The body, through its blackness, lets us know that it is the Civil Rights Movement that is being referred to. Were the body another colour, this association might not be made. Here we see an excellent example of how race is a floating signifier, as Stuart Hall has argued.[5] In the twenty-first-century United States, black skin carries meaning; it signifies.

The card's meaning is also contingent upon paratextual factors: the fact that this e-card is intended to be sent in celebration of Black History Month ensures that the allusion to Martin Luther King – and through him, to the heroic civil rights narrative – is reinforced. Thus, in order to comprehend the message contained in this card, one needs to be familiar with the mythology and cultural codes of the contemporary United States. In other words, this card has an implied reader–viewer – an American citizen who is cognizant of the tradition of Black History Month and its significance, and who is, of course, aware of the cultural practice of sending greeting cards to mark important occasions.

Although the actual reader–viewer of the greeting card may be of any race or background, I would venture that the implied one is an African American. And I offer this hypothesis because of a grammatical detail that I think merits further consideration. The single-word sentence 'Dream' is also an injunction, an imperative: it impels the reader to action, to dreaming. The card bears an inspirational message as it urges the reader to dare to dream of great things, even in the face of adversity – like Martin Luther King who, in spite of segregation and racism, could dream that his daughters would 'one day live in a nation where they will not be judged by the colour of their skin but by the content of their character'. Meanwhile, the body, seen from the back, is anonymous, permitting the viewer to identify with him, to take his place. In comparison to the image, the word is printed in a diminutive size and font, but the simplicity of the word only serves to accentuate the nobility of its message. The black body emerging into the light from the dark ground of the image further supports that message with its visual metaphor of a brighter future. Dreaming is for idealists, but those who know the story of the heroic Civil Rights Movement, know that it ended in victory. Without this knowledge of the end of the heroic narrative of civil rights and the moral of its story, the motivational message of this e-card cannot be grasped.[6]

This e-card indicates how widespread a particular narrative of civil rights has become, but it also demonstrates that historical consciousness in contemporary societies is constructed and perpetuated across various media. This is important to note, because it suggests that historians who are interested in using the insights of narratology to critique historical narratives cannot afford to limit themselves to textual analyses of historical writing. Indeed, as new media becomes increasingly predominant, techniques drawn from the analysis of visual culture and semiotics may become essential tools for historians seeking to understand and to critique the various historical narratives that circulate in society.

The Heroism of the Heroic Narrative

As with greeting cards, semiotic and narratological analyses can equally be applied to academic historical writing. And the heroic narrative of civil rights is, after all, also disseminated by historians in their written texts. There are numerous narrative histories of the civil rights struggle, but due to space limitations in this chapter I will take only one example, Harvard Sitkoff's well-known book, *The Struggle for Black Equality 1954–1992*. I would like to focus on one passage in particular, the one in which the historian introduces the Montgomery bus boycott:

> Mrs Rosa Parks said no. Her feet hurt. Politely yet firmly, the 42-year-old brown-skinned seamstress said no a second time. Some black passengers on the bus, fearful for Parks's safety, and their own, shook their heads; others exclaimed 'Lawd, Lawds', expecting a violent reprisal. The driver sternly insisted again that she move back and give up her seat to a standing white man. That was the law. Parks held fast. Weary after her long hard day of holiday-season work at the men's alteration shop of the Montgomery fair department store, she wanted to remain seated for the rest of her ride. On that fateful first of December 1955, Parks demurred again, defying the cannons of white supremacy.
> 'Are you going to stand up?'
> 'No' . . .
> The Black Panther publicist Eldridge Cleaver would later write about that moment: 'Somewhere in the universe, a gear in the machinery had shifted'.[7]

To describe what the author tries to do in this passage, we could refer to the analytical distinction that narratologists sometimes draw between narration and description. These two elements of a narrative can, in principle, be distinguished from one another, even though where the one begins and the other ends has been a question of debate among scholars.[8] The passage cited above can also be analysed on these two levels.

On the level of narration, it should be noted that the passage not only opens the second chapter of Sitkoff's book, but it also marks the starting point of the story of the heroic Civil Rights Movement that he recounts throughout the book. Parks's direct action on a Montgomery bus is here emplotted as an inaugural event in the story of civil rights. This placement is significant – it plays a central role in determining the contours of the plot of the heroic narrative. In order to mark the importance of this event in his plot, and in history, Sitkoff chooses to slow his narration and recount Rosa Parks's actions in detail. In any narrative, and especially in a narrative that covers an expanse of calendar time as long as Sitkoff's book, the narration can be sped up or slowed down, which is to say that a minute can be recounted in a paragraph, and a decade can be recounted in a sentence. The choice of slowing or speeding the narration belongs to the author, and it can be deployed as he or she pleases. Here Sitkoff has chosen to dedicate a page to an episode that lasted only a few minutes, and of course, he does this for a reason: precisely to mark it as a heroic event and a turning point in the story he is telling.

At the same time, on the level of description, this passage serves as an allegory for non-violent resistance, and for the heroism of the Civil Rights Movement in general. It defines the mood and the atmosphere of the era that will be described in the subsequent pages. Rosa Parks's direct-action protest is presented in great detail as a heroic and simple act of defiance against injustice. The passage seems to emphasize the stark contrast between the simplicity of the monosyllabic utterance 'no' on the one hand and, the enormous heroism and historical importance of its significance on the other. The 'no' appears in the first sentence and is repeated throughout the passage, each sentence explaining more of what is at stake in Parks's refusal to give up her seat. Like the word 'dream' discussed above, the 'no' also contains deeper connotations: it is not only a refusal to stand up, it is a rejection of systemic injustice, even in spite of the knowledge that doing so would put her at great risk. The bravery of her protest is emphasized by the fearful remarks of the other passengers, '*Lawd, Lawds*'; their dialect indicates Southern-ness. Narratives of the Civil Rights Movement are often littered with references to the 'simple courage and undeniable virtue' of the movement's activists, and this vignette conveys that courage and virtue in dramatic fashion.

Lower down in the passage, Sitkoff quotes the Black Panther, Eldridge Cleaver, in order to underline the historical importance of the event. Although Cleaver did not participate in the Montgomery bus boycott and only came to prominence in the late 1960s, Sitkoff uses his words because they clearly express the historian's own view that Parks's defiance changed the course of history. Obviously, there are no gears in the universe, but citing Cleaver's figurative language enables Sitkoff to shift speeds in the plot. The reference to Cleaver also functions as a prefiguration: a character who will appear later in the story, in the chapter on Black Power, is cited here anticipating his own coming. The view that Parks's actions marked the beginning of a coherent story that would continue until the late 1960s is thus reinforced. The story is opened here, but the closure of the story is also anticipated, because in the heroic narrative of the civil rights movement, the rise of Black Power – here personified by Cleaver – is the end of the story.

The 'Long Civil Rights Movement'

But when did the story of the Civil Rights Movement really end? Many historiographical debates have focused on the question of beginnings and endings of historical periods, and the historiography of the Civil Rights Movement is no exception. Did the Civil Rights Movement begin in Montgomery and end in Memphis, or did it begin much earlier, in the 1930s, as the proponents of the 'long Civil Rights Movement' would have it? Did the rise of Black Power really signal the demise of civil rights, or is it better to speak of a continuous struggle throughout the so-called Black Power era? These very interesting problems of periodization can also be examined from the perspective of narration.

It is no coincidence that beginnings and endings are of crucial importance in both historiography and in a narration. History writing takes a narrative form, as Hayden White has shown us, when the historian chooses to explain historical data by emplotment.[9] Beginnings of historical periods are thus often also the beginnings of historical narratives. Because, in a narrative, the beginning and ending of the story frame the sequence of events that form the plot, they play an essential role in determining the syntagmatic arrangement of those events, and hence endow those events with a narrative meaning. This helps to explain why the question of the temporal boundaries of a given period of history can become such a contentious issue – or why, indeed, the choice of a specific start or end date sometimes seems automatically to imply a particular view on the way that the period hangs together. To be sure, the dates that begin and end historical periods are tied to real and important historical events, but the choice to place said events at the beginning, middle or end of a given narrative belongs to the author.[10]

In her essay 'The Long Civil Rights Movement and the Political Uses of the Past', Jacquelyn Dowd Hall challenges the heroic narrative of civil rights that we have been discussing so far, arguing that it 'distorts as much as it reveals' about the past.[11] According to Dowd Hall, it is the 'New Right' that has played a large role in disseminating a particular narrative of civil rights that effectively purifies the movement of its more radical elements; and it did so for ideological reasons. How does this purification operate? Amongst her critiques, Dowd Hall takes issue with the main characters chosen for the heroic story of civil rights, in particular the focus on the 'defining figure' of Martin Luther King as 'frozen in 1963, proclaiming "I have a dream" during the march on the Mall'. She laments the fact that much of King's legacy has been obscured, and that his 'democratic socialism' and opposition to the Vietnam War have consequently been minimized. Moreover, the focus eclipses a panoply of other, often more radical members of the Civil Rights Movement who operated at the grass-roots level.

Although she does not make the theoretical claim explicit in her text, Dowd Hall's insightful criticism of said narrative, in fact, centres on the framing of its time span. Starting in 1954, it 'proceeds though public protests' until the story comes to a close with the Voting Rights and Civil Rights acts.[12] 'Then comes the decline', writes Dowd Hall, referring to the way the rise of Black Power and other radical movements of the late 1960s and early 1970s are presented in this narrative.[13] The historiographical implication of the shortened time frame of the 'dominant' narrative of civil rights, is clear:

> By confining the civil rights struggle to the South, to bowdlerized heroes, to a single halcyon decade, and to limited, noneconomic objectives, the master narrative simultaneously elevates and diminishes the movement. It ensures the status of the classical phase as a triumphal moment in a larger American progress narrative, yet this undermines its gravitas. It prevents one of the most remarkable mass movements in American history from speaking effectively to the challenges of our time.[14]

At the crux of Dowd Hall's critique, then, is an important argument about narrative. Yet while she convincingly names and criticizes this narrative of progress, she does so without explaining how it functions. How, for example, does a short time span produce a 'bowdlerized' view of the movement? One answer, in my view, can be found in the way that beginnings and endings structure emplotment. The dates themselves reveal that the narrative is King-centric. The Montgomery bus boycott marks the emergence of King onto the political scene. The end of the narrative is, of course, the date of King's death. If one thinks that the civil rights years are mostly about Martin Luther King and the so-called 'Big Four' civil rights organizations, then these dates seem to offer a logical periodization. King is the central subject of the heroic narrative of civil rights.

Dowd Hall offers an alternative narration of civil rights.[15] Her historiographical operation can, from a narratological perspective, be described in very simple terms: by elongating the time frame in order to produce a 'long Civil Rights Movement' she actually constructs an entirely new plot, with another beginning, middle and end. By shifting the plot in this way, the main character of the 'classical phase', Martin Luther King, is reduced in importance, as he becomes one character alongside many others. In fact, in Dowd Hall's account, there is a shift of narrative subject: it is no longer the civil rights coalition that is at the centre of the story, but rather a broader range of black groups. This is why she and other scholars who take the long view tend to speak less about the Civil Rights Movement and more of the 'black freedom struggle' — an expression that captures a much broader range of groups.[16]

Exploding Black Power

The 'narrative breach' between civil rights and Black Power, that Dowd Hall speaks of, has been the topic of renewed interest of scholars in the field 'Black Power studies'. According to one of the leading thinkers of this group, historian Peniel E. Joseph, Black Power studies seek to re-examine and to challenge the historiographical tradition that has devoted a great deal of attention to the 'heroic' years of the Civil Rights Movement but tended to neglect the significance of Black Power, and to characterize it as

> a destructive, short-lived, and politically ineffectual movement that triggered [a] white backlash [and] urban rioting, and severely crippled the mainstream civil rights struggle. Black Power's classical period of 1966–1975 is most often characterized as a kind of fever dream dominated by outsized personalities who spewed words of fire that make this a justly forgotten era. Moreover, histories of the New Left tend to blame Black Power radicalism for inspiring white radicals towards a simplistic and tragically romantic view of 'revolutionary' violence.[17]

Black Power scholars have challenged traditional views of Black Power in a number of ways, and one of the main tactics has been to problematize the distinction between the 'non-violent' Civil Rights Movement and the 'violent' Black Power movement. This has been achieved primarily by showing the continuities between these periods and by highlighting instances of Black Power-type politics outside of the spatio-temporal boundaries in which the movement has traditionally been situated. Indeed, against the view that Black Power was primarily a phenomenon of the late 1960s that was concentrated in urban milieux, Black Power historians have incisively pointed out the presence of 'self-defence' groups during the southern US civil rights struggle — groups that often protected non-violent demonstrators. Peniel E. Joseph, who wrote the first narrative history of Black Power, uses this strategy when he begins his story not in 1966 in Mississippi, but in the 1950s with the arrival of Malcolm X in Harlem.[18] The first chapters of his book are a series of vignettes about radical figures like Malcolm X, who have conventionally been associated with the Black Power movement. But by showing how these figures were keenly aware of what went on in the south of the country, and that indeed they often interacted with this movement, both as critics and as supporters, Joseph succeeds in blurring the line between civil rights and Black Power periods.

Meanwhile the non-violent/violent distinction which supposedly separates civil rights from Black Power has also been the subject of much criticism, as historians have argued that many figures who are called 'violent' actually advocated self-defence. Thus, Jeffery Ogbar has remarked on the irony that although Malcolm X is considered to be an advocate of violence, he mostly avoided it, while the non-violent Martin Luther King was constantly enveloped in violence.[19]

Another way to critique the traditional view of the Black Power period would be to show how this periodization is a narrative construct. This is not to say that the people and events that we associate with Black Power are invented or imagined. Rather it is only to point to the ways in which they have been brought together to form a coherent historical period known as 'the Black Power era' is a function of the way they have been figured by historians in their texts.

We can again turn to a passage in Harvard Sitkoff's book to illustrate this point. Compare his account of the Montgomery bus boycott with his account of the birth of Black Power below:

> On August 11, however, just five days after Johnson signed the voting rights act, the most destructive race riot in more than two decades began in Watts . . . That explosion of bitterness over unfulfilled African-American hopes for dignity and equality sparked a succession of 'long, hot summers'. The violent upheavals hopelessly splintered the Civil Rights Coalition, hastened the decline of CORE and SNCC, and virtually ended significant white support, both financial and political, for the movement. Just as the struggle had hit its stride, the riots cut the legs off the runners best equipped to stay the course successfully. The era of nonviolence ended. The age of Malcolm X's angry heirs began. Strategies of social change gave way to expressions of rage. 'Black Power' drowned out 'Black and White together'. 'Burn, Baby, Burn' supplanted 'Freedom Now'. By the end of 1968, 259 African-Americans had died, over eight thousand had been wounded, and some fifty thousand had been arrested. In the nearly 300 race riots and disturbances since 1965, an estimated half million blacks had participated in the burning and looting. An equal number of Americans served in Vietnam in 1968. The war in Asia had among its many unintended consequences the destruction of racial reform. As the US disgorged it firepower into Vietnam and the ghettos burst into flames, the hopes of the blacks went up in smoke, and King's dream turned to ash.[20]

This passage of text establishes a tone and perhaps a mood for the ensuing chapter on Black Power. Sitkoff evokes what he perceives to be the atmosphere of the 'Black Power era', and heavily emphasizes the themes of anger, fire and violence to this end. That Sitkoff describes this period as 'the age of Malcolm X's angry heirs', in which presumably rational civil rights 'strategies' of social change gave way to 'rage', tells us much about how he views the political value of Black Power groups.

Sitkoff's emphatic use of metaphors of fire and explosion are not simple literary flourishes intended to enliven his prose, however. Rather, it is precisely by linking the rhetoric of Malcolm X with urban riots, the Vietnam

War and the decline of King's dream in a metaphorical relation that 'Black Power' is constituted as a coherent period. It should be clear that there is no immediate causal relation between these things: it is not that Malcolm X called for the Watts riots (he was assassinated several months before), or that the Watts riots were an explicit rejection of Martin Luther King or the Civil Rights Movement. The link between the real fires that engulfed Los Angeles buildings and the angry rhetoric of Black Power activists is primarily figurative.

It has often been pointed out, even by contemporaries, that Black Power was always a nebulous concept that was understood differently by many of its proponents, and was not used by many of those whom historians associate with the term. Although so-called Black Power groups were 'radical' in their outlook, they often had little in common with each other, and in fact were sometimes bitterly opposed. Indeed, groups like the SNCC under Stokely Carmichael, the Black Panther Party, the US organization and the Nation of Islam, had numerous differences and were often at odds with each other. But such differences are elided by the suggestion that they were all manifestations of the same fiery zeitgeist.

But presenting Black Power in this way also has important political implications. By casting it as a pyrogenic movement, Black Power is discredited before the claims and critiques put forward by activists at that time have even been laid out or presented. And in this, Sitkoff's characterization is representative of a great deal of historical writing on Black Power, which views the period as being marked by illogical explosions of emotion as opposed to calculated political organizing. Some contemporaries of Black Power also saw it in these terms. For example, Allen J. Matusow's 1969 essay on the SNCC presents the thesis that Black Power was the product of the frustration and anger of non-violent student activists in Mississippi in the mid-1960s. Matusow argued that 'the true significance of Black Power lies not in the doctrines into which it evolved but in the historical circumstances that gave birth to it'.[21] And those circumstances, he goes on to explain, were a burnout among civil rights workers in Mississippi: 'SNCC's frustrations exploded intellectually in the formulation of Black Power doctrines, but ghetto rage took the form of the riot'.[22] By troping Black Power ideology as explosive, Matusow succeeds in moving unproblematically from Mississippi to Los Angeles in one sentence.

In both Sitkoff's and Matusow's work, the Watts riots stand as an allegory for the Black Power era in general; this is due in part to the perceived symbolism of the burning, looting and destruction that took place, as well as to the timing of the riot no less than five days after Lyndon Johnson had signed the Voting Rights Act. Presented in this way, Black Power indeed seemingly emerges all of a sudden, like an unwelcome and ungrateful explosion, at the very moment the Civil Rights Movement was achieving success. This construal of Black Power has obvious political implications: the groups and individuals associated with Black Power are disparaged, even vilified and separated from the Civil Rights Movement, which, placed in a juxtaposition to Black Power as its opposite, looks even more heroic.

Conclusion

In this chapter, I have attempted to show that multimedia narratological and semiotic analysis can offer useful approaches for historians. But narratological theory following the work of earlier historians, especially Hayden White, can be further augmented by transmedial and cross-disciplinary methods. Indeed, as more and more historical information is now disseminated across media that are both visual and textual, such methods of analysis will become all the more important for historians. The examples that I have presented here were taken up with the aim of showing how narrative choices influence and even construct objects of historical study, and demonstrating that particular dominant narratives can become so naturalized that they become almost common sense. The image and message of the e-card depends upon the pre-existing knowledge of that narrative; the card becomes a metonym for the heroic narrative of the Civil Rights Movement that has been disseminated through other texts and images, and the image of the e-card in turn references and reinforces that standard narrative, thus perpetuating it further. The historiographical narratives of the Civil Rights Movement and Black Power are scholarly choices to be sure, but they are also the result of narrative and figurative strategies. Such strategies constitute the historical meaning that is said to reside in the events. Different narrations of civil rights have their own political implications: They can work to sideline aspects of the continuing struggle for civil rights, in favour of a triumphal tale of progress in which persistent inequality is obscured, but they can also highlight the continuities of the black freedom struggle, linking the protests and activism of the 1960s with events today.

Kenan Van de Mieroop teaches history at Utrecht University in the Netherlands. He is also a co-founder of the International Network for Theory of History. He publishes on topics relating to the theory and philosophy of history and public history. His work has analysed public historical engagements with black history in the United States and in France from a comparative perspective.

Notes

1. Romano and Raiford, *Civil Rights Movement*, xii.
2. Ibid., xxi.
3. Arnesen, 'Reconsidering the Long Civil Rights Movement'.
4. Mitchell, *Picture Theory*.
5. Jhally, *Stuart Hall*.
6. Elsewhere, I have argued that the Black History Month now celebrated in the United States often tends to resemble motivational speech to young African Americans (Van de Mieroop, 'On the Advantage and Disadvantage of Black History Month for Life'.)
7. Sitkoff, *Struggle for Black Equality*, 37–38.
8. Genette, 'Boundaries of Narrative', 5.
9. White, *Metahistory*, 7.
10. It might also be imposed by convention, or by the request of other historians or readers.
11. Dowd Hall, 'Civil Rights Movement'.
12. Ibid., 1234.
13. Ibid.
14. Ibid.
15. Dowd Hall, 'Civil Rights Movement', 1254.
16. Carson, 'Civil Rights Reform'.
17. Joseph, 'Historians and the Black Power Movement', 8.
18. Joseph, *Waiting 'Til the Midnight Hour*.
19. Ogbar, *Black Power*, 42.
20. Sitkoff, *Struggle for Black Equality*, 184.
21. Matusow, 'From Civil Rights to Black Power', 383.
22. Ibid., 377.

Bibliography

Arnesen, Eric. 'Reconsidering the Long Civil Rights Movement'. *Historically Speaking* 10(2) (2009), 31–34.

Carson, Clayborn. 'Civil Rights Reform and the Black Freedom Struggle', in Charles C. Eagels (ed.), *The Civil Rights Movement in America* (Jackson: University Press of Mississippi, 1986), 19–37.

Dowd Hall, Jacquelyn. 'The Long Civil Rights Movement and the Political Uses of the Past'. *The Journal of American History* 91(4) (2005), 1233–63.

Genette, Gerard. 'Boundaries of Narrative', translated by Ann Levonas. *New Literary History* 8(1) (1976), 1–13.

Jhally, Sut. *Stuart Hall: Race, the Floating Signifier*. Northampton, MA: Media Education Foundation, 1996.

Joseph, Peniel E. 'Historians and the Black Power Movement'. *OAH Magazine of History* 22(3) (2008), 8–15.

———. *Waiting 'Til the Midnight Hour: A Narrative History of Black Power in America*. New York: Henry Holt and Company, 2007.

Matusow, Allen J. 'From Civil Rights to Black Power: The Case of the SNCC, 1960–66', in Barton J. Bernstein and Allen J. Matusow (eds), *Twentieth-Century America: Recent Interpretations*, 2nd edn (New York: Harcourt Brace Jovanovich, 1972), 367–83.

Mitchell, William John Thomas. *Picture Theory: Essays on Verbal and Visual Representation*. Chicago: University of Chicago Press, 1994.

Ogbar, Jeffrey. *Black Power: Radical Politics and African American Identity*. Baltimore, MD: Johns Hopkins University, 2005.

Romano, Renee, and Leigh Raiford (eds). *The Civil Rights Movement in American Memory*. Athens, GA: University of Georgia Press, 2006.

Sitkoff, Harvard. *The Struggle for Black Equality, 1954–1992*. New York: Hill and Wang, 1993.

Van de Mieroop, Kenan. 'On the Advantage and Disadvantage of Black History Month for Life: The Creation of the Post-racial Era'. *History and Theory* 55 (2016), 3–24.

White, Hayden. *Metahistory: The Historical Imagination in Nineteenth-Century Europe*. Baltimore, MD: Johns Hopkins University, 1973.

CHAPTER 11

Media Narratives of 1970s Left-Wing Terrorism

Jörg Requate

A terrorist attack can be conceived as a kind of visible climax to a story of which the beginning and subsequent course has, up until that point, been largely unknown to the public. When on 11 September 2001 the planes crashed into the towers of the World Trade Center, it was completely unclear which story was concealed behind it and which story should be told.

The media have a fixation on the immediate topicality of current events, involving an obligation that forces them not only to portray these events, but also to categorize them and to immediately produce a narrative. But from the point of view of the victims, the shape of the narrative is already predetermined: it is a tragedy and the terrorist attack a peripeteia in their life story. People die, are seriously injured, lose family members and friends – that morning they had a normal life which has now been superseded by a completely unforeseeable, tragic turn of events. From the perspective of the narration technique used by the media, this story is in principle simple. It is relatively easy to reconstruct, can be reproduced simultaneously multiple times for each single individual and his/her fate. In contrast, the position of the perpetrator presents a much larger challenge in the narrative technique. Research on terrorism rightly emphasizes that in essence terrorist attacks are to be understood as a communication strategy. But what exactly should be conveyed and to whom is frequently only discernible in fragments, and a consistent message cannot always be established. In the cases of September

Notes for this section begin on page 237.

11th, the terrorist attacks of 2015/16 in Paris, and in many other cases, one initially knew nothing about the perpetrators, their life stories, their personal motives, the concrete background or the sequence of events leading up to the attacks. And even if it were possible to collate more details, the fact that preparations for a terrorist attack are of course kept secret means that much remains open and unresolved. Nevertheless, it seems inevitable that the media repeatedly use the new details to compose new stories, which are in turn part of a media metanarrative, defining their own role as crucial for the reconstruction of events and the clarification of crimes.

Although these observations apply absolutely to a discursive handling of terrorist attacks, one can nevertheless establish major differences between how comprehensively and in which manner each story is told about the terrorist attacks themselves, terrorist groups in general, and the interaction between these groups and the state. The terrorism of the 1970s, and most particularly left-wing terrorism, proves to be particularly productive in this respect, which is anything but a coincidence. Three closely related points converged here. Firstly, particular actions, especially the kidnapping and taking of hostages, were frequently employed by terrorist groups, primarily in the 1970s, as a type of 'mini-series' of actions, which constantly supplied material for a dramatic story with an indeterminate outcome, for days and sometimes even for weeks on end, and which were conveyed, so to speak, by the media in real time.[1] These types of actions – and this is my second point – were an unmistakable feature of a communication strategy, which was accompanied in addition to the attacks themselves by 'public relations exercises'. Although these 'public relations exercises' were operated by the different groups with varying intensity, the RAF (Red Army Faction) and the Red Brigades, as well as Palestinian groups, the Basque ETA (*Euskadi Ta Askatasuna*) and the IRA (Irish Republican Army), all had a strong media presence, especially in the 1970s. Letters claiming responsibility, communiqués and political statements and demands were issued to the press and were guaranteed attention. Thirdly, in consequence, a great number of the protagonists of the terrorist groups were well known and enjoyed a certain type of fame, which in turn offered the great advantage of personalization options to the media narrative.

Thus, the media did not just accompany the terrorist attacks and the government responses to them, but they were directly involved in them and provided at the same time an interpretative framework and a narrative structure. This is evident not least from the fact that the role of the media was an integral part of the examination of left-wing terrorism, and of the way society dealt with it. After repeated reference has already been made to the fact that the media played an important role in achieving an understanding of the RAF, Jan Henschen has recently argued that the RAF must be regarded as an actual 'media project', even more than is customary so far. The mutual penetration of media and terrorist practice therefore has to be analysed even more intensively. According to Henschen, 'event and symbol, operation andits representation, presence and past, are and were the interlocked basic figures of "being RAF" and "acting RAF"'.[2] Here Henschen also emphasizes the peculiar interweaving of documentation and fictionalization. In fact, the RAF and their environment were from the start always in some indirect and some direct form the subject of fictional descriptions. The fictional versions – notably Böll's novel and the film version of 'Die verlorene Ehre der Katharina Blum' – dealt with the role of the media in a particularly effective and succinct way. Even though the individual portrayals deviated from each other to a great extent and presented widely different interpretations, and the coverage in the media, the fictional representations and the academic debate on this subject provided a very contradictory picture, a certain basic narrative can nevertheless be established. Even if all of the players involved had their share in the development of these narratives, the media representation established the central guidelines. The media representation provided not only the initial chronological categorization of the attacks – including their beginning and ending, which are fundamental to all narrativization – but also created the framework for the debate as a whole through the generation of attention. Martin Steinseifer has put forward the argument that a central function of the media coverage was to establish a connection between the events relating to the RAF and to depict them as a series of acts that had a tendency to escalate.[3] According to the overall narrative perspective, 'the terrorists' and 'the state' were diametrically opposed. The historians Sylvia Schraut and Klaus Weinhauer recently emphasized that this dichotomous point of view was also dominant in academic literature until the beginning of the 1990s: 'Established scholarly narratives about political violence, the (nation) state and related gender codes were questioned. These traditional narratives were at the same time state-centred and very dichotomous: they (the terrorists) fought against us (the state and society)'.[4]

Daniel Fulda emphasizes that the construction of opposition is also a central instrument for narrative within the historiography, and he continues by stating that 'structuring the infinitely ramified process of human actions in time according to the "dramaturgical model" can give rise to the coherence and meaningful development implied in the collective singular "History"'.[5] The provocation of the state by a small group thereby created a firm dramaturgical framework, which was established by the media but which had an effect on the historiography. One of the most important German publications on the subject of left-wing terrorism from this period carried the title 'Angriff auf das Herz des Staates' [Attack on the heart of the state]. This is interesting in as much as the contributions to the book endeavour to create a very differentiated picture, and they discuss the problems related to the term terrorism: 'terrorists are bad guys (similar to 'drug dealers'). It is even justifiable to bomb their towns and camps, as can be seen with recent events in the Near East . . . Terrorists are State enemies on a national level, in our country they are enemies of the constitution'.[6] In spite of this criticism on a demonizing segregation and homogenization of terrorists, the book with the title that it was given was nonetheless registered fully in the dichotomous narrative, and thus followed the media logic of generating attention and the corresponding narrative.

Schraut and Weinhauer note a significant departure in the consideration of terrorism during the late 1990s. According to them, the dichotomous, polarizing point of view in the media representation was replaced in academic circles by a perspective that was increasingly informed by cultural history: the RAF historians have become increasingly concerned with the issues of the culture of memory, while connecting the history of terrorism and the general history of political violence, and dedicating more attention to the interaction between the state, a media-dominated society and social movements.

Nevertheless there are also similarities between the media and the academic representations: whereas on the one hand the protagonists of the so-called first generation of terrorists – in particular Ulrike Meinhof, Gudrun Ensslin and Andreas Bader – were people whose life stories were well known and identifiable to the general public; on the other hand, this applied a great deal less, at least initially, to members of the so-called second generation. After the reunification of Germany and the consequent discovery of former terrorists living in the GDR, together with the fact that these and other former terrorists took a public stand, meant that certain people moved more into the focus of interest. This applied, in fact, not only to the perpetrators but also the victims, and their respective fates increasingly became a subject of discussion. The attention given to the perpetrators and victims had a direct relation to the personalization mechanisms in the media. The individual fates provided the perfect material for personal stories – but it was impossible to incorporate them into an overall coherent narrative.

Fighting the State – Hunting the Terrorists

If one searches for the origins of the dichotomization of terrorism and the state, Ulrike Meinhof's statement below regarding the release of Andreas Baader had a central function, published in 1970 in *Spiegel* magazine. Ulrike Meinhof's jump out of the window was the jump to the other side, to the sphere outside society, and the article made it clear that there could no longer be any bridges or links between the two sides, but only a battle:

> And we say, of course, the cops are pigs, we say, the guy in the uniform is a pig and not a man, and so we have to tackle him. That means, we are not to talk to him, and it is wrong to talk with these people at all, and of course one can shoot. Because it is not our problem that they are people, insofar as it is their function or their job to protect the crimes of the system, to defend and represent the criminality of the system. And if we have to deal with them, then they are simply criminals, then they are just pigs. There is a very clear-cut front.[7]

A more extreme demarcation between 'we' and 'the system' is hardly possible, whereby the 'we' is defined by the unconditional support of the RAF's position. This demarcation between themselves and the state, associated with their self-presentation as martyrs willing to accept death in order to achieve their goals, is a feature that without exception pervades the programmatic statements of the RAF.[8] The relentless hunt for the 'Public Enemy No.1' was the answer to this declaration of war. After a newly founded 'special terrorism unit' had started its work on 1 February 1971, the pressure on the search was not only greatly increased, but was correspondingly accompanied by the media: 'Last week the Bonn Security Group gave the alarm fifty times per day, day in and day out,' according to *Spiegel* on 22 February 1971, 'and made the police to be called out in the towns and the country, in the north and the south'; and 'Hunted: Public Enemy No. 1', according to Springer's *Welt am Sonntag* and the Munich *Abendzeitung*. The enemy appeared to be everywhere – as if the invasion from the Wega had started. 'We have not had such a group of desperados since the end of the war', concluded Bonn's chief security officer, Dr Günther Nollau. The police officer Heinz Müller from Lower Saxony described the atmosphere in the police squads as like having 'a lion let loose'. Böll's formulation '6 against 60 million' lines up with this directly, even if he was then trying to break down this situation. However, the frame of the manhunt narrative had already been fixed, and had been personalized in the media representation by one of the main protagonists. This personalization escalated further on the publication in 1997 in academic circles of the double biography by the historian Dorothea Hauser, *Bader und Herold: Beschreibung eines Kampfes*, which was widely registered in the media. One of the central consequences of this dichotomous escalation of the struggle between terrorist groups and the state, and the state's hunting of the criminals, was that all of those individuals who attempted to withdraw their commitment to the state came under considerable pressure to justify themselves. This was made especially clear by the disputes revolving around the 'sympathizers', the 'accomplices', the 'Klammheimlichen', and last but not least the supposedly 'left-wing solicitors'.[9] It is noticeable that the perspective of precisely those who saw themselves as being 'caught between the front lines' is particularly present in the films of the 1970s and 1980s. Volker Schlöndorf's *Die verlorene Ehre der Katharina Blum*, Margarethe von Trotta's *Die Bleierne Zeit*, Reinhard Hauff's *Messer im Kopf*, and last but not least the episodic film *Deutschland im Herbst* all convey without exception an oppressing atmosphere, in which the protagonists get caught directly between the fronts of a threatening and apparently hermetic state power and a mostly diffuse terrorist threat. Fassbinder's performance in *Deutschland im Herbst* is particularly impressive; he plays an individual who is desperate and well and truly crushed by the knowledge that he cannot deal with the political circumstances. In Reinhard Hauff's film *Stammheim*, which reconstructs the trial based on the trial records, the courtroom is depicted as the place where the state power manifested by the judges stands face to face with those who were about to destroy the country. Both sides appear here as totally unable to communicate, as wholly unable to build a basic communicative bridge. As with the other films mentioned, the audience was left behind feeling helpless and depressed between the two fronts.

At the end of the 1990s, Heinrich Breloer chose a completely different approach to the subject in his 'documentary drama film *Todesspiel*, in which the events surrounding the kidnapping and murder of Hanns Martin Schleyer, as well as the associated hijacking of the Lufthansa plane 'Landshut' were reconstructed. Also, Breloer represented the events in a narrative of dichotomous confrontation, although he was clearly shifting its perspective. In his case, two irreconcilable opponents were also standing opposite each other, but the methods of portrayal had changed radically. Whereas the state was depicted in the films of the 1970s and 1980s as largely hermetic, and personified by a mask-like and cypher-like police, Breloer now showed the representatives of the state as individuals who often struggle with themselves and their decisions, which caused them concerns. By contrast, Breloer gave the terrorists mask-like, non-individual traits, which were dehumanized to a certain extent. The earlier films did not in any way endorse the acts of the terrorists, but the decision to employ violence appeared to partly stem here from an act of desperation, which, although not justifiable, was shown as a product of specific circumstances and developments. Whereas in the films of the 1970s and 1980s it was the members of a left-wing milieu who were shown as those who got caught between the fronts, Breloer brought the actual victims of the terrorist attacks into the foreground, not only the passengers and crew members of the 'Landshut' but especially the president of the Federal Employers' Association, Hanns Martin Schleyer. Breloer portrayed Schleyer completely in the role of the victim, showing his human reactions, whereas his national socialist past hardly played a role at all. This shifting of roles comes particularly to the fore during Schleyer's interrogation by the RAF. The audience does not see Schleyer as sitting in the dock, but the person being interrogated unmasks the kidnappers. As Julia Schumacher expresses in her work on Breloer's film, owing to the characteristic style of the documentation film and its closeness to the facts, the film is central for a significant redefinition of society's perspective on the RAF, and particularly of the Deutscher Herbst.[10]

Books written by journalists form an important link between the media's preoccupation with the issue and interest from academic circles, a relatively large number of which deal with left-wing terrorism and its protagonists. The significance of Stefan Aust's book on the 'Baader-Meinhof-Complex', first published in 1985, can hardly be overestimated here.[11] Following its publication in 1985, this book has since been reissued several times, and parts of it have been thoroughly revised and supplemented. The book is justifiably considered to be a 'standard reference work' on this subject, not least because Aust relates the events with a mixture of intensive journalistic research and personal involvement – he got to know Ulrike Meinhof whilst working with her on the magazine *konkret*, and in 1970 he brought Meinhof's daughters back from Sicily to their father in Hamburg on his own. However, what is also evident is that Aust's account does not hide the gaps in knowledge, but fills them by use of narrative techniques, meaning that in certain neuralgic sections there is repeatedly a mixture of fiction and verifiable accounts, which is hard to disentangle.[12] Aust supplies, in the form of a report, an exciting portrayal of a whole series of criminal cases, which were still fresh in the memories of the readers of the first editions, and which were subsequently reproduced repeatedly in the media. Aust's account of 1985 concluded with a dramatizing résumé: '47 fatalities. That is the end result of seven years of "underground warfare" in the Federal Republic of Germany. These seven years changed the Republic'. Aust thus emplots the criminal cases as one historical episode and as one historical drama. This plot structures his whole account and bestows upon the story a continuous effectiveness. The fact that the producer Bernd Eichinger decided to make a film many years later based on the events from the book, which was released in 2008, confirms the continuing faith and interest in this way of framing the RAF-past. The film's success proved Eichinger to be correct, giving the media's treatment of the subject a renewed impetus. Wolfgang Kraushaar, the historian and an expert on the history of the RAF, made the following criticism of the film: it wanted cinema-goers to 'now savour the adventure playground of the RAF whilst consuming popcorn and alcopops'.[13] The statement 'the RAF sells' has been true for a long time. Indeed, it is undeniable that Aust's established mix of exciting criminal story with dramatic historical meaning encourages one to recount the story repeatedly, while adding in some cases a large number of new aspects, in others just a few.

Kraushaar's observation that the 'RAF sells' also applies to the academic evaluation of the subject. Just one part of Kraushaar's numerous publications regarding the history of left-wing terrorism follows the narrative of the criminal case that needs to be solved. This applies to Kraushaar's book *Die Bombe im jüdischen Gemeindehaus* [Bomb in the Jewish Community Hall], which, as Kraushaar proves, had been planted by Albert Fichter, who was a member of the Tupamaros West Berlin. One can readily observe in this book, but also in other books by Kraushaar, how a 'distanced' historical analysis alternates with a journalistic narration of an exciting criminal case. Under the chapter title 'Der Bombenleger', Kraushaar recounts in great detail Albert Fichter's story about the bomb that did not detonate.[14] The changes from the present to the past tense clearly represent his switches between a more analytical, enlightening style and a more emotional storytelling style.

One can gain an even clearer view of the extent to which the terrorist attacks of left-wing groups (which have still not yet been fully solved) hold a high fascination when reading Kraushaar's book about Verena Becker and her possible direct involvement in the murder of Siegfried Buback.[15] Kraushaar puts forward the conjecture here that Verena Becker already had contact with the Federal Office for the Protection of the Constitution during the time of the 'Deutscher Herbst', and that the state has to this day no interest in a complete clarification of the crime. Ultimately this remains an allegation, as in Kraushaar's case, that is very vague and not verifiable. The fact that a book on this subject was published in 2010 can only be explained by the connection to the comprehensive narrative of the criminal case and by the unwavering interest of the media. Thus, it was relatively easy for Michael Buback, the son of Siegfried Buback, the chief federal prosecutor who was assassinated, to generate interest in the media for his questions that were still unsolved, and to contribute in this way to an update of the criminal story of the RAF.[16]

The journalist Butz Peters' latest book, which is titled *1977: RAF gegen Bundesrepublik* [1977: The RAF against the Federal Republic of Germany], is another indication that it is still attractive to relate the history of the RAF as a criminal story. In 2004, Peters had already published a story about the RAF, which essentially drew its strength from an action-packed narrative, turning the reader into a direct witness of the struggle between the RAF and the state. The new book follows the same chronological and narrative pattern:

> The overture to the Deutscher Herbst begins in the spring, on Maundy Thursday. A misty, dull day. A petrol pump attendant is surprised – it's just after half past eight in Karlsruhe. Heinrich Wagner is standing behind his cash desk and observes through the window of his salesroom something strange next to a petrol pump. Two men are standing there with a Suzuki GS 750. The bike is absolutely like a rocket – we are in the year 1977, and it is the fastest mass-produced machine in the world.[17]

The legal authorities have been concerned with the open questions until today, or at least until the recent past, and the criminal story of the RAF still captivates its readers today.

The Generation Narrative

Discourse on the 'generations' has for a long time been firmly established in academic debates – sociological as well as historical. Like 'the working class' or 'the bourgeoisie', the concept of 'generation' fulfils a narrative function – that is, it attributes a subject status with its own options of action to a collective actor, a group of people, that one does not find as such in the sources.[18] The generations model is firmly integrated in most explanations regarding the worldwide cultural awakening and the associated protests of 1968. The historian Gerd Koenen puts forward the argument in his book on the 'red decade' that the year 1968 was in essence about 'an extraordinary conflict between world war generations and postwar generations'.[19] It would be difficult to find another plausible explanation. The concept of generation provides a narrative coherence to the events of '1968', and presents them as a comprehensive, global history. In the character of Che Guevara, Koenen sees an association between the '68 protest movement and the militancy emerging from it. The youth culture of these years was focused on the already dead Ernesto Che Guevara.[20] 'Everyone had read his records from the Cuban civil war and they did not find it strange, for instance, to read macho eulogies about "the hardy and noble warriors", who cried, "because they did not have the honour to be first in line in the case of battle and death"'.[21] The author and literary academic Hans Egon Holthusen also observed in the glorified admiration for Guevara's heroism a unifying bond for the young people of the '68 generation: 'these . . . young people, who were extremely hostile to authority and were disrespectful, experienced, somehow for the first time, the epiphany of heroism'. Che Guevara was a character for them who 'united the classical elements of the heroic in a chemically pure ratio: selflessness, unconditionality, contempt of death, generosity of spirit and – cruelty'.[22] Guevara thus became an idol of the youth, who allowed themselves to be fascinated by supposedly heroic violence. The narrative framing presented the move to terrorism, although it was only implemented by individuals, as a collective project of 'the 1968 generation'.

In 1977, the South African author Jillian Becker published a book with the title *Hitler's Children: The Story of the Baader-Meinhof-Gang*, which tries to explain the phenomenon of the RAF to English-speaking readers. However, she does not really make a connection between national socialism and the RAF, as is suggested by the title. Nevertheless, this 'Nazi connection' was at the centre of the generation narrative, which on the one hand socialized the conflict between the RAF and the state, and on the other hand personalized it. Socialization, here, means that the conflict as established in the confrontation narrative between the state and a group was located on a social level, whereby its roots were situated in the national socialistic past. It is of secondary importance here that this aspect remained vague in the book.

The personalization was significantly more tangible. The life stories of Ulrike Meinhof and Gudrun Ensslin were in the focus of the account, and they exercised a considerable fascination on the media from the start. The fact that the well-known journalist Ulrike Meinhof and the pastor's daughter Gudrun Ensslin went underground called for explanations, and the generation approach attempted to place the individual life paths into a social and historical context.

The autobiographical novel *Die Reise* [The journey] by Bernward Vesper, the deceased former partner of Gudrun Ensslin, was also published in 1977. Vesper was a son of the nationalist poet Willi Vesper, and the novel, or rather the fragment of a novel, appeared to be both a reckoning with the 'generation of Auschwitz' and an admission of the failure of his own generation. In his review, Heinrich Böll included the title of the book by Jillian Becker, and considered the novel to be proof of the observation that 'we are all "Hitler's children"', whether we are directly guilty or not'. It is not without reason that a key moment in Vesper's book is the night of 2/3 June 1967, when the student Benno Ohnesorg was shot dead by a policeman during a demonstration in West Berlin against the visit of the Shah of Iran. In Vesper's portrayal, Gudrun Ensslin called out during a discussion about the incident: 'They will murder us all – you know what sort of pigs we have to deal with – it's the Auschwitz generation that we're dealing with – one can't discuss anything with people who started Auschwitz. They have weapons and we have none. We have to arm ourselves as well'.[23] Gerd Koenen emphasizes that it is rather doubtful that this episode, which was probably based on the recollections of the SDS activist Tilmann Fichter, actually transpired in this manner. Koenen considers this episode to be proof that 'the political and social generation debate could free itself from every personal conflict between parents and children', and thereby strengthens the generational narrative.

The interpretation of the "68 movement' in terms of a generational conflict remains one of the fundamental narrative frames to this day – in spite of its details having been subjected to a wide range of criticism. The youth protest movement, however, was worldwide, although this conflict in the Federal Republic of Germany developed an additional intensity due to Germany's national socialistic past. The media regarded the conflict between parents and children as an ideal plot in order to narrate the extremely violently charged confrontation between the 'Baader-Meinhof-group' and the state in terms of a family drama. This narrative frame thus privatized political matters and politicized private matters: narrative framing is both ethically and politically loaded, as Hayden White already argued back in 1973.

According to the historian Hanno Balz in his work on the relationship between the state, terrorists and sympathizers, terrorism 'had become above all in conservative discourse an issue affecting parents, and ultimately a question of possibly wrong upbringing'.[24] This type of parenting, however, was represented in particular by the Springer newspapers as a private tragedy, and not as an individual failure of parents. In fact, parenting appeared to have altogether become a problem in this changing society. In a statement in *Die Welt* in 1977: 'there has been a widespread general denunciation of fathers in the many attempts to understand the rebellion of the 1960s and 1970s. These fathers were doubly condemned – by a past for which they themselves were hardly responsible and by a future of which they allegedly had no understanding – and they saw themselves being sent into a corner by their sons and daughters'.[25]

The traditional idea of 'order' appears to have been turned upside down: whereas children used to be sent into a corner, the children have now assumed the moral authority to judge their parents and their generation. Ultimately the loss of the father's authority was thus put on a par with the purported state's loss of authority. According to the underlying narrative's logic, the terrorists' fight became a fight against the fathers' generation and the state that embodied them. The fact that it was not just the 'sons' but also the 'daughters' who rebelled against their real and fictitious fathers appeared to call for an explanation. In this context, Dominique Grisard has put forward the argument that the 'Oedipal rivalry myth' has to be seen as a 'structuring element of histories and stories of the RAF and their motifs'.[26] Grisard sees a type of 'vulgar Freudianism' at work, above all in the media coverage. It was suggested here that the female terrorists had penetrated into a field of violence 'reserved for men' and had become masculine. The masculine women thus also became competitors of the fathers, challenging their power.

In any case, male and female terrorists thus became indicators of a societal and gender order that had fallen apart. The members of the founding generation of the RAF had already destroyed their families in various ways, thus also destroying the nucleus of society. This narrative motif of a generational conflict that destroyed families reached its climax in 1977. When Susanne Albrecht took part in the assassination attempt on her own godfather Jürgen Ponto, terrorism appeared to have finally become the bloody generational conflict, which had been transported into the actual family.[27]

Another aspect was added to the generational narrative through the image of 'Hitler's children', that has already been cited. Where the members of the RAF saw themselves as fighters against the 'Fascist state' and the fathers' generation representing this state, the image of 'Hitler's children' suggested a sort of heritage of violence that originated in Fascism. When later on Silke Maier-Witt self-critically said, 'in trying not to be like my father, I ended up being even more like him. Terrorism is close to Nazism', she brought both motifs of the generational narrative together. In her fixation on violence, the rebellious daughter became an heiress to the National Socialist ideology.

The continuing attractiveness of the generational narrative in relation to the RAF is again apparent in the context of more recent films, in which RAF terrorism is no longer specifically made a subject of discussion, but appears as a shadow of the past. Films like Christian Petzold's *Die innere Sicherheit* [The state I am in] (2000) or Hans Weingartner's *Die fetten Jahre sind vorbei* [The Edukators] (2004), 'reveal a generational gap between 1968ers and 1989ers' according to Ilka Rasch in her analysis. The author attributes the directors of both films to the '89er' generation, who got the young generation to settle the score in respect of the RAF violence in their films.[28] The narrative motive of violence linked to a particular generation is thus once more repeated.

The Dissolution of the Narrative into Single Stories

In the 1980s, the RAF evolved more and more into a sort of phantom group. They struck out with a series of assassinations, amongst others on Alfred Herrhausen, the chairman of Deutsche Bank, on Karl Heinz Beckurts, the Siemens manager, and on Ernst Zimmermann, the chairman of MTU, but otherwise they remained for the most part invisible. The members of the second generation were in prison or had disappeared – some of them were in East Germany, as was only discovered after 1990. By and large, the members of the third generation were unknown to the outer world. This situation changed radically in the 1990s, when for various reasons especially members of the so-called second generation reappeared in the public sphere. Initially Peter Jürgen Boock played a central role here, who had already broken ties with the RAF in 1980. He not only submitted a plea for clemency to the Federal President in 1988 but also supplied the first life story of one of the RAF terrorists with his book *Abgang*. However, he wrote this in the form of a novel, in which fiction and actual occurrences were inextricably mixed.[29] With his book and associated interviews, Boock attracted intense public interest, although after the fall of the Berlin Wall it turned out that some of his information — especially about his own role — was not correct. This happened after some of Boock's previous comrades started to contradict his version of the RAF story.

Not only Boock, but also a lot of the individuals wanted in connection with the attacks of the 'Deutscher Herbst' were now seizable in a double sense, and had a great deal of attention directed at them in the media. Some of them, in particular Silke Maier-Witt and Inge Viett, sought public attention themselves. Silke Maier-Witt distanced herself very clearly from her past, and Inge Viett came to terms with hers by writing books. Finally, Volker Schlöndorff produced a film from her autobiography, which had the title *Die Stille nach dem Schuss*. Others, for instance Susanne Albrecht, again became the object of public interest, although they made every effort to avoid it. She attracted intense attention due to her unusual family history — the friendship of the two families Albrecht and Ponto, and Susanne Albrecht's role in the attempted kidnapping of Jürgen Ponto, which ended in his murder.

Some years later her story proved to be an important initiator for a more thorough examination of victims and their families. With her book *Für die RAF war das System, für mich der Vater*, Anna Siemens completely transferred attention onto the (families of the) victims for the first time, who were able to express their opinions in the book and subsequently in other interviews. In addition, Juliane Albrecht, Susanne's older sister, and Corinna Ponto, Jürgen Ponto's daughter, reappraised their family history in a joint book and in interviews. On the other hand, Michael Buback, Siegfried Buback's son, repeatedly made public statements and called for steps to be taken to uncover the exact truth about the gunman who had murdered his father.

However, any hope of attaining transparency soon vanished. Apart from Peter-Jürgen Boock, other members of the RAF had also on various occasions since the 1990s made statements in the media; but these statements neither helped to finally clarify open questions regarding the exact sequence of events, nor did they shed light on their life stories. A certain amount of doubt was always present concerning the statements made by Peter-Jürgen Boock, who had a high degree of prominence in the media, because his first accounts about his role turned out to be untrue. Others withdrew completely from public attention, and others again refused to say anything about the events of the crime. This applied to Knuts Folkerts, Karl-Heinz Dellwo, Lutz Taufer, Bernd Rössner, Christian Klar and others. Some of the interviews that they gave from their imprisonment were enlightening to the extent that real individuals came into view, rather than just names, and they attempted to set their own narrative against the picture of their senseless and ruthless acts. They regarded themselves as political fighters, who had waged a hard but justified war of resistance. They considered the terrorist attacks to be part of a long armed struggle against the state, which in this phase demanded the use of particular violent methods, while during other periods more peaceful strategies were given priority.

For this view, Bernd Rössner's statement was symptomatic. He declared in retrospect that their war was justified and that victims are simply part of it.[30] The statements given in the interviews definitely did not form a complete narrative, because the explanations of their own actions were too fragmentary and inconsistent. These remarks only made sense at the level of individual histories, with which the various participants tried to bring their individual life stories into shape. Not surprisingly the perpetrators and the victims configured their stories in very different ways, meaning that it is impossible to integrate them into one coherent narrative – other than in a narrative of lives that had been damaged or destroyed in one way or another.

All in all, when one again asks which role the media have played in the framing of the narratives concerning the history of the RAF, one can only conclude that the media not only shaped the image of terrorism as a whole, but also of the individual terrorists and of the individual victims. The crimes themselves had an immediate resonance in the media – also the manhunts, the arrests, the trials and the hunger strikes. Furthermore, the media constituted the central location for debates on the phenomenon – in a journalistic, documentary and artistic way. In addition to this, the media repeatedly offered a platform to those individuals who wanted to express their opinions in interviews. Not only was the confrontation narrative of the state vs. terrorists firmly established by the media, but also the generational narrative, and the diffusion of these narratives into single stories was substantially supported by the media's tendency to personalize. In principle, these narratives and the personalizations that had a tendency to disperse them proceeded alongside one another and overlapped, admittedly with certain displacements: whereas at the beginning of the 1970s the central figures of the RAF were individuals and members of a certain generation, the confrontation narrative of the later 1970s and 1980s became progressively more dominant. After the end of the 1980s, people with their differing life stories came back into the foreground.

It is obvious that the media were not satisfied with merely the role of documentarists, and instead they developed their own agenda. In connection with the RAF, Cordia Baumann spoke of films and literature functioning as 'legend forces', above all regarding the fictional debates on the subject.[31] The self-perception of the journalistic and documentary debates on the issue are above all aimed to 'de-mythologize' the RAF and to solve remaining puzzles. Also, the dust cover of Stefan Aust's book on the RAF, published in 1984, exemplifies this motive: the book claims to tell the story of the RAF and to elucidate the political and societal background, 'and destroys thereby the myth of the terrorists as a community, which has pledged loyalty'. The 'ZDF-History' series on the RAF explicitly presented itself as 'Detectives of the past', and Breloer's film *Todesspiel* echoes a similar claim of 'enlightenment'. Michael Buback's insistence on uncovering the truth about his father's murder fitted perfectly in this media agenda. It would definitely be a serious misunderstanding if one were to see the 'myth producers' in the fictional accounts, and the 'myth investigators' in the journalistic/documental accounts. It is obvious that the media themselves have contributed to the 'mythologization' in their journalistic/documental accounts, and thus the ductus (characteristic style) of the 'de-mythologization' is already part of a new media narrative.

Jörg Requate is professor of West European history at the University of Kassel. He has published widely in different fields of European history, especially in media history, the history of political violence, and the history of justice. Among his recent publications are: 'TV-Duell à la française? Das Hochamt des Präsidentschaftswahlkampfs in seiner Genealogie und Bedeutung', in *Frankreichjahrbuch 2017* (Wiesbaden, 2018); 'Modernisierung im Zeichen Amerikas? Politische Kommunikation in Frankreich und der Bundesrepublik Deutschland in den "langen" 1960er Jahren', in Johannes Großmann and Hèlène Miard-Delacroix (eds), *Deutschland, Frankreich und die USA in den 'langen' 1960er Jahren* (Stuttgart, 2018); 'Terrorismus in der Mediengesellschaft: Kommunikative Strategien links- und rechtsterroristischer Gruppen in der Bundesrepublik', in Nicolas Bonnet et al. (eds), *Sociétés face à la terreur (de 1960 à nos jours): Discours, Mémoire, Identité* (Dijon, 2017).

Notes

This chapter was translated by Jane Parsons-Sauer.

    1. Cf. Weimann and Winn, *Theater of Terror*, who examined the phenomenon by taking as an example the hijacking of a TWA plane in Lebanon in 1985.

    2. Henschen, *Die RAF-Erzählung*, 10.

    3. Steinseifer, *'Terrorismus' zwischen Ereignis und Diskurs*, 35. Compare Kenan van de Mieroop on the media representation of the 'peaceful' civil rights movement versus the 'violent' black power movement in this volume.

    4. Schraut and Weinhauer, 'Terrorism, gender, and history', 29.

    5. Fulda, 'Historiographic Narration', 2.

    6. Hess et al., 'Vorbemerkung: Terrorismus-Diskurs und Wissenschaft', 9.

    7. 'Natürlich kann geschossen werden', *Der Spiegel*.

    8. Cf. the diverse texts in: ID-Verlag, *Rote Armee Fraktion*.

    9. Cf. Balz, *Von Terroristen*.

    10. Cf. Schumacher, *Filmgeschichte als Diskursgeschichte*.

    11. Aust, *Der Baader-Meinhof-Komplex*.

12. Cf. Kellerhoff, 'Stefan Austs Standard-Werk zur RAF'.
13. Kraushaar, 'Warum die RAF bis heute verklärt wird'.
14. Kraushaar, *Die Bombe im jüdischen Gemeindehaus*, 234ff.
15. Kraushaar, *Verena Becker und der Verfassungsschutz*.
16. Buback, *Der zweite Tod meines Vaters*; Buback, *Wer erschoss Siegfried Buback?*
17. Peters, *1977*, 21.
18. Cf. Ankersmit, *Narrative Logic*; Fulda, 'Historiographic Narration', 2.
19. Koenen, *Das rote Jahrzehnt*, 77.
20. Ibid., 85.
21. Ibid.
22. Holthusen, 'Che Guevara', 1065f.
23. Becker, *Hitler's Children*, 88.
24. Balz, *Von Terroristen*, 238.
25. Neander, 'Väter und Söhne'.
26. Grisard, 'History of Knowledge', 90.
27. Cf. Balz, *Von Terroristen*, 241.
28. Cf. Rasch, 'Generation Gap'.
29. Cf. the article in *Der Spiegel* magazine by Vollmer, 'Die Suche nach dem Ausweg'.
30. Cf. the ZDF History documentary, 'Die RAF – Phantom ohne Gnade', available through: https://www.youtube.com/watch?v=rMgre0f1-BA, 43:30 (last accessed 31 May 2016)
31. Baumann, *Mythos RAF*.

Bibliography

'"Natürlich kann geschossen werden"': Ulrike Meinhof über die Baader-Aktion'. *Der Spiegel* 25 (15 June 1970), 74.
Ankersmit, Franklin. *Narrative Logic: A Semantic Analysis of the Historian's Language*. The Hague: Nijhoff, 1983.
Aust, Stefan. *Der Baader-Meinhof-Komplex*. Hamburg: Hoffmann und Campe Verlag, 1985.
Balz, Hanno. *Von Terroristen, Sympathisanten und dem starken Staat: Die öffentliche Debatte über die RAF in den 70er Jahren*. Frankfurt a.M.: Campus-Verlag, 2008.
Baumann, Cordia. *Mythos RAF: Literarische und filmische Mythentradierung von Bölls 'Katharina Blum' bis zum 'Baader-Meinhof-Komplex'*. Paderborn: Ferdinand Schönigh, 2012.
Becker, Jillian. *Hitler's Children: The Story of the Baader-Meinhof Terrorist Gang*. Washington, DC: AuthorHouse, 1977.
Buback, Michael. *Der zweite Tod meines Vaters*, 2nd edn. Munich: Droemer-Knaur, 2009.
———. *Wer erschoss Siegfried Buback? Zwischenbilanz der Nachforschungen von Michael Buback*. Leonberg: Public Lounge, 2009.
Fulda, Daniel. 'Historiographic Narration', in Peter Hühn et al. (eds), *The Living Handbook of Narratology* (Hamburg: Hamburg University, 2014). http://www.lhn.uni-hamburg.de/article/historiographic-narration (last accessed 30 March 2017).
Grisard, Dominique. 'History of Knowledge, Terrorism and Gender'. *Historical Social Research* 39(3) (2014), 82–99.
Henschen, Jan. *Die RAF-Erzählung: Eine mediale Historiographie des Terrorismus*. Bielefeld: Transcript, 2013.
Hess, Henner, et al. 'Vorbemerkung: Terrorismus-Diskurs und Wissenschaft', in Henner Hess et al. (eds), *Angriff auf das Herz des Staates: Soziale Entwicklung und Terrorismus*, Vol. 1 (Frankfurt a.M.: Suhrkamp, 1988), 9–14.

Holthusen, Hans-Egon. 'Che Guevara: Leben, Tod und Verklärung'. *Merkur* 23(259), 1051–67.
ID-Verlag (ed.). *Rote Armee Fraktion: Texte und Materialien zur Geschichte der RAF*. Berlin: ID-Verlag, 1997.
Kellerhoff, Sven Felix. 'Stefan Austs Standard-Werk zur RAF'. *WeltN24* (4 September 2008). https://www.welt.de/kultur/article2393134/Stefan-Austs-Standardwerk-zur-RAF.html (last accessed 2 June 2016).
Koenen, Gerd. *Das rote Jahrzehnt: Unsere kleine deutsche Kulturrevolution*. Cologne: Fischer, 2001.
Kraushaar, Wolfgang. *Die Bombe im jüdischen Gemeindehaus*. Hamburg: Hamburger Edition, 2005.
———. *Verena Becker und der Verfassungsschutz*. Hamburg: Hamburger Edition 2010.
———. 'Warum die RAF bis heute verklärt wird'. *Welt* (7 September 2008). https://www.welt.de/kultur/article2408097/Warum-die-RAF-bis-heute-verklaert-wird.html (last accessed 10 December 2020).
Neander, Joachim. 'Väter und Söhne', *Die Welt* (5 November 1977).
Peters, Butz. *1977: RAF gegen Bundesrepublik*. Munich: Droemer-Knaur, 2017.
Rasch, Ilka. 'The Generation Gap: The Reappropriation of the Red Army Faction in Contemporary German Film', in Laurel Cohen-Pfister and Susanne Vees-Gulani (eds), *Generational Shifts in Contemporary German Culture* (Rochester, NY: Camden House, 2010), 184–204.
Schraut, Sylvia, and Klaus Weinhauer. 'Terrorism, Gender, and History – Introduction'. *Historical Social Research* 39(3) (2014), 7–45.
Schumacher, Julia. *Filmgeschichte als Diskursgeschichte: Die RAF im deutschen Spielfilm*. Münster: Lit Verlag, 2012.
Steinseifer, Martin. *'Terrorismus' zwischen Ereignis und Diskurs: Zur Pragmatik von Text-Bild-Zusammenstellungen in Printmedien der 1970er Jahre*. Berlin: De Gruyter, 2011.
Vollmer, Antje. 'Die Suche nach dem Ausweg'. *Der Spiegel* (23 May 1988), 192–95.
Weimann, Gabriel, and Conrad Winn. *The Theater of Terror: Mass Media and International Terrorism*. New York: Ex-library, 1994.

CHAPTER 12

Time Travel as Running around in Circles

The Popular Historical Novel and the Sense of Historicity in Today's Society

Daniel Fulda

Since the 1980s, historical subject matters have become increasingly important in popular literature, where the focus lies mainly on a broadly 'realistic' narration of the eventful adventures of underdog heroes and heroines with a high identification factor. What is 'popular' is generally not measured solely by the properties of a thing (e.g. a novel) or merely by the breadth of its reception, but results from a combination of both. Schematic narrative styles and stereotypical conceptions of history make it easier for a historical novel to become 'popular', but they are neither a guarantee nor a necessary condition for it. In the case of the popular historical novel, it should enable the reader to experience an effortless 'consumption of the past'[1] by sparing him/her the impositions of two adjacent discourses: the sobriety and methodological complexity of scholarly historiography as well as the challenging of his/her usual perspectives through sophisticated fiction.[2]

By focusing on the historical novel as the most successful textual genre dealing with history, and especially on its popular sector, which literary studies rarely address,[3] I hope to gain an answer as to what form of historicity is dominant in our present age. Does 'historicity' today mean that we think in terms of high rates of decay because we experience how each novelty is almost immediately overtaken by an even newer one? Or must present historicity be described as the extension of the present into the past? To answer this question, I will analyse narrative techniques, on the one hand, and data

Notes for this section begin on page 252.

from a reader survey that I conducted amongst students, on the other. This is of importance, because although historical perspectives – and history as a whole – are 'constructed' in narratives,[4] they only become culturally accepted through the readers' reception of these acts of narration. The element of reception has gained in importance in recent years with reference to theories of narrativity and historiography. Empirical studies have, however, been rare, and are 'of particular necessity'.[5] As the survey was carried out among German students, the majority of the analysed texts are written in German, but most of them were translated into several languages, and they do include a number of bestsellers that were originally written in English.

Contracting or Expanding Present?

What extent does the present have? Saint Augustine replied: none. Hans Ulrich Gumbrecht (2014), professor of comparative literature at Stanford and 'global intellectual', argues that we are witnessing an unprecedented *expansion* of the present. Only a few years earlier, other prominent authors had established the opposite diagnosis, namely that the age in which we are living is dominated by a sense of the present being in a state of *contraction*. 'Contraction of the present' means that the period in which 'we can count on some consistency in our living conditions' is becoming ever shorter.[6] According to the idea of a contracted present, the past, which is characterized by the fact that its conditions and rules deviate from those that are currently valid, is seen to have elapsed only a short time ago, perhaps no more than a few years ago, or even less.[7] When cultural and social change begin to accelerate, the border between what is seen as the 'different' past and the 'familiar' present moves closer towards the position of the spectator in the present. The expected future duration of the present appears to be similarly shortened – that is to say, we assume that the near future will be different from today's circumstances. The present seems to be shrinking at both ends; at the same time life seems to have shifted more and more into remembered pasts and expected futures.

This contracting of the present should not be mistaken for a new phenomenon. Its origins can be located some two to three hundred years ago as a constitutive component of modernity since its genesis in the eighteenth century. Since then, Western societies have devoted a great deal of effort in defining themselves in relationship to a past that is perceived to be 'different'.[8] What is new in recent times, the philosopher Hermann Lübbe argues, is merely the heightened speed at which a state of affairs that was only recently 'present' turns into the past. What slips into the past tense has not necessarily become uninteresting. On the contrary, according to Lübbe our 'shortened stay in the present' results in a greater interest in the past, which comes to seem more familiar and safer than the present precisely *because* it is no longer in danger of becoming old.[9] Whether one agrees with this theory or not, the cultural tendency that it seeks to explain is hard to ignore – namely, that the past has never been so present in the public sphere, from politics to the entertainment industry.[10] Today,

> this trend is reflected in such indicators as increasing numbers of visitors to historical exhibitions and museums; considerable public interest in controversies among historical experts; and the prominence of historical topics in new and old media, in documentary and fictional genres, [and] in performative forms (theme parks, living history and re-enactments). Numerous websites on the Internet, articles on Wikipedia, CD-ROM productions and historical computer games attest the phenomenon's expansion into the digital media. We witness these trends all over the world, in the global North as well as increasingly in the global South.[11]

This is also the starting point for Gumbrecht's argument, although he develops a very different view of the relationship between past and present on these grounds. According to him, 'pasts flood our present', meaning that 'the border' between both has become 'porous'.[12] Because we are no longer able to leave the past behind us, he says, 'the present has turned into a dimension of expanding simultaneities'. Rather than prioritizing expansion over contraction, Gumbrecht's objection to Lübbe's thesis is more fundamentally based on what he considers to be the dissolution of 'historical time' in modernity ('historical time' is Gumbrecht's term for what I would call the genetic model of history, invented around 1800). According to him, we no longer perceive either the past as complete or the future as 'an open horizon of possibilities'. We still speak of history, but it no longer represents a vectored or (despite all the catastrophes of the twentieth century) meaningful process in which newness is constantly produced.[13] Where Lübbe diagnoses acceleration, Gumbrecht sees the entire system as having collapsed.

History Sells! But Why?

Popular historical novels, including serial novels, can boast sales and print runs of several million copies within the space of a few years. For example, *Das Geheimnis der Hebamme* [The secret of the midwife], a novel based in the Middle Ages, was published in November 2006; sequel novels followed in 2007, 2008, 2010 and 2011.[14] When the final volume of the series appeared in October 2011, over two million copies of the first four books had already been sold. The fifth volume automatically hit the top of the bestseller lists and subsequently remained in the top twenty for over ten weeks.[15] Even more successful than Sabine Ebert's *Hebammen* series is *Die Wanderhure* [The wandering harlot] by Ingrid Klocke and Elmar Wohlrath. In the series, begun in 2004, is a married couple known by their collective pseudonym 'Iny Lorentz'. By the time its film adaptation was broadcast by German television, the first volume had already sold 1.6 million copies.[16] The film attracted an audience of almost 10 million viewers (Germany has 82 million inhabitants), making *Die Wanderhure* the most successful television film of 2010. Two more *Wanderhure* films followed in 2012, the first of which was again the most successful German television film of the year. *Das Geheimnis der Hebamme* was also adapted for television in 2016. The *Wanderhure* novels were translated into eleven languages, including English, in June 2014.[17]

Such novels can hardly be described as works of art. As can be seen from the serialized book titles, their goal is to make the most of repetitive narrative schemes and provide a sense of familiarity to the reader, rather than offer thought-provoking narratives. There are, of course, further *Wanderhure* novels, altogether seven volumes.[18] None of these sequels corroborate the positive view put forward by the research on the historical novel as a genre: 'a disruptive genre, a series of interventions [that] have sought to destabilize cultural hegemonies and challenge normalities';[19] nor do not confirm the thesis recently presented by Jerome de Groot that 'popular historical texts are interested in communicating the complexity of communication, representing the past in such a way as to allow an insight into the strangeness of what is called "history"'.[20] But most readers access this genre through these very novels. They are therefore more meaningful in terms of socially popular conceptions of history than more ambitious novels.

In 2011/12, I held a lecture series at the University of Halle on 'The Historical Novel'. In the first lecture I conducted a survey on the reading patterns of the students. Ninety-seven participants completed the questionnaire,[21] providing sufficient data to minimize a random distribution of answers.[22] The results, in particular relating to the popular market segment, are telling: my students are well acquainted with this sector, and value it highly. Their expectations for a historical novel were informed considerably by the narrative models of popular examples of the genre, or were at least similar to these. Formal qualities or the reflection on questions of historical representation in literary texts were less important. The answers provided – especially by female participants – illustrate how the popular historical novel, with its successful marketing strategies and its strong presence in the media, has reached the academic world and is, indeed, valued by educated readers.[23]

As their favourite historical novel, female participants listed, for example:
- *Die Wanderhure* (2004, English translation: *The Wandering Harlot*, 2011) – eight students

- *The Pillars of the Earth* (1989, German translation: *Die Säulen der Erde*, 1990) by Ken Follet – seven students
- *Pope Joan* (1996, German translation: *Die Päpstin Johanna*, 1996) by Donna W. Cross – six students

Three participants each listed the following:
- *Das Lächeln der Fortuna* [Fortuna's smile] (1997) by Rebecca Gablé, pseudonym of Ingrid Krane-Müschen
- *Outlander/Cross Stitch* [title in the US/UK] (1991, German translation: *Feuer und Stein*, 1995) by Diana Gabaldon
- *Die Vermessung der Welt* (2005, English translation *Measuring the World*, 2006) by Daniel Kehlmann

These novels are all, of course, bestsellers. Emmanuel von Stein[24] provides the following figures for 2009: total books sold by Rebecca Gablé: 3.2 million; *The Pillars of the Earth*: 4.2 million (in Germany!); the total number of books sold in Germany by Diana Gabaldon: over 8 million. *Die Vermessung der Welt* sold 6 million worldwide.

Kehlmann's *Die Vermessung der Welt* is a very artistic text, highly estimated by critics, and thus quite an oddity among the other novels mentioned. Notably, it is not the best-ranked literary text mentioned by the participants; by far the most commonly mentioned novel was Patrick Süskind's *Das Parfum* [Perfume] (1985), which was listed twelve times. Kehlmann's and Süskind's novels are relatively unusual among historical novels, in that they have gained critical acclaim and a broad, even global readership.[25] If, however, one compares references made to popular novels and to these two more literary texts, the dominance of the popular novels is clear (27 versus 15). Presumably, Süskind and Kehlmann are familiar amongst student readers because they are often included in the high school curriculum.

The best-known author by far is Ken Follet – a clear majority of my students have read his novels (57 out of 97) and 90 per cent know him 'at least by name' (88 out of 97).[26] This result is hardly surprising, since Follett's *Pillars of the Earth* initiated the boom in novels set in the Middle Ages, which began in the early 1990s, and most of the 'favourite novels' listed by participants are set in the same period.[27] (Exceptions are *Outlander/Cross Stitch* and the two 'literary' texts. *Die Vermessung der Welt* is set in the early nineteenth century and revolves around the mathematician Gauß and the researcher and traveller Alexander von Humboldt; *Das Parfum* tells the story of a brilliant but criminal French perfume maker during the reign of Louis XV; *Outlander/Cross Stitch* takes place mainly during the Jacobite Rising of 1743–46.)

Historical novels with leading female protagonists who bravely assert themselves in a misogynistic world and hence actively seek their own happiness – usually embodied in a man who is as muscular as he is sensitive – are much liked in popular literature. All the above-mentioned novels, except R. Gablé's, have such protagonists. Despite their precarious social position, they prove themselves to be superior in terms of sensibility, tactical nous and strength of character. This superiority can also be seen in their medical knowledge, and the healing powers with which Ebert, Cross and Gabaldon equip their main protagonists, show all the signs of female fantasies of empowerment. Whereas the male heroes demonstrate their potency by inflicting brutal damage on each other with their weapons, the heroines' power of healing must be seen as a traditionally feminine as well as politically correct alternative to this violence.

Further explanations for the commercial success of popular historical novels can be found in the participants' answers regarding what they value most about historical novels. Here it is important to note that women – who represent the vast majority of the readership – most often pointed to qualities associated with popular literature in their replies: the majority (almost 60 per cent, 48 out of 81) replied that they liked historical novels best 'if they have an adventuresome plot', followed by novels 'in which a love story is important' (48 per cent, 39 out of 81); and in third position (44 per cent, 36 out of 81) came novels 'in which the historical setting is depicted in detail'. The fact that a historical novel is 'formally interesting' by virtue of its 'multiple points of view and different temporal levels' was mentioned in 43 per cent (35 out of 81) of the replies.[28] Historical novels are thus appreciated by students of literature less for their artistic merit than for their accessibility. They are of interest not so much as literary pieces that create supplementary meaning through complex linguistic composition, but rather for their characteristics more usually associated with popular writing (adventure and romance stories) and also because of their historical outlook. Thematic excitement and plasticity are of more importance than artistic considerations.

Narrative Techniques: Suggestion of Familiarity in History

What does the success of popular historical novels tell us about our sense of historicity in today's society? Many of the findings thus far seem to support Lübbe's theory: from the perspective of the publishing industry, these novels underline what he has termed the acceleration and contraction of the present. This acceleration can be seen in the fact that these novels 'age' or become outdated very quickly due to their production in rapid succession, and that they are usually read over no more than a couple of days, as shown from discussions in the relevant fan forums. A yearly publication of a 600-page novel seems to be almost mandatory for authors in order to maintain their fan base. Following an often quick and exhilarating reading experience, most readers automatically turn their attention to the sequel or film adaption of the novels; numerous readers' only contribution to the various forums are posts about how excited they are about the next instalment.

The long-elapsed premodern and most frequently medieval past in these novels provides a counterbalance to the rush of contemporary society, because the ancient worlds of the popular historical novel are depicted as well established and clearly structured. In the words of one of these authors: 'Nothing is as safe as the past; it is straightforward and the social structures were simpler. Everyone knew where they belonged'.[29] Initially these ancient worlds seem strange, but the novels make them understandable by providing numerous and often detailed explanations. This means that the reader can feel more at home in the recently cleared woodlands of twelfth-century East Germany than in the current post-unification times. The strictly regulated symbolic nature of premodern society, which is the subject of persistent explanations by the narrator, makes the readers' orientation far easier, as does the overly simplistic distinction between good and bad.[30] Those novels are published in series of up to seven sequels, which only serves to reinforce this suggested familiarity. It would not be too far-fetched to say that these novels thereby serve precisely the preterite 'compensation . . . for a lost sense of familiarity created by the speed of change', which has been identified by Hermann Lübbe as a characteristic of today's society.[31]

It would be mistaken to assume that this concept of a compensatory past automatically implies the existence of idyllic social conditions. This is by no means necessary, and seems, indeed, to be undesirable, as it would make the depicted world less exciting and deny the reader the seemingly expected 'pleasurable fear'.[32] Injustice and violence seem to be the order of the day in these historical novels, and they are rather forcefully depicted. Moreover, the static social order and pre-emancipatory gender roles are unambiguously criticized. On the other hand, these adversities do provide a certain clarity – the necessity to emancipate oneself from such impositions forms the core belief of the protagonist with whom readers are meant to identify, and presumably of the readers themselves.[33] Sabine Ebert has emphatically speculated on this relationship:

> The people of those times were squeezed into a tight corset; if they wished to free themselves they had to do so with cunning tricks. It is easy to see parallels with the East [of Germany] today; people can empathize with this, and I intended them to do so.[34]

The contemporary popular novel breaks with the passive role of women, which was the norm embodied by leading protagonists in traditional pulp fiction; it does, however, uphold the 'affirmation of the readers' value judgments and behavioral'.[35]

The readers' expectations about historical novels today, namely 'identification with a character and thus the experience of history in one's own eyes', are completely in line with these findings.[36] Two-thirds of my female students (53 out of 79) and also the relative majority of male students (6 out of 13)[37] considered this to be the main purpose of the genre. The most important function according to concepts developed by academic critics since the 1980s,[38] namely 'showing that all historical knowledge is constructed', is of interest only to a small minority (4 per cent [3 out of 79] of female and 15 per cent [2 out of 13] of male participants).

Contrary to what 'historiographic metafiction's critical preponderance'[39] would lead us to assume, there is a 'non-complex' reading expectation among the students of German literature that I surveyed, and this 'non-complex' reading expectation goes beyond a mere attraction to specific individual popular novels. One can conclude that more complex historical novels are also read on these grounds[40] – a clear majority of almost two-thirds (60 out of 93) of the students wished to identify with a character in order to 'experience' history first-hand.[41]

One could assume that this identification process is by no means easy, even in the case of those popular novels that focus on private stories that are told in close relation to the heroes/heroines, usually from their own perspective. Is the fate of a travelling prostitute or a young midwife who departs on a voyage into the wilderness with a group of settlers not too different from the experiences of modern readers? This difficulty is not only due to the different social conditions, but also to the equally dissimilar worldviews and mentalities. It would be incorrect to say that popular novels convey the impression that the society of the Middle Ages is quite similar to ours. A few differences are displayed quite blatantly, from human defencelessness against the elements and deficient hygiene to arbitrary violence and the subordination of women. However, the ways in which people thought and felt in past ages are portrayed without any major deviations from those of today. This includes the self-awareness of the characters, their conception of society, their manner of speaking, their sense of happiness, and their sexuality. Religiosity is usually expressed in the form of mere verbal adornments – or as a mask behind which brutality and striving for power can be found lurking. Most notably, the novels' protagonists view themselves as individuals and follow goals in life that we would consider to be desirable. Their sense of injustice correlates with our contemporary feelings regarding what is unjust, and they view their circumstances as being man-made and hence within their own power. With this supposed 'common humanity', these novels thus invite readers to an identificational experience of the past – and obviously do so with considerable success.

These novels depict, in a way, actors of this day and age slipping into old-fashioned costumes. The actors themselves seem to personify a timeless general human nature but in fact they represent the norms and habits of our own present-day *juste milieu*. The reader is thus provided with easy access to every version of history through his own norms and habits. That the reader then encounters unfamiliar elements only goes to increase the excitement of the journey through time. Such accessibility, however, is of no use to a form of historical understanding that tries to explore the 'otherness'[42] of past times, which literary critics like to emphasize.

Time Travel through an Expanding Present

Some texts offer readers more than a mere metaphorical 'journey through time', as they feature time travel as a central part of the plot. In *Outlander/ Cross Stitch*, the first instalment of Diana Gabaldon's Highland series (which sold over 7 million copies in twelve years in Germany alone),[43] the heroine suddenly travels in time from the twentieth century back into the eighteenth century, where she lands in the middle of the English–Scottish battles, which featured centrally in *Waverley*, Sir Walter Scott's paradigmatic arch-text published in 1814. If the reader chooses to accept this fantastic element from the outset – and more than two-thirds of my female students (55 out of 79) were prepared to do so – this can function as a superbly universal means of explaining why the heroine refuses to accept corporal punishment as unproblematic, why she rejects the medicinal properties of dried mouse ears and, most importantly, why she refuses to accept the traditional subordination of women. In short, it explains why the protagonist views the Scot(t)ish highlands of 1743 through the eyes of her modern-day readers.[44] It is easy to view the motif of time travel critically, in historical novels in particular, not least because it undermines all attempts at verisimilitude through historical accuracy. On the other hand, one must admit that it makes the narration of a popular historical novel that much easier.[45] The point that I would like to stress here is that time travel is a suitable and characteristic motif for this genre because the entire popular branch of the historical novel relies on the catapulting into the past of present-day characters with whom readers can identify.

This results in what Gumbrecht terms the 'expansion of the present', and indeed this seems to me to be perhaps the most characteristic feature of the popular historical novel, because the unconditional effort towards empathy turns every past era into little more than the present in historical guise.[46] Indeed, it is by no means unusual to wear medieval costumes at Sabine Ebert's readings. Both the motif of time travel and, perhaps even more so,

Figure 12.1 'Continuation of Reality by Other Means'. Picture taken from the front page of the *Frankfurter Allgemeine Zeitung* (3 November 2009), photographer: Daniel Pilar.

the general suggestion that one is able to travel through time by reading popular historical novels, point towards a 'an expanding present' precisely by substituting spatial difference for historical distance, as Gumbrecht's metaphor shows.[47] The poetics of time travel in the popular sector of the market takes this substitution literally by depicting the understanding of past societies and their peoples as being as simple as merely moving to another place.

I have already mentioned Gumbrecht's notion that the present has changed into 'a dimension of expanding simultaneities'.[48] What this means can be clearly seen in Figure 12.1. What we see here is a scene from the American Civil War, namely the 'The generals of the confederate army ... eating breakfast before the battle of Cold Harbor', as the photo caption explains. This battle witnessed the last great victory of the Confederates, and it did indeed take place – originally in 1864. It was re-enacted on 11 September 2009 on a military training ground in Lower Franconia in Germany. Such re-enactments have experienced a boom since the 1990s; there are some ten thousand people involved in the 'living history' community in Germany alone.[49] This picture illustrates two major aspects of my argument: as with the popular historical novels, these costumes are by and large true to life. What is modern, however, is the breakfast enjoyed by the confederates – the toasts and margarine highlight the anachronistic nature of the situation. But it is important to note that this scene would also be anachronistic if the men were eating crushed oats or bread from the field kitchen, because the people acting here are our own contemporaries. Their thoughts and feelings are those of today, because they know what has happened since 1864 – and they are careful to maintain a low cholesterol diet. The characters in the popular historical novel also act in this manner with one major exception: the narrator avoids displaying the toast and margarine openly on his table. And this is my second point here. The historical accuracy of the costumes conceals a basic anachronism both in the situation depicted in the picture and in the popular historical novels.

The fundamentally anachronistic model of mentality in the popular novel is not designed to be open to scrutiny – and indeed, it generally goes unnoticed, as my survey shows: 73 per cent (71 out of 97) of my students claim that their own reading experiences of historical novels provide a 'sense of the life in different times', and 60 per cent (58 out of 97) say that they 'make past ways of thinking and feeling' comprehensible. By contrast, barely one-sixth of my students agree with the radically opposite opinion that 'historical novels are fictions that convey no appropriate knowledge' of the past (16 per cent, 15 out of 97). Most of my students would not agree with Alfred Döblin's dictum – often cited by scholars of literary studies – that 'the historical novel is firstly a novel and secondly not history'![50] Viewed against the background of the constructivism, broadly acknowledged in the academic world, that the historical novel has cultivated for well over a hundred years, my students' trust in the historicity of the genre is somewhat surprising. To compare it with the picture of the Confederates eating breakfast, one could say that the bread wrappers and tubs of margarine – as symbolic equivalents of anachronistic mentalities – are simply not recognized.

One reason for this could be that historical novels generally rely on a vast collection of historical material, including primary sources and secondary literature. In literary narratives of history, historical 'facts' function as mere 'material', and are important only in terms of their treatment. In the popular historical novel, by contrast, the dependence on detailed historically verified events, places and practices are important in themselves – the blatant historicity provides these texts with a socially accepted value that their trivial plot and their lack of linguistic complexity would otherwise negate. Sabine Ebert in particular seeks to legitimize her books by referring to her comprehensive investigation and her extreme attention to detail, but other authors also point out the historical models on which they have based their characters.[51] Historiographical postscripts are the norm, and glossaries and bibliographies are often included.

The characters' mentalities, however, at no point achieve the purported historicity, as their self-awareness and their goals are those of this day and age. This too is hardly surprising; historicity in these areas would probably demand too much of most authors and would be sure to reduce the chances of successfully gaining a broad readership – after all, the main attractiveness of these books is that the readers find their own ideal identities and beliefs in novels set in the Middle Ages. The pretension to historicity actually increases the attraction of this affirmative framework because it conveys a confirmation of the self even through the seemingly foreign or strange, and in so doing, these novels conceal the circularity involved in the process.

Beyond the 'Age of History'?

The popular historical novel seems to confirm Gumbrecht's diagnosis that the genetic model of historicity is no longer dominant in our time ('We no longer live in historical time').[52] The narrative technique analysed here is by no means new, however, and was already in full flow in nineteenth-century novels and cultural practices dealing with history. The leading values and guiding social principles of this age were also projected back into the Middle Ages[53] so that the reader was under the impression that he too was a crucial part of the progress that has unfolded throughout the course of history.[54] In the German historical novel of the nineteenth century, the primary value to be conveyed was the emancipation of the liberal and nationally oriented citizen whose appearances 'in historical costume' were a massive success with readers – one prominent example being Gustav Freytag's six volume cycle *Die Ahnen* [Our forefathers] (1872–1880).[55] The narrative scheme of the texts that I have discussed here has hardly changed: a new concept – namely the emancipation of women – has merely replaced the old guiding value of 'participation of the male protagonist for the good of the nation state'.[56] Likewise, nineteenth-century critics' reception of Freytag's *Ahnen* also shows that anachronisms (particularly in the mentalities of the characters) were also only rarely recognized in this era.[57]

The fact that an arch-historicist such as Freytag wrote about past ages that were in fact expanded presents could also lead us to question Gumbrecht's belief that this process is a new phenomenon that only appeared in the 1980s.[58] This scepticism is confirmed by the fact that Gumbrecht himself actually rehearses important elements of the critique of bourgeois historical culture already articulated by Friedrich Nietzsche as early as 1874 in *On the Use and Abuse of History for Life* (1874), the second *Untimely Meditation*, for example his complaint that 'the broad present, with its concurrent worlds, has, always and already, offered too many possibilities; therefore, the identity it possesses – if it has one at all – lacks clear contours'.[59] An analysis of both the historical novel at the start of the twenty-first century and in the nineteenth century shows that Gumbrecht's theory needs to be amended: expansions of the present are not new, nor have they superseded other forms of historicity, because we can still observe tendencies towards a contracting present and even a traditional historicist belief in historical progress.

Daniel Fulda is chair of modern German literature at the University of Halle-Wittenberg, and has been visiting professor in Paris (École pratique des hautes études), Lyons (ENS) and Notre-Dame. His research focuses on the interrelation between historiography and aesthetics, on contemporary literature, and on the cultures of erudition in the eighteenth and nineteenth centuries. His books include *Wissenschaft aus Kunst: Die Entstehung der modernen deutschen Geschichtsschreibung 1760–1860* (de Gruyter, 1996); *Schau-Spiele des Geldes: Die Komödie und die Entstehung der Marktgesellschaft von Shakespeare bis Lessing* (Niemeyer, 2005); and '*Die Geschichte trägt der Aufklärung die Fackel vor': Eine deutsch-französische Bild-Geschichte* (mdv, 2016). Among his articles in English are: 'Historiographic Narration', Peter Hühn et al. (eds), *Handbook of Narratology*, 2nd edn, vol. 1–2 (de Gruyter, 2014), vol. 1: 227–40; and 'Between Archival Research and Aspirations to Leadership in Society: 19th-Century Germans as Practitioners in History', in Efraim Podoksik (ed.), *Doing Humanities in Nineteenth-Century Germany* (Brill, 2019), 59–82.

Notes

This chapter was translated by Barry Murnane and Catherine Ballériaux.

1. Berger, Lorenz and Melman, *Popularizing National Pasts*, 19.
2. Lechner, *Histories for the Many*, 16–17.
3. See Hughes, *Historical Romance*. Based on a chart of favourite books as voted on by German television viewers, see: Jürgensen, *Die Lieblingsbücher der Deutschen*. This hit list includes popular novels such as *The Pillars of the Earth*, *Pope Joan* and *Outlander/Cross Stitch*, to which I will refer in this chapter. For popular fiction in the context of modern culture, see McCracken, *Pulp*. From a historians' perspective, see Berger, Lorenz and Melman, *Popularizing National Pasts*.
4. Fulda, 'Historiographic Narration'.
5. Korte and Paletschek, 'Geschichte in populären Medien und Genres', 48. See Nitz and Petrulionis on the tasks of narratology concerning history: 'One of the first tasks of cultural analysts should be to study empirically how people "consume" history and to examine which cognitive frames of meaning making they apply in order to come to an understanding of how the past is (re)created in collective memory'. Nitz and Petrulionis, 'Towards a Historiographic Narratology', 4.

6. Lübbe, 'Die Modernität', 150. All translated quotes are the translator's own. See also Rosa, *Social Acceleration*, 75–77.

7. It should be apparent that this refers to what is considered to be the present in a specific cultural and social framework, rather than the present in physical terms, which is, of course, completely inelastic.

8. Schiffman, *Birth of the Past*.

9. Lübbe, 'Die Modernität', 3.

10. Ibid., v.

11. Korte and Paletschek, 'Popular History Now and Then', 7.

12. Gumbrecht, *Our Broad Present*, xiii.

13. Koselleck, *Futures Past*, 33–34.

14. In 2009 – the year without a *Hebammen* novel – Sabine Ebert published the novel *Blut und Silber* [Blood and silver], which is set slightly later in the Saxon Middle Ages and includes a descendent of the midwife as the leading character. All of these novels are published by Droemer Knaur in Munich.

15. Jauer, 'Die Bestseller', 44.

16. Hieber, 'Die verlorene Ehre der Marie Schärer', 33.

17. The other languages are Latvian, Hungarian, Dutch, French, Italian, Spanish, Portuguese, Polish, Czech and Russian. Sabine Ebert's *Hebammen* novels were translated into Polish, Czech, Hungarian and Albanian.

18. The title of the fifth volume, *Töchter der Sünde* [Daughters of sin] (2011), is also semantically related to the earlier titles, albeit in metaphorical variation. The 'Iny Lorentz' novels are published by Droemer Knaur in Munich, too.

19. De Groot, *Historical Novel*, 139; De Groot, *Remaking History*, 2.

20. De Groot, *Remaking History*, 226.

21. The questionnaire consisted of 18 questions, most of which offered a series of possible answers.

22. Incidentally, the participating students registered no particular affinity with the historical novel. In response to the question 'Do you like historical novels?', almost two-thirds (63 out of 97) answered 'no more than other novels'; and the answer 'I like them a great deal' was only slightly better represented than 'I don't like them at all' (20 and 14 respectively).

23. That the readership for such schematic literature is by no means restricted to readers with less educated backgrounds is an established consensus. In the 1980s, for example, it was established that the level of education among female readers increased in relation to the 'modern love-story' novels that began appearing from the mid-1980s. See Thiel, *Liebe, Sex und Karriere*, 12–13. These were strong and independent working women, not readers with an academic background.

24. Von Stein, 'Oh du schöne Ritterzeit . . .', 25–27.

25. Süskind, *Das Parfum*; Kehlmann, *Die Vermessung der Welt*.

26. Follett's popularity was no doubt reinforced by the four-part television adaptation of *Pillars of the Earth*, produced and shown by Sat.1 in the autumn of 2010.

27. Young, *The Middle Ages in Popular Culture*.

28. The least favoured answers were 'when a text includes fantastic elements, e.g. time travel' (35 per cent, 28 out of 81) and 'stories about battles or voyages of discovery' (30 per cent, 24 out of 81). Different reasons to those options provided in the questionnaire were mentioned by only 11 of the 81 female students.

29. Gablé, cited in Schmitz, 'Die Königin des historischen Romans'.

30. Wolfgang Hardtwig and others have made similar observations in relation to popular enactments and the marketing of history. See Hardtwig and Schug, 'Einleitung', 12–13.

31. Lübbe, *Im Zug der Zeit*, 3.

32. Nusser, *Trivialliteratur*, 692.

33. Hassemer, 'Das Mittelalter der Populärkultur'.
34. Ebert, cited in Pergande, 'Die Geburt der Hebamme', 12.
35. Nusser, *Trivialliteratur*, 139–40. See also: Gelder, *Popular Fiction*.
36. The quotations in this paragraph denote the wording used in my questionnaire.
37. The total number of answers to this question is slightly lower because four of the students provided no answer or did not answer according to the suggested answers as requested.
38. See Hutcheon, *Poetics of Postmodernism*.
39. See Johnston and Wiegandt, 'Introduction', 11.
40. A glance in the respective internet chat rooms underlines how readers of popular fiction openly compare complex literary texts such as *Das Parfum* with novels such as *Pope Joan*.
41. Johnston and Wiegandt have now established a similar diagnosis in terms not of the reception but of the production: 'Even as the freshly coined term "historiographic metafiction" was gaining currency in critical discourse, a new generation of novelists were beginning to betray a growing interest in historical fiction as a way of gauging modes of historical experience'. Johnston and Wiegandt, 'Introduction', 12.
42. De Groot, *Historical Novel*, 2.
43. Jürgensen, *Die Lieblingsbücher der Deutschen*, 86.
44. In my survey, only one male student had read a book written by Gabaldon.
45. Time travel is by no means an unusual motif in the genre of historical love stories.
46. Diana Wallace also speaks of a 'masquerade'. Wallace views this as a partly positive process in so far as she identifies a process of self-fashioning in all identities. Whether or not female readers are able to reflect upon this premeditated construction of 'cosmetically' adjusted history is by no means certain, but the results of my survey offer little support for this understanding. See: Wallace, *The Woman's Historical Novel*, 21.
47. Gumbrecht, *Our Broad Present*, 48, 54, 60.
48. Ibid., xiii.
49. On re-enactments as a form of time travel in this sense, see Fenske, 'Abenteuer Geschichte'.

On American Civil War re-enactments, see Hochbruck, 'Reenacting Across Six Generations 1863–1963'.

50. 'Der historische Roman ist erstens Roman und zweitens keine Historie': Döblin, 'Der historische Roman und wir [1936]', 169.
51. Ebert, 'Jede Figur ein Stück von mir', 66.
52. Gumbrecht, *Our Broad Present*, xiii.
53. See Niemeyer, 'Im Spiegel der Geschichte', 211: 'When the bourgeois reader of 1850 looked in the literary mirror of the historical novel he especially saw himself.'
54. See Korte and Paletschek, 'Popular History Now and Then', 98.
55. See Eggert, *Studien zur Wirkungsgeschichte*, 176–77, 182; and Lonner, *Mediating the Past*. The print runs in the nineteenth century are naturally far less than those of today; *Ingo*, the most successful installment of the *Ahnen*, sold well over half a million copies between 1872 and 1920.
56. See Eggert, *Studien zur Wirkungsgeschichte*, 184.
57. Ibid., 177–81.
58. See Gumbrecht, *Our Broad Present*, 28–31.
59. Ibid., xiii.

Bibliography

Berger, Stefan, Chris Lorenz and Billie Melman (eds). *Popularizing National Pasts: 1800 to the Present*. New York: Routledge, 2012.

Döblin, Alfred. 'Der historische Roman und wir [1936]', in Walter Muschg (ed.), *A.D., Aufsätze zur Literatur: Ausgewählte Werke in Einzelbänden*, Vol. 7 (Freiburg i. Br.: Walter, 1963), 163–86.

Ebert, Sabine. '"Jede Figur ein Stück von mir". Autoren-Interview'. *DB mobil – was uns bewegt* 10(11) (November 2009).

Eggert, Hartmut. *Studien zur Wirkungsgeschichte des deutschen historischen Romans 1850–1875*. Frankfurt a. M.: Klostermann 1971.

Fenske, Michaela. 'Abenteuer Geschichte. Zeitreisen in der Spätmoderne. Reisefieber Richtung Vergangenheit', in Walter Hardtwig and Alex Schug (eds), *History Sells! Angewandte Geschichte als Wissenschaft und Markt* (Stuttgart: Steiner, 2009), 79–90.

Fulda, Daniel. 'Historiographic Narration', in Peter Hühn et al. (eds), *Handbook of Narratology*, 2nd edn, Vol. 1–2 (Berlin: de Gruyter, 2014), 227–40.

Gelder, Ken. *Popular Fiction: The Logics and Practices of a Literary Field*. London: Routledge, 2004.

Groot, Jerome de. *The Historical Novel*. London: Routledge, 2009.

———. *Remaking History: The Past in Contemporary Historical Fiction*. London: Routledge, 2016.

Gumbrecht, Hans Ulrich. *Our Broad Present: Time and Contemporary Culture*. New York: University of Columbia Press, 2014.

Hardtwig, Walter, and Alex Schug. 'Einleitung', in Walter Hardtwig and Alex Schug (eds), *History Sells! Angewandte Geschichte als Wissenschaft und Markt* (Stuttgart: Steiner, 2009), 9–17.

Hassemer, Simone Maria. 'Das Mittelalter der Populärkultur: Medien – Designs – Mytheme'. Unpublished PhD thesis, Albert-Ludwigs-Universität Freiburg i. Br., 2016. Retrieved from https://www.freidok.uni-freiburg.de/data/10612 (last accessed 11 December 2020).

Hieber, Jochen. 'Die verlorene Ehre der Marie Schärer'. *Frankfurt Allgemeine Zeitung* 33 (5 October 2010).

Hochbruck, Wolfgang. 'Reenacting Across Six Generations 1863–1963', in Sarah Willner, Georg Koch and Stefanie Samida (eds), *Doing History: Performative Praktiken in der Geschichtskultur* (Münster: Waxmann, 2016), 97–116.

Hughes, Helen. *The Historical Romance*. London: Routledge, 1993.

Hutcheon, Linda. *A Poetics of Postmodernism: History, Theory, Fiction*. London: Routledge, 1988.

Jauer, Markus. 'Die Bestseller'. *Frankfurter Allgemeine Zeitung* 44 (5 October 2011).

Johnston, Andrew James, and Kai Wiegandt. 'Introduction', in Andrew James Johnston and Kai Wiegandt (eds), *The Return of the Historical Novel? Thinking about Fiction and History after Historiographic Metafiction* (Heidelberg: Winter, 2017), 9–18.

Jürgensen, Christoph (ed.). *Die Lieblingsbücher der Deutschen*. Kiel: Ludwig, 2006.

Korte, Barbara, and Sylvia Paletschek. 'Geschichte in populären Medien und Genres: vom Historischen Roman zum Computerspiel', in Barbara Korte and Sylvia Paletschek (eds), *History Goes Pop: Zur Repräsentation von Geschichte in populären Medien und Genres* (Bielefeld: transcript, 2009), 9–60.

———. 'Popular History Now and Then: An Introduction', in Barbara Korte and Sylvia Paletschek (eds), *Popular History Now and Then: International Perspectives* (Bielefeld: transcript, 2012), 7–11.

Koselleck, Reinhardt. *Futures Past: On the Semantics of Historical Time*. Transl. and with an Introduction by Keith Tribe. New York: Columbia University Press, 2004.

Lechner, Doris. *Histories for the Many: The Victorian Family Magazine and Popular Representations of the Past. The 'Leisure Hour', 1852–1870*. Bielefeld: Transcript, 2016.

Lonner, Alyssa A. *Mediating the Past: Gustav Freytag, Progress, and German Historical Identity*. Oxford: Lang, 2005.

Lübbe, Hermann. 'Die Modernität der Vergangenheitszuwendung', in Gunther Scholz (ed.), *Historismus am Ende des 20. Jahrhunderts. Eine internationale Diskussion* (Berlin: Akademie, 1997), 146–54.

———. *Im Zug der Zeit: Verkürzter Aufenthalt in der Gegenwart*, 3rd postscript edition. Heidelberg: Springer, 2003.

McCracken, Scott. *Pulp: Reading Popular Fiction*. Manchester: Manchester University Press, 1998.

Niemeyer, Lisa. 'Im Spiegel der Geschichte: Geschichtspopularisierung im historischen Unterhaltungsroman der 1850er Jahre', in Walter Hardtwig and Alex Schug (eds), *History Sells! Angewandte Geschichte als Wissenschaft und Markt* (Stuttgart: Steiner, 2009), 200–215.

Nitz, Julia, and Sandra Harbert Petrulionis. 'Towards a Historiographic Narratology: Résumé'. *Siegener Periodicum zur internationalen empirischen Literaturwissenschaft* 30(1) (2011), 1–6.

Nusser, Peter. *Trivialliteratur*. Stuttgart: Metzler, 1991.

Pergande, Frank. 'Die Geburt der Hebamme'. *Frankfurter Allgemeine Sonntagszeitung* 12 (27 December 2009).

Rosa, Hartmut. *Social Acceleration: A New Theory of Modernity*. Translated and Introduced by Jonathan Trejo-Mathys. New York: University of Columbia Press, 2013.

Schiffman, Zachary Sayre. *The Birth of the Past*. Baltimore, MD: Johns Hopkins University Press, 2001.

Schmitz, Rolf. 'Die Königin des historischen Romans'. *Welt online* (30 May 2010). Retrieved 11 December 2020 from http://www.welt.de/print-wams/article615631/Die_Koenigin_des_historischen_Romans.html.

Stein, Emmanuel von. 'Oh du schöne Ritterzeit . . .'. *Börsenblatt* 176(33) (2009), 25–27.

Süskind, Patrick. *Das Parfum: Die Geschichte eines Mörders*. Translated by John E. Woods. New York: Vintage International, 1986.

Thiel, Christian. *Liebe, Sex und Karriere: Die Modernisierung des trivialen Liebesromans*. With a Foreword by Peter Nusser. Hamburg: Argument, 1991.

Wallace, Diana. *The Woman's Historical Novel: British Women Writers, 1900–2000*. Basingstoke: Palgrave Macmillan, 2005.

Young, Helen (ed.). *The Middle Ages in Popular Culture: Medievalism and Genre*. Amherst, NY: Cambria Press, 2015.

Part IV

NATIONAL HISTORIES

CHAPTER 13

National Narratives in Chinese Global History Writing

XUPENG ZHANG

Historians are living in a golden age of global narratives, in which global history is not merely possible but is unavoidable.[1] They have endeavoured in both post-nation-states and nation-states to break away from the old framework of national history, and to draw a new world picture by means of global history. With the increasing interconnectedness of the world, the history of the nation-state, having been developed in isolation, is now increasingly integrated into a narrative system that emphasizes interaction and entanglement. As a result, the face of world history is not the same as it was before. But on the other hand, in terms of the importance of local experience in global narratives and the challenge to power relations embedded in them, national narratives, rather than disappearing, are becoming a prerequisite for highlighting the diversities of global history.[2] In non-Western countries, especially those with long traditions of historical writing, national narratives will play, through strategies of rearrangement, emplotment and representation – an important role in constructing global pasts that is different from those that have prevailed in the West. Accordingly, although there will be some degree of conflict, the emergence of global narratives does not suppress long-standing national narratives but instead gives them the opportunity to speak their own words and put their own local experiences into global narratives, making them more open and more inclusive.

Notes for this section begin on page 277.

The Rise of Global History in China

The rise of global history in China is almost synchronous with its rise in the West. In the West, global history received official international attention in academic circles in 2000, when, at the 19th International Congress of Historical Sciences that was held in Oslo, Norway in that year, one of important themes was global history.[3] In China, Capital Normal University in Beijing took the lead in setting up China's first Global History Research Center in late 2004, and, in cooperation with the US World History Association, organized an international conference on 'World History Teaching in the World' held in October 2005. This was the first time that global history, as a research approach and perspective, entered the horizon of the public and of academia in China. In the wake of these initiatives, the systematic introduction into China of global history theories and methodologies began. Moreover, the Global History Research Center published its annual *Global History Review* in 2008, only two years after the *Journal of Global History* was inaugurated in London in 2006. Since then, the *Global History Review* has published 18 volumes, and has become semi-annual. As for books related to global history, *Globalization and Global History*, edited by Yu Pei, was published in Beijing in 2007. It was the first collection on global history published in China, basically reflecting Chinese scholars' understanding and knowledge of global history at the time. Just one year before, a book with the same title had been published in the West.[4]

Chinese scholars have shown a continuing enthusiasm for global history ever since. A search in the database of China National Knowledge Infrastructure (CNKI) reveals that from 2004 to the present, 464 articles that contain the term 'global history' in their titles have been published (last accessed 12 December 2019), showing an upward tendency year by year, whereas in 1997–2003 only 8 such articles appeared. In short, since 2004 scholars have paid notably more attention to global history than they had previously, recognizing the advantages that it has over traditional world history, and its potential as a historical research approach in the global era. Under the influence of global history, in many fields of research such as the long-established ones of economic history, history of cultural exchange, and historical geography, or the more recently developed ones of climate history, environmental history and maritime history, there appears to be a move to take 'global' as an important starting point and analytical tool for investigating topics that historians had previously studied from long-term and large-scale perspectives. In consequence, people have been given fresh perspectives on the past. It can be said that a 'global turn' in current historical research in China has now occurred.[5] Enthusiasm for global history, in addition, is also reflected in the founding of a number of global history research institutions. In December 2014, following the lead of the Global History Research Center at Capital Normal University, an Institute for Global History was set up at the Beijing Foreign Studies University – a rather striking initiative for a university that has long focused on the teaching and researching of foreign languages. In June 2016, an Institute for Global and Transnational History was established at Shandong University, a university long known for its focus on Chinese ancient history and Confucianism.

The efflorescence of global history in China can be attributed to both internal and external factors. On the one hand, it is a consequence of the globalization of global history. Although global history originated in the West, its methods and ideas have been accepted by many non-Western scholars in recent years, making it a global historical phenomenon. On the other hand, global history meets the intrinsic needs of Chinese historians, especially world historians. First, global history overcomes the disadvantages of world history studies, which took the nation-state as its narrative foundation. In the traditional conception of world history in China, world history is the sum of foreign histories, excluding Chinese history. It basically takes the vertical development of national history as its main thread and pays no attention to the horizontal relations between different nations. Consequently, only with difficulty is it able to convey a sense of the world as a totality. Second, global history breaks with the Western-centred narrative framework that prevailed in China's previous version of world history writing, in which the West was given much greater attention than non-Western countries – an emphasis that was justified by the argument that China needed to learn from the successes of the West. As a result, the developmental and expansive history of Western civilization constituted the main part of world history as researched and taught in China. Third, global history meets the need that Chinese historians have for a new grand narrative in the global era. For a long time, the paradigms of revolution and modernization have been the two grand narratives through which Chinese historians have sought to explain the historical development of modern China and the world.[6] However, the influence and explanatory power of these two paradigms have been declining in recent years. Historians need a new grand narrative in terms of which to narrate and explain the epoch, and the world in which they live. Fourth, global history can provide the rising China with a vision and attitude that a major country should have in looking at the world, and it can also provide references and experiences for China as it attempts to solve its share of global issues.

Of the four internal reasons for the rise of global history in China, the first two can be attributed to the universality of global history. That is to say, these two reasons are applicable both to explaining the rise of global history in other countries, and to the internal logic of the globalization of global history, which militates against Western-centrism. The universality of global history actually reflects a recent trend in international historiography – that is, from national history to transnational history, from local perspective to global perspective, and from single context to multiple contexts. The roots of this transformation lie both in globalization itself and in the reflection on the nature of the nation-state, the spatial turn of historical research and the contemporary value of historical writing that followed therefrom. A great number of historians have come to recognize that historical events will gain the significance and value that the national or any other local perspective cannot show if they are examined in a larger space.[7] In other words, historical events, as a result of being analysed in multiple contexts, will reveal their relations with diverse spaces and groups, by which their richer connotations will be produced. History thus becomes a complex weaving together of all coexisting histories with different narratives, different temporal signifiers and different significance. In this interweaving they share overlapping spaces; they are brought into relation with one another, often with causal consequences, but without being assimilated one to the other. As Lynn Hunt points out, such reflection, from a global perspective, on the past of humankind offers a new purpose for history: understanding our place in an increasingly interconnected world.[8]

The last two reasons for global history's rise, compared with the first two, involve what we can call the particularity of global history – that is, its mission of meeting the different and special needs of each country into which it is introduced. This means that in order to understand why global history has sprung up in China we need to analyse China's concrete reality. Generally speaking, China's openness to global history is inextricably linked with the current situation of historical research and the social reality in China. Since the 1980s, historical research in China has undergone continuous development and transformation. New fields of research have opened up and are expanding, and new theories and methods are continually emerging, although most of them deriving from the West. As a result, historians' interests and priorities in research are also changing. Especially since the beginning of the twenty-first century, historians' interests have been concentrated more on social history and cultural history. They pay more attention to local, regional and even individual issues than to any grand narrative. Meanwhile, there has emerged a phenomenon of fragmentation and de-ideologization in historical research, and many major issues have been put aside. Such master narratives as revolutionization and modernization, prominent in previous historical studies, have been criticized for having so many unstated presuppositions.[9] Historians seem to be in an era of what Jo Guldi and David Armitage have called 'short-termism'.[10] Accordingly, it has become necessary to reclaim grand narrative, but a different grand narrative, one capable of incorporating diverse historical phenomena and events into a teleological framework. Global history seems to be an option that provides a general and long-term analytical perspective for current historiography, and that complements the materialist conception of history, which has been the guiding thread of historical research in China.

As the purpose of history is often conceived as serving the present, it is reasonable to suppose that China's historical experience and real achievements should become a significant source for revising and improving the current views of globalization at a time when the depth and breadth of China's participation in globalization are increasing day by day. History, especially global history, should be a fundamental medium for interpreting the relations between China and globalization, offering a narrative useable for Chinese historians' reconstructing of their understandings of a globalized world. A considerable number of Chinese scholars hold that global history should no longer be regarded merely as an exotic import from the West; rather, they have closely linked it with China's practice of globalization. The developments and changes brought about by global history can provide a beneficial reference for China's innovation of globalization theory.[11] In this sense, global history, or rather, a localized global history, offers the possibility of providing China with the knowledge and experience of looking into and coping with globalization. Its advocates hold that it must also reflect China's global consciousness and values. As was emphasized in the establishing of the Institute for Global and Transnational History in Shandong University, the purpose of the institute is 'to draw wisdom from global history, and to probe into the formation process and historical experience of global governance system academically so as to provide constructive historical basis and policy-making recommendations for China's participation in global governance'.[12] Similarly, Sebastian Conrad has pointed out that 'in public discourse, globalization is sometimes seen almost as a political instrument of the Chinese state. Global history is therefore not generally regarded as a methodological alternative, but as a context in which the growth of the nation can be explained and promoted'.[13]

The particularity of global history means that each country, nation and cultural tradition has its own unique understanding of it. Accordingly, the connotations and meanings of global history are diverse, and its application has varied purposes. Although the narrative of global history aims to encompass the 'global', global history does not have a 'standard version'. Global history cannot be other than diverse and entangled with various local factors. For China, the nation-state still occupies an important position in current political, economic and cultural reality and discourses. It remains an important framework for present-day historical writing. Thus, even with global history the goal is not to transcend or dissolve the nation-state but to reshape understanding of the concept of nation-state within a larger scope of time and space. As Thomas Bender pointed out in discussing American history in a global age, 'it will do historiography no good to work free of the nation and its ideology only to embrace the ideology and process of globalization. Such a move promises new blindnesses, and there is, besides, the danger of complicity, conscious or not, in a triumphalism that justifies the current phase of capitalism'.[14] What Bender said indicates clearly that global history is not diametrically opposed to national history. Especially for countries like China, wherein national consciousness is still prevalent in public discourse, only by working hand in hand with national history can global history really be rooted in the tradition of Chinese historiography. Therefore, in China's discourse of global history, national narratives, instead of being declined, will highlight its due value.

National Narratives and Global History

National narratives are the product of Chinese modern historical consciousness, which originated from the collapse of the idea of *tianxia* (under heaven), which was based on the distinction between Hua and Yi, also known as Chinese–Barbarian dichotomy. Since the Western Zhou Dynasty (11th century BC – 771 BC), *tianxia* had always denoted the largest space for China to imagine and practise its political and cultural power. The *tianxia* system took China as the centre of the world, and constantly absorbed surrounding areas into its order. However, in the second half of the nineteenth century, under the impact of Western powers, the *tianxia* system collapsed virtually overnight, and was replaced by the modern world system based on nation-states. The frustrations caused by China's encounters with the West, and the sense of loose ends that resulted from the fall of traditional values, forced China to re-evaluate itself and the world. New conceptions of China and the world developed, through two approaches that were diametrically opposed to each other with respect to time. One conception was future-oriented, looking forward to China's becoming, through struggle, a true nation-state, the ascent to which would allow it to become an active participant in the modern world. The other conception was past-oriented, seeing in the denial, or at least the serious reform, of China's past the key to China's entry into the new time. Both approaches regarded history as a tool for reconstructing the Chinese nation's self-identity. On one hand, historians began to study world history (which in China means 'foreign' history) in the hope of using the successes of Western countries as exemplars from which China might learn. On the other hand, historians set about reforming China's old historiography in order to create a new historiography aimed at serving the present and the future. In 1902, Liang Qichao (1873–1929), the founder of modern Chinese historiography, published a paper 'The New Historiography', in which he called upon the Chinese to study world history in order to understand China's position in the world today. His aim was to rewrite Chinese history in the light of Western evolutionary thought, which in his view represented the successful experience of the West. In this way China's stagnant dynastic history would give way to a national history pointing towards the future.[15] Liang Qichao, and many other leading historians who came after him, such as Fu Sinian (1896–1950), Gu Jiegang (1893–1980) and Lei Haizong (1902–1962), by repeatedly recounting national narratives on which they pinned China's future, indeed succeeded in making the Chinese nation a subject of history, and thus carried out a crucial step in China's movement towards the world and towards modernity.[16]

In the first half of the twentieth century, and even for a long time afterwards, Chinese national narratives, no matter whether adopting a revolutionary or a modernization discourse, mainly expressed an appeal to establish a modern nation-state on a par with the West. To this end, the memory of the traumatic past and the expectation of a better future were deployed as indispensable factors in these narratives.[17] However, for historians, presentism – that is, the pragmatic principle that history should serve the real needs of China – was the most important impetus promoting the development of national narratives. In contrast to the temporalities, or 'regimes of historicity', prevailing in the West, in China there was no divide between the 'space of experience' in the past and the 'horizon of expectation' aimed towards the future.[18] Instead, in Chinese historiography, past experience, whether embodied in stories of failure or in stories of success, is presented as giving an unbroken impetus to the present and as pushing China into the future. At the juncture (rather than divide) that is the present, an accord is reached between the remembered past and the anticipated future, forming a resultant force that enables historians to consciously combine historical knowledge with practical action, maximizing the real effects of national narrative. The intensely pragmatic concern manifested by national narratives in contemporary Chinese historiography is no doubt an inheritance from the tradition of *Jingshi zhi yong* (applied governance, or statecraft) in ancient Chinese historiography. Even in the present era of globalization, national narratives are still active in the historians' writing, which point to the issues of reality that are urgent for practice – namely, that China not only has the ability to participate in global affairs but also, as a responsible country, to provide a new vitality and capacity for leading to new directions in globalization.[19]

Consequently, current Chinese global history writing cannot be separated from the value and significance of Chinese national narratives, and may even be within the framework of those narratives. This seemingly paradoxical issue, present in Western global history writing, finds its legitimacy in

Chinese global history. In his discussion of Third World literature, Fredric Jameson pointed out that all Third World texts are necessarily read as 'national allegories': even those texts that are seemingly private and invested with a personal libidinal dynamic are seen as projecting, in the form of national allegory, the embattled situation of Third World public culture and society.[20] Jameson's interpretation of Third World texts may be somewhat stereotyped, and there is also a risk of reducing their diversity to a single pattern.[21] Nonetheless, his argument that the telling of the individual story and of individual experience in Third World texts cannot avoid the whole laborious telling of the experience of the collectivity itself is revelatory of how national consciousness haunts Third World texts.[22] It will be helpful to analyse and understand national narratives in Chinese global history writing.

In constructing an alternative model of global history, Chinese historians attend first to the Western origins and characteristics of global history, and then endeavour, correspondingly, to create a global history that incorporates Chinese local experiences, thus amending the 'universal' understanding of global history. This alternative model not only embodies the diversity of global history, but also creates conditions for the emergence of national narratives. For Chinese historians, global history is diverse, and has different representations in different countries and regions, because each nation has a peculiar relationship with the past and has its rich memory heritage, which determines that there cannot be only one model in global history. This the position articulated by Yu Pei, with his notion of 'global history in national historical memory', which is based on the recognition that different countries and nations have distinct historical thinking and understanding, and therefore make different historical value judgements. As a new approach to historical understanding, global history is a historical thinking that cannot be regarded as focusing only on Western culture, or it will fall into the pit of Western/globalization ideology.[23] Considering that history is a form of memory, Chinese historical consciousness is passed down via its own historical memory. This historical memory is based on the unbroken tradition of the recording, collection and sorting of historical facts by Chinese historians. Consequently, Chinese historians' understanding of global history must proceed from the perspective of Chinese national historical memory.[24]

However, the creation of 'global history in national historical memory' is not just a matter of cultural transmission. It also has great significance in reality, in the destiny and future of a nation. In Yu Pei's view, the globalization led by the West has threatened the diversity of cultures. As an important part of national culture, historical memory determines the survival and development of a nation. If a nation loses its own historical memory, it loses its independent national culture, as well as its foundation for standing out within the family of nations in the world.²⁵ Hence, to emphasize global history in the memory of Chinese nation is to emphasize on the autonomy of Chinese culture.²⁶ Although global history takes the 'global' as its basic content, there is no single, universal understanding of these contents. The Chinese nation has its own global history rooted in its own national historical memory, as do other nations.²⁷

On the other hand, memory also means forgetting, and hence an excluding of others from the sites of memory. Is it possible that the so-called 'global history in national historical memory', by excluding other cultural experiences and collective memories, becomes a new ethnocentric historical narrative no different from Eurocentrism? In response to this question, Yu Pei argues that the emphasis on national historical memory in global history is not a matter of cultural conservatism or of parochial nationalism, because a nation's historical memory is both living and open. Such a historical memory will revise and reflect upon itself in the light of the new characteristics of new times. It will also strive to develop and enrich itself by continuing to absorb the outstanding cultural achievements of other nations. National historical memory is thus reflexive and inclusive; it does not simply stress exclusion and differences. It is consistent with the intrinsic value of global history. In fact, global history can live within the nation only if it connects with national historical memory. Only in this way can it combine with the immediate needs of the nation, and guide the nation to the future. As Yu Pei asserts, 'in the new historical circumstance, we should have our own global history that is situated inside our national historical memory. Only in this way can we continue to substantiate our historical memory, enrich its resources and play a larger role in the great task of China's revival'.²⁸

The 'global history in national historical memory' that Yu Pei envisages aims to reshape China's cultural consciousness and self-awareness in the era of globalization. It also seeks to call attention to the Western ideology behind global history. Yu Pei argues that in the past, the globalization process was not a 'global' process but was a process led by the West, with the United States at its centre. Likewise, 'global history' was not a history for the 'globe' but one incorporating, implicitly or explicitly, the residues of Western-centrism.²⁹ In a similar vein, Qian Chengdan has suggested that when Chinese scholars fail to insist on understanding global history from a national standpoint, they have tended not to notice the concealed features of Western globalization ideology. For example, Chinese scholars too often fail to notice that advocacy for a transcending of national standpoints amounts to a denial of the present-day rationality of the nation-state. The outcome is a form of global history that ends up offering a covert defence of Western hegemony over the world.³⁰ Qian's reflections on global or world history, like Yu Pei's, start from a national standpoint. However, unlike Yu Pei's retrospections of national historical memory, Qian's analysis of the rationality of global history starts with the current research work of historians.

Qian first points out two different purposes of historical research: one is to understand the past, to satisfy people's curiosity about the past, and to seek the truth of history; the other is to identify the relevance of the past to the present, or to draw lessons from the past to serve the present.[31] In Qian's view, the study of national history should be undertaken for both purposes. However, the study of world history is mainly for the second purpose. The reason for this is that in studying world history Chinese people have interests, perspectives, and consciousness quite different from those of non-Chinese. For Chinese people, it is more important to see what they might learn from and what they might find inspiring in the history of foreign countries. Consequently, for them, the exploration of historical details is less important than the meaning of drawing lessons from history.[32] Qian contends that there is a very commendable tradition in the study of world history in China – namely, a strong concern for issues of one's own era. Taking the actual needs of social development in China as an example, he points out that when China faced invasion by foreign powers and consequently had the need to maintain national independence, world history studies focused on Sino-foreign relations and on the national liberation; when China was immersed in the process of social liberation, world history focused on revolutions, as well as on the histories of political systems in all countries; and when China entered the period of reform and opening, world history turned to the modernization of Western countries.[33] It is not hard to see that, in Qian's view, the lesson-drawing function of world history studies is even more important than its truth-seeking function.

Qian here obviously makes two distinctions in history or the past. One belongs to purely academic research, purposing to inquire into details, truth and objectivity; the other is included in the realm of serving the present needs, providing experience, examples, lessons and admonition for the present. World/global history studies are mainly placed in the second field, the ultimate goal of which is to serve the real needs of the country, nation and people. The distinction between these two functions of historical research made by Qian is reminiscent of Michael Oakeshott's division of the past. In his *Experience and its Modes*, Oakeshott divides the past into 'historical past' and 'practical past'. The so-called historical past refers to 'what really happened', which is the historical reality that historians should study and investigate. It exists mainly in academic research and represents neutrality and objectivity. As long as the historian is patient and fortunate enough, he can discover the true features of the past.[34] The practical past, however, is completely different from the historical past. It comes from people's past practical experience. It is often used to demonstrate the effectiveness of present and future actions, and exists more in memories, beliefs, myths and legends. The value the practical past is not its authenticity but its connection with the present and its guidance to the present.[35] Applying this distinction to Qian, we can see that Qian's two-level division of history aims to explore the 'practical' connotation or practicality of world/global history studies, and then to exert its functions of providing past references, guiding the present and anticipating the future, which provides new historical resources for the development of countries and nations. Qian's doing makes global history accord with national narratives, and also enables national narratives to expand and continue in a new global context.

Qian's emphasis on the practical functions of world history is in line with Yu Pei's reconstructing of global history in national historical memory. Both affirm a need for national narratives in global history. This position reflects different global views of history, and even different cultural values and historiographical traditions as between Chinese and Western scholars. As for Ge Zhaoguang, although he does not make the above distinction between Chinese and Western forms of global history, he also believes that national history is still important in the prevailing era of global history. Ge further asserts that the reason why the West could give birth to a global history 'beyond nation-states', while China and even East Asia still needed to uphold the importance of national history, has to do with the differences between the historical developments of the East and the West. Ge argues that from the perspective of political history there is a big difference between East Asia and Europe, especially with regard to the formation and development of the state, and the influence of state on culture.[36] First of all, East Asia did not have a universal religion (such as Catholicism) that transcended the 'state' and 'imperial power', offering a medium for communication and identification among various countries. Consequently, the people of East Asia lacked the basis for mutual recognition in culture and belief. Second, there were no large-scale population movements, ethnic migrations, or regime changes between China, Japan and North Korea. Consequently, the borders, nationalities and cultural boundaries between these three countries were generally stable and clear. Major historical events that shaped politics, culture and identity formation were normally rooted in and dominated by state or dynasty. Third, before the nineteenth century, East Asia lacked a community of intellectuals (a 'Republic of Letters') that could unite across nation-state boundaries. On the contrary, intellectuals from different countries adhered to distinct national positions. Finally, China did not have actual control of neighbouring countries, although historically it had the status of a suzerain state. In modern times, however, East Asian countries have gradually established their respective subjectivities, with ideological traditions and national languages, and have also constructed unique respective histories. As a result, it is difficult for East Asia to become a community that transcends the nation-state. Nation or country is still important for its history.[37]

Ge regards the cultural community in a broad sense as the basis and premise for generating the idea of global history. Seeing that East Asia cannot form a cultural community like Europe, and East Asian intellectuals cannot set up a Republic of Letters as European and American intellectuals did, it is easy to understand why it is difficult for China to generate a global history that transcends the nation-state. In Ge's view, while paying more attention to global history, China must adhere to the value of national history and national narratives. He bases this view not on the claim assumption that global history is a master narrative that embodies Western ideology, but rather on the particularity of the development of Chinese history. In other words, the highly homogeneous culture and political system formed in China's history results in its natural adoption of the national mode in historical narrative, having more obvious internal vein than other super-national narratives.[38] So the repeated emphasis on the importance of national history in trend of global history, as pointed out by Ge, is not the expansion of nationalist historiography but the vigilance against nationalist historiography; tracing and sorting out the origins, traditions, concepts and systems that are shaped historically and closely related to current nationalist consciousness will restrain nationalist historiography.[39] More importantly, writing national history in the context of global history will allow people to see the historical changes in the concept of 'nation'. If this is done, the writing of the nation-state history will still make sense.[40]

Constructing a Global History with Chinese Characteristics: The Predicaments and Possibilities in Theory and Practice

As Yu Pei's global history as 'national historical memory', or Qian's 'practical' world history, or Ge's open rather than closed national history clearly show, national history and global history are not completely opposite or incompatible. National narratives should have a place in the global discourse. An emphasis on national narratives in global history does not mean establishing a confrontational stance, but means rethinking the significance of global history and national history in the present; or rather, it means contextualizing such highly ideologized concepts as 'nation' and 'global', and recognizing that they are always in constant development and change. They should not be confined to a single unit of time and space. The existence of national narratives also shows that there should be different understandings and applications of global history. Only by localizing or absorbing various local discourses can global history truly achieve its potential of diversity and inclusiveness. It is in this sense that there is a theoretical and practical possibility to build a global history with Chinese characteristics.

What, then, is global history with Chinese characteristics? In answering this question, Yu Pei made the following three points: global history must consciously take the materialist conception of history as its theoretical foundation; it should thoroughly reject Western-centrism; and it should not deviate from the reality of Chinese history, which should be included in the broad background of contemporary Chinese social development.[41] In a 2010 interview, Yu Pei further discussed this issue, particularly emphasizing that global history should present China's values and reflect China's current problems:

> Our research on global history manifests our standard of value judgement, our view of history, our values, our Chinese people's feeling, and our Chinese people's understanding of the historical reality; and what is more, we should build our understanding of global history on the basis of our understanding of global reality.[42]

Yu Pei added that global history is a new history that best reflects the spirit of the present, but only if it is attentive to complex issues rooted in the reality of contemporary China and of the world. Only in this way can global history convey a sense of history and a sense of the times, and combine them to reflect the spirit of the times.[43] The idea of building a global history with Chinese characteristics put forward by Yu Pei represents a general expectation and aspiration of Chinese global historians – that is, to create a global history that combines nationality, reality and the spirit of the times, and integrates it, with an open attitude, into the trend of global historiography.

However, a question that urgently needs to be resolved is: What kind of theory is needed to build a global history with Chinese characteristics, and where does this theory come from? Historical materialism is obviously the guiding theory of historical research. But historians still need a more operable method or theory to 'make a specific analysis of specific issues'. However, so far, global history with Chinese characteristics has not reached the 'theoretical' height that can guide the specific studies. Absence of theory is obviously not conducive to the construction of a global history with Chinese characteristics. It also makes the study of specific aspects of history more like a reproduction of Western global history – an unpersuasive, rather mechanical application of Western experience to Chinese history. As Ma Keyao pointed out:

> So far we have only one historical theory, which has its roots in the West. The countries of Asia, Africa and Latin America have not developed their own historical theories, although they have a long history. Western theory indeed has its rationality, but it also has its limitations, for it only looks at the world from Western circumstances. Many of these limitations are Eurocentric

discourses that we want to go beyond. The Third World countries do not have their own historical theories, and so up to now we have not yet achieved this kind of transcendence.[44]

Similarly, Zhang Kaixuan, in his reflection on the study of modern Chinese history, emphasized that:

> to some extent, Chinese historiography, especially modern Chinese historiography, has been marginalized by international academia, which holds that it lacks its own theoretical thoughts, independent thinking, research characteristics, even its own style. It is a sad thing if the so-called 'bringing into line' of Chinese historiography with international norms means following the line of one particular country, regarding its historiographical trend as if it were ours.[45]

The absence of theory in historical writing is itself a historical issue, although it appears like a practical problem. This is closely related to the fact that in modern times, Chinese historians, in order to reshape China's historicity and nationality, rushed to embrace Western theories while giving up traditional methods of Chinese historiography. Since the late Qing Dynasty (1840–1912), the two Western theories that have had the most impact on Chinese historiography are positivism (or 'scientism') and evolutionism. Liang Qichao once pointed out that the lack of a scientific spirit and of an objective research attitude was the reason why Chinese historiography lagged behind the West. As he said:

> We must acknowledge that the reason why European and American historiography made progress in the past century lies in the fact that European and American historians know how to use scientific methods to examine historical resources. . . . Our country's historians do not know how to use scientific methods to deal with historical sources, and therefore they do not know that there are mistakes and falsities in their books.[46]

Furthermore, evolutionism has subverted the traditional ideas of Chinese historians, leading to dramatic changes in their understanding of history. An obvious example is that the moral judgements in traditional Chinese historiography no longer take specific good and evil acts or an attentiveness to the welfare of the people as standards, but instead ask whether people and institutions have successfully adapted themselves to the universal trend of evolution. As Xia Zengyou (1863–1924) argued: 'It comes to be taken as right and proper that the weakest will go to the wall and that the powerful are to be obeyed. These notions come to be widely accepted, and had a great impact on the world. The law of the jungle is now taken as common sense'.[47] It is precisely on the basis of the acceptance of these views as *exempla* of 'common sense', summoned up from Western historical experience, that historians have gradually realized that Chinese history is no longer particular, and instead identify with the universality of Western history, even the universal value of Western theory.[48] At the beginning of the twentieth century, Liang

Qichao, among other Chinese historians, first proposed using Western theory to reform Chinese traditional historiography in the name of a 'New History'. Subsequently, in the 1980s, when China opened its doors and restarted the modernization process, the transformation and internationalization of historiography was once more put on the agenda. Many Western theories and historical methodologies, such as modernization theory, world system theory, the theory and method of the Annales School, postmodern history, new culture history and global history, have been introduced into China and have profoundly influenced the research paradigms, research fields and even writing styles of Chinese historians. Our ability to look back upon, and to grasp the historical background and rationality of, the Western theories that have entered China allows us to judge those theories more objectively. On the one hand, the importation of these theories has promoted the renewal and development of Chinese historiography; on the other hand, it has also exposed the atheoretical character of Chinese historiography.

However, just as late-developing countries have an advantage over developed countries in the process of industrialization, China, as a late-developing country in theory production, may be able to see the disadvantages and deficiencies of Western theory more clearly than is the case in Western countries, leading to the possibility of breakthroughs on the theoretical level.[49] Of course, theoretical breakthroughs are nothing without integration into the practice of history. It is a proper and reasonable choice to prioritize a return to concrete historical research over theory construction. New theories can only properly emerge through the practice of history and the updating and development of current historical studies. As Ma Keyao advocated, 'Third World historians . . . should re-examine their own civilization, their own history, and the history of the world as well. They should establish their own system of historical theory according to their own understanding, and with reference to the achievements of historical theories in the world'.[50]

A global history with Chinese characteristics does not simply highlight China's importance in global history, nor does it simply increase the amount of 'Chinese content' in global history.[51] Rather, it emphasizes a global history with no centrality, a global history that is based, rather, on the connection and interaction between different countries, regions and civilizations. Non-centrality does not deny that a particular country or region may be at the centre of global interaction at some stage of historical development. Such a history emphasizes that the historical status of the countries in the central position is not formed in isolation, but is instead the result of global interaction. Non-centrality also means the rejection of any centralist narrative in global history writing: the history and reality of 'non-central' countries or regions cannot be explained merely by the historical experience of 'central' countries or regions. Although this seems to be common sense, people often jump into another centralism unconsciously after they have rejected the dominant centralism. Rigid thinking of this sort risks impairing the study of global history. For example, in his *Mongol Conquests in World History*, Timothy May challenges the claim made in traditional European and Asian historical writings that the Mongol conquest was bloody, cruel and barbaric. May subverts this view, proposing instead the idea of the 'Chinggis Exchange' – that is, he holds that in the period of *Pax Mongolica* Mongolians had a profound and basically positive impact on the world in terms of trade, forms of warfare, administration, religion, plague control, migrations and cultural exchanges. Consequently, the world made by the Chinggis Exchange was completely different from what it had been before.[52] However, while May did jump out of the previous narrow framework by writing a history of the Mongol Empire not centred on the perspective of Europe or Asia, in putting the Mongol Empire at the centre he underplayed its destructive impact on Eurasian civilizations, especially the Arab, Turkic and Russian civilizations.

Given that no theory has yet been established that makes possible a description of the global past of mankind in general, it may not be necessary for Chinese historians to start from the global when practising global history. On the contrary, they should first look at their own country's history, and then, based on a new understanding of that history, gain a new understanding of world/global history. Here are two issues to which we should be particularly attentive.

First, we must see that 'China' – whether as a cultural or as a political community – is not immutable: instead, it is constantly changing, interwoven with the surrounding areas. For example, John E. Herman's *Amid the Clouds and Mist* examines the interaction between the central government and the local authority of Nasu Yi in south-west China from the Song to the Qing dynasty. Although it is quite inappropriate to use the term 'colonization' to refer to the relation between the central government and the local ethnic minority, the book, with its 'from below' perspective, nonetheless gives us fresh insight from its thorough analyses of the responses and reactions of Nasu Yi to the central government as it gradually became more unified.[53] Similarly, Bin Yang's *Between Winds and Clouds* describes how Yunnan became politically integrated into the central government: over time, it was broken off from its older trade system, which had been focused on the Indian Ocean, and was incorporated into the trade system centred on China.[54] From the intricate and complex relations between the central and the local discussed in the two books, we can see, also, changes in the concept of China. Similarly, in a series of recent articles and writings, Ge Zhaoguang has emphasized that we should understand the complexity and diversity of China in its historical context. In his *Zhai zi zhongguo* [Here in 'China' I Dwell], he sought to show how 'historical China' is a moving 'China' by examining the changes of dynasties, ethnic groups and borders in Chinese history.[55] His dynamic understanding of 'China' in history helps us to break out of a rigid mode of thinking, allowing us to see how 'China' has been formed by diverse cultures and multiple 'places'. In this way, a historian can get rid of fixed, inherent ideas about the history of his or her country or nation, in this case putting China into the world in a more tolerant way, and then examining and balancing the relations between Chinese history and global history. This sort of move is foundational for building an open rather than closed mode of China-oriented global history.

Second, examining China in a transnational or global context will help us to recognize that today's China is not only the result of the collaborative development of inner forces, but also the consequence of international and even global factors. China's political territory is vast and its cultural space is wide, and many different countries and civilizations are located around it. For a long time, it was interaction and comparison with these countries and civilizations that brought about China's self-recognition. However, this recognition came from an internal, 'emic' perspective, lacking an 'etic' perspective from outside. Ever since the inception of the modern times, under the double attacks of Japanese civilization and Western civilization, traditional China witnessed an 'unprecedented transformation for millennia'. At this time, the 'emic' perspective fails to offer an adequate explanation, which means that the 'etic' perspective has become indispensable. Ge Zhaoguang has pointed out that '[w]hen we discuss historical China, we have to involve Asia and even the world, because "China" is not a self-contained historical world. All historical discussions have to be placed in the background of "world" or "Asia", or at least in the background of "East Asia"'.[56] In line with this view, Ge proposes the viewpoint of 'looking at China from the periphery'. Specifically,

> reconstructing a new reference system that uses the periphery as the 'other' to understand cultural China historically would not only make the study of traditional history and culture have the significance of establishing identity, but could also enable people to clearly distinguish historical China on the move from the present political China. At the same time, our observing the ever-changing 'historical China' in history and culture from the reactions of the 'periphery', in fact, is trying to have a new understanding of 'present China' itself.[57]

Not only that, such a perspective counters self-centrism in historical writing, by re-examining China in a transnational or global context. Jörn Rüsen has pointed out that, in the era of globalization, historiography increasingly depends on transnational and cross-cultural approaches.[58] However, a kind of ethnocentrism that is deeply rooted in modern historical consciousness is still entrenched. This ethnocentrism shows itself in the following three ways: by asymmetrical evaluation, by teleological continuity and by centralized perspective. Only by jumping out of China and looking back at it with exotic eyes, then reconstructing China's perception of itself in a transnational context, can we build an equal rather than a provincial, and a pluralistic rather than an egocentric, perception of the world. This new understanding of self and world will be an important methodological prerequisite for the construction of a Chinese model of global history.

Conclusion

In a retrospective article on world history studies in twentieth-century China, the authors articulated the following expectations concerning world history studies in twenty-first century China.

> By taking root in the rich soil of our national culture, putting in order and carrying on the excellent achievements of historical studies in China, we can merge with the great unification of cultures in the world. Such a move will help to create an open-minded Chinese school of historical thinking, sharing the same language as historians all over the world yet having our own Chinese character. Only in so doing can we enrich historical studies in the world and make our own contribution.[59]

As these authors write, only by combining of nationality and world-ness can Chinese global history writing make a contribution to the formation of a global history with more universal significance. In order to achieve this, it is imperative to rethink and sort out the history of China, freeing it from confinement in the existing framework of national history, and opening it to a transnational and global context. Such a global history will eventually produce a re-spatialized national narrative, which will become a link between China's national past and global present. Although this new national narrative retains a nation's past experience and aspirations, it does not mean narrow-minded nationalism, much less methodological nationalism. The spatial basis for its existence – open rather than closed, inclusive rather than exclusive – will finally dissolve the linear temporal consciousness of nationalist discourse, from which self-centred historical consciousness grows.

In the golden age of global narrative, national narratives still have significance. However, national narratives as here envisaged are intended not to emphasize the uniqueness or superiority of national history, but rather to balance the relations between national history and global history by showing the value of local experience and by enriching the diverse understandings of global history. Similarly, such national narratives are no longer a memory of hatred, trauma or conflict. Rather, they will become an important medium for reaching equality, respect and consensus by demonstrating and expressing claims based on difference and diversity. Only on the basis of equality and mutual recognition can historians truly understand that the universal value of global history lies in the transcendence of those conceptions of space that have long dominated many academic, and other, ways of conceptualizing the past.[60]

Through the particularity brought about by national narratives, historians can use a roundabout way to achieve the universality of global history. Historians have reason to believe that regardless of the modes of expression of, or the position taken by, global history, the fundamental starting point is to seek the unity of human society and the universal laws in world history. Unity means to seek common ground while reserving differences, although it is hard to find a value acceptable to all human beings. Here, it is perhaps appropriate to cite and share Liu Xincheng's views:

> The essential aim of world history, namely, the study of the universal quality of the human past . . . It is this nature of the endeavour that has lent world history its academic legitimacy without which this academic discipline would come to nothing. It is perhaps more realistic, I believe, for us to start from the current discourse structure (despite its strong Western orientation) and make piecemeal corrections and amendments so that we can come nearer to consensus.[61]

Acknowledgements

I would like to thank Professor Allan Megill, University of Virginia, for improving my English.

Xupeng Zhang is a professor at the Institute of Historical Theory, Chinese Academy of Social Sciences in Beijing, China. His research focuses on European intellectual history, historical theory and global history. He publishes many papers in these fields. He is the author of several books, including *The Concise History of Western Civilization* (2011); *The Studies of Cultural Theory* (co-authored with Ping He, 2014); and *Philosophy of History and Historical Theory of Our Times* (co-authored with Q. Edward Wang, 2020).

Notes

1. Klein, 'In Search of Narrative Mastery', 298.
2. Davis, 'Decentering History'; Mignolo, *Local Histories/Global Designs*.

3. Sogner, *Making Sense of Global History*.
4. Yu, *Quanqiuhua yu quanqiushi*; Gills and Thompson, *Globalization and Global History*.
5. Zhang, 'Characteristics and Trends'.
6. Li, 'From Revolution to Modernization'.
7. Bender, 'Introduction', 9.
8. Hunt, *Writing History*, 10.
9. Li, 'Rewriting Modern Chinese History', 99–100.
10. Guldi and Armitage, *The History Manifesto*, 2.
11. Liu, 'Quanqiu lishi guan', 22, 24.
12. Zhao, 'Shandong daxue'.
13. Conrad, *What Is Global History?*, 208.
14. Bender, 'Introduction', 12.
15. Liang, *Xin shixue*, 85.
16. Duara, *Rescuing History*, 33–48.
17. Wang, *Jindai zhongguo de shijia yu shixue*.
18. Koselleck, *Future Past*; Koselleck, *Practice of Conceptual History*; Hartog, *Regimes of Historicity*.
19. Dittmer and Yu, *China, the Developing World*.
20. Jameson, 'Third World Literature', 69.
21. Ahmad, 'Jameson's Rhetoric of Otherness', 8.
22. Jameson, 'Third World Literature', 85–86.
23. Yu, 'Quanqiu shi', 23.
24. Ibid., 28.
25. Ibid., 18.
26. Ibid., 29.
27. Ibid., 30.
28. Ibid., 30.
29. Yu, 'Shijie wenming jincheng zhong de quanqiu shi', 9.
30. Qian, 'Shijie shi yanjiu de ruogan wenti', 7.
31. Qian, 'Fasheng de shi guoqu', 7.
32. Qian, 'Gongne yu dingwei', 7–8.
33. Qian, 'Shijie shi yanjiu de shidai guanhuai', 5.
34. Oakeshott, *Experience and its Modes*, 106.
35. Ibid., 104–5.
36. Ge, 'Zai quanqiu shi chaoliu zhong'.
37. Ibid., 27.
38. Ge, *Zhai zi zhongguo*, 30.
39. Ge, 'Zai quanqiu shi chaoliu zhong', 28.
40. Ibid., 29.
41. Yu, 'Quanqiuhua he "quanqiu lishi guan"', 7.
42. Yu, 'Quanqiuhua yishi xingtai he quanqiu shi', 48.
43. Ibid.
44. Ma, 'Wo dui shijie tongshi tixi de sikao', 25.
45. Zhang, 'Zou ziji de lu', 105.
46. Liang, *Zhongguo lishi yanjiu fa*, 123.
47. Xia, *Zhongguo gudai shi*, 404.
48. Wang, *Jindai zhongguo de shijia yu shixue*, 39–40.
49. Gerschenkron, *Economic Backwardness*.
50. Ma, 'Wo dui shijie tongshi tixi de sikao', 26.
51. Littrup, 'Lishi zhong de daxiao he yuanjin', 24.
52. May, *Mongol Conquests*.

53. Herman, *Amid the Clouds and Mist*.
54. Yang, *Between Winds and Clouds*.
55. Ge, *Zhai zi zhongguo*, 31.
56. Ge, *Hewei 'zhongguo'*, 3.
57. Ge, *Zhai zi zhongguo*, 294–95.
58. Rüsen, 'How to Overcome Ethnocentrism'.
59. Xiang et al., 'Ershi shiji zhongguo de shijie shi yanjiu', 109.
60. Sachsenmaier, *Global Perspectives*, 2.
61. Liu, 'Quanqiu shiguan zai zhongguo', 187.

Bibliography

Ahmad, Aijaz. 'Jameson's Rhetoric of Otherness and the "National Allegory"'. *Social Text* 17 (1987), 3–25.
Bender, Thomas. 'Introduction: Historians, the Nation, and the Plenitude of Narratives', in Thomas Bender (ed.), *Rethinking American History in a Global Age* (Los Angeles: University of California Press, 2002), 1–21.
Conrad, Sebastian. *What Is Global History?* Princeton, NJ: Princeton University Press, 2016.
Davis, Natalie Zemon. 'Decentering History: Local Stories and Cultural Crossings in a Global World'. *History and Theory* 50(2) (2011), 188–202.
Dittmer, Lowell, and George T. Yu (eds). *China, the Developing World, and the New Global Dynamic*. Boulder, CO: Lynne Rienner Publishers, 2010.
Duara, Prasenjit. *Rescuing History from the Nation State: Questioning Narratives of Modern China*. Chicago: Chicago University Press, 1995.
Ge, Zhaoguang. *Hewei 'zhongguo'* [What is 'China': Territory, nation, culture and history]. Hong Kong: Oxford University Press, 2014.
———. 'Zai quanqiu shi chaoliu zhong guobie shi yaiyou yiyi ma?' [Is there any meaning for national history in the trends of global history?]. *Zhongguo wenhua* [Chinese culture] 2 (2012), 26–30.
———. *Zhai zi zhongguo: Chongjian youguan 'zhongguo' de lishi lunshu* [Here in 'China' I dwell: Reconstruct a historical discourse on China]. Beijing: Zhonghua shuju, 2011.
Gerschenkron, Alexander. *Economic Backwardness in Historical Perspective: A Book of Essays*. Cambridge, MA: Harvard University Press, 1962.
Gills, Barry K., and William R. Thompson (eds). *Globalization and Global History*. London: Routledge, 2006.
Guldi, Jo, and David Armitage. *The History Manifesto*. Cambridge: Cambridge University Press, 2014.
Hartog, François. *Regimes of Historicity: Presentism and Experiences of Time*, translated by Saskia Brown. New York: Columbia University Press, 2015.
Herman, John E. *Amid the Clouds and Mist: China's Colonization of Guizhou, 1200–1700*. Cambridge, MA: Harvard University Press, 2007.
Hunt, Lynn. *Writing History in the Global Age*. New York: W.W. Norton, 2014.
Jameson, Frederic. 'Third World Literature in the Era of Multinational Capitalism'. *Social Text* 15 (1986), 65–88.
Klein, Kerwin Lee. 'In Search of Narrative Mastery: Postmodernism and the People without History'. *History and Theory* 34(4) (1995), 275–98.
Koselleck, Reinhart. *Future Past: On the Semantics of Historical Time*, translated and with an introduction by Keith Tribe. New York: Columbia University Press, (1985) 2004.

———. *The Practice of Conceptual History: Timing History, Spacing Concepts*, translated by Todd Samuel Presner et al. Stanford, CA: Stanford University Press, 2002.

Li, Huayin. 'From Revolution to Modernization: The Paradigmatic Transition in Chinese Historiography in the Reform Era'. *History and Theory* 49 (2010), 336–60.

———. 'Rewriting Modern Chinese History in the Reform Era: Changing Narratives and Perspectives in Chinese Historiography', in Q. Edward Wang and Georg G. Iggers (eds), *Marxist Historiographies: A Global Perspective* (London: Routledge, 2016), 87–103.

Liang, Qichao. *Xin shixue* [New history]. Beijing: Shangwu yinshuguan, 2014.

———. *Zhongguo lishi yanjiu fa* [The research method of Chinese history]. Shijiazhuang: Hebei jiaoyue chubanshe, 2000.

Littrup, Leif. 'Lishi zhong de daxiao he yuanjin' [Big and small, and distant and close in history]. *Lishi jiaoxue* [History teaching] 1 (1991), 23–24.

Liu, D. 'Quanqiu lishi guan: Lixiang yu xianshi zhijian de paihuai' [Global view of history: Lingering between ideal and reality]. *Shixue jikan* [Collected papers of history studies] 5 (2015), 21–24.

Liu, Xincheng. 'Quanqiu shiguan zai zhongguo' [Global view of history in China]. *Lishi yanjiu* [Historical research] 6 (2011), 180–87.

Ma, Keyao. 'Wo dui shijie tongshi tixi de sikao: Fang Ma Keyao jiaoshou' [My reflections on the system of world history: An interview with Professor Ma Keyao]. *Lishi jiaoxue wenti* [History teaching and research] 2 (2008), 21–26.

May, Timothy. *The Mongol Conquests in World History*. London: Reaktion Books, 2011.

Mignolo, Walter D. *Local Histories/Global Designs: Coloniality, Subaltern Knowledge, and Border Thinking*. Princeton, NJ: Princeton University Press, 2012.

Oakeshott, Michael. *Experience and its Modes*. Cambridge: Cambridge University Press, 1986.

Qian, Chengdan. 'Fasheng de shi "guoqu", xiechulai de shi "lishi": Guanyu lishi shi shenme de sikao' [What happened is the 'past', what is written is 'history': Reflections on what history is]. *Shixue yuekan* [Journal of history science] 7 (2013): 5–11.

———. 'Gongne yu dingwei: guanyu shijie shi xueke de liangdian xiangfa' [Function and location: Two thoughts on the discipline of world history]. *Shijie lishi* [World history] 2 (2011), 7–8.

———. 'Shijie shi yanjiu de ruogan wenti' [Some issues on world history studies]. *Lishi jiaoxue* [History teaching] 20 (2012), 3–9.

———. 'Shijie shi yanjiu de shidai guanhuai' [The concerns of times in world history studies]. *Renmin ribao* [People's daily], 13 April 2014, 5.

Rüsen, Jörn. 'How to Overcome Ethnocentrism: Approaches to a Culture of Recognition by History in the Twenty-First Century'. *History and Theory* 43 (2004), 118–29.

Sachsenmaier, Dominic. *Global Perspectives on Global History: Theories and Approaches in a Connected World*. New York: Cambridge University Press, 2011.

Sogner, Solvi (ed.). *Making Sense of Global History: The 19th International Congress of the Historical Sciences Oslo 2000*. Oslo: Universitetsforlaget, 2001.

Wang, Fansen. *Jindai zhongguo de shijia yu shixue* [Historians and historiography in modern China]. Shanghai: Fudan daxue chubanshe, 2010.

Xia, Zengyou. *Zhongguo gudai shi* [The ancient history of China]. Shijiazhuang: Hebei jiaoyue chubanshe, 2000.

Xiang, Xiang, et al. 'Ershi shiji zhongguo de shijie shi yanjiu' (World history studies in twentieth-century China). *Xueshu yuekan* [Academic monthly] 8 (1999), 99–109.

Yang, Bin. *Between Winds and Clouds: The Making of Yunnan (Second Century BCE–Twentieth Century CE)*. New York: Columbia University Press, 2009.

Yu, Pei. 'Quanqiuhua he "quanqiu lishi guan"' [Globalization and 'global view of history']. *Shixue jikan* [Collected papers of history studies] 2 (2001), 1–9.

———. 'Quanqiuhua yishi xingtai he quanqiu shi: Fang Yu Pei yanjiuyuan' [Global ideology and global history: An interview with Professor Yu Pei]. *Lishi jiaoxue wenti* [History teaching and research] 2 (2010), 41–50.

——— (ed.). *Quanqiuhua yu quanqiushi* [Globalization and global history]. Beijing: Shehui kexue chubanshe, 2007.

———. 'Quanqiu shi: minzu lishi jiyi zhong de quanqiu shi' [Global history in national historical memory]. *Shixue lilun yanjiu* [Historiography quarterly] 1 (2006), 18–30.

———. 'Shijie wenming jincheng zhong de quanqiu shi' [Global history in the process of world civilizations]. *Guangming ribao* [Guangming daily], 8 June 2007, 9.

Zhang, Kaixuan. 'Zou ziji de lu: Zhongguo shixue de qiantu' [Go your own way: The future of Chinese historiogrphy]. *Jinan xuebao* [Journal of Jinan University] 3 (2005), 101–7.

Zhang, Xupeng. 'The Characteristics and Trends of Historical Writing in the People's Republic of China since 1978'. *Historiein* 14 (2014), 43–60.

Zhao, R. 'Shandong daxue chengli quanqiu shi yu kuaguo shi yanjiuyuan' [An institute established in Shandong University]. 6 June 2016. Retrieved from http://cnews.chinadaily.com.cn/2016-06/06/content_25619691.htm (last accessed 11 December 2020).

CHAPTER 14

Narratives of Brazilian History

From Liberal to Politically Incorrect

Valdei Araujo

Introduction

In this chapter, we seek to understand how the conceptual modernization affects and is affected by changes in the historical narrative. We are well acquainted with the Koselleck's thesis on the emergence of a new experience of history between 1750 and 1850, particularly the notion of reality as a progressive totality, but we still need a better understanding of how concrete historical narratives are transformed during this complex process.[1] In other words, categories as democratization, politicization, ideologization and temporalization can be used as heuristic tools for the study of the modern nationalization of narratives in the *Sattelzeit* period. As I intend to demonstrate for the Brazilian context, the national narratives react to and produce the modern historical experience that encompasses the process of gaining independence.

We believe that by analysing the historiographical narrative it is possible to understand not only the experience of this history at play at each moment, but also its ideological implications,[2] the politico-social effects and the projection of institutional models that condition the production and reproduction of historiography. In this chapter, we will examine two emblematic cases that indicate the profound transformations of Brazilian

Notes for this section begin on page 301.

society in the past two centuries. The first, an attempt to systematize the history of Brazil as an independent nation, was written by a national in 1826, and the second was a popular recent work (2009–12) that has received great visibility and provoked strong reactions. Both cases are introduced by a brief contextualization with the political-institutional conditions for the writing of history that help to understand the meaning and scope of these narratives.

'Primitive' Accumulation of Narratives: The King's Arrival as a Narratological Force

The transfer of the Portuguese Court from Lisbon to Rio de Janeiro in 1808 began a period of unprecedented historical acceleration in the Luso-American world. Contemporaries were unanimous about the memorable character of this event, which not only reinforced the specificity of America in the Portuguese Empire, but also gave the former colony a new historical value.

The perception that a new empire was born gave the present functions of mythical foundation that was able to guide the gaze towards the future in a time of uncertainties. This attempt to probe the future from the present was recorded by the frequent quotation of Leibniz's statement 'the present is pregnant with the future', used as a kind of mantra for the most diverse political actors of the time. Gradually there emerged the experience of the present as a time of transition to a brighter future that could be anticipated.

The presence of the court also meant the introduction of printed media into Brazil, deepening the reformist project of recruiting local elite, generally educated in Coimbra, for administrative positions. The new court needed to mobilize broader sections of the public opinion through a more systematic use of print, whether in the form of pamphlets, newspapers or the sponsorship of books published by the royal press, now based in Rio de Janeiro. The project of economic reconstruction of the kingdom required a broader and systematic knowledge of colonial territories and histories. These two functions led to a multiplication of historical memories in this period, producing an ambivalent effect of greater identification with the monarchy, but also a growing awareness of the differences of reality and interest between its American and European parts.

In addition to local accounts, the Napoleonic invasion deepened the diaspora of Portuguese-Brazilian scholars in Europe, also multiplying point-of-views and narratives. This was the case for the influential newspaper *Correio Brasiliense*, published in London by the Luso-Brazilian man of letters

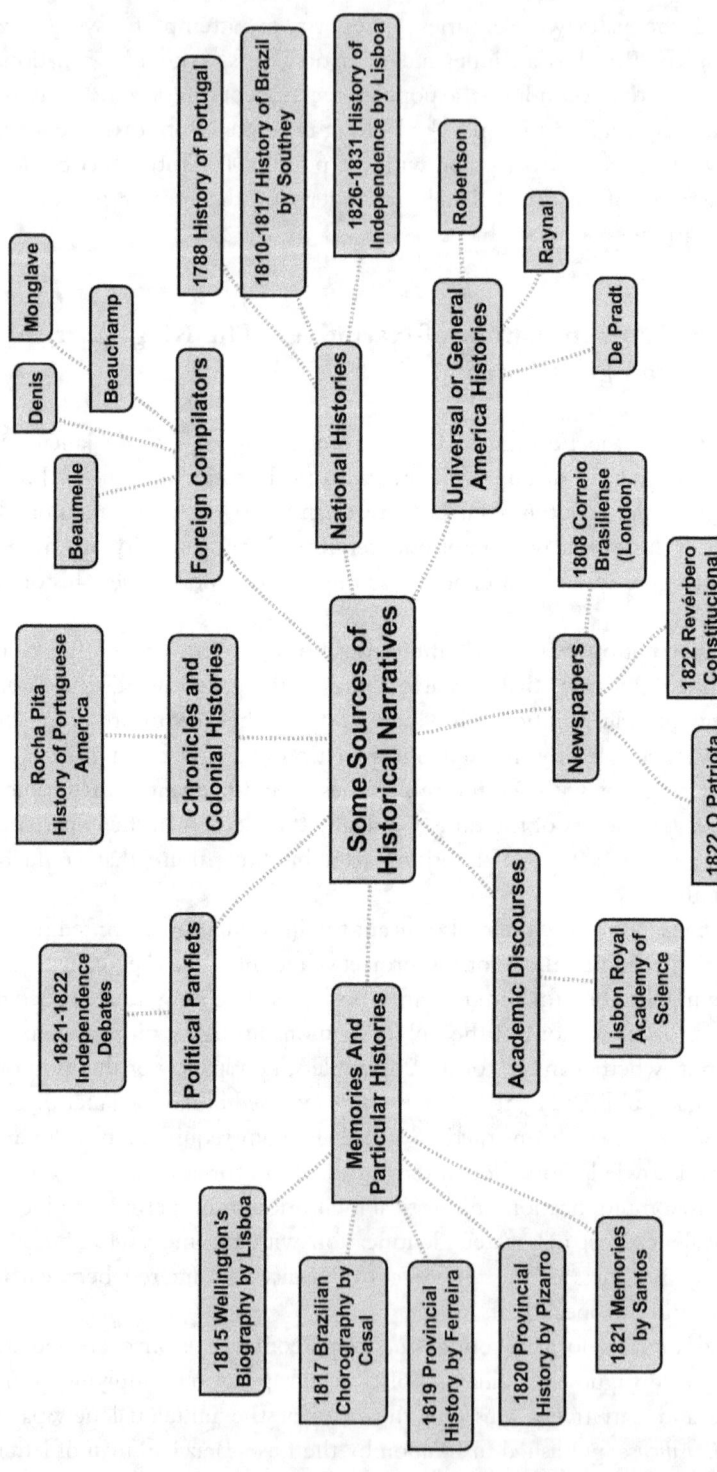

Figure 14.1 Main sources of historical narratives. © Valdei Araujo.

Hipólito da Costa. In its pages, history is a moral guide, a judge and guardian of posterity, but also a source for philosophical reflection capable of revealing the destiny of people.

For this last point, the enlightened reading of the Roman historian Tacitus, especially his *Germania*, was central.[3] The love of freedom and their institutions present in the Portuguese nation were originally inherited from this 'barbarian' people. It is inside these enlightened master narratives that some main contemporary events, especially the Napoleonic expansion – cause of the court's migration to Brazil – were understood as the threat of a return to 'universal despotism' similar to the Romans, thus preventing 'the progress of civilization'.[4]

In general, we can say that these master narratives can be organized into three major successive waves, which are not mutually exclusive: restoration, regeneration and emancipation narratives. The narratives of regeneration were based on reinterpretations of the Portuguese past, searching for principles to reinforce the kingdom in its time of crisis. In its enlightened form, these narratives are linked to Pombal's time and to the discourse of Portuguese reformism. In these narratives, the history of Portugal was understood as marked by successive moments of decay caused by different historical forces. In the early nineteenth century, the Portuguese-Brazilian scholars, trained in Coimbra and somehow involved with the Lisbon Royal Academy of Sciences, could find the Golden Age and restorative principles in a twelfth-century rural country, averse to luxury; or in the Portugal of the Great Navigations of the fifteenth and sixteenth centuries; or even in the Germanic past, into which were projected mythical notions of a love of freedom and a primitive constitution, evoked to legitimize the absolutist foundations of the monarchy. In narratives of restoration, Brazil's place was a sort of natural resource to be exploited rationally, since a new relationship could be established between metropolis and colonies, a relation more akin to ancient than to modern models. It was those narratives of restoration that oriented the meaning of the court's migration. A fact that could be understood as a defeat was meant as a great event for the restoration of the kingdom from the forces of its American part.

As the court was taking root in the new continent, new narratives produced from Brazil sought to make sense of these events. We can say that the narratives of restoration begin to be displaced by narratives of regeneration. It was no longer a matter of recovering the old kingdom in its former greatness, but of designing a new Portugal from its American portion. Especially with the political restructuring in the form of the United Kingdom of Portugal, Brazil and Algarve cemented in 1815, part of the literate elite and urban middle class began to imagine a new Portuguese nation – an empire, with a permanent seat in America.

The final defeat of Napoleon's troops in 1814, and the growing political dissatisfaction in the ancient kingdom led to double pressure for the King's return and the promulgation of a constitution. This combination led to the Port revolution in 1820, the return of King John VI in 1821, and, already in a scenario of narratives of emancipation, the Declaration of Brazilian Independence in 1822. The effort of reformist policy to promote greater knowledge of the colonial territory turned out to amplify awareness of the differences between metropolis and colony, and the emergence of new symbolic pilgrimage centres such as Rio de Janeiro.

This process can be documented by the diversity of sources for the history of Brazil that were produced from 1808 onwards. Provincial histories, chorographies and dissertations mobilized the colonial past. The reading of old chronicles and histories helped to produce narratives of progress that gave a new meaning to the end of the old colonial system. As long as this progressive movement could be identified with the reign of John VI, these narratives helped to consolidate the regeneration project on new foundations of an empire between two worlds. With the absence of the king and the reconstruction of the social pact that began with the new court, these narratives were redesigned on both sides of the Atlantic.

The Narratological Experience of Brazilian Independence

The son of John VI was left in Rio as the Brazilian regent and declared independence in 1822, receiving the title of Peter I, constitutional emperor of Brazil. In 1823 a Constituent Assembly was organized, but after several conflicts with the new emperor, it was dissolved by force. Several leaders who had played important roles in the independence were exiled. In 1824, the emperor, supported by ministers of his trust, passed the first constitution, allowing the monarch to exercise a 'moderating power', granting to the emperor several prerogatives, such as choosing the senators and presidents of provinces. In addition to this first political crisis, the new empire needed to fight provinces that had remained faithful to the Lisbon courts, struggled for the recognition of independence by the European powers, especially Britain and Portugal, and, from 1825, engaged in a territorial war on the southern frontier.

With greater freedom of the press in the period after independence, the historical narratives took a central role in political disputes and in the building of legitimacy for the newly established powers. Some new government agents in Europe were asked to recruit foreign scholars to write favourably about the Brazilian cause. It was in this context that, in 1823, a brief history of independence was published by the French La Beaumelle entitled *On [the]*

Empire of Brazil, and in 1824, the book *Brazilian Empire Independence Presented to European Monarchs*, by the also French Alphonse Beauchamp.[5]

In 1825, the emperor commissioned one of the most influential scholars during his father's reign to write a history of independence. José da Silva Lisboa, Viscount of Cairo, who then planned a work in ten parts as a general history of Brazil that would culminate in the account of the independence with the title *History of the Most Important Political Events of [the] Brazilian Empire*. Only four volumes of the work appeared between 1826 and 1830, and it was interrupted by political pressures and the author's death.

According to the original plan, the work would begin with the history of the Portuguese Great Navigations, a context with which the discovery of Brazil should be associated, and end with the bestowal of the Constitutional Charter in 1824. The first volume, published in 1826, in fact addresses the Great Navigations, the discoveries and the early years of colonization. But the planned sequence was abandoned by order of the emperor, who wanted to see the volumes on the most recent history published earlier. The next three volumes were then devoted to the last part of the planned history, narrating the events between 1821 and 1822.

In general, we can say that the great national narrative produced by Silva Lisboa seeks to understand political emancipation as the fulfilment of a providential plan, and at the same time as a demonstration of the civilizing forces driving Brazilian history. Being born out of the Great Navigations, which opened up global trade and spread the Christian religion, Brazil was destined to be a great commercial empire able to equalize the balance of power in the New World, being the first American constitutional monarchy. In a narrative in which the actions are organized by a hidden providential force that gives meaning to constant conflicts resulting from ambitions and human weaknesses, Silva Lisboa produces a comic history, in the sense given by White, with the effects of a conservative conciliation.

One of the sources of motion of this narrative is the belief that the political world can be understood as an eternal conflict between the principles of freedom and authority. One of the epigraphs of the work is a passage from *Vita Agricola* by Latin historian Tacitus:

> Primo statim beatissimi Imperii ortu res olim dissociabiles miscuit, Principatum ac Libertatem . . .
> Nunc redit animus: non pigebit rudi et incondita voce memoriam praesentium temporum composuisse.[6]
>
> [Since the beginning the opulent empire blended things hitherto incompatible: Principate and Freedom . . .
> Now the spirit returns: he will not regret having collected the memory of the present times with unskilful and unadorned voice.]

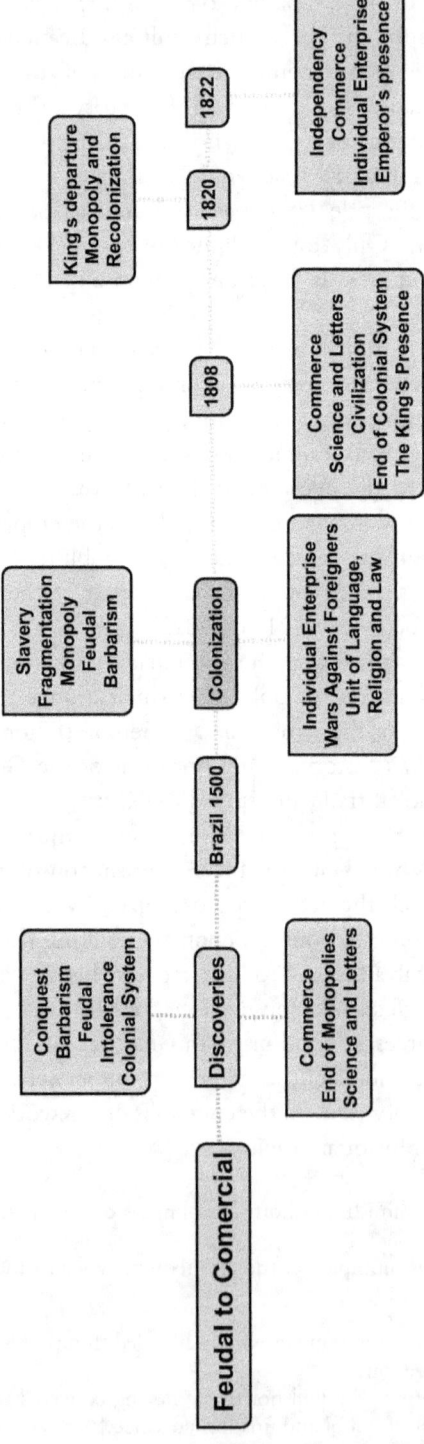

Figure 14.2 The feudal to commercial master narrative. © Valdei Araujo.

Or, in the Tacitian original, just to illustrate the freedom with which the text is handled, I transcribe the full passage below, highlighting the parts used by Silva Lisboa:

> *Nunc* demum *redit animus*; et quamquam *primo statim beatissimi* saeculi *ortu* Nerva Caesar *res olim dissociabiles miscuerit, principatum ac libertatem*, augeatque cotidie felicitatem temporum Nerva Traianus, nec spem modo ac votum Securitas publica, sed ipsius voti fiduciam ac robur adsumpserit, natura tamen infirmitatis humanae tardiora sunt remedia quam mala; et ut corpora nostra lente augescunt, cito exstinguuntur, sic ingenia studiaque oppresseris facilius quam revocaveris.... *Non* tamen *pigebit* vel *incondita* ac *rudi voce memoriam* prioris servitutis ac testimonium *praesentium* bonorum *composuisse*.[7]

We know that for the Luso-Brazilian men of letters, an author like Tacitus represented a familiar set of ideas and themes. In the passage assembled for Silva Lisboa, the key idea is a response to the conflict between civic virtue and empire. The first part of the quote says that for the first time, and Silva Lisboa refers to the reign of Peter I, empire and liberty were in harmony. In its original context, Tacitus is referring to the principate of Nerva and Trajan, in which he says he had the freedom to write history and in which the Roman virtues were slowly being restored.

We then have two possible readings. On the one hand, the first statement produces a simile in which Nerva and Trajan can be approximated to King John VI and D. Pedro I. As in any simile, one party owes its expressive power to another – in this case, the Roman history is the model through which the Brazilian context can be understood by readers. On the other hand, in its specific content, the passage responds positively to the big question of the eighteenth century about the possibility of combining a strong government, such as a monarchy, with freedom, as the citizens of a commercial and polite society could not have the same kind of virtues as those of the ancient republic.

Even using Tacitus's words (nothing is added), Silva Lisboa composes a new expression adapting the meaning of the passage to the aims of his work, deleting words and even reversing the order of periods, so that the words, which in Tacitus had a certain function, assume other meanings. It is then important to note that Silva Lisboa deliberately omits mention of the Tacitian 'first servitudes'. It seems clear that the author avoids the confrontation between past and present, which was so important in the Roman original context. It would not be difficult to continue the simile identifying the colonial period with the 'first servitudes' referred to by Tacitus, but Silva Lisboa seems to deliberately avoid this parallelism in search of a more conciliatory interpretation. In any case, the exclusion of this possibility seems consistent with the ambivalent sense of the Portuguese legacy in his work.

After a long historiographical debate, the first chapter describes the new nation's territory, emphasizing its natural borders, suggesting its providential donation, and highlighting the uniqueness of its wide expanse and resources:

> No less unique, and without parallel in the history of empires, is that such a large area of geological physiognomy superior to Europe was occupied by the smallest European nation, both in territory and population, by which have been owned for more than three centuries, now conserves the integrity of the original discovery, with the same religion, language and law, and even with increased strength and splendour, despite at various times have been invaded, in several provinces, by the French, English, Spanish and Dutch, as will be seen in the course of this history. Thus, as far as the weak human reason reaches, it seems not to be against reason that Brazilians can say with religiosity, and pride – behold the finger of God.[8]

In that context, it seemed to many members of the political elite that the biggest challenge of independence was to maintain the integrity of the national territory, threatened by internal and external conflicts. This short paragraph is a good example of what I would call 'pocket narratives'. They are short retrospective passages that give the reader the ability to realize the principles of experience that confirm a diverse and unfamiliar reality. These fragments facilitate memorization, presenting in an epigrammatic way the most important themes. These short syntheses or recapitulations ensure the circulation of guiding narratives even among those who do not have the time or the opportunity to read the entire work. One of the functions of these pocket narratives was to facilitate repetition and memorization, organized as they were around 'myths', such as the natural unity of the territory, the uniqueness of the empire, its providential destiny, and so on. As myths, they cannot withstand critical analyses, but constantly reinforced they become actual.

Another narrative reinforcing structure is the use of footnotes in the production of temporal connections. Constantly notes create the necessary connections between beginning and end, highlighting the narrative teleological connections that turn the diverse events into a pre-figurative force. This is the case, for example, with the passage in which the author explains that the words he uses to describe the geography of Brazil at the beginning of his book were taken from a speech by the British king celebrating the migration of the Portuguese Court in 1808. The chronological order is interrupted by the introduction of a later or earlier event, which guides the reading experience. Consequently, the fact that both the birth and acclamation of Pedro I took place in the same month in which the first king of Portugal swore that he saw Christ in Ourique field, promising him that he should establish a great empire through him and his descendants, is pointed out in a note as a providential sign, but with the ambivalent observation that such speculations would be incompatible with nineteenth-century taste. In the more personal part of the footnote, Silva Lisboa believes he could state his providential creed without compromising the rational decorum required by a modern national history.

The following chapters describe the discovery of oceanic islands, the route to India and America. Following the Scottish and British Enlightenment, of whose authors he was a regular reader and translator, especially of the works by Burke, Robertson, Hume and Adam Smith, Silva Lisboa praises the end of the monopoly of Italian cities as a consequence of the Great Navigations. He especially approves because, according to him, this was a process without wars or insult against other nations. Therefore, the Portuguese should be recognized as those who opened up the paths to progress for Europe.

But this promising prospect was interrupted because the 'spirit of conquest, inertia and greed, frustrating largely the providential gifts, slowing the natural progress of civilization and perfectibility of mankind, and causing untold misery, not only to people discovered, but also to its discoverers and their offspring'.[9] Human nature and the rudeness of the times prevented the progress of civilization, introducing great social evils as slavery, religious intolerance and the spirit of conquest. This semi-barbarous state is understood as a continuation of feudal principles. But instead of writing an ironic enlightened narrative that simply condemns these actions, Silva Lisboa claims to understand them in their historical context, as the role of the Catholic Church in international affairs, reprehensible in nineteenth century but an essential civilizational force in the past.

The discovery of Brazil is explained by the commercial expansion and providential action. The Portuguese fleet was on a commercial mission to India, and the discovery of a new land was an act of chance or providence. In a controversial move, he prefers to call this event a 'finding' of Brazil and not a discovery.[10] The claim implies a double movement: it links Brazil to the expansion of trade and at the same time disconnects it from the less noble reasons of conquest and dominion. Thus, he responds to and distorts the opinions of Robertson and R. Southey, quoted as authorities in this matter, who in their histories also stressed the accidental character of Brazilian discovery. He refuses to believe that any historical event could be the work of chance, using the idea of providence both as a cognitive resource and as a way of transferring the Portuguese providential myth to Brazil. It is worth noting, however, that at no point is the providential hand turned into sufficient grounds. Nor is the inclusion of miraculous actions in the main narrative allowed at any point. An ultimate belief in the meaning of history as an organic process is persistently stated.

With this conceptual movement, the history of Brazil and its independence can be narrated as the fulfilment of a providential and civilizational destiny. The Portuguese colonization is depicted as slovenly and as marked by

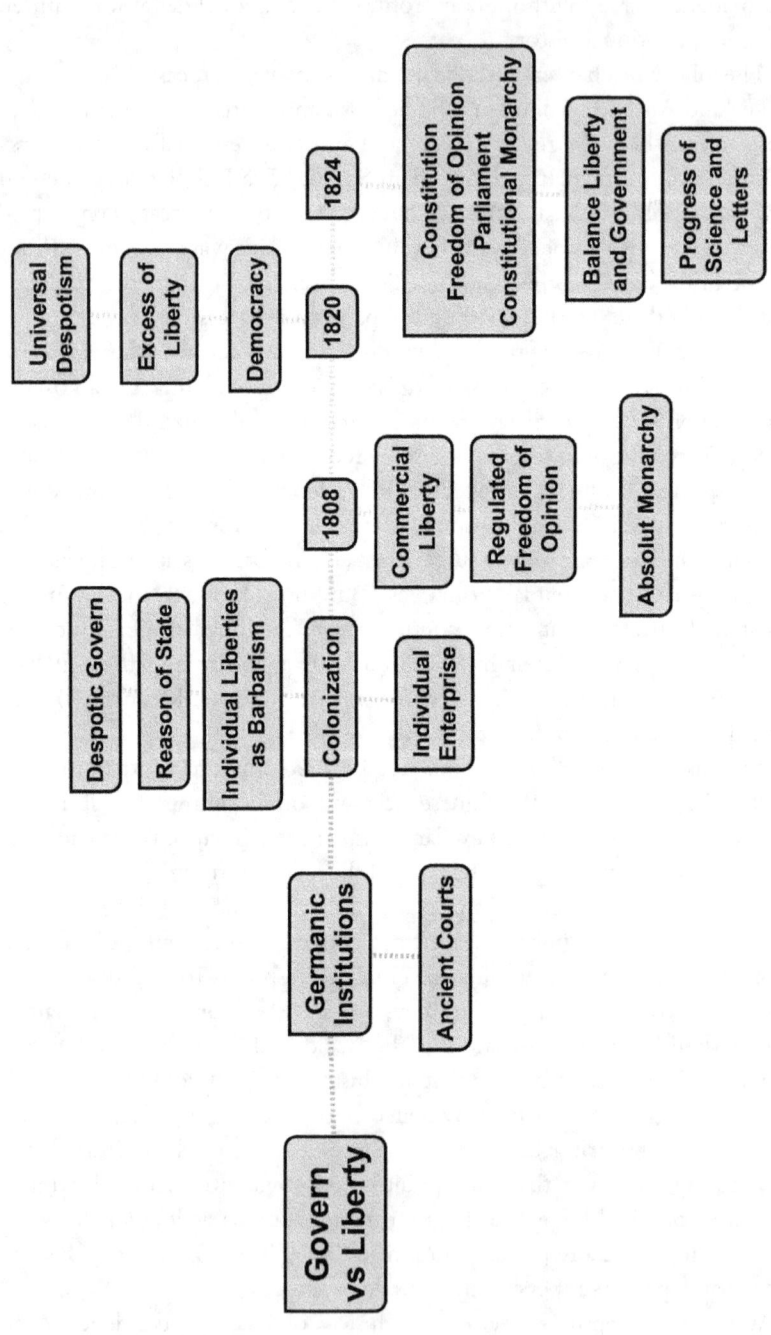

Figure 14.3 The conflict between govern and liberty master narrative. © Valdei Araujo.

anti-commercial principles such as monopoly, religious intolerance and other feudal practices. According to him, this 'ancient colonial system' was reinforced by the Treaty of Utrecht at the beginning of eighteenth century. Nonetheless, despite these impediments, the colony prospered and progressed through the initiative of its inhabitants, as is highlighted in the general epigraph of the work, a quote from the *History of Brazil* by Robert Southey: 'discovered by chance, it is by individual industry and enterprise, and by operation of the common laws of nature and society, that this empire has risen and flourished, extensive as it is now, and might as it must one day become'.[11]

The barbaric, feudal and colonial 'ancient system' would be reversed only with the arrival of the court in 1808, a historic period that Silva Lisboa had already dealt with in previous works. But, as ever in his history, this progress is never linear or smooth, but is always compromised by human weakness and ambition, especially among peoples with whom civilization had not reached a degree of perfection. According to him, in a Europe still marked by revolutionary movements and projects of universal empires, Portugal, recently freed from French rule, was a victim of these same forces in the liberal revolution of 1820. In a clever inversion, he interprets the liberal revolution as a plot between Spanish and Portuguese radical democrats to unite the peninsula under one government, recolonize America and impose on Europe their universal ambitions. The anti-Napoleonic narratives, deeply inspired by Burke, are repurposed to depict Portuguese liberal despotism that would eventually force Brazilians either to declare their independence or to be reduced to feudal domination. Thus, Silva Lisboa uses a Burkean language to describe how 'revolution' spread throughout Brazilian provinces, threatening its territorial integrity.

Reacting to measures that he believes will restore the trading privileges of the metropolis and deprive Brazil of its political centre, the young prince of Bragança fulfils his destiny as Brazilian '*libertador*', preserving the integrity of the American empire revealed by its origins and history. To emancipate Brazil from the corrupt Portugal is now regarded as the only way of regenerating the Portuguese nation.

Silva Lisboa portrays Pedro I as a Burkean hero, capable of uniting in his person the aura of a noble presence, moderation and political conciliation. This image was meant to counterbalance the warlike character that contemporaries generally attributed to the prince. During a military revolt, he wrote, 'His PRESENCE haunted all spirits. No one dared to deny the command to the Prince of the Nation'.[12] In another passage, in which he describes how the emperor's presence had resolved a provincial revolt, he compares this political aura of legitimate and ancient princes to the halo that forms around certain planets and stars.[13] Thus, the young prince becomes a moral force able to unite the nation, also against internal enemies, some of them attached to local allegiances. Against those, in a direct reference to Burke, he writes, 'Nations are not geographical areas, but moral Essences'.[14] He claims that they should not be faithful to their local commitments, but to the very idea of the nation embodied in its commercial vocation, providential destiny, and now, a conciliatory hero.

He sees the theme of the charisma of nobility and others involving the creation of honorific orders and commendations as an opportunity to defend these feudal institutions as necessary devices for general education. To him, the codes of chivalry were a historical force that had helped to civilize the European Middle Ages, polishing manners and institutions. As the Brazilians are still far from achieving the perfect civilization, forces like religion and nobility should play a central role in the nation's moral education. Of course, the nation itself seems to be formed by different temporalities, from the natives' savagery to the barbarous practices spread to a greater or lesser extent throughout the vast territory. Thus, constitutional monarchy appears as the political solution most appropriate to the century and to the particular conditions in Brazil, which required freedom but also a strong government. It is this balance that his history ascribes to Pedro I's government.

The aim of writing history was to demonstrate and defend the civilizational model represented by the empire in its monarchical-constitutional form. Its function was to educate the public on its truths, polish manners and so prepare the conditions for its own development as a literary enterprise, because without freedom and good government there are no conditions for the progress of letters. Therefore, the circularity between letters and civilization is another dimension of the metanarrative that organizes the account. The commercial manners could lead to the decay of virtue, as many authors argued; at this point, the good government should act as an antidote in order to guide the commonwealth, even if men were no longer able to identify these virtues. As part of a good government, the historian should help with controlling modern times through firmness in moral values and rationality, seasoned by circumstances.

The age of discoveries announced the commercial and civilized future of Brazil, although it had to go through 'barbarism' represented by the colonial system as a kind of Middle Age, marked by the influence of powerful families and their fiefdoms. A different narrative line transfers providentialist expectations of Portugal's history, organized around the Ourique miracle, to the American context. The empire promised to the Portuguese by Christ was finally materialized in Brazil. While the first narrative can be understood as a history of freedom, the second roots the legitimacy of government in a dynastic basis. The harmonization of commercial freedom and providential destiny, between freedom and authority, would find its perfect historical

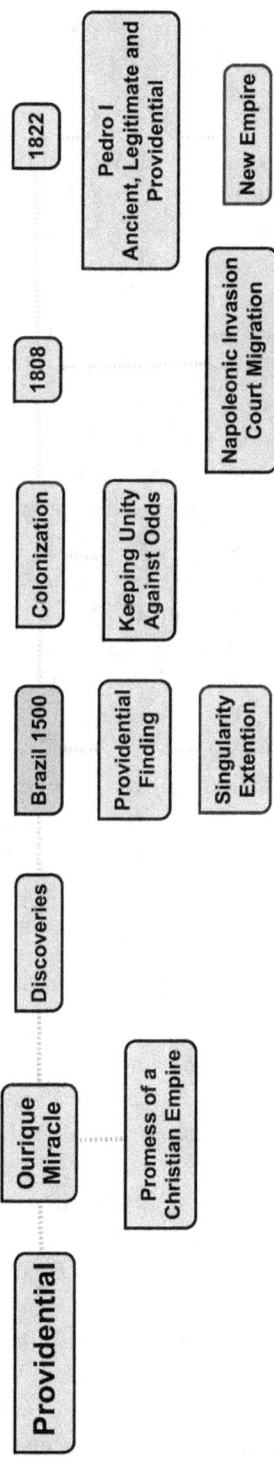

Figure 14.4 The providential master narrative. © Valdei Araujo.

form in the constitutional monarchy and restore the balance of power in the Americas dominated by republics. The young nation could finally be conscious of the gap between the old and the new, Europe and America, Portugal and Brazil.

An episode from 1830 is quite emblematic of the institutional conditions for writing history. The political and financial crisis of the empire was used by Silva Lisboa's adversaries as a pretext to undermine the continuity of his projected work. Some senators had proposed cutting the funding for a scribe who assisted the historian.[15] Viscount de Alcântara opened the debate, arguing that the amount budgeted for the scribe should be restored.[16] He said cutting it was unfair after the nation had chosen Silva Lisboa to write its history, a history that it needed. The clerk received 365 milreis annually, an amount considered modest for a public employee at the time. Opposing him was Senator Nicolau Vergueiro, who, despite insisting on the cost-saving aspects of the cut, did not fail to indicate his doubts about the relevance and legitimacy of the project, since he considered the writing of history to be a private subject, in which the state should not interfere. He also questioned the validity of contemporary written of history by its protagonists, 'because men are always swayed by the passions that surround them, without sensing this themselves: so this is speculation from the man of letters, not the government, and therefore it should be eliminated'.[17]

Everything seemed to point to a great conflict concerning contemporary historical representations, something like the image conjured by Vergueiro of truth emerging from the political struggle. The function of the press as a space for criticism was mentioned by both sides of the debate, but that did not answer the social need to have access to historical narrative in a more or less cohesive way. While pointing to the freedom of the press as a condition of truth in his work, Cairu evoked ancient examples of sponsorship and patronage of kings and nobles. Without sponsorship, history, especially modern history, would not be possible. But how could one prevent sponsorship from compromising impartiality? Even accepting Cairu's argument that the freedom of the press and Partisan struggle would serve as critical instances, the question remained: Why should the state fund one historical work and not the many others that could be written? Vergueiro's position was consistent with his image of a historiography mediated by public debate. But would this model then be able to produce the kind of complete, documented, philosophical historical narratives that was desired and requested by modern nations?

By the end of the decade, in 1838, the Instituto Histórico e Geográfico Brasileiro was created, which, with support from the imperial state, would establish the basis to the disciplinarization of the writing of Brazil's history. This was a process that only during the twentieth century took on the professional autonomy model as mediation between state funding and epistemological independence. Although this relation between nation-state and historiography has never been free of conflict or ambivalence, in the past decades the problem has once again become prominent, suggesting that the institutional and epistemological basis of the modern national solution is being questioned again.

A Contemporary Historical Narrative: What Is a Politically Incorrect Historiography?

It is since 2013 that we have been witnessing the progressive questioning of democracy's reach in Brazil. In that year, diverse subjects who were unsatisfied with their political representation and the Brazilian state on different levels went to the streets in great numbers. Diverse segments of the social forces released in 2013 act on the social legitimation of the political-juridical manoeuvre that in 2016 led to the impeachment of Dilma Rouseff, the winner of the general elections in 2015. Since historiography has always been closely related with the foundations of the nation-state and its institutions, challenges to the historical narratives and their political use emerge from all sides of the political-ideological spectrum.

Aggressive questioning of the mediating functions of university and human sciences is one of the main concerns of this movement. The emergence of an 'identity right', supported by great economic groups interested in weakening the state, the civil and political society on a Partisan basis feeds a cultural war of unprecedented scale in Brazil.[18] The growth of expectations of the subalternized groups welcomed, although with deep ambiguities, in the successive governments of the Worker's Party between 2003 and 2016, equally contributed to the questioning of the limits of traditional politics. These two waves of dissatisfaction gain visibility in the so-called 'June 2013 journeys', which put Brazil in the sequence of subsequent manifestations in the style of the 'Arab Spring', marked by new mediation through social media. In the university spaces, we can see increasing questioning of programmes and bibliographies supposedly indifferent to the new demands of the social collectives that demand that their questions, knowledge, epistemology and presence be recognized in the curriculums and classrooms.

The loss of space afforded to history in the high school curriculum, a project that emerged before the impeachment, but which the fragile conditions of democracy helped to accelerate, resulted in a new high school model that abolishes or reduces the obligatory status of teaching history in this segment of basic education. This is another very concrete example of doubt being cast upon the relation between historians and professional historiography and the state, democracy and society.[19] This scenario of fragmentation and dispute became more evident in historians' and non-historians' reactions to the diverse options for future instruction in history that were projected in the National Common Curricular Base, putting to different sides the demands for recognition and reception of the identity struggles and spaces of the disciplinary traditions such as ancient history.

The increasing politicization of this deflation flag and the attacks against the humanities is evident, with all its risks, in the 'School Without Party' movement, as it calls itself. Its goal is nothing more than tutelary of teachers' autonomy, with the teaching of history being the main target of these initiatives. As historian Marco Napolitano has highlighted, to the 'right identity' movement, the humanities are a left-doctrinal apparatus and to the liberal right they would represent a waste of money on dubious performance.[20]

In the social media, historians are more exposed. Just like other specialists, they need to negotiate their authority in spaces other than those academically controlled. On Facebook, Twitter, YouTube, blogs and other media, this space of lacking differentiation in discourse grows. In these spaces, the historian simultaneously speaks as a citizen, specialist and pamphleteer (party militant), without the internal protocols or codes that give expressions in the context of an academic discipline differentiation and authority. Ordinary citizens, on the other hand, have greater access than ever to the means of communication diffusion. Commentaries and other means of expressing opinion acquire a 'personal' and massive strength, not to mention the appropriation and distortion of these new ways of behaving by political and business groups, be it by the renewed propaganda formula, or by the use of robots capable of inducing behaviours. Another challenging element in this conjuncture is the secret policy that organizes the economy of the algorithms and codes of the big companies that control and shape this new social reality.

From the point of view of scientific production, despite the recent reversal provoked by the cutting of funds and by failed expectations raised by laws that expanded the budget for science and education, the evaluations generally are positive. The model of research in historiography and in the humanities adapted itself to the evaluative logic built during the past decades. The quantity and quality of the scientific production, the number of graduate programmes, periodicals and researchers have been growing solidly. But even here we can find signs of some model depletion, be it in the risk of productivism, or by the insulation of this production whose social impacts are currently rediscussed.[21] Nothing seems to have revealed more clearly the complexity of this problem than the memory battles over the meaning of the civil–military dictatorship. This perception has led varied efforts in the search of new ways of mediation between academic historiography and its public, both in the teaching of history and in the debates of public history.

Under these conditions of setbacks to values and democratic structures, the struggle for the regulation of the historian's profession opened a healthy debate on the need for rethinking the curriculums and models of the graduation courses on history that we currently have in Brazil. The current scenario does not seem to show superficial movements but a new status quo. Therefore, it is urgent to understand how we might not just adapt to it but work to extract from this new situation its emancipatory potentialities. How can we defend democracy's ampliation, and re-found the pact between historiography and democratization that has been marking modern history, even without ignoring the ambivalences and setbacks in this relation? In the search for answers, it is important that we amplify our comprehension of how this new situation translates into historical narratives. To this end, in the last section, we will talk about the most successful narrative of what we can call the 'new identity right'.

The *Politically Incorrect Guide to the History of Brazil* was published in 2009 by the journalist Leandro Narloch, who had worked in one of the most influential conglomerates of the Brazilian media, Editora Abril. The project has a great audience, and became a franchise with various volumes that approached subjects like Latin American history, philosophy, universal history, soccer and many others. Narloch chooses as an opponent what he calls 'traditional history', and the first volume of the series is dominated by a partisanship vision committed to the left's ideology and 'political correctness'. This year, the original book has been converted into a television show produced for the History Channel.

The book, in its second edition published in 2012, is organized in a thematic-chronological structure divided into the following sections: Indians, Black People, Writers, Samba, Paraguay's War, Aleijadinho, Acre, Santos Dumont, Empire and Communists. One of the characteristics already identified by the critics is the tendency to personify historical phenomena. All of them become figures operating to a logic of villains or bandits.[22] Historical periods, such as the 'Empire' or the diversity of the indigenous people are treated as individual characters.[23] Another structuring and decisive element of the book in its reception is the author's concept of a 'new history', as a way of legitimizing his project as an update of the historiographical reviews that the 'politically correct' would have blocked from reaching the schools or the public in general. Thus, a lot of the argument is structured through the pragmatic quotation and interpretation of recent historical research.

Despite the thematic emphasis and the personification, it is possible to highlight the structural narrative of Brazil's history that organizes the book. The driving force of the process incorporated in the characters is a philosophy of evolutionary history, debtor of social Darwinist elements and cultural racism widespread in Brazilian society. The history of humanity would be a result of the competition between people and distinct cultures in which the stronger ones inherit and transmit the civilizational heritage – usually reduced to material and technological culture. Thus, after trying to demonstrate that the indigenous Brazilian and American people (he does not seem to acknowledge these differences) were full of addictions, under the pretext of demolishing an image supposedly idealized by the politically correct history, Narloch searches for answers to explain the technological and political inferiority of the indigenous people, using the traditional procedure of classifying them as Neolithic people. In truth, states the author, the arrival of Europeans on the American continent was a type of reconnection of two fields of humanity that had been separated for fifty thousand years.[24] The author thereby follows the theory of the continent's settlement via the Bering Strait. In the end, for the indigenous people, colonization would have been a great opportunity to appropriate a higher culture.

In another moment, after saying that the indigenous, for their isolation [sic] in America 'didn't know the wheel',[25] he alerts his readers that they should restrain the desire of considering them 'naturally incapable', because they just suffered from the distance from more developed civilization that would have emerged from the conflicts between Asia, Africa and Europe: 'The clash of civilizations made technology spread. By wars, achievements or even by commercialization, technology and new customs passed from culture to culture'.[26] Thus, as in Silva Lisboa's report, the history of Brazil really starts in 1500 with the arrival of the Portuguese and civilizations clashing.

The other sections re-enact this plot in order to naturalize conflict and competition as the only forces effective in explaining history. Black people, enslaved, were actually partners in this business, in Africa and in Brazil, where, when they could, they also owned slaves. Using a logic of inversions, he promises to his readers in the introduction a kind of redemption from the debate of the effects of black slavery: 'And there are a lot of European descendants thinking they are guilty of the slave trade, although most of their ancestors immigrated after slavery had been extinguished'.[27]

In addition to the social groups that demand reparation and recognition, another target to be deconstructed is the heroes 'invented' by the professors and historians of the left, labelled as traditional historiography, confused with any discourse that can be classified as nationalist or patriotic. Mobilizing new research, partially quoted, and a wide range of anecdotes, characters and episodes connected to moments of contestation of the order are ridiculed. Among these are expressions of popular culture such as Samba, national cuisine, political leaders, writers, artists and celebrated intellectuals. All of them would be minor or less original than what the 'teachers' would have us believe.

It is only in the second edition of the book that Narloch decides to insert some of his 'heroes', who would have been erased or diminished by left-wing historiography: the Bandeirantes and the Imperial period (1822–1889), represented, as always, by individuals – in this case, the Emperor D. Pedro II and conservative politicians – who would have barred the radicalism of the French Revolution! Along similar lines, he mobilizes part of a revisionist historiography to celebrate the last Brazilian dictators (1964–1985) as heroes of an effort of national salvation against the communist threat. But even in the evaluation of the economic miracle of the years of the dictatorship, the role of the state as a historical force is annulled: 'The government's work in the early years of the regime was simply to not disturb the free initiative'.[28]

The work that promised a history without morality or lessons ends with the following paragraph, the balance of economic growth of the last fifty years: 'There is even a motive to betray the proposal of this book and to express an ecstasy of patriotism. Long live the capitalist Brazil'. Thus, in a very traditional way, his narrative returns to the beginning: in 1500, with the Europeans and the conflict – competition – of cultures, the spirit of capitalism contributed to Brazil. Its history is that of the struggle of exceptional men, descendants or emulators of a stronger culture, who, despite the state and the resentment of the weakest, through individual enterprise, have made and make the history of Brazil.

Valdei Araujo is professor of theory and history of historiography at the Universidade Federal de Ouro Preto, Brazil. He is currently chief editor of *Revista Brasileira de História*. He has published regularly about the history of concepts in nineteenth-century Brazil and on the contemporary experience of time in a global perspective. Among his most recent publications are *Atualismo: como a ideia de atualização mudou o século XXI* (2nd rev. edition, Milfontes, 2019); *Do Fake ao Fato: (des)atualizando Bolsonaro* (Milfontes, 2020); and *Almanaque da Covid-19: 150 dias para não esquecer* (Milfontes, 2020).

Notes

1. Koselleck, *Futuro Passado*.
2. 'Therefore, this choice of plot is significant for the (hi)story being narrated, as it is for history in general. Historiographic narration creates a meaning that may vary greatly, thereby revealing something of the historiographer's ideological intentions.' Fulda, 'Historiographic Narration'.
3. Pocock, *Barbarism and Religion*.

4. Da Costa, 'Análise do folheto impresso', 44.
5. Medeiros, *Plagiário*, 19, 75.
6. Lisboa, *História Dos Principais Sucessos*, 1.
7. 'Now at last heart is coming back to us: from the first, from the very outset of this happy age, Nerva has united things long incompatible, Empire and liberty; Trajan is increasing daily the happiness of the times; and public confidence has not merely learned to hope and pray, but has received security for the fulfilment of its prayers and even the substance thereof. Though it is true that from the nature of human frailty cure operates more slowly than disease, and as the body itself is slow to grow and quick to decay, so also it is easier to damp men's spirits and their enthusiasm than to revive them ... But after all I shall not regret the task of recording our former slavery and testifying to our present blessings, albeit with unpractised and stammering tongue.' Tacitus, *Agricola*, Cap. III, pp. 170–73.
8. Lisboa, *História Dos Principais Sucessos*, 2–3.
9. Ibid., 11.
10. Ibid., 44.
11. Southey, *History of Brazil*.
12. Lisboa, *História Dos Principais Sucessos*, X.I, 60.
13. Ibid., X.II, 79.
14. Ibid., X.II, 20.
15. Kirschner, *José Da Silva Lisboa*, 268.
16. Senado Federal, *Anais do Senado Federal*, 9.
17. Ibid., 11.
18. There is an intense global debate about the limits and the consequences of identity politics in the recent conjuncture. See: Lilla, *The Once and Future Liberal*.
19. The attempt to reduce the debate on education to numbering and literacy, widely sponsored by the OECD, without a political confrontation, will lead to a deepening of this trend.
20. Napolitano, 'As Ciências Humanas'. See also Rodrigues, 'Escola Sem Partido' on the judicial ideology of the movement. The author proposes to return to the deepening of the dimensions of collegiality as a horizon of progressive repression of the demands for greater social participation in the school and academic environment.
21. Araujo, 'O Regime de Autonomia'.
22. Bonaldo, 'Quando a Odebrecht Construiu Salvador'; Malerba, 'Acadêmicos Na Berlinda'.
23. Pimenta et al., 'A Independência e Uma Cultura de História No Brasil'.
24. Narloch, *Guia Politicamente Incorreto Da História Do Brasil*, 124.
25. Ibid., 386.
26. Ibid., 404.
27. Ibid., 80.
28. Ibid., 4289.

Bibliography

Bonaldo, Rodrigo Bragio. 'Quando a Odebrecht Construiu Salvador: A Narrativa Jornalística Da História Na Coleção Terra Brasilis, de Eduardo Bueno (1998–2006)'. *Revista Tempo e Argumento* 9(20) (2017), 130–61.
Costa, Hipólito José da. 'Análise do folheto impresso, em Lisboa, a fim de mostrar o Estado presente da Inglaterra'. *Correio Braziliense* ou *Armazém literário*, Vol. I (São Paulo: Imprensa Oficial do Estado [1808] 2002), 37–56.

Fulda, Daniel. 'Historiographic Narration', in Peter Hühn et al. (eds), *The Living Handbook of Narratology*. Hamburg: Hamburg University, 2014.

Kirschner, Tereza C. *José Da Silva Lisboa, Visconde de Cairu: itinerários de um ilustrado luso-brasileiro*. Brasilia: Editora Pucminas, 2009.

Koselleck, Reinhart. *Futuro Passado*. Edited by PUC-Rio. Rio de Janeiro: Contraponto, 2006.

———. *The Once and Future Liberal: After Identity Politics*. New York: Harper, 2017.

Lisboa, José da Silva. *História Dos Principais Sucessos Políticos Do Império Do Brasil*. 4 Vols. Rio de Janeiro: Tipografia Imperial e Nacional, 1825–1830.

Malerba, Jurandir. 'Acadêmicos Na Berlinda Ou Como Cada Um Escreve a História?: Uma Reflexão Sobre o Embate Entre Historiadores Acadêmicos e Não Acadêmicos No Brasil à Luz Dos Debates Sobre Public History'. *História da Historiografia* 15 (2014), 27–50.

Medeiros, Bruno F. *Plagiário, à Maneira de Todos Os Historiadores*. Jundiaí, São Paulo: Paco Editorial, 2012.

Napolitano, Marco. 'As Ciências Humanas e a Guerra Cultural No Brasil – Brasileiros'. *Portal Os Brasileiros* 1 (26 June 2017). https://controversia.com.br/2017/07/26/as-ciencias-humanas-e-a-guerra-cultural-no-brasil/ (last accessed 6 November 2020).

Narloch, Leandro. *Guia Politicamente Incorreto Da História Do Brasil*. São Paulo: Leya (Kindle Edition), 2012.

Pimenta, João Paulo G., et al. 'A Independência e Uma Cultura de História No Brasil'. *Almanack* 2(8) (2014), 5–36.

Pocock, John G.A. *Barbarism and Religion: Narratives of Civil Government*. Cambridge: Cambridge University Press, 1999.

Rodrigues, Henrique E. '"Escola Sem Partido": A Escola Do Nosso Tempo?' *Associacão Nacional de História* (2016). https://anpuh.org.br/index.php/2015-01-20-00-01-55/noticias2/diversas/item/3594-escola-sem-partido-a-escola-do-nosso-tempo (last accessed 6 November 2020).

Senado Federal. *Anais do Senado Federal* [Proceedings of the Senate], Vol. 3, 10 September 1830.

Southey, Robert. *History of Brazil. Part I*. London: Printed for Longman, Durst, Rees, Orme and Brown, Paternoster Row, 1810.

Tacitus. *Agricola*. London: Wlliam Heinemann, 1914.

CHAPTER 15

Changing LUK

Nation and Narration in the First and the Third Editions of Life in the United Kingdom

ARTHUR CHAPMAN

Introduction

Narrative involves structure, patterning the representation of time. Narrative has been understood as continuity, in the sense that narrative acquires 'unity' by 'implicit reference to a continuous subject' to whom differing predicates are attributed at $Time_1$, $Time_2$, $Time_3$ and so on.[1] Narrative has been understood as emplotment: first, cyclically, beginning with an initial situation of equilibrium between forces or states of affairs, and moving through a variable number of iterations to a subsequent re-establishment of equilibrium; and second, tropically, in terms of archetypal patterning and plot genres.[2] Narrative has also been understood in cognitivist and constructivist terms, as emerging through interactions between readers, who apply sense-seeking schemata as they read, and structural features of texts.[3] This chapter explores narrative grammatically, focusing on the grammatical relations through which narration is constructed, and, in particular, on how relationships of transitivity weave together actors, their actions and those they act upon into narrative patterns and 'who/whom' relationships.[4] It focuses on grammar for two reasons: first, in order to explore the hypothesis that this level of analysis can be particularly effective in revealing shifts and contrasts in the political and ideological strategies

---

Notes for this section begin on page 323.

deployed by authors in narrative construction; and, second, to explore the hypothesis that a granular analysis of grammatical relationships can facilitate the operationalization of narrative typologies and categories for the purposes of empirical research.

This chapter applies grammatical analysis of narrative to a case study of a changing official story – the 'history' chapter in the UK Home Office's publication *Life in the United Kingdom* (*LUK*). The case is of interest, first, as an example of an 'official' narrative – it allows us to explore how practical pasts are constructed through narrative – and second, because it has been revised twice, it allows interactions between practical pasts and changing presents to be analysed.

Texts and Method

LUK was created to serve the residency and citizenship requirements of the Nationality, Immigration and Asylum Act, 2002, and to help to prepare candidates for tests that must be passed as one precondition for a successful application for permanent residency status in the UK and, subsequently, for citizenship.[5] The guide is now in its third edition – it was first published in 2004, revised in a second edition in 2007 and substantially rewritten in a third edition in 2013.[6] All editions of *LUK* contain a range of information about the present-day UK, but there is also a chapter on national history. Here I provide a comparative analysis of the history chapter in the first edition and the one in the third edition of *LUK*.

The two chapters vary in length. The third edition's history chapter is longer than that in the first edition, being 54 rather than 25 pages long, and representing 30 per cent rather than 17 per cent of *LUK* as a whole. Both editions of the chapter contain a discursive narrative account of British history, but the third edition's chapter contains approximately 21 pages of illustrations, bullet-pointed biographical material and self-assessment lists of points on which understanding should be checked. Nevertheless, counting their main narrative text only, the two chapters are comparable in size, both being approximately 11,000 words long (see Table 15.1, below). In order to make a strict 'like for like' comparison, my analysis focuses almost exclusively on the main text of these two chapters.

Orientation

LUK aims to provide political education. In the first edition, the focus is on 'those institutions, values and beliefs that the four nations [of the United

Kingdom] have in common . . . the laws and customs of the constitution, the crown as a symbol of unity and, for over three centuries, parliamentary and representative government'.[7] In the third edition, the focus is now stated to be on 'fundamental values and principles [that] those living in the UK should respect and support . . . based on history and traditions and . . . protected by law, customs and expectations'.[8]

The historical narrative presented in *LUK* aims to serve orientational needs and arguably expresses 'anxiety' of the kind that Rüsen sees as driving all historical meaning making.[9] As van Oers has argued, the first guide emerged from the context of the Oldham riots of 2001 – a moment at which concerns about what policy discourses termed 'community cohesion' and 'social exclusion' were raised and addressed through a multiculturalist response.[10] The third edition of the guide arose, circuitously, in response to the London bombings of 2005, in a context where liberal multiculturalism was perceived by many policymakers as having failed, and where it was increasingly eclipsed by policies stressing participation, community and shared values.[11]

The guide's function is to help to prepare new residents to demonstrate their knowledge about life in the UK in officially administered multiple-choice tests aimed at assessing their mastery of the information that *LUK* contains.[12] Because of controversy occasioned by historical errors in the text of the first edition of the history chapter, history was excluded from testing under the first two editions of the guide; this was re-introduced with the third edition.[13] Whatever the pedagogic merits and demerits of the proposition that cohesive national identity can be built by ensuring 'mastery' of narrative content alone, narratological questions arise, namely: How do these texts mobilize historical narrative for practical purposes? And how do the guides differ in their narrative strategies and in the types of historical narrative that they construct?

Constructing a 'National Story'

Textual Relationships to Readers and to the Past

The first and the third editions of *LUK* differ in their titles and in the titles of their history chapters. The first edition is subtitled *A Journey into Citizenship* and the third *A Guide for New Residents*. Whereas 'a journey' suggests a gradual process, 'a guide' does not. Whereas 'citizenship' grants a political status, the term 'resident' grants rights but not political agency. Although the second subtitle is the most accurate in practical terms, since passing a test based on *LUK* is a necessary condition for 'permanent residency', the subtitles do, nevertheless, construct their readers differently.[14] The first subtitle positions readers as active – *they go* on a journey. The third edition positions the text itself as active – *it gives* guidance *to* its readers.

The titles of the history chapters contain striking differences also. The first edition's history chapter is entitled 'The Making of the United Kingdom' and the third edition's is entitled 'A Long and Illustrious History'. The former is explicit in identifying its subject ('the United Kingdom') and in identifying a dynamic process of change to be narrated (the UK's 'making'). The latter is, literally, adjectival and attributes predicates ('long' and 'illustrious') to a 'history' that appears to be static – it just 'is' these things in continuity over time. In terms of the typical 'tasks' that Allan Megill has identified historical writing as performing, one can say that the first chapter title suggests an explanatory purpose – a narrative account of a process – *how* the UK was 'made'; but the third edition's chapter title suggests just a descriptive and attributive aim – attaching positive qualities to a history.[15]

The first edition's history chapter begins with introductory text explaining its aims:

> To understand a country well and the character of its inhabitants, some history is needed . . . What follows tries to be a coherent if brief narrative of how the different nations came together. However, it also mentions some events and persons, which, while not always important parts of that narrative of the making of the British state, are often mentioned in books, newspapers, broadcasts and sometimes in conversation, and might puzzle new arrivals to our shores.[16]

The aims are, then, to provide a historical background that can enable contemporary Britain to be understood but also to provide the historical elements of what Hirsch calls 'cultural literacy' – the knowledge needed to understand national media and everyday conversation – a precondition, in Anderson's account, for 'national' imagining and belonging.[17] No explanation of aims is present in the third edition's history chapter, although the function of the guide as a whole is explained as being to enable readers acquire 'a broad general knowledge of the culture, laws and history of the UK' – a 'cultural literacy' aim.[18]

The first edition's introductory text also foregrounds the inevitability of interpretation, and the personalized and subjective nature of the history that it presents: 'Any account of British history is . . . an interpretation. No one person would agree with another [about] what to put in, what to leave out, [or] how to say it'.[19] No equivalent comment is present in the third edition, which presents *a* history without foregrounding its constructed nature. The contrast between the 'personal' approach taken by the first text and the 'impersonal' approach presented in the second text is apparent also in the use of pronouns. The narrator is literally present in the text in first edition, identifying with those whose history is narrated through the use of the first-person plural ('we' appears fifteen times) and the pronoun 'our' (nine times). Narrative identification of this kind is absent in the third edition's history chapter, where 'we' is used three times only and to explain the usage of terms rather than to assert identity with the narrated past.

Both editions' history chapters establish relationships of continuity with the past that they narrate by noting instances where the past is still present today; however, this occurs twice as frequently in the third edition's chapter (forty instances) as in the first edition's chapter (twenty instances).

Narrative Framing and Thematic Coherence

A further striking difference in the structure of the two texts is apparent in their overall narrative framing.[20] After the prefatory paragraph on purpose and interpretation that we have discussed above, the first edition's chapter opens with a section entitled 'What's in a Name?',[21] which is largely in the present tense, and features the first-person plural; it concludes with a section entitled 'Today', which again is largely in the present tense and is similar in its frequent use of 'we'.[22] Neither text features a continuous narrative subject , as one might have expected, on Danto's model referenced at the start of this chapter: some sections narrate the actions of Romans, some of kings, some of the Scots, some of Britain, and so on. This lack of a continuous narrative subject is unsurprising; although both texts aim to provide a history for the present, when tracing developments over millennia it is clear that no historical 'British' subject has existed throughout this long period. Ultimately, 'Britishness is a constructed identity . . . created by legal magic in 1707' through the Act of Union.[23]

Despite the lack of a continuous narrative subject, the first edition still manages to construct a degree of overall narrative coherence by thematic means. Themes – notably diversity – are introduced in 'What's in a Name?', then reappear at a number of points in the narrative (for example, on page 19) and recur in the concluding section, which explicitly draws out continuities over time: 'We have been . . . a multinational and multicultural society for a long time now without losing [either] our overarching British identity or our . . . cultural [or] national identities'.[24]

Things are very different in the third edition's history chapter. The thematic unities constructed in the first edition have been removed – at the start and the end and for the most part throughout. The chapter begins immediately to narrate, without any prefatory theme-embedding comment, and continues in the same manner throughout.

Representing the Past: What?

We have seen that the two chapters construct contrasting relationships to the past, but do they structure the content of their narratives in similar or in contrasting ways?

Table 15.1 The first and the third editions' history chapters compared: chapter titles, and the distribution of content by word count.

Period	1st Edition Section Titles	Word count	3rd Edition Section Titles	Word count
[Not applicable]	What's in a Name?	504	[Not present]	0
Pre-1066	Early Britain	807	Early Britain	1,207
1066–1480s	The Middle Ages	1,247	The Middle Ages	1,387
1480s–c.1700	The Early Modern Period	2,616	The Tudors and Stuarts	2,463
c.1700–c.1900	Stability and the Growth of Empire	3,005	A Global Power	3,039
c.1900–1945	The 20th Century	980	The 20th Century	1,490
1945–Present	Britain since 1945	1,984	Britain since 1945	1,348
		11,143		10,934

Both chapters are divided into sections and subsections. Table 15.1 below compares section titles, corresponding time periods and the number of words devoted to each period.

Although the third edition's chapter lacks the section 'What's in a Name', discussed further below, the overall structures of the two chapters are very similar – they share periodization and four of the six period titles.

Figure 15.1 below restates word count data in terms of the percentage of each text devoted to each time period.

Except for the pre-1066 period, to which the third edition gives fuller coverage, the ratio between 'time of narration and narrated time' is nearly identical in both texts: the last two sections, covering c.1900 to the present, represent 26 per cent of both texts; the period c.1700 to c.1900 represents 27 per cent of both texts; and the period from the 1480s to 1700 represents 22 and 23 per cent of the two texts, respectively.[25]

Differences begin to emerge at the level of subsection headings, but the two texts remain more similar than different. There were forty subsection headings in the first edition's chapter and fifty in the third edition's chapter. Twelve of these are identical in both chapters (e.g. 'The Welfare State') and eighteen are very similar (e.g. 'The Republic or The Commonwealth' and 'Oliver Cromwell and the English Republic'). Ten that are present in the first edition are absent in third edition (e.g. 'Domestic Politics 1951–1979'), and an additional ten have been added in the third edition (e.g. 'Exploration, Poetry and Drama'). Subheadings were coded into content categories – for example, 'political' (e.g. 'The Origins of Parliament') and 'sociocultural' (e.g. 'Social Change in the 1960s'). Table 15.2 compares category coding for the subsection headings in the two narratives in terms of percentage totals.

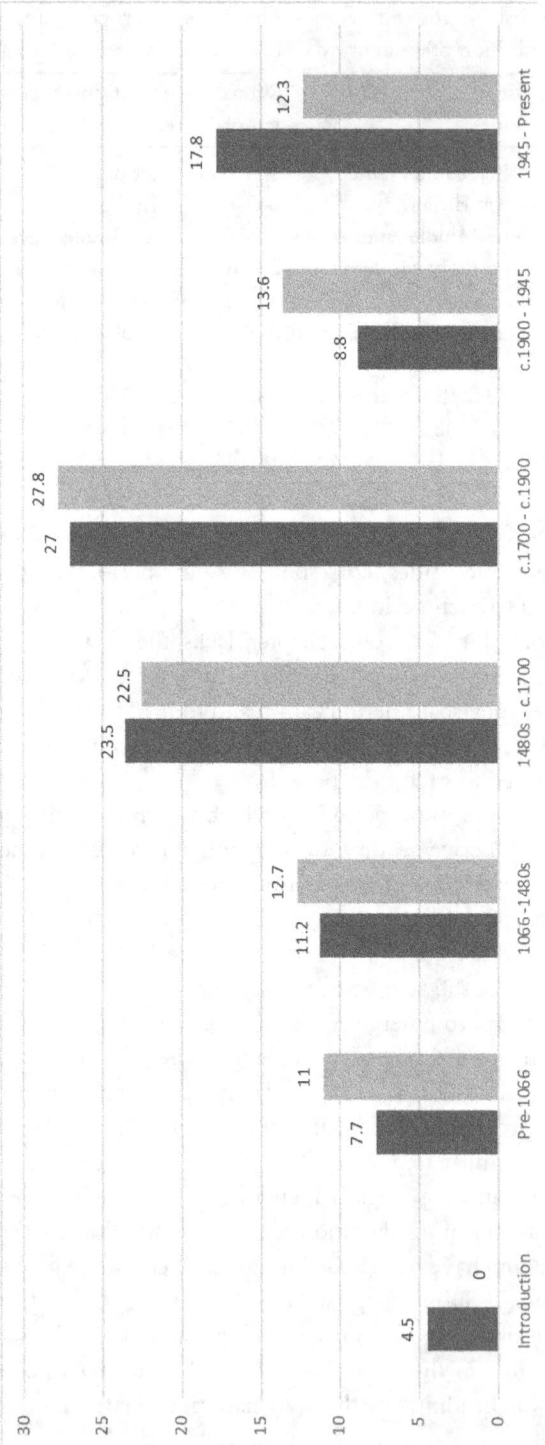

Figure 15.1 The first and the third editions' history chapters compared: distribution of content between time periods, stated in percentages. © Arthur Chapman.

Table 15.2 The first and the third editions' history chapters compared: the incidence of subsection headings coded under content categories.

Category	1st Edition Category incidence (count)	1st Edition Category incidence (percentage)	3rd Edition Category incidence (count)	3rd Edition Category incidence (percentage)	Percentage incidence compared (1st Edition minus 3rd Edition)
Political	32	50.8	40	46.0	4.8
Social Policy	3	4.8	2	2.3	2.5
Unclassified	1	1.6	0	0.0	1.6
Trade and Economics	8	12.7	10	11.5	1.2
Sociocultural	4	6.3	6	6.9	-0.6
Migration	3	4.8	5	5.7	-0.9
Military	10	15.9	15	17.2	-1.3
Religion	2	3.2	5	5.7	-2.5
Culture	0	0.0	4	4.6	-4.6
	63	100.0	87	100.0	

Note: 'N' in the table is greater than the number of headings because headings were often coded under more than one category.

The table suggests that, again, the two guides are more similar than different in terms of the overall organization of their content: in both, the three most important categories are the 'political', the 'military' and 'trade and economics', accounting for 79.4 per cent (first edition) and 74.7 per cent (third edition) of items coded. The first edition's subsection headers are marginally more focused on politics (by +4.8 per cent) and social policy (by +2.5 per cent) and marginally less focused on culture (by -4.6 per cent) and religion (by -2.5 per cent) than the third edition's headers.

Representing the Past: How?

Even where content is structured in similar ways at the level of topic and subtopic headings or in terms of thematic content, the contrasting presentation of material can differ at the level of the sentence:

- What is 'theme' in one text can become 'rheme' in another, and can be foregrounded or backgrounded as a result;
- Predication can ascribe differing properties to the same objects through denotation or connotation; and
- The agents narrated and their modes of relationship can vary significantly through 'transitivity' – 'who/whom' relationships established by allocating agentive and non-agentive roles to narrative 'participants'.[26]

In order to explore the extent to which the two history chapters were similar or different at the level of the sentence and sentence grammar, four parallel episodes were selected for analysis. Episodes with contemporary significance in national memory culture were identified, indicated by the fact that they have been publicly memorialized in the period since the first publication the guide:

- Magna Carta, whose 800th anniversary was marked in 2015;
- The Battle of Agincourt, whose 600th anniversary was marked in 2015;
- The abolition of the slave trade in the British Empire, whose 200th anniversary was marked in 2007; and
- The First World War, the centenary of which began to be marked from 2014 onwards.

Like most events celebrated officially, these commemorations have often been controversial.[27] It seems probable that the ways in which these episodes are treated in *LUK* will be revelatory of the approach that our two editions take to constructing national identity narratives.

The text relating to these four episodes from the first and the third editions of *LUK* was inputted to NVivo and analysed deductively – data was coded data to transitivity categories.[28] Transitivity analysis is a fine-grained mode of grammatical analysis that, in effect, asks the question '*Who* does *what* to *whom?*' of any text to which it applies. Specifically, this text was analysed in terms of:

- *Participants* present and their distribution to the roles of 'Actors' (the subjects of verbs) and 'the Acted-upon' (semantic objects);
- *Processes* used in the narratives to construct the actions narrated, in the form of verbs; and
- *Circumstances* included in the narratives to construct the situation, or context in which the process/es articulated by verbs took place.

TRANSITIVITY ANALYSIS: PARTICIPANTS

Participants in narratives can be represented as agents – 'actors' (the subjects of verbs) – or as 'acted-upon' (semantic objects). Participants can, in turn, be foregrounded – positioned before the verbs that they govern / are governed by – or backgrounded – positioned after these verbs. Actors can be omitted, so that processes appear without the explicit attribution of agency. These five possibilities are illustrated by the codes and quotations below. Items were coded as: (1) 'Agent before the verb'; (2) 'Acted-upon after the verb'; (3) 'Agent after the verb'; (4) 'Acted-upon before the verb'; and (5) 'No agent'. The last quotation illustrates both (4) and (5).

(1) *The new Labour Party*, born out of discontent at poverty and the class system;[29]
(2) In 1215 the great barons forced a charter of rights from *a tyrannical King John*;[30]
(3) The first formal anti-slavery groups were set up by *the Quakers*;[31]
(4)/(5) *All the resources of new technologies, of bureaucratic control and fervid patriotism* were used and exploited.[32]

In the first and the second of these possibilities, semantic 'who/whom' relationships are fully realized at text level. In the third and the fourth, some semantic components are backgrounded or absent: in the third, action is thematized not agency, and in the last two the acted-upon are thematized and actors are absented.

All participants in the four episodes were coded using these categories. In total 133 items were coded in the first edition, and 142 in the third edition. Figure 15.2 identifies the extent to which items in these categories play a greater role in the third edition's text (positive values) and the extent to which items in these categories play a greater role in the first edition's text (negative values), expressed in percentages.

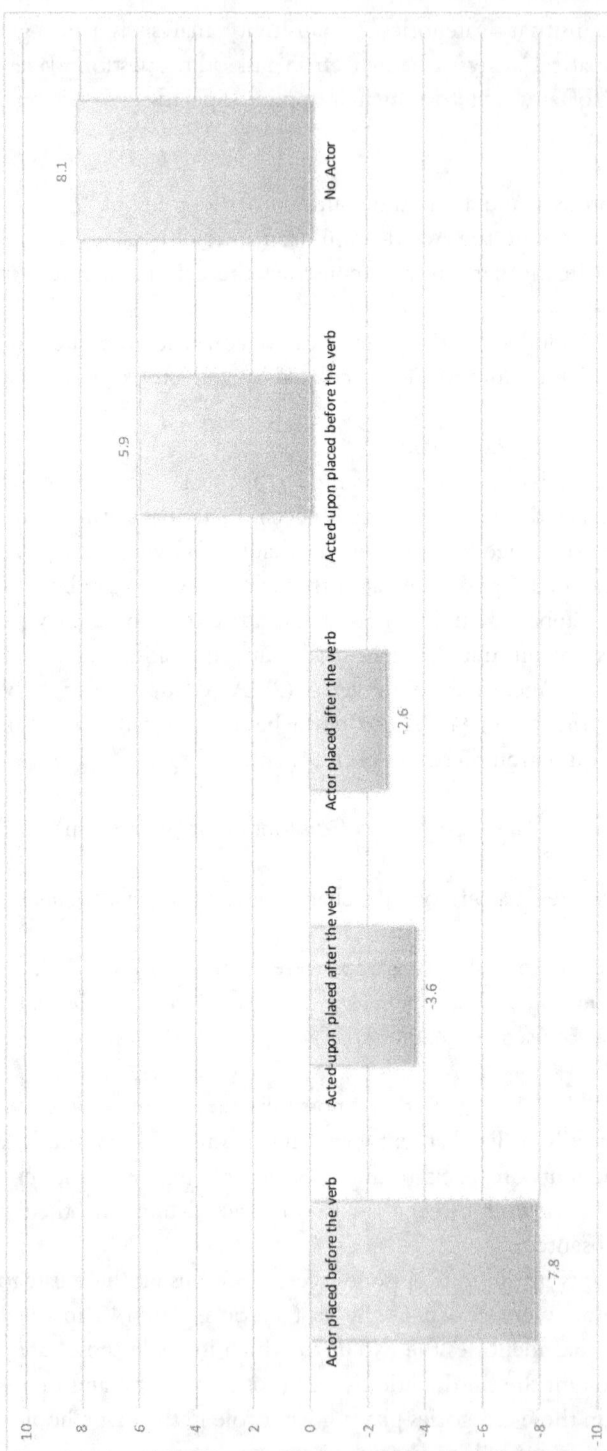

Figure 15.2 The first and the third editions' history chapters compared: differences in the incidence of participants in the roles of 'Actor' and 'Acted–upon', and their location before and after verbs in the two the narratives, stated as percentage differences. Negative values indicate greater incidence in the 1st Edition text, and positive values indicate greater incidence in the 3rd Edition text. © Arthur Chapman.

The figure indicates that semantic and text-level features align more clearly in the first edition than in the third, and that the backgrounding and the absenting of agency are more prevalent in the third edition.

TRANSITIVITY ANALYSIS: PROCESSES

The processes included in narratives can be of various types – 'Actors' can be the subjects of verbs that identify their actions, their thinking, their motivations, what they say, and so on.

Processes were coded as: (1) 'Material' (acting/doing); (2) 'Mental' (thinking, knowing, feeling, desiring, believing); (3) 'Relational' (having/being); (4) 'Existential' (is/are, were/was); and (5) 'Verbal' (saying, telling). This coding is exemplified in the examples below:

(1) The largest rebellions of the Welsh had *been put down*;[33]
(2) The kings of England constantly *attempted to* control the kings of Scotland;[34]
(3) The numbers attending Parliament *increased*;[35]
(4) In Scotland, the English kings *were* less successful;[36]
(5) In the nineteenth century, historians and statesmen *presented it as* a charter of liberties for all.[37]

The prevalence of particular process types is likely to be consequential for the depth with which a narrative characterizes actors. Narratives dominated by the first ('Material') and fourth ('Existential') of these process types focus on *externalities* – what was the case, and what was done. Narratives dominated by the second process type ('Mental') focus on *internalities* – perceptions, beliefs and intentions. Narratives in which the fifth process type ('Verbal') plays a significant role focus on what was said (*dramatization*) and/or on what has been said subsequently (*interpretation*).

All processes in the four episodes were identified, and coded using these categories. In total 80 items were coded in the first edition's text, and 83 in the third edition's text. Figure 15.3 below presents this coding in the same manner as Figure 15.2 above.

The figure indicates that the features of external narrative are more prevalent in the third edition, and that internalities and dramatization and/or interpretation are more prevalent in the first edition of the history chapter.

TRANSITIVITY ANALYSIS: CIRCUMSTANCES

The circumstances included in narratives can be of various types: information can be provided about the contexts in which actions occur, about the qualities of actors or the qualities of those they act upon, and so on. Circumstances were coded as identifying: (1) features of 'Context/situation'; (2) 'Means (how/

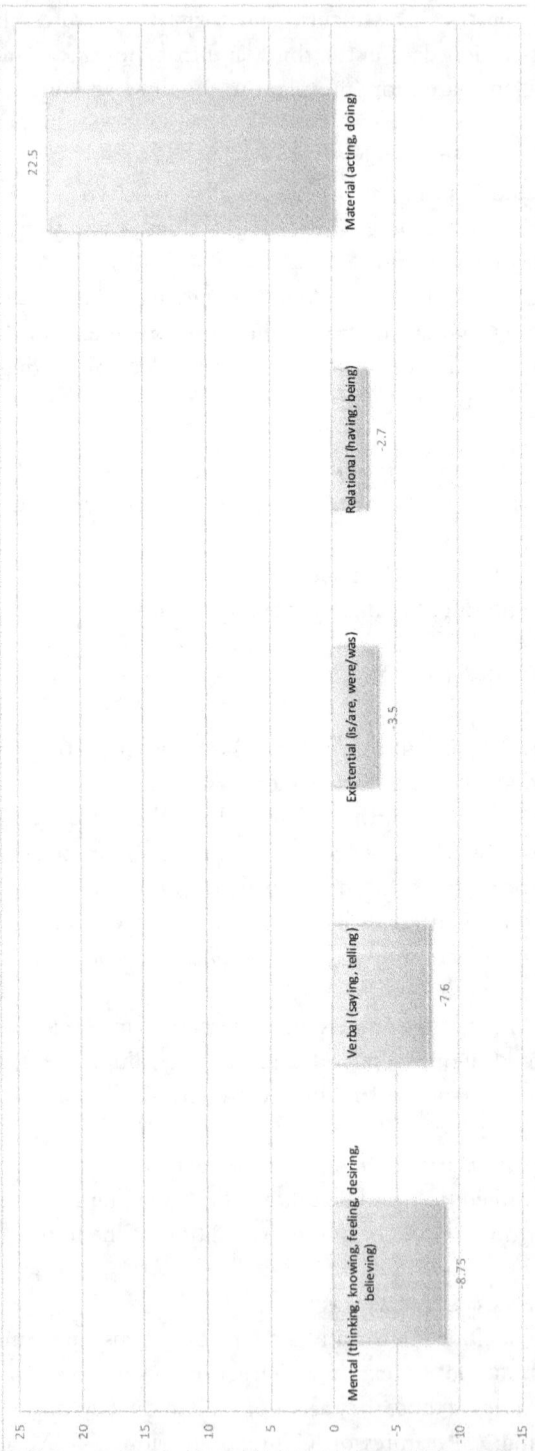

Figure 15.3 The first and the third editions' history chapters compared: differences in the incidence of processes by process type (e.g. mental, material) in the two narratives, stated as percentage differences. Negative values indicate greater incidence in the 1st Edition text, and positive values indicate greater incidence in the 3rd Edition text. © Arthur Chapman.

with what?)'; (3) 'When? (temporal location)'; (4) 'Qualities' (e.g. predicates of states of affairs or individuals); (5) 'Significance' (explicit evaluation); (6) 'Extent/scale'; (7) 'Who/What?' (e.g. text specifying additional participants); (8) 'Why? (cause /reason)'; and (9) 'Where? (spatial location)'. This coding is exemplified below:

(1) Ten(s) of thousands died in mid-passage *chained in the overcrowded holds of the slave ships*.[38]
(2) To control the kings of Scotland *by supporting rival claimants to the throne*.[39]
(3) *By the middle of the 15th century* the last Welsh rebellions had been defeated.[40]
(4) William Wilberforce, *an evangelical Christian and a member of Parliament*.[41]
(5) *The most terrible and bloody war since* the wars of religion three centuries before.[42]
(6) *Only a small part of the population* was able to join in electing the members of the Commons.[43]
(7) Huge castles, *including Conwy and Caernarvon*, were built.[44]
(8) The English parliament survived *because it was more broadly based than others*.[45]
(9) They worked . . . *in mines in South Africa*.[46]

The prevalence of particular circumstances is likely to have consequences for the narrative 'tasks' performed by a text.[47] In ideal-typical terms, a pure *descriptive chronicle* would be likely to be dominated by circumstances of types (3) (temporal location), (7) (Who/What) and (9) (spatial location); an *explanatory narrative* by circumstances of types (1) (context/situation), (2) (means) and (8) (cause/reason); and an *evaluative narrative* by circumstances of types (4) (qualities of states of affairs or individuals) and (5) (significance).

All circumstances in the four episodes selected for analysis in the two narratives were identified and coded using these categories. In total 90 items were identified and coded in the first edition, and 100 in third edition. Figure 15.4 below presents this coding in the same manner as Figures 15.2 and 15.3 above.

Neither of these two editions of the history chapter are ideal-typical: circumstances likely to typify a *descriptive chronicle* ('where' and 'what'), and circumstances likely to typify an *explanatory narrative* ('why') are prevalent in the third edition; circumstances likely to typify an *explanatory narrative* ('context/situation' and 'means'), and circumstances likely to typify an *evaluative narrative* ('qualities') are prevalent in the first edition. This analysis does, however, surface a clear difference in the types of historical narration that the two editions' history chapters engage in, as summarized in Table 15.3

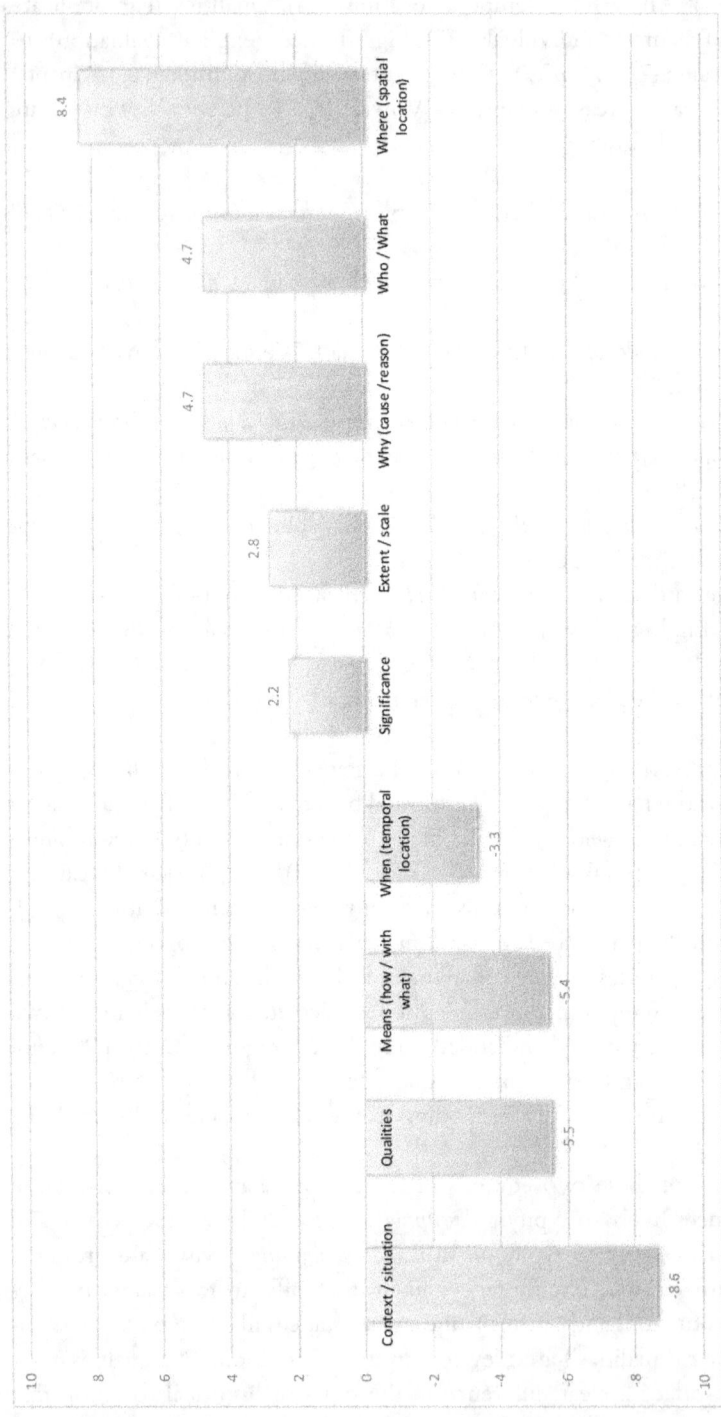

Figure 15.4 The first and the third editions' history chapters compared: differences in the incidence of circumstances by circumstance type (e.g. temporal, spatial) in the two the narratives, stated as percentage differences. Negative values indicate greater incidence in the 1st Edition text, and positive values indicate greater incidence in the 3rd Edition text. © Arthur Chapman.

Table 15.3 Narrative Types prevalent in the history chapters of the first and third editions of *LUK*.

Narrative Type	1st Edition	3rd Edition
Descriptive chronicle	✗	✓
Explanatory narrative	✓	✓
Evaluative narrative	✓	✗

above. There appears to be some regression in the sophistication of the historiographic tasks attempted by the history chapters between the first and the third editions of *LUK*.

TRANSITIVITY ANALYSIS: QUALITATIVE ILLUSTRATION

The foregoing analysis has pointed to some clear and to some suggestive differences in the narrative texture of the two history chapters examined. What do these formal differences amount to in practice?

In the case of Magna Carta, it is apparent in both texts that the common people were not participants in the narrative or direct beneficiaries of the charter, with the third edition's text stating that 'King John was forced by his noblemen to agree to a number of demands' and that the charter 'protected the rights of the nobility'.[48] However, only the first edition's text is explicit in offering direct interpretive comment on these aspects of the charter:

> In the nineteenth century, historians and statesmen presented it as a charter of liberties for all. But in fact it had little in it for ordinary people, even though centuries later a myth grew up that made it sound like a modern charter of human rights. This was not so, but it did show that in England the power of the king was not absolute.[49]

The sections of both texts that discuss Agincourt also discuss English wars against Wales, Scotland and Ireland.[50] Whereas the third edition's text has the English kings fighting – the 'English kinds fought with the Welsh, Scottish and Irish . . .' and 'fought with France' – in the first edition they 'put down' rebellions in Wales, 'destroy' Welsh power and 'claim' the French crown – all terms that add evaluative connotations not present in the verb 'fought'. Whereas in third edition's narrative the English language is 'introduced' to Wales, the first edition chooses instead to have it 'imposed'. The descriptions of Agincourt in both texts also differ in analogous ways, although this time it is the first edition that is less directly evaluative in its linguistic choices. In first edition, the battle is presented as one of a class ('great pitched battles, such as Agincourt'), and the fact that it was 'celebrated in Shakespeare's play of *Henry V*' is noted in parenthesis, but in the third edition the battle is characterized in a directly celebratory manner, as 'One of the most famous battles of the Hundred Years War' in which 'King Henry V's vastly outnumbered English army defeated the French'.[51]

In the cases of both Agincourt and the conquest of Wales, the texts differ in their representation of agency, with the first edition attending to actors other than the English. We are told that 'Welsh survived among the common people and a bilingual class of small landowners. Language and culture are remarkably resistant to political power'.[52] Whereas the third edition concludes by saying that 'the English left France in the 1450s', the first edition's narrative gives agency to the French, and concludes by noting that the English 'were driven out by continual small-scale actions by the French, almost guerrilla warfare, and eventually by civil war at home'.[53]

Similar contrasts in appraisal and agentification are apparent in the two texts' treatment of the slave trade.[54] Both texts acknowledge the dependence of British economic prosperity on the trade, but whereas the first edition calls it 'evil' the third edition describes the trade as 'booming'. The form in which agency is realized in sentence structure tends, in the third edition's text, to minimize the role of Britain in the trade. Captured Africans are described as coming ('Slaves came') from West Africa — a description that is accurate as a statement of their geographical origin, but that also appears to attribute agency to the slaves: the acted-upon are thematized and located in the agentive position before the verb — they 'came', they were not 'taken'. They are further described as 'travelling on British ships' — again, a form of words that puts captured Africans in the subject position in an active role. The first edition's text has 'British ships' in the subject position, 'supplying' colonies with 'men and women seized or bought in West Africa' to work on the sugar, cotton, and tobacco plantations, a trade on the basis of which named British cities are described as 'flourishing'. The first edition tells us that 'tens of thousands died in mid-passage, chained in the overcrowded holds of the slave ships', whereas the third edition simply states that the conditions in the ships in which the slaves were travelling were 'horrible'. Before the third edition explains the trade, it tells us that 'While slavery was illegal within Britain itself, by the 18th century it was a fully established overseas industry, dominated by Britain and the American colonies' — a form of words that distances slavery from Britain, locating it 'overseas'.[55] The first edition's text, by contrast, narrates the '1769' Somerset case, and argues that there were many thousands of slaves in Britain for most of the eighteenth century whose status was affected by the ruling.[56] Both texts are inaccurate to an extent (the Somerset ruling dates from 1772), but the first edition is more accurate than the third whose inaccuracies tend to paint Britain in a more favourable light than the record allows.[57]

Attributions of agency differ in similar ways in the treatment of slave trade abolition and its consequences in the two texts. Whereas both texts mention slave uprisings, only the first edition grants them a role in bringing about abolition. Whereas the first edition attributes agency to 'public opinion in Britain', which 'led to the abolition' under the influence of 'evangelical Christians like William Wilberforce ... and ... slave revolts in the West Indies', the agentive roles in the third edition's text are taken by Wilberforce who, along with other abolitionists, 'succeeded in turning public opinion against the slave trade'.[58] The activities of the British state subsequent to the abolition of slavery are presented very differently in both texts also. Whereas the first edition states that 'the British navy patrolled the Atlantic to stop slave ships of any other nation', the third edition is more explicitly evaluative and states that 'The Royal Navy stopped slave ships from other countries, freed the slaves and punished the slave traders'.[59] Where the third edition presents the Navy as an agent of freedom and justice, the first edition opens the Navy's role up to interpretation, concluding that it 'can be endlessly debated whether they were then creating international law or whether they were, in the eyes of other nations, breaking it'.[60]

The treatment of the First World War in the first edition is much briefer than in the third edition – the former covers it in 70 words and the latter in 249.[61] The third edition's text begins with the assassination in Sarajevo, explains its role as a 'trigger', identifies 'other factors', names the combatant countries on both sides, notes the contribution of imperial troops and the extent of casualties, before concluding by stating that 'The First World War ended at 11.00 am on 11th November 1918 with victory for Britain and its allies'.[62] By contrast, the first edition's text focuses explicitly on significance, evaluating the war comparatively ('the most terrible and bloody war since the wars of religion three centuries before'), explaining how 'new technologies ... bureaucratic control and fervid patriotism were used and exploited' to prosecute the war, describing an aspect of the war that came 'to dominate popular imagination', noting postwar 'recriminations' directed 'at the generals' and 'the older generation', and concluding by saying: 'War memorials became a common sight in nearly every town and village in Britain, usually Christian crosses inscribed with the names of the dead'.[63] Where one text closes with victory, the other closes with casualties and mourning.

Conclusion: Restructuring the National Story

In terms of the content to be narrated, then, this chapter has shown that there are substantial continuities between these narratives presented in the first and the third editions of *Life in the UK*, and that, despite some variation, they do not differ significantly at the level of the 'fabula' or basic story. Both are very similar in terms of the overall organization of their content and the types of history that they include (Table 15.1); and, also, in terms of the relationships that they construct between the 'time of narration and narrated time', and the proportions of text covering differing categories of content.[64]

At a macrolevel, then, and in terms of content to be narrated, one can say that little changes between the 2004 and 2013 editions. Although there are many instances where new content is introduced in third edition, such as the addition of lists of combatant countries in the First World War, and instances where the first edition content is deleted in the third edition, such as the Somerset Case, the lineaments of the first edition can very clearly be traced in the third edition. Most, though not all, of the content is retained, and key purposes of the narrative remain constant in both texts – for example, to narrate the development of parliamentary democracy and to narrate the unification of four nations into one United Kingdom. Continuities in overall content are apparent also in the absences common to both texts, notably the lack of reference to the labour movement: trade unions figure only once in both narratives, and appear, as it were, from nowhere in an account of the crises of the 1970s, when both texts concur in averring, it was generally agreed that they had become too powerful.[65] What this power consisted in, where it came from and why and how it came to be regarded as excessive all remain unaccounted for in both texts.

Despite these continuities in content to be narrated, this chapter has demonstrated significant differences in the manner in which these contents are narrated. The two texts differ markedly, as we have seen, in the relationships that they aim to construct with their readers and with the past, and in the tasks they set out to perform, as indicated by their titles. The texts differ also in the prevalence of both explicit interpretive discourse and thematic narrative framing in the first edition, and their absence in the third.

In addition to these global differences, contrasts in the narrative strategies adopted by each text are revealed by sentence-level grammatical analysis focused on 'who/whom' patterns of transitivity. There is a greater prevalence in the third edition of the absenting of agency, of external narration, of the features of an ideal-typical chronicle, and so on. In Rimmon-Kenan's terms, then, we can say that the two narratives differ more in their 'texts' and their 'narrations' than in their 'story', and these differences in emplotment are largely realized through a rewriting of the grammar of narration of the text at sentence level.[66]

In addition to surfacing such differences at sentence level, grammatical analysis has proved valuable in operationalizing macro-contrasts in narrative types (see Table 15.3). As was noted in the discussion on patterns of transitivity above, the presence or absence of different types of narrative – for example, an explanatory dramatization narrating internal features of agents such as their motivations and perceptions – can be determined by examining the extent to which particular types of process or circumstance are present in a text's narrative discourse. Granular grammatical analysis, then, enables these two texts to be systematically differentiated, and also points to analytical tools likely to be of wide application in the narrative analysis of historical texts more generally.

Arthur Chapman is associate professor of history education at UCL Institute of Education, University College London. He is managing editor of the *History Education Research Journal*, and series editor of the *International Review of History Education* and of UCL Press's *Knowledge and the Curriculum* book series. His recent publications include the translated collection of essays *Desenvolvendo o Pensamento Histórico: Abordagens conceituais e estratégias didáticas* (W.A. Editores Ltda) and the edited collection *Knowing History in Schools: Powerful Knowledge and the Powers of Knowledge* (UCL Press).

Notes

1. Danto, *Narration and Knowledge*, 326.
2. Todorov, *Poetics of Prose*; Frye, *Anatomy of Criticism*; White, *Metahistory*.
3. Bordwell, *Narration in the Fiction Film*; Fulda, 'Historiographic Narration', 7–9.
4. Halliday and Matthiessen, *Halliday's Introduction to Functional Grammar*; Chapman, 'On the Grammars of School History'; Chapman and Hale, 'Understanding What Young People Know'.
5. Van Oers, *Deserving Citizenship*; Brooks, *Becoming British*.
6. Home Office, *Life in the United Kingdom* (2006, 2007, 2013). I use the 2006 8th impression of the 2004 first edition text in the analysis reported here.
7. Home Office, *Life in the United Kingdom*, 2006, 18.
8. Home Office, *Life in the United Kingdom*, 2013, 7.
9. Rüsen, *History: Narration, Interpretation, Orientation*.
10. Van Oers, *Deserving Citizenship*; Home Office, *Community Cohesion*.
11. Todorov, *Inner Enemies of Democracy*; Van Oers, *Deserving Citizenship*.
12. Van Oers, *Deserving Citizenship*; Brooks, *Becoming British*.
13. Glendinning, 'Citizenship Guide Fails its History Exam'.
14. Brooks, *Becoming British*, 100–103.
15. Megill, 'Recounting the Past'.
16. Home Office, *Life in the United Kingdom*, 2006, 17.
17. Hirsch, *Cultural Literacy*; Anderson, *Imagined Communities*.
18. Home Office, *Life in the United Kingdom*, 2013, 7.
19. Home Office, *Life in the United Kingdom*, 2006, 17.
20. Leerssen, 'Setting the Scene', 73.
21. Home Office, *Life in the United Kingdom*, 2006, 17–18.
22. Ibid., 41–42.
23. Brooks, *Becoming British*, 56.
24. Home Office, *Life in the United Kingdom*, 2006, 42.

25. Eckel, 'Narrativizations of the Past'.
26. Halliday and Matthiessen, *Halliday's Introduction*; Barthes, *Mythologies*; Chapman, 'On the Grammars of School History'.
27. See, for example: Strachan and Kennedy, 'Should the Country Spend £55m'; and Kettle, 'It Will Soon be Time'.
28. Coffin, Donohue and North, *Exploring English Grammar*; and Halliday and Matthiessen, *Halliday's Introduction*, 83.
29. Home Office, *Life in the United Kingdom*, 2006, 36.
30. Ibid., 21.
31. Home Office, *Life in the United Kingdom*, 2013, 43.
32. Home Office, Life in the United Kingdom, 2006, 36.
33. Ibid., 20.
34. Ibid., 20.
35. Home Office, *Life in the United Kingdom*, 2013, 23.
36. Ibid., 21.
37. Home Office, *Life in the United Kingdom*, 2006, 21.
38. Ibid., 31.
39. Ibid., 20.
40. Home Office, *Life in the United Kingdom*, 2013, 21.
41. Ibid., 21.
42. Home Office, *Life in the United Kingdom*, 2006, 36.
43. Home Office, *Life in the United Kingdom*, 2013, 23.
44. Ibid., 21.
45. Home Office, *Life in the United Kingdom*, 2006, 21.
46. Home Office, *Life in the United Kingdom*, 2013, 43.
47. Megill, 'Recounting the Past'.
48. Home Office, *Life in the United Kingdom*, 2013, 22.
49. Home Office, *Life in the United Kingdom*, 2006, 21.
50. Ibid., 20–21; Home Office, *Life in the United Kingdom*, 2013, 21.
51. Home Office, *Life in the United Kingdom*, 2013, 21.
52. Home Office, *Life in the United Kingdom*, 2006, 20.
53. Home Office, *Life in the United Kingdom*, 2013, 21; Home Office, *Life in the United Kingdom*, 2006, 20–21.
54. Home Office, *Life in the United Kingdom*, 2006, 31–32; Home Office, *Life in the United Kingdom*, 2013, 42–43.
55. Home Office, *Life in the United Kingdom*, 2013, 42–43.
56. Home Office, *Life in the United Kingdom*, 2006, 31–32.
57. National Archives, *Slave or Free?*
58. Home Office, *Life in the United Kingdom*, 2006, 32; Home Office, *Life in the United Kingdom*, 2013, 43.
59. Home Office, *Life in the United Kingdom*, 2013, 43.
60. Home Office, *Life in the United Kingdom*, 2006, 32.
61. Ibid., 36; Home Office, *Life in the United Kingdom*, 2013, 53–55.
62. Home Office, *Life in the United Kingdom*, 2013, 55.
63. Home Office, *Life in the United Kingdom*, 2006, 36.
64. Eckel, 'Narrativizations of the Past', 35.
65. Edgar, 'The British History New Citizens Must Learn'; Home Office, *Life in the United Kingdom*, 2006, 39; Home Office, *Life in the United Kingdom*, 2013, 66.
66. Rimmon-Kenan, *Narrative Fiction*, 3–4.

Bibliography

Anderson, Benedict. *Imagined Communities: Reflections on the Origin and Spread of Nationalism.* London: Verso, 1991.

Barthes, Roland. *Mythologies: The Complete Edition.* New York: Hill and Wang, 2013.

Bordwell, David. *Narration in the Fiction Film.* London: Routledge, 1985.

Brooks, Thom. *Becoming British: UK Citizenship Examined.* London: Biteback Publishing Ltd, 2016.

Chapman, Arthur. 'On the Grammars of School History: Who Whom?' *Public History Weekly* 4(11) (2016). https://public-history-weekly.degruyter.com/4-2016-11/on-the-grammars-of-school-history-who-whom/ (last accessed 4 April 2018).

Chapman, Arthur, and Rebecca Hale. 'Understanding What Young People Know: Methodological and Theoretical Challenges in Researching Young People's Knowledge and Understanding of the Holocaust'. *Holocaust Studies: A Journal of Culture and History* 23(3) (2017), 289–313.

Coffin, Caroline, Jim Donohue and Sarah North. *Exploring English Grammar: From Formal to Functional.* London: Routledge, 2009.

Danto, Arthur C. *Narration and Knowledge.* New York: Columbia University Press, 2007.

Eckel, Jan. 'Narrativizations of the Past: The Theoretical Debate and the Example of the Weimar Republic', in Stefan Berger and Chris Lorenz (eds), *Nationalizing the Past: Historians as Nation Builders in Modern Europe* (Basingstoke: Palgrave Macmillan, 2008), 26–48.

Edgar, David. 'The British History New Citizens Must Learn: No Radicals, No Homosexuals, No Holocaust'. *Guardian,* 11 March 2013. http://www.theguardian.com/commentisfree/2013/mar/11/battle-britain-history-new-uk-citizens (last accessed 4 April 2018).

Frye, Northrop. *Anatomy of Criticism: Four Essays.* Princeton, NJ: Princeton University Press, 2000.

Fulda, Daniel. 'Historiographic Narration', in Peter Hühn et al. (eds), *The Living Handbook of Narratology* (Hamburg: Hamburg University, 2014). http://www.lhn.uni-hamburg.de/article/historiographic-narration (last accessed 4 April 2018).

Glendinning, Lee. 'Citizenship Guide Fails its History Exam'. *Guardian,* 29 April 2006. https://www.theguardian.com/uk/2006/apr/29/immigration.immigrationpolicy (last accessed 4 April 2018)

Halliday, Michael A.K., and Christian M.I.M. Matthiessen. *Halliday's Introduction to Functional Grammar.* Abingdon: Routledge, 2014.

Hirsch, Eric D. *Cultural Literacy: What Every American Needs to Know.* New York: Random House, 1988.

Home Office. *Community Cohesion: A Report of the Independent Review Team Chaired by Ted Cantle.* London, 2001. https://dera.ioe.ac.uk/14146/ (last accessed 17 November 2020).

———. *Life in the United Kingdom: A Guide for New Residents.* London: The Stationary Office, 2013.

———. *Life in the United Kingdom: A Journey to Citizenship.* London: Her Majesty's Stationary Office, 2006 (8th impression of the 2004 text 'with minor amendments').

———. *Life in the United Kingdom: A Journey to Citizenship.* London: The Stationary Office, 2007.

Kettle, Martin. 'It Will Soon be Time to Drop our Oppressive Remembrance Rituals'. *Guardian,* 23 October 2015. http://www.theguardian.com/commentisfree/2015/oct/23/agincourt-remembrance-day-national-ritual (last accessed 4 April 2018).

Leerssen, Joep. 'Setting the Scene for National History', in Stefan Berger and Chris Lorenz (eds), *Nationalizing the Past: Historians as Nation Builders in Modern Europe* (Basingstoke: Palgrave Macmillan, 2008), 71–85.

Megill, Allan. 'Recounting the Past: Description, Explanation and Narrative in Historiography'. *The American Historical Review* 94(3) (1989), 627–53.

National Archives. *Slave or Free?* London. http://www.nationalarchives.gov.uk/pathways/blackhistory/rights/slave_free.htm (last accessed 4 April 2018).

Rimmon-Kenan, Shlomith. *Narrative Fiction: Contemporary Poetics*. London: Routledge, 1992.

Rüsen, Jörn. *History: Narration, Interpretation, Orientation*. New York: Berghahn Books, 2005.

Strachan, Hew, and Alison L. Kennedy. 'Should the Country Spend £55m to Commemorate the First World War?' *Guardian*, 25 May 2013. http://www.theguardian.com/commentisfree/2013/may/25/first-world-war-commemorations-debate (last accessed 4 April 2018).

Todorov, Tzvetan. *The Inner Enemies of Democracy*. Cambridge: Polity, 2014.

———. *The Poetics of Prose*. Ithaca, NY: Cornell University Press, 1977.

Van Oers, Ricky. *Deserving Citizenship: Citizenship Tests in Germany, the Netherlands and the United Kingdom*. Leiden: Martinus Nijhoff Publishers, 2014.

White, Hayden. *Metahistory: The Historical Imagination in Nineteenth-Century Europe*. Baltimore, MD: Johns Hopkins University Press, 1973.

Analysing Historical Narratives
Concluding Remarks

Stefan Berger and Chris Lorenz

Varieties of Historical Narratives: Their Mediatization, Spatialization and Politicization

Overlooking the case studies collected in this volume – and assuming that they are a fair and up-to-date sample of the wide variety of the kind of narratives representing 'the past' – this collection in itself is an argument for the thesis that the history of historical writing needs to move away from just looking at professional historians. The subfield of historical writing called historiography emerged out of the extremely high self-esteem of historians as a professional body of men (and traditionally they were largely male) who had assumed, qua their professionalism, the sole authority about the past.[1] Envious of novelists, whose books often had and continue to have a much longer shelf life than those of historians, they often began writing about themselves as a means of letting the world know about their significance. It is characteristic that historiography as a subdiscipline enjoyed its greatest popularity among historians in countries where the status of the historical profession was high, such as Germany. In countries where history had a much lower status in comparison, such as Britain and the Netherlands, historiography was not particularly popular and was widely regarded as a deviation from the real craft of historical writing. However, during the

---

Notes for this section begin on page 342.

course of the long nineteenth century, professional historians in many parts of the Western world managed to make an authoritative claim over the past which made them useful to governments and social movements alike – in fact, to anyone who had a political claim that involved a mobilization of the past for their particular aims. Hence professional historians did indeed become 'prophets of the nation',[2] and they were vital for movements like the communists, who sought to reinterpret the past as the history of class wars, as Karl Marx had famously stated.[3] For religious movements and movements of ethnic and other minorities, history was an equally powerful vehicle to further their particular objectives. The women's movement, the peace movement, the environmental movements – they all mobilized history in order to make specific political claims.[4]

All of this propelled professional historians to a standing they had not possessed before the advent of history as a university subject. Before the eighteenth century, when history was largely the handmaiden of theology, a wide range of people – not at all restricted to the universities and academies – could write histories. Historians had a much lower status in society then, as they were just one among many professions, disciplines and cultural fields concerned with the past. Interestingly, in the twenty-first century, we are witnessing in some respects a decline in the authority of the professional historian and a return to a more multipolar, kaleidoscopic and multidisciplinary historical writing, where 'amateurs' once again play a prominent role.[5] Today, most people who want to know about history, indeed who want to know about anything at all, will immediately refer to the internet and Wikipedia; and whilst professional historians are undoubtedly active as authors on Wikipedia, they remain anonymous. Unlike in the nineteenth and twentieth centuries, their professional status no longer gives them a guaranteed public credibility. And, of course, many Wikipedia authors writing on history are not at all professional historians. Arguably, in the twenty-first century, we have moved full circle to the time before the eighteenth century, when history was practised by a great number of people from diverse professional backgrounds. Indeed, journalists in the media have often become far more influential commentators on historical matters than professional historians. Whilst the latter still do occasionally write for the print media and appear on television, and whilst some even have their own Twitter, Facebook or Instagram accounts, they are running after a trend that has, by and large, bypassed them. Long gone also are the times when leading academic historians, like Ernest Lavisse, were the authors of school textbooks. Today's generation of textbook authors are their own little profession. Hence, in a volume on historical narratives, we thought it important to deal with popular forms of historical writing and with schoolbooks just as much as with professional historical writing.

In this contemporary context of historical writing it strikes us as vitally important to pay closer attention to the media in which historical narratives have been narrated. On the one hand we can observe how historical narratives are more and more present in an ever-growing variety of diverse media (especially digital media), whilst on the other hand we can see how the media are producing new historical narratives.[6] Furthermore, historical narratives are translated from one medium to another. So far, we know too little about what happens in these processes of translations from one medium into another. Are certain narrative strategies more suitable to one medium than to another? Especially with regard to the digital turn in the humanities, there is an urgent need to examine what this means for more traditional historical narratives. In this volume Robbert-Jan Adriaansen has examined historical narratives on Instagram and concluded that they produce their own distinct forms of narrating the past that are completely different from more traditional forms. By contrast, Markku Jokisipilä, who has examined the internet presence of national histories of Britain, Germany and Finland, paying special attention to Wikipedia, found that 'the historical information available online appears to be rather old-fashioned in both form and content'.[7] Traditional master narratives of old-fashioned national histories, focusing on political and military history, were among the most widespread and most popular on the internet; so we cannot conclude that the new media *necessarily* brought and bring a change of narrative. They, and also those institutions working with the new media such as museums and heritage sites, no doubt tend to prioritize 'experience' and 'authenticity' over professional historians' analyses of the past, thus favouring oral histories and visual evidence over historians' reports.

Philippe Carrard, however, has pointed out that in contrast to popular storytellers and writers of fiction, professional historians in principle *only* write about the 'inner experiences' – thoughts, feelings – of historical actors as far as these experiences can be critically reconstructed from primary sources (like diaries, letters, memoirs and interviews).[8] This evidential restriction obviously creates serious limits to the scope of experience that historians can include in their narratives in comparison to fictional authors and other storytellers, who can freely roam inside the hearts and minds of their characters. It is this restriction that many present-day readers and viewers, who tend to identify the showing of emotions with authenticity, are experiencing as 'distanced' and 'unauthentic'. Hence, with the advances of the new media, an increasing gap is opening up between the consumption of the past and the historians' claim that only they can reproduce the past accurately.[9] 'Unprofessional' narratives proliferate, especially those of the 'contemporary witness' and their memories – with the witness being a traditional enemy of the historian.[10] At the same time, however, Carrard points out that cultural historians have opened up a more mediated understanding of experience in comparison with the idea of experience being somehow direct, authentic and unframed. This is so because historians of mentality and of emotions have reconstructed the *changes* in the ways in which people have experienced love, death, childhood, fear and sexuality over time, thereby historicizing *all* common sensical frames of experience[11] – including the very notion and frame of 'contemporary witness'.[12]

The historical narratives produced by the new media are directly related to the memory boom that started in the 1980s and has proliferated to immense proportions since then. Memory narratives on the past have, however, been increasingly disconnected from professional historians' narratives, which is why Aleida Assmann has argued: 'The historian has lost his monopoly over defining and presenting the past. What is called the "memory boom" is the immediate effect of this loss of the historian's singular and unrivalled authority'.[13] The historical consciousness of people is rooted in those memory narratives far more than in the accounts of professional historians, although we should not underestimate to what extent the historians' discourse is part and parcel of wider memory narratives. Some memory scholars, like Wulf Kansteiner, have argued that the new technologies and their representation of the past would in the future determine much more than interpersonal relations how historical narratives and historical consciousness would be shaped. Computers and interactive video game technology, he argued, will have the power to construct virtual pasts that influence the historical consciousness of real people[14] – although one could question with Jeffrey Barash whether it makes sense to call *all* ideas about the past 'historical' if they are not supported by methodically checked historical evidence.

Barash has recently made a philosophical argument in favour of restoring the fundamental distinction between the concepts of history and memory – after at least twenty-five years of 'memory craze', during which memory has been ascribed to a wide variety of phenomena like archives, statues, landscapes and nations[15] – and to realize again that the faculty of memory is restricted to individuals and what they experience in face-to-face, interpersonal communication. Barash, of course, emphasizes with Halbwachs the inescapable collective forms and media in which individual memories are framed, but his fundamental point is that collective carriers of collective memory do not exist, as Halbwachs had sometimes suggested. The concept of collective memory can, therefore, only be conceived in a metaphorical sense – that is, as the memories that the members of several generations share because they were transmitted in their interpersonal communication. Consequently, collective memory has a temporal stretch of three to four generations, and is subject to a continuous process of simultaneous expansion and contraction: it is the 'horizon of experience' that travels with the generations through time. After the past is no longer a part of collective memory, the only access to it is through the methods of history according to Barash, who also emphasizes the increasing formative power of the mass media in the domain of collective memory in the contemporary period.[16]

The new media, which also includes film, seem to reintroduce to narratives of the past 'liminal' and 'grotesque' experiential elements that, as Hayden White has argued, were removed from history by the advances of professional history writing.[17] History as graphic novel, as enactment, as living history and as television have all been producing narratives that tend to equate emotionality with authenticity. We agree with Wolfgang Hardtwig and Erhard Schütz that these mediated narratives need to be taken seriously in their own right. They are not just popularizations of academic history but they follow their own narrative conventions, which have to explored far more thoroughly.[18]

Apart from a relative loss of importance of professional historical narratives and their increasing mediatization, we can also see, among historians, a desire to move away from the Western-centric look at the history of historiography that has long dominated this subfield of the historical profession.[19] This volume welcomes this trend, and through its three contributions on Brazil, China and Japan seeks to extend the analysis of historical narratives beyond the Western-centric canon of history writing. The nineteenth-century Brazilian narratives that are discussed by Valdei Araujo demonstrate how entangled the narratives of Portugal and Brazil were at the constitutive moment of a Brazilian national historical consciousness during the time when the Portuguese court fled from Napoleon's advancing armies to Brazil. Historical narratives, by combining stories of progress and modernization with the advances of national historical consciousness, were vital in underpinning the move of Brazil to an independent nation-state in the nineteenth century. In the twenty-first century, Araujo argues, the conflict between the political left and the political right also finds expression through historical narratives. Right-wing non-professional histories produced by journalists working for the right-wing media in Brazil challenge what they present as a left-wing-infested academic history writing that has allegedly falsified the history of the country. Xupeng Zhang's account of the recent rise of global history in China demonstrates how the Marxist-trained historians in China have long adopted Western ways of narrating the past and are, in a post-Marxist China, seeking to relate to what they perceive as the most advanced forms of historical writing in the West – in other words, global history. On the other hand, he also shows how they inflect these Western forms of historical writing with a Chinese peculiarity, making Chinese narrativizations of the global far more

Sinocentric and nationalist than its Western variants. One could see this kind of local adaptation of a global phenomenon as the historiographic variety of 'glocalization'.[20]

Whilst Araujo deals partly with non-professional historians, Zhang restricts himself to professional historians and Naoki Odanaka deals with writers of school textbooks in Japan. A greater concern with non-Western historical narratives would, however, move us even further away from a concentration on professional history writing. Many non-Western civilizations, after all, wrote history and sought to develop historical consciousness through other genres, such as family histories on the Indian subcontinent, which worked through oral history and storytelling.[21] The ancient Chinese historian Sima Qian had an entirely different understanding of historical narrative from that promoted by professional Western historians.[22] The tradition of neo-Confucian history writing in China and the Far East more generally promoted very different forms of historical narrative from those imported by Western historians.[23] Of course, with the conquest of the world by the 'globalizing' West from the sixteenth century onwards, ideas of professional history writing and its specific ways of narrating the past also started to spread globally. By the late nineteenth and early twentieth centuries, many historians outside the West had a keen interest in studying Western ways of 'scientifically' writing the past. Yet nowhere did they produce simple copies of Western historical narratives. Instead they frequently adapted those Western narratives and produced hybrid forms of historical narratives that took older traditions and understandings of writing history and merged them with the new forms, travelling on the back of Western colonialism and imperialism. Hence colonial and postcolonial history writing in the global South cannot simply be perceived as a copy of Western forms of historical writing.[24] In Latin America, creole forms of historical writing preceded or were at least contemporaneous with the professionalization of historical writing in Europe, producing an interesting mixture of nativist oral traditions and 'scientific' Western history.[25] Investigations into non-Western historical narratives need to focus much more on those interdependencies of, and circulations between, Western and non-Western forms of colonial and postcolonial history writing.

A closer look at the spatial dimensions of historical narratives that are particularly prominently discussed in the section on national historical narratives indicates a need to give up the separate study of spatial scales that was established in historical writing in the course of the nineteenth century. Local, regional, national and transnational histories cannot be narrated in isolation from one another, but only by taking into account their interconnectedness. Institutionally they often continue to remain separated from one another. Thus, in Germany, for example, the tradition of *Landesgeschichte* is supposed to look at local and regional history only, whilst many historiographies across the world know the institutional separation of national history, still often perceived as the most important form of history, and world history – the latter being seen as everything that is not national history. All of this has, for a long time, hindered the emergence of historical narratives relating the local, regional, national and transnational, and of interwoven narratives of space. Territorialities have long been extremely contested. The strong nationalization of historical writing in the nineteenth century has led to a hierarchy of space, in which local and regional spaces were subsumed under national ones. They became building blocks of national histories, but were at the same time restricted to this. Many historians lost a sensitivity to local and regional spaces as spaces of resistance to nationalizing policies, and as spaces that often thrived on transnational connections. Border spaces, in particular, were spaces where the local and the regional transcended the national, and border narratives stressed intensive cross-border contact throughout the ages.[26] So far, national historical narratives have predominantly sought to integrate border regions into national histories, thereby ignoring their interjecting, overlapping and shared narratives with territories outside of the borders of the nation-state. Yet various forms of territoriality have always found their own historiographies attempting to put specific territorialities into narrative form. Thus, narratives of cities, regions, nations and nation-states, as well as stateless nations and narratives of empire, all stood next to each other and related their spatial focus to that of others.[27] Gabriele Lingelbach, in her contribution to this volume, reminds us how some of the best contemporary global history has skilfully interrelated local, regional, national and transnational spaces in its narrativizations of global processes.

The politics of historical narratives is not only visible in relation to spatial preferences, but also in terms of a wide range of ideological positions espoused via historical arguments. The politics of historical writing underpinned left-wing and right-wing political movements, Communism and Fascism, and it supported religious fundamentalisms just as it underlined the demands of gender equality. Liberal democracies also mobilized history in attempts to bolster its legitimacy vis-à-vis challenges to liberal democratic forms of governance. All these aspects are reflected in the various contributions to this volume. Herman Paul, for example, deconstructs secularization narratives as political thought structures within which specific phenomena in the history of the West in the twentieth century are structured. Textbooks on ancient Persia, as Björn Onken argues in his chapter, have oscillated between a perpetuation of orientalist attitudes and the desire to address the consequences of Western colonialism and imperialism. Both positions are intensely related to contemporary political choices. Daniel Wimmer shows how the narrative construction of space in the Middle Ages is connected to specific political projects in the contemporary world. Naoki Odanaka demonstrates in relation to Japanese school textbooks that they cannot, despite government control mechanisms, be neutral in their politics or objective in their presentation of the past; rather, their narratives imply clear political and normative choices. Mario Carretero and Everardo Perez-Manjarrez underline how maps in schoolbooks have served nationalist political purposes; and Jörg Requate emphasizes how narratives of terrorism all come with their own political agendas. Daniel Fulda in his analysis of contemporary historical novels, arrives at the conclusion that they serve a very wide variety of different political objectives.

Unsurprisingly we find a close alignment of historical narratives to political projects in the section on national historical narratives in this volume, although the political objectives are usually not stated explicitly and may be camouflaged under epistemological or methodological flags, as Pierre Bourdieu argued long ago and as Wulf Kansteiner argues in his analysis of the 'politics of comparison' in Timothy Snyders 'Bloodlands'.[28] We already referred to the espousal of right-wing politics by popular Brazilian national histories, and to the strong nationalist message in Chinese global histories. Arthur Chapman, in his analysis of the historical narratives surrounding British citizenship tests, also finds history attached to the political project of nationalization. Hence, our analyses of historical narratives have time and again drawn attention to political functionalization and prioritization, as well as power imbalances that go a long way in explaining why some historical narratives have been more popular and widespread than others. Nevertheless, all narratives that claim to be 'historical' simultaneously imply a 'reality claim', (as we have argued in the Introduction) that translates into a claim to truth and objectivity – and this leads us back to historical narrative and the theory of history.

Historical Narratives and Historical Theory

In the Introduction we observed a remarkable imbalance between the extended theoretical discussions about history and narrative on the one side, and the quite limited number of empirical attempts to analyse narrative strategies of historians on the other – professional or otherwise. Now it is time to check how far theoretical claims concerning narrative in history – especially those formulated by White, like the construction of a temporal beginning, middle and ending, and the construction of a plot, as well as the claims of postnarrative theory concerning truth and objectivity – have surfaced in the contributions in this volume, and how our empirical findings relate to narrative theory. We will structure our conclusions according to seven observations.

The *first* observation we want to make is pretty basic but probably not superfluous – namely, the fact that, as postnarrative theory of history posits, the historians in this volume do compare historical narratives with other historical narratives when they make claims about the past. So indeed, and in contrast to fictional narratives, historical narratives necessarily and openly talk to each other, and through the sources to the past.[29] Moreover, our historians do evaluate historical narratives comparatively in connection to their capacity to explain the information derived from a variety of sources and perspectives: the more sources and perspectives they explain, the more justified is their claim to the epistemological quality of the narrative (i.e. its 'relative objectivity') it seems. On this ground, historians tend to prefer narratives that integrate a larger variety of perspectives than their competitors over narratives that only focus on one or two perspectives. This appears to be the reason why Requate and Lingelbach in their case studies prefer narratives that integrate the perspectives of both the 'perpetrators' and the 'victims' over narratives that focus exclusively on one *or* the other.[30]

This argument is also present in Kansteiner's critique of Snyder's 'biases' and in his remarks on Holocaust historiography, although Kansteiner proposes to analytically disentangle the quality of the narrative's perspective from the quality of its descriptive contents, and from the quality of its arguments – and to regard these three dimensions as separate qualities of historical works. Remarkably, in comparison with the 'narrative holism' of White and Ankermit, who both located the defining characteristics of narrative on the level of the *complete text* and not on the level of the singular statements it contains,[31] Kansteiner's variety of narratology locates 'the issue of narrative' again on the level of singular descriptive statements, thereby returning to a kind of 'narrative atomism' – and thus to the kind of philosophical analysis of narrative – that Arthur Danto practised in his *Analytical Philosophy of History* of 1965. Although Kansteiner identifies 'at least four different textual layers' in historical texts and is making a distinction between 'small-scale' and 'large-scale' descriptions, his own textual analysis almost exclusively deals with singular statements of the 'Stalin was a Georgian' type. Also, in contrast to Ankersmit, Kansteiner does not see narrative explanation as being opposed to causal explanation, and nor does he recognize the metaphorical ('perspectival') properties of narrative. Instead – following Carola Smith – he connects metaphor to argument.[32] His proposal is in line with Ann Rigney's critique of White's view of narrative plotting as 'one size fits all',[33] and also with Philippe Carrard's earlier analysis of the 'limits of narrativity' in historiography.[34] All in all, our cases support the idea that comparing historical narratives is guided by at least some intersubjective epistemological criteria, which obviously does not mean that these criteria guarantee a professional consensus. Lingelbach's observation that narrative conventions may vary between national traditions also suggests that expecting a consensus among historians is not realistic – even in principle.[35]

The *second* basic observation we want to make is that the historians in this volume no longer act like all-knowing narrators, as had been the case when Roland Barthes analysed the writing of history in the 1960s.[36] As Lingelbach observes, historians are using an authorial voice in narrative as soon as they engage in a debate on several representations of history and discuss their pros and cons. As soon as historians acknowledge the fundamental discursive, or argumentative, character of historical narratives – as historians of historiography do, almost by definition – the position of the all-knowing narrator is no longer available for them, and they are forced to 'come out' epistemologically in practice, so to speak. The fact that many historians still are reluctant to take on this role explicitly does not contradict this observation.

This leads us to the *third* observation concerning the narrative construction of historical time, namely the construction of periodization.[37] Looking especially at the chapters of Herman Paul on narratives of 'secularization', of Kenan van de Mieroop on narratives of the 'civil rights movement', of Jörg Requate on narratives on 'RAF-terrorism' and of Gabriele Lingelbach on narratives of 'globalization', there can be little doubt that these authors all emphasize the fundamental importance of periodization by narrative plotting, including the conclusion that different periodizations of the same topic (Civil Right Movement, globalization, terrorism) imply different beginnings, middles and endings. So, with the help of periodization, the historian creates a basic order in processes of change. The circumstance that not all historical narratives focus primarily on temporal change – as Kansteiner posits for *Bloodlands*, and as Carrard posits for much of the Annales historiography[38] – does not contradict this observation, so here too narrative theory of history appears to make explicit some characteristics of historical practice.

As to the narrative construction of periodization, there is no difference between Herman Paul, with his critical attempt to 'deconstruct' the (meta-) narrative of secularization as a misguided ('sociological') idea derived from modernization theory, and the other authors just mentioned. However, Herman Paul is questioning the fundamental claims to truth and objectivity of secularization narratives as such, because in his view they are discredited by thinking in terms of fixed stages and of teleology. This is indeed in contrast to the other authors who analyse their historical narratives without questioning their claims to truth and objectivity in principle. This does not, of course, mean that van de Mieroop, Requate and Lingelbach do not compare the narratives they analyse in terms of epistemological qualities (for instance, scope and coherence), because they all do, using a variety of arguments. Van de Mieroop, for instance, leaves no doubt that in his view the narratives on the Civil Rights Movement that delimit the black struggle in time to the 'reasonable' and 'peaceful' actions under the leadership of Martin Luther King, that ended in a succesful 'black emancipation' – are epistemologically inferior to narratives with a wider scope and coherence that include the 'radical' Malcolm X and the 'violent' Black Panther movement, as integral parts of the 'continuing' history of the peaceful and violent struggles for black lifes and rights (cf. 'Black Lives Matter'). Obviously, van de Mieroop prefers more 'complex' over 'dichotomous' narratives because the first can clarify that good/reasonable and bad/violent are not dichotomous moral properties of individuals, and that peaceful people may become violent under certain circumstances – and the other way around. Similarly, Requate is quite clear that in his eyes the later, more differentiated generational narratives of RAF terrorism are more adequate in epistemological terms than the early, dichotomous 'us against them' ('6 against 60 million') stories.

Our *fourth* observation concerns the construction of plots in historical narrative. Although in the Introduction we already established – against the narrativist thesis – that not all histories are narrative (see Adriaansen in this volume), and that not all narratives are plotted (as Rigney argued),[39] most of our historians have identified plots in the narratives analysed here. Both Herman Paul and Gabriele Lingelbach, for example, argue that the plot of the narratives about 'religion/secularization' and 'globalization' that they analysed was basically – although not necessarily, as Lingelbach emphasizes – a story of decline (that is, of the declining autonomy of those who were integrated in the 'world system'), while Kenan van de Mieroop presents us with standard histories in which progress – history as the march of freedom – was the plot ('the romantic/heroic story of American triumph'). Given the fact that, in the standard histories he analyses, the Civil Rights Movement is interpreted as part of American 'national' history – not as part of the history of American racism, nor as the after-history of American black slavery – the 'romantic plot' (White) was to be expected because American national history has predominantly been plotted as the 'history of progress' (in terms of America's 'exceptionalism' and its 'Manifest Destiny').[40]

Something similar goes for the ways in which the national histories of China and Brazil have been plotted, as we could learn from the chapters by Xupeng Zhang and Valdei Lopez de Araujo. Therefore, national history writing as a narrative genre and 'romantic plotting' still seem to be intimately connected. In stark contrast to these, Jörg Requate offers us narratives with a dramatic plotting, in which generations – especially fathers and sons – are pitted against each other like in a classic Greek tragedy. So, although the 'Grand Narratives' ('metanarratives') were famously declared dead by Lyotard in 1979, in the practice of history writing – and in the rest of 'historical culture' – they still seem to be very much alive in most parts of the globe. Given the continuing presence of both the plots of decline and of progress in historical narratives, only the cyclical pattern – Nietzsche's 'eternal return of the same'[41] – seems to be missing in the cases analysed in this volume.

Our *fifth* observation concerns the issue of narrative focus. It is thematized in several chapters, especially those of Lingelbach, Lianeri and Kansteiner. Lingelbach makes clear that every global historian must find a solution to the problem of how to connect phenomena on the global macrolevel and phenomena on the local microlevel – and all levels in between. Individual historians use various narrative techniques to zoom in on the local and out to the global, and every decision to zoom in or out not only produces an epistemological benefit but also an epistemological cost. Zooming in, for example, produces the possibility of re-enacting in individual lifeworlds, including emotions ('empathy'), but makes it impossible to simultaneously explain the mechanisms of the global market 'system' that conditions the lifeworlds of the actors of globalization. So the choice of focus on the micro/macro scale by the global historians, and the decisions they take where and when in the narrative to zoom in and out in a spatial sense, determines what their narratives make visible and what is kept in the narrative dark. This observation confirms our earlier remark concerning the interplay between spatial levels in historical narratives – between the national, subnational and supranational.

Alexandra Lianeri also addresses issues of 'narrative focusing' in Thucydides' narrative of the War of the Peloponnese with the concept of 'the gaze'. In her case, the zooming in and out does not primarily refer to differences on a spatial scale (local–global) but to differences on a temporal scale (earlier–later). This difference in time scale also determines what is presented as visible or invisible, and for whom; this is a well-known narrative characteristic of crime stories, which commonly contain flashbacks and fore-sights, and therefore do not adhere to chronological time. Lianeri argues that Thucydides is systematically changing the ex-post, 'teleological' perspective of the historian with the perspectives of the actors, the Athenians, who did not know that they were losing this war – until they lost it (among other things by losing their lives).[42] Lianeri argues that for Thucydides 'the gaze of the dead' is the privileged narrative focus, and suggests that he thereby was anticipating Koselleck's arguments concerning the 'privileged gaze' in history writing of those who are the losers of wars. Koselleck famously argued that the losers of wars tend to be better historians than victors because they have experienced the quintessence of 'historical experience': that is, that the important things in life do not usually go according to plan and often fail miserably.[43]

Wulf Kansteiner analyses the explicit attempt by Snyder in *Bloodlands* to 'restore the humanity' of the anonymous victims of the Soviet and Nazi mass murders by giving a few of them back their individuality amidst the statistics of death. Snyder tried to do so by combining the 'numerical' approach to these mass murders, which was typical for their perpetrators, with a 'humanistic' approach to four of their victims. According to Kansteiner, however, Snyder's attempt to construct a narrative with a 'double focus' – on both the perpetrators and the victims – on balance fails miserably. Although Snyder is credited with including the 'taboo topics' of sexual mass rape and cannibalism into his picture of the 'Bloodlands', in the end the narrator remains one-eyed, predominantly relying on statistics of death. His story therefore remains an example of single-focus perpetrator history: 'a study of killing – written on the basis of the killers' documents and from their perspective' (Kansteiner, this volume).

Our *sixth* observation concerns the political dimension of historical narratives that was emphasized by White. Many of our chapters (Paul, van de Mieroop, the national histories) confirm indeed that historical narratives show a clear 'elective affinity' to political positions, and are inextricably connected to political discourses. Kansteiner's analysis of *Bloodlands* showed how an author, by means of categorizing and comparing in specific ways, can 'spin' a narrative so that it clearly carries political messages: no method, including statistical method, is politically innocent.[44]

What our cases also show is that quite a few narratives about the past are simultaneously the 'stories that people live by' – because people not only tell stories about their own lives, but also live according to the stories they tell themselves. This 'double character' of narratives was not clarified by the theories of narrative as developed by either White or Ankersmit, who both emphasized the fundamental 'gap' between historical narratives and the amorphic and chaotic character of what happened in the past. Some of our cases, however – those dealt with by Herman Paul, Kenan van de Mieroop and Jörg Requate are good examples – suggest a clear and direct continuity between the narratives that historians are telling and the narratives that specific groups of people are telling themselves, and/or are being told by the media, about what they basically are.[45] As the 'stories that people live by' are also the 'stories that people act upon', historical narratives may therefore have a clear *performative* dimension – because they help to construct *practical* identities. This connection has not been elucidated in the (dominant) narrative theories that we dealt with in the Introduction.[46] So we can conclude that although narrative theory has often been interpreted as bringing the 'linguistic turn' to history and philosophy of history – and thus to historians and philosophers of history – in its best-known varieties it did not highlight the constitutive function of historical narrative for everyday life, nor did it highlight the interpenetration between historical and popular narratives, or the consequences of this interconnection for history. These practical aspects of historical narratives have primarily been elucidated by narrative philosophers with a background in phenomenology, like Paul Ricoeur and David Carr.[47] This leads us to our last observation, which deals with two aspects of historical narrative that are also not dealt with by mainstream narrative theory: intermediality and personalization.

Our *seventh* observation concerns the fact, highlighted by both van de Mieroop and Requate, that 'historical consciousness' of individuals and groups in the 'online age' no longer primarily derives from written narratives about the past, which have been the undisputed core business of narrative theory in history.[48] Instead it primarily derives from various 'extra-textual' – especially visual – media.[49] This observation is not, of course, brand new because it is more or less foundational for popular history and visual history; but its implication is not restricted to popular and visual history, as both Requate and van de Mieroop have pointed out. This is so because the representations of modern phenomena like 'terrorism' (and, one could add, 'Trumpism', 'the Islamic Caliphate' and 'the refugee crisis') are not only primarily constructed by, but are also dependent on, the media: the media are not just reporting 'what is going on out there' but they are involved as actors themselves. In Requate's chapter, for example, representatives of the media are communicating with the terrorists and are thus acting as their 'messengers'. Because of this fundamental fact, the phenomenon of 'terrorism' cannot be separated in history from the role played by the media and their ways of framing this phenomenon. This constitutive role of the media in the construction of phenomena like 'terrorism' and 'Trumpism' increases complexity for contemporary historians because they inevitably have to deal with two characteristics of medial communication: the simultaneity of documenting and of fictionalizing the phenomena on the one hand, and the personalization of the phenomena on the other – the incarnation of phenomena by specific individuals. This 'personalization' of the historical is somewhat ironic, because the social historians of the 1960s and 1970s primarily sought alternative representational modes for the narrative mode of history – especially derived from the social sciences – because they identified narrativization with personalization. Thrown out through the front door, narrativization now seems to be entering through the journalistic back door of history.

Requate addresses the simultaneous factual reporting in the press of RAF terrorism on the one side, and the transformation of RAF terrorism into fiction and films on the other. Inevitably the simultaneous framing of terrorism in factual and fictional narratives conditioned each other, as was the case with the representation of RAF terrorism as 'a war between two generations', and of the perpetrators as 'Hitler's children'. Books authored by journalists later functioned as the bridge between the medial and the historical representations.

The 'personalization mechanism' in the media explains, according to Requate, why over time both the perpetrators and the victims of RAF terrorism were increasingly framed as individuals with specific family backgrounds. This mechanism, which is also known from popular history, enables the reader/viewer/listener/player to develop empathy for the protagonists in narratives – which, of course, was an insight not unknown to historians and historical theorists inspired by the 'Verstehen/Understanding' tradition (and Snyder's *Bloodlands*, although predominantly based on statistics, also contains this insight, as we have seen).[50] Along this way, narrators of history are able to frame political matters as private, and private matters as political – an insight rooted in '1968'. We can find this in historical documentaries – for example, by Ken Burns and Claude Lanzman, in the quasi-historical films of Steven Spielberg, and in the work of professional historians.[51]

The historical novelists, who invented the 'personalization mechanism' and who gave birth to the historical narrative as a genre in the first half of the nineteenth century – a birth that was denied by the 'scientific' historians in the second half of that century – thus seem to have returned to history through a 'detour' in the media in order to claim their credits (and, maybe, their intellectual fathership). However this may be, the spectacular renewed public success of the historical novel, both in its written as its film series variety (see Fulda's chapter) – strongly suggests that, for professional historians, ignoring the grounds of this renewed success may be risky. This is not, of course, to suggest that the historical novel represents the only existing narrative model for future success in history; for example, one 'impersonal' macro-history, Jared Diamond's *Guns, Germs and Steel* – a book inspired by evolutionary biology and geography – became an impressive bestseller, despite it being explicitly non-narrative.[52] So, all in all, it seems safe to conclude on the basis of this volume that for the foreseeable future 'the issues of narrative' will remain in the centre of both historical theory and a reflexive historical practice.

Stefan Berger is professor of social history at Ruhr-University Bochum, where he also directs the Institute for Social Movements and is executive chair of the Foundation History of the Ruhr. He is also an honorary professor at Cardiff University in the UK. He has published widely in the comparative history of social movements and labour movements, the history of deindustrialization and industrial heritage, nationalism and national identity studies, the history of historiography and historical theory. Among his most recent publications are *The Making of the New History: Historiographical Developments since the 1980s* (Cambridge University Press, 2021); *Writing History: Theory and Practice*, co-edited with Heiko Feldner and Kevin Passmore (3rd rev. edn, Bloomsbury, 2020); and *The Engaged Historian: Perspectives on the Intersections of Politics, Activism and the Historical Profession* (Berghahn Books, 2019).

Chris Lorenz was professor of historical theory at Leiden University and professor of German historical culture at VU University Amsterdam. Since 2016 he has been an international research associate at the Ruhr-University Bochum. He has widely published on historical theory, historiography and on higher education. His publications include *De Constructie van het Verleden* (Boom, 2008, 9th.rev.edn); (ed.), *'If you're so smart why aren't you rich? Universiteit, Markt & Management* (Boom, 2008); (with co-editor Berber Bevernage), *Breaking Up Time: Negotiating the Borders between Present, Past and Future,* (Vandenhoeck, 2013) and *Entre Filosofía e Historia. Volumen 1: Exploraciones en Filosofía de la Historia,* and *Volumen 2: Exploraciones en Historiografía* (Prometeo Libros, 2015).

Notes

1. Tollebeek and Porciani, 'Institutions, Networks and Communities'.
2. Gramley, *Propheten des deutschen Nationalismus*.
3. Wang and Iggers, *Marxist Historiographies*, 1–16.
4. Berger and Cornelissen, *Marxist Historical Cultures*, 1–32.
5. Berger, 'Professional and Popular Historians'.
6. See especially, Rigney, 'When the Monograph is no longer the Medium'.
7. Jokisipilä, 'The Internet and National Histories', 325.
8. Carrard, 'Historiographic Discourse and Narratology'.
9. de Groot, *Consuming History*.
10. Sabrow and Frei, *Die Geburt des Zeitzeugen*.
11. Carrard, 'Historiographic Discourse and Narratology'.
12. Sabrow and Frei, *Die Geburt des Zeitzeugen*.
13. Assmann, 'Re-framing Memory', 39. Assmann does not claim, however, that 'memory' is an alternative 'method' for studying 'the past', in the ways that historians do; only that 'memory' is also about what 'the past' *means* for present-day individuals and collectivities. Therefore she is pleading for a *complementarity* of the 'historical' and the 'memorial' ways of handling the past. See Lorenz, 'Time and Space', 47–49.
14. Kansteiner, 'Alternate Worlds'.
15. For a critical analysis of the emergence of 'memory' in historical discourse, see Klein, *From History to Theory*, 112–38.
16. Barash, *Collective Memory*, 114–68.
17. White, *Content of the Form*, 66.
18. Hardtwig and Schütz, *Geschichte für Leser*.

19. Hence recent surveys of the history of historiography have taken a global approach. See Iggers, Wang and Mukherjee, *A Global History*; Woolf, *A Global History of History*.

20. For an outstanding comparison of the historiography of global histories in China, the US and Germany, see Sachsenmaier, *Global Perspectives*.

21. Chatterjee, 'King of Controversy'.

22. Durrant, *The Cloudy Mirror*; Hardy, *World of Bronze and Bamboo*.

23. Kwong, 'Rise of the Linear Perspective'; Wang, 'Modern Historical Consciousness'.

24. Chatterjee, *The Nation and its Fragments*.

25. Rappaport, *Politics of Memory*.

26. Frank and Hadler, *Disputed Territories*.

27. Middell and Roura, *Transnational Challenges*; Ghobrial, 'Global History and Microhistory'; Iriye and Saunier, *Palgrave Dictionary of Transnational History*.

28. Bourdieu, 'The Specificity of the Scientific Field'.

29. Authors of fictional narratives may also 'talk to each other', but they do not do so 'necessarily', nor 'in the open'.

30. Although this is not the place to deal with the discussion on perpetrators, victims and bystanders in the Holocaust, the analytical value of this categorization is usually also judged in terms of its ability to integrate a variety of perspectives. See Morina and Thijs, *Probing the Limits*.

31. See Ankersmit, *Narrative Logic*, chapter 3; and Kuukkanen, *Postnarrativist Philosophy of Historiography*, 30–50 and 68–97.

32. For critical analyses of the views of Ankersmit and White, and of the idea that metaphors are arguments, see Lorenz, 'Can Histories Be True?' and Mitrovic, *Materialist Philosophy of History*.

33. Rigney, 'History as Text', 193.

34. Carrard, 'History and Narrative'.

35. See Landwehr's defence of a fundamental, non-reducible pluralism in history in his *Die anwesende Abwesenheit der Vergangenheit*.

36. Barthes, 'Discourse of History'.

37. For a more detailed analysis of the issue of periodization, see Lorenz, 'The Times They Are a-Changin''.

38. Carrard, *Poetics of the New History*.

39. Rigney, 'History as Text'.

40. Smith, 'Seven Narratives'. See also: Bender, *A Nation Among Nations*; Novick, *That Noble Dream*; Breisach, *American Progressive History*.

41. Nietzsche, *Gay Science*, 341f.

42. Paul Ricoeur has argued that the interplay between temporal levels – between 'lived' time and chronological time – is a fundamental characteristic of narrative as such, and is exemplified in plotting. See Ricoeur, *Time and Narrative*.

43. Koselleck, 'Transformations of Experience', 76–83.

44. See Bourdieu, 'The Specificity of the Scientific Field'; Steinmetz, *Politics of Method*.

45. It is important to note that continuity is *not* the same as identity: historical identity is *not* the same as practical identity, although they are connected, as Emil Angehrn, Paul Ricoeur and Charles Taylor have argued on a philosophical level. See Angehrn, *Geschichte und Identität*; Laitinen, Taylor and Ricoeur on 'Self-Interpretations and Narrative Identity' in: Huttunen, Heikkinen and Syrjälä, *Narrative Research*.

46. For White's ambivalences in case, see Lorenz, 'It Takes Three to Tango'.

47. See Ricoeur, *Time and Narrative*; Carr, *Time, Narrative and History*.

48. Hayden White touched upon this issue in his 1992 article on 'the modernist event', but he did not connect his analysis in case with his earlier work on narrative. See White, 'Modernist Event'.

49. See Rigney, 'When the Monograph is no Longer the Medium'.

50. For the 'Verstehen/Understanding' tradition, see Lorenz, *Konstruktion der Vergangenheit*, chapters 6–8.

51. Claude Lanzmann's documentary *Shoah* (1985), Ken Burns's *The Civil War* (1990) and Steven Spielberg's film *Schindlers List* (1993) have undoubtedly exerted an influence on the rise of historical 'perpetrator research' (*Täterforschung*) concerning the Second World War – a field of historical research that is usually seen as originating in Christopher Browning's pathbreaking *Ordinary Men* (1992).

52. Diamond, *Guns, Germs and Steel*, even strongly suggests that from a 'scientific' viewpoint the narrative 'Verstehen' approach represents a dead end for historians.

Bibliography

Angehrn, Emil. *Geschichte und Identität*. Berlin: De Gruyter, 1985.
Ankersmit, Frank. *Narrative Logic: A Semantic Analysis of the Historians Language*. The Hague: Martinus Nijhoff Publishers, 1983.
Assmann, Aleida. 'Re-framing Memory: Between Individual and Collective Forms of Constructing the Past', in Karin Tilmans, Frank van Vree and Jay Winter (eds), *Performing the Past: Memory, History and Identity in Modern Europe* (Amsterdam: Amsterdam University Press, 2010), 35–50.
Barash, Jeffrey. *Collective Memory and the Historical Past*. Chicago: University of Chicago Press, 2016.
Barthes, Roland. 'The Discourse of History'. Translated by by Stephen Bann. *Comparative Criticism* 3 (1967), 7–20.
Bender, Thomas. *A Nation among Nations: America's Place in World History*. New York: Hill and Wang, 2006.
Berger, Stefan. 'Professional and Popular Historians: 1800 – 1900 – 2000', in Barbara Korte and Sylvia Paletschek (eds), *Popular History Now and Then: International Perspectives* (Bielefeld: transcript, 2012), 13–30.
Berger, Stefan, and Christoph Cornelissen (eds). *Marxist Historical Cultures and Social Movements during the Cold War: Case Studies from Germany, Italy and Other West European States*. Basingstoke: Palgrave Macmillan, 2019.
Bourdieu, Pierre. 'The Specificity of the Scientific Field', in Charles C. Lemert (ed.), *French Sociology: Rupture and Renewal since 1968* (New York: Columbia University Press, 1981), 257–93.
Breisach, Ernst. *American Progressive History: An Experiment in Modernization*. Chicago: University of Chicago Press, 1993.
Browning, Christopher R. *Ordinary Men: Reserve Police Batallion 101 and the Final Solution in Poland*. New York: Harper, 1998.
Carr, David. *Time, Narrative and History*. Bloomington: Indiana University Press, 1991.
Carrard, Philippe. 'Historiographic Discourse and Narratology: A Footnote to Fludernik's Work on Factual Narrarive', in Jan Alber and Greta Olson (eds), *How to Do Things with Narrative: Cognitive and Diachronic Perspectives* (Berlin: De Gruyter, 2018), 125–40.
———. 'History and Narrative: An Overview'. *Narrative Works* 5(1) (2015), 174–96.
———. *Poetics of the New History: French Historical Discourse from Braudel to Chartier*. Baltimore, MD: Johns Hopkins University Press, 1995.
Chatterjee, Kumkum. 'The King of Controversy: History and Nation-Making in Late Colonial India'. *American Historical Review* 110(5) (2005), 1454–75.

Chatterjee, Partha. *The Nation and its Fragments: Colonial and Postcolonial Histories*. Princeton, NJ: Princeton University Press, 1993.

Diamond, Jared. *Guns, Germs and Steel: The Fates of Human Societies*. New York: W.W. Norton, 1997.

Durrant, Stephen W. *The Cloudy Mirror: Tensions and Conflicts in the Writings of Sima Qian*. Albany: State University of New York Press, 1995.

Frank, Tibor, and Frank Hadler (eds). *Disputed Territories and Shared Pasts: Overlapping National Histories in Modern Europe*. Basingstoke: Palgrave Macmillan, 2011.

Ghobrial, John-Paul A. (ed.). 'Global History and Microhistory'. *Past and Present* 242, supplement 14. Oxford: Oxford University Press, 2019.

Gramley, Hedda. *Propheten des deutschen Nationalismus: Theologen, Historiker und Nationalökonomen (1848–1880)*. Frankfurt am Main: Campus, 2001.

Groot, Jerome de. *Consuming History: Historians and Heritage in Contemporary Popular Culture*. London: Routledge, 2008.

Hardtwig, Wolfgang, and Erhard Schütz (eds). *Geschichte für Leser: Populäre Geschichtsschreibung in Deutschland im 20. Jahrhundert*. Stuttgart: Franz Steiner, 2005.

Hardy, Grant (ed.). *World of Bronze and Bamboo: Sima Qian's Conquest of History*. New York: Columbia University Press, 1999.

Huttunen, Rauno, Hannu Heikkinen and Leena Syrjälä (eds). *Narrative Research: Voices of Teachers and Philosophers*. Jyväskylä: SoPhi Academic Press, 2002.

Iggers, Georg G., Q. Edward Wang and Supriya Mukherjee. *A Global History of Modern Historiography*. London: Routledge, 2008.

Iriye, Akira, and Pierre-Yves Saunier (eds). *The Palgrave Dictionary of Transnational History*. Basingstoke: Palgrave Macmillan, 2009.

Jokisipilä, Markku. 'The Internet and National Histories', in Stefan Berger, Chris Lorenz and Billie Melman (eds), *Popularizing National Pasts: 1800 to the Present* (London: Routledge, 2012), 308–30.

Kansteiner, Wulf. 'Alternate Worlds and Invented Communities: History and Historical Consciousness in the Age of Interactive Media', in Keith Jenkins, Sue Morgan and Alun Munslow (eds), *Manifestoes for History* (London: Routledge, 2007), 131–49.

Klein, Kerwin Lee. *From History to Theory*. Berkeley: University of California Press, 2011.

Koselleck, Reinhardt. 'Tranformations of Experience and Methodological Change: A Historical-Anthropological Essay', in Reinhardt Koselleck (ed.), *The Practice of Conceptual History: Timing History, Spacing Concepts* (Stanford, CA: Stanford University Press, 2002), 45–83.

Kuukkanen, Jouni-Matti. *Postnarrativist Philosophy of Historiography*. Basingstoke: Palgrave, 2015.

Kwong, Luke. 'The Rise of the Linear Perspective on History and Time in Late Qing China'. *Past and Present* 173 (2001), 157–90.

Landwehr, Achim. *Die anwesende Abwesenheit der Vergangenheit: Essay zur Geschichtstheorie*. Frankfurt a.M.: S. Fischer Verlag, 2016.

Lorenz, Chris. 'Can Histories Be True? Narrativism, Positivism and the "Metaphorical Turn"'. *History and Theory* 37 (1998), 309–29.

———. *Konstruktion der Vergangenheit: eine Einführung in die Geschichtstheorie*. Cologne: Böhlau, 1997.

———. 'It Takes Three to Tango: History between the "Historical" and the "Practical" Past'. *Storia della Storiografia/ Geschichte der Geschichtsschreibung* 65(1) (2014), 29–46.

———. '"The Times They Are a-Changin": On Time, Space and Periodization in History', in Mario Carretero, Stefan Berger and Maria Grever (eds), *Palgrave Handbook of Research in Historical Culture and Education* (Houndmills: Palgrave, 2017), 109–33.

———. 'Time and Space', in Stefan Berger and Bill Niven (eds), *The Cultural History of Memory*, vol. 6. (London & New York: Bloomsbury, 2020), 31–51.
Middell, Matthias, and Lluis Roura (eds). *Transnational Challenges to National History Writing*. Basingstoke: Palgrave Macmillan, 2013.
Mitrovic, Branko. *Materialist Philosophy of History: A Realist Antidote to Postmodernism*. New York: Rowman & Littlefield, 2020.
Morina, Christina, and Krijn Thijs (eds). *Probing the Limits of Categorization: The Bystander in Holocaust History*. New York: Berghahn Books, 2018.
Nietzsche, Friedrich. *The Gay Science*. New York: Vintage, 1974.
Novick, Peter. *That Noble Dream: The 'Objectivity Question' and the American Historical Profession*. Cambridge: Cambridge University Press, 1988.
Paul, Herman. *Hayden White: The Tropological Imagination*. London: Polity, 2011.
Porciani, Ilaria, and Jo Tollebeek (eds). *Setting the Standards: Institutions, Networks and Communities of National Historiography*. Basingstoke: Palgrave Macmillan, 2012.
Rappaport, Joanne. *The Politics of Memory: Native Historical Interpretation in the Columbian Andes*. Durham, NC: Duke University Press, 1998.
Ricoeur, Paul. *Time and Narrative*, vol. 3. Chicago: University of Chicago Press, 1988.
Rigney, Ann. 'History as Text: Narrative Theory and History', in Nancy Partner and Sarah Foot (eds), *The SAGE Handbook of Historical Theory* (London: SAGE Publications, 2013), 183–202.
———. 'When the Monograph Is No Longer the Medium: Historical Narrative in the Online Age'. *History and Theory*, Theme Issue 49 (December 2010), 100–117.
Sabrow, Martin, and Norbert Frei (eds). *Die Geburt des Zeitzeugen nach 1945*. Göttingen: Wallstein, 2012.
Sachsenmaier, Dominic. *Global Perspectives on Global History: Theories and Approaches in a Connected World*. Cambridge: Cambridge University Press, 2011.
Smith, Allan, 'Seven Narratives in North American History: Thinking the Nation in Canada, Quebec and the United States', in Stefan Berger (ed.), *Writing the Nation: A Global Perspective* (Basingstoke: Palgrave Macmillan, 2007), 30–62.
Steinmetz, George (ed.). *The Politics of Method in the Human Sciences: Positivism and Its Epistemological Others*. Durham, NC: Duke University Press 2005.
Tollebeek, Jo, and Ilaria Porciani. 'Institutions, Networks and Communities in a European Perspective', in Ilaria Porciani and Jo Tollebeek, *Setting the Standards: Institutions, Networks and Communities of National Historiography* (Basingstoke: Palgrave Macmillan, 2012), 3–28.
Wang, Q. Edward. 'The Rise of Modern Historical Consciousness: A Cross-cultural Comparison of Eighteenth-Century East Asia and Europe'. *Journal of Ecumenical Studies* 15(1) (2003), 74–95.
Wang, Q. Edward, and Georg G. Iggers (eds). *Marxist Historiographies: A Global Perspective*. London: Routledge, 2016.
White, Hayden. *The Content of the Form: Narrative Discourse and Historical Representation*. Baltimore, MD: Johns Hopkins University Press, 1987.
———. 'The Modernist Event', in Vivian Sobchack (ed.), *The Persistence of History: Cinema, Television, and the Modern Event* (New York: Routledge, 1996), 17–38.
Woolf, Daniel. *A Global History of History*. Cambridge: Cambridge University Press, 2011.

Index

THIS INDEX WAS COMPILED BY RAMESHA JAYANEHTHI

Abu-Lughod, Janet L., 100
aesthetic, aesthetics, 3, 7, 11, 52, 58, 73, 168, 197, 198, 199, 202
Africa, Africans, 100, 102–4, 107, 152, 154–55, 172–75, 179, 209, 218, 271, 320
  South, 231, 317
  West, 106, 320
Age of Revolution, the, 152
agency
  narrative, 16, 58, 64, 80n, 90, 105, 165, 170, 178–79, 181, 306, 313, 315, 320–22
  new, 8
agentive role, 312, 321
  non-agentive role, 312
Alexander, the Great, 120, 123, 125
amateurs, 328
American civil war, 249, 254n
anachronism, 29, 250, 251
'Analytical Philosophy of History'. *See* Danto, Arthur
anarchism, 19n
Anderson, Benedict, 181, 307
Ankersmit, Frank, 4, 5–7, 10, 34, 193, 335, 339
Annales (school), 3–4, 11, 19a, 159, 273, 336
artefacts, 5, 167
arts, 1, 137
Athenians, 10, 31–42, 44–55, 338
anthropology, 19n, 159, 160, 181
Argentina, 169–70

Armitage, David, 263
Asia, 107–10, 152, 155, 175, 218, 271, 274–75, 300
  Central Asia, 152, 154, 157
  East Asia, 151–52, 154–55, 157, 269–70, 275, 332
  South Asia, 152, 154, 157
  Southeast Asia, 152, 154
  West Asia, 117, 125, 134, 152
Assmann, Aleida, 330
Assyrians, 122
Auschwitz, 61, 63, 68–69, 72, 76–77, 191–92, 194, 196–97, 206n, 232
Aust, Stefan, 229, 236
Australia, 75, 154, 162n
autonomy, 1, 267, 297–98, 337
'The Autonomy of Historical Understanding. *See* Mink, Louis

'Bader und Herold: Beschreibung eines Kampfes' (1997). *See* Hauser, Dorothea
Baltic States, 52, 66
Barash, Jeffrey, 330–31
Barth, Karl, 91
Barthes, Roland, 2, 39, 210, 336
Baumann, Cordia, 236
Becker, Jillian, 231–32
Belarus, 52, 66, 69, 71, 72
Belgium, 66
Bender, Thomas, 264
Berger, Stefan, 1, 341
Berkhof, Hendrik, 90–93

This index was compiled by Ramesha Jayaneththi

Bible, the, 121
black emancipation, 337
Black History Month, 210, 212, 221n
Black Panther movement, 337
Black Power, 209, 214–20
Black Power movement, 217, 237n
Blanchot, Maurice, 42, 44, 45
Blight, David, 211
'Bloodlands' (2010). *See* Snyder, Timothy
Bolsheviks, 58, 66
border, 8, 109, 133, 142, 167, 173, 241–42, 269, 275, 290, 333
Bourdieu, Pierre, 334
bourgeoisie, 121, 123, 231
Brazil, 17, 282, 283–97, 299–301, 331, 334, 337
    Rio de Janeiro, 283
Breloer, Heinrich, 228
Brewitt-Taylor, Sam, 84
Britain, 16–17, 88, 103, 109, 119, 286, 307–9, 320–21, 327. *See also* England, the United Kingdom
British Empire, the, 312
'Bruchstücke, Aus einer Kindheit 1939–1948' (1996). *See* Dössekker, Benjamin
Burns, Ken, 341

Canada, 75
capitalism, 162n, 264, 301
    post-, 88
Carr, David, 340
Carrard, Philippe, 11, 329
Carretero, Mario, 164, 168, 179
Catholicism, Catholic, 90, 138, 269, 291
centralism, 274
century
    eighteenth, 1, 11, 110, 121, 149, 152, 157, 162, 177, 248, 252, 289, 293, 320, 328
    nineteenth, 1, 11, 14, 19n, 76, 85–6, 88, 90, 103, 120, 122, 131, 133, 149, 157–58, 160, 162, 167, 177, 244, 251–52, 264, 269, 285, 290–91, 301, 315, 319, 328, 331–33, 341
    seventeenth, 91, 174
    twentieth, 12, 19n, 19, 62, 90, 100, 117–19, 123–24, 144, 161, 165, 196, 242, 248, 265, 272, 276, 296, 328, 332–33
    twenty-first, 14, 19, 144, 174, 212, 252, 262, 276, 328, 331
Certeau, Michel de, 11
Che Guevara, Ernesto, 231
China, 16, 154, 160, 260–77, 331–32, 337
China National Knowledge Infrastructure (CNKI), 260
Christians, Christianity, 14, 88, 91, 132, 133–34, 136–37, 139– 143, 321, 151
chronicles, 286, 317, 319, 322
chronology, chronological, 2, 3, 71, 100–2, 107, 120, 124, 151, 162n, 170, 225, 230 290, 299, 338, 343n
'Church and People in an Industrial City' (1957). *See* Wickham, Edward Ralph
citizen, citizenship, 17, 30, 33, 65, 69–72, 103, 164, 182, 212, 251, 289, 298, 305–6, 334
civil rights, (narrative), 209, 212–13, 215–18
Civil Rights Movement. *See* movement
civil society, 84, 88, 92
Cold War, 61, 68, 152
colony, colonial, 14, 75, 103–4, 167, 174, 177–81, 283, 286, 289, 293–94, 320, 332, 334
communication, 8, 55–6, 77, 191–94, 204, 223–24, 243, 269, 298, 330, 340
    digital forms of, 15
    new, 193
    visual, 192
communicative act, 8, 340
communicative relationship, 9
communism, 13, 333
    anti-, 65
conformism, 91
constructivism, 250
Conrad, Sebastian, 263
contextualism, 3
Cornford, F.M., 29
Cox, Jeffrey, 84
Cromwell, Oliver, 309
Crusades, the, 134–42, 145n
Cuban civil war, 231
cultural, culture
    European, 117, 121–22
    historical, 191, 196, 203, 251, 338
    indigenous, 179

literacy, 30
memory, 59, 61, 72, 75–76, 226
Muslim, 137
non-European, 124
popular, 15, 197–98
racism, 300
studies, 2, 145n
Cyrus, the King, 11–12, 117–24

Danto, Arthur, 1, 7, 308, 335
'Das Geheimnis der Hebamme' (2006), 242–43
death-images, 44, 45, 55
democracy, 53, 153, 210, 297–99
 parliamentary, 322
Denmark, 119
Der Spiegel, magazine, 226–27
Derrida, Jacques, 174
despotism, 121, 124, 285, 293
determinism, 30, 34, 36, 44
 historical, 31–32, 45
 historiographical, 32
Deutschland im Herbst (1978), 228
Dewald, Carolyn, 33
Diamond, Jared, 341
diaspora, 283
Die Ahnen (1872), 251
Die Wanderhure, (2004), 243
disciplines, 1, 10, 160, 165, 328
discourse, 1, 30, 41–43, 52–53, 56–57, 60, 121–22, 210, 231, 233, 240, 254n, 263–65, 270, 272, 276–77, 285, 298, 300, 306, 322–23, 330, 339
 historical, 12
 historiographical, 40
'The Discourse of History'. *See* Barthes, Roland
discovery, 6, 8, 110, 162, 180, 226, 287, 290–91
discursive, 6, 80n, 85, 92, 166, 174, 210, 224, 305
 mode, 53, 79n
 constellation, 2
diversity, 77–78, 110, 133, 142–43, 266, 270, 275, 277, 286, 299, 308
division of labour, 103, 108
Dobbelaere, Karel, 84
Dössekker, Bruno, 10
Dowd Hall, Jacquelyn, 215–17
Dutch. *See* Netherlands

East Asia. *See* Asia
Ebert, Sabine, 246, 248, 250
Egypt, 120, 123–24
empire, 16, 35, 62, 112, 117, 119–25, 153–54, 158, 274, 283, 285–90, 293–96, 299, 309, 312, 333
empiricism, empirical, 5, 8, 17, 20n, 52, 55, 60, 62, 68–69, 77–78, 92, 90, 171, 241, 252n, 305, 334–35
emplot, emplotment, 3, 7, 11–12, 18n–19n, 132, 133, 138, 141, 143, 168, 191, 193, 203, 215–16, 259, 304, 322
England, 88, 90, 152, 157, 159, 315, 319
 Sheffield, 88–91 (*see also* Britain)
Enlightenment, 84, 121, 291
epistemology, epistemological, 2–4, 6–7, 9, 21n, 44, 52, 58–59, 76, 297, 334
Epple, Angelika, 100
equality, 333, 277, 333
 inequality, 107, 220
essentialism, 166
Estonia, 168
ethnic cleansing, 52, 66
ethnicity, 65, 70, 72, 143, 166, 170
 multi-ethnic, 58
ethnocentrism, 276
Eurasia, 157, 274
Eurocentrism, 16–17, 267
Europe, European
 countries, 15, 19n, 64, 72, 85, 108–9, 123, 133, 156–58, 300
 culture, 121–22
 Eastern Europe, 61, 66, 70, 75, 77
 memory, 63
 modern, 11, 125, 151
 narratives, 84–93, 100, 103–4, 107
 non-European, 124, 154
 supremacy, 118–19
 Western Europe, 61, 65, 133, 143
evolutionism, 272
exceptionality, 71, 77, 166

Facebook, 298, 328
fact, factual, 2–5, 8, 10, 16, 19, 35, 51, 58–63, 72, 74–77, 79n, 80n, 90, 179, 250–51, 266, 340
factuality pact, 11, 20, 21
fake-news, 2
Fascism, 234, 333

This index was compiled by Ramesha Jayaneththi

Feyerabend, Paul, 3–4
fiction, fictionalizing, 2–11, 19, 53, 55, 101, 165, 225, 229, 234, 236, 240, 242, 246–47, 250, 252n, 329, 335, 340–41
 non-, 53, 55, 80n
film, 2, 73, 78, 90, 168, 196–98, 225, 228–29, 234–37, 243, 246, 331, 340
Finland, 329
Follet, Ken, 244
Forceville, Charles, 194
Foucault, Michel, 43, 160
France, French, 3, 66, 89, 135–36, 142, 148–49, 159, 162n, 174, 220, 244, 253n, 286–87, 290, 293, 319–20
French Revolution, the, 5, 11, 19n, 152–53, 155–56, 301
Freytag, Gustav, 251
Friedländer, Saul, 11, 78, 80n
Fulda, Daniel, 85
Funeral Oration, 32, 36–37

Gambia, 102–3, 105, 113n
Geisteswissenschaften, 1
gender, 225, 233, 333
 history, 159
Genette, Gérard, 32
genocide, 15, 52, 61, 63, 66, 78
Georgia, Georgians, 58, 168, 335
Germania, 285
Germany, German, 11, 14, 18n, 61, 63–66, 68, 70–74, 76, 80n, 86–87, 117–25, 134, 136, 138, 145n, 159, 225–26, 229, 230, 232, 241, 243–44, 246–49, 251–252n, 285, 327, 332, 343n
 Berlin, 62, 91, 230, 232
 Berlin Wall, 149, 196, 234
 East, 234, 246
 German Empire, 122–23
global
 history, 13, 16, 17, 63, 99–107, 109–11, 231, 259–77, 331, 333
 historian, 99–102, 271, 338
 readership, 244
Global History Review (2008 onward), 275
Global History Research Center, China, 260–61
globalization, 2, 16, 99, 104–6, 110, 133, 143, 149, 153, 155–56, 160, 260–67, 275, 336–38

actors of, 338
history, 99
'soft globalization', 110
glocalization, 106, 332
Gorbahn, Katja, 124
Gorski, Philip, 92
Gossman, Lionel, 5, 19n, 20n
grammatical
 analysis, 17, 313, 322–23
 relationship, 304–5
Grazia, Victoria de, 100
Great Britain. *See* Britain, the United Kingdom
Greece, Greek, 29, 30, 32, 37–38, 40, 46, 47n, 69, 117–25, 149, 152, 154, 338
Greenwood, Emily, 40–41
Grethlein, Jonas, 33, 34
Gruzinski, Serge, 100
Gumbrecht, Hans Ulrich, 241–42, 248–49, 251–52
Guldi, Jo, 262

Halbwachs, Maurice, 330
Hardtwig, Wolfgang, 253n, 331
Hartog, François, 148–49, 151, 153, 196
Hashtags, 15, 191, 193, 195, 199, 200, 202–4
Hauff, Reinhard, 228
Hauser, Dorothea, 227
Hegel, Georg Friedrich Wilhelm, 122
Henry V, king, 319–20
Henschen, Jan, 224–25
Herder, Johann Gottfried, 121
heritage, 15, 75, 191, 196, 234, 266, 300, 329, 341
heriosm, heroic, 15, 19, 61, 120, 123, 125, 135, 168, 170–71, 178, 180–81, 210–17, 220, 231, 245, 247, 294, 300–1
Herodotus, 33, 123
Hinz, Felix, 124
historian
 global, 99–102, 271, 338
 Greek, 31
 non-professional, 332
 professional, 12, 20n, 327–30, 332, 341
 Roman, 30
historical
 actors, 30–34, 36, 40–41, 44–45, 170, 329

consciousness, 30, 45, 161n, 204–5, 212, 264, 266, 276, 330–32, 340
didactics, 1, 11, 13, 19n, 57
maps, 164–65, 167–75, 177–81
materialism, 271
profession, 3, 18, 327, 331, 342
reality, 6, 10, 35, 37, 85, 268, 271
historicism, 87, 88, 91, 93
historicity, 131–34, 141–42, 148–49, 240, 245, 250–52, 265, 272
historiography, 18, 19n, 29–30, 44–45, 77–78, 101, 112, 132, 142, 144, 149, 158–59, 162, 163n, 167, 169, 179, 215, 225, 240–41, 252, 262–65, 270–73, 275, 282, 296–1, 327, 331, 335–36, 342
   Greek, 29
   international, 262
   non-modernist, 158
   revisionist, 301
   western, 149, 179
history
   comic, 287
   comparative, 18, 60
   European, 11, 61–62
   didactics, 1, 13, 19n, 21n, 57
   digital, 7, 16
   fake, 10
   global, 13, 16–17, 63, 99–7, 110–11, 231, 259–92, 331–32
   local, 13, 90, 104–6, 110, 259, 262, 266, 270, 332–33
   medieval, 14, 131–34, 141–44
   national, 16, 64, 161n, 259, 261–65, 268–70, 276, 291, 305, 333, 337
   popular, 340–41
   professional, 53–54, 331–32
   regional, 331
   social, 3, 159, 262
   transnational, 261–63, 332
'History of Cotton'. *See* Riello, Giorgio
'History of Niumi'. *See* Wright, Donald R.
history of progress, 56, 337
Hitler, Adolf, 10, 61, 65–69, 75, 80n, 119, 231, 234, 341
Hitler's War (1977). *See* Irwing, David
Hoekendijk, Johan Christiaan, 87, 91
Holocaust, 5, 10, 11, 13, 51, 61–63, 67–70, 73–74, 76–79, 79n–80n, 192, 197–98, 200–1, 335

humanism, 151, 153
Hume, David, 291
Hungary, 66, 72
Hunt, Lynn, 262
Hunter, Virginia, 38
identity
   collective, 132–33
   concept of, 144n
   national, 15, 18, 166, 170, 180, 306, 312, 342
   regional, 167, 169, 308
   right, 297–99
   social, 165

ideologization, 17, 262, 282
   de-ideologization, 262
illocutionary assertive, 9
immersivity, 8
immigration, 305
imperialism, 14, 123, 152, 332, 334
indigenous people, 178–81, 299–300
India, 107–8, 119, 125, 143, 154, 157, 173, 274, 291, 299, 332
   Hindus, 157
Indian Ocean, 107–8, 143, 247
individuality, 93, 339
Indo-European languages family, 119
Indo-Germanic people, 119
Industrial Revolution, the, 152–53, 155, 157
industrialization, 89, 273
   deindustrialization, 18
Instagram, 15, 191–99, 202–5, 328–29
Iran, 117, 119, 121, 124, 154, 232
Ireland, 319
Irving, David, 10
Islam, Islamic, 14, 143, 151, 154–54, 219, 340
Israel, 123
   Jerusalem, 136, 138–40
Italy, Italian, 119, 291

Japan, Japanese, 14, 72, 147–51, 153–55, 157–61, 162n, 163n, 269, 275, 331–32, 334
   Meiji Restoration, 155, 158, 163n
Jackson, Michael J., 91, 93
Jameson, Fredric, 266
Jenkins, Keith, 4
Jews, 61, 63, 66–73, 76, 78, 80n, 136, 139, 143, 157

Jokisipilä, Markku, 329
Jonker, Gerdien, 122, 124
Johnson, Lyndon, 218–19
Joseph, Peniel E., 217
journalists, journalistic, 16, 132, 229–32, 236–37, 239, 328, 331, 340–41

Kaixuan, Zhang, 272
Keyao, Ma, 273
King, Martin Luther, 209, 211–12, 215–16, 218–19, 337
Koselleck, Reinhart, 32, 44–45, 282, 338
Korea, 160
   North Korea, 269
Kuukkanen, Matti-Jouni, 6–7, 11

Lacan, Jacques, 31
Landesgeschichte, 332
Lanzman, Claude, 341
Latin America, 171, 179, 271, 299, 332
Lavisse, Ernest, 328
Lehrbuch der Geschichte (1912). *See* Neubauer, Friedrich
Leibniz, Gottfried Wilhelm, 283
Leningrad, 68, 72
liberal, 178, 282
   democracies, 333
   multiculturalism, 306
   revolution, 293
   right, 298
   theology, 89, 91
Life in the United Kingdom (LUK) (2004), 305–21
linguists, 52–53, 192
linguistic turn, 12, 52, 54, 78, 79n, 339
linguists, 52–53, 192
Lisboa, Silva, 287, 289, 291, 293, 296, 300
literature, 1, 3, 73, 101, 121, 225, 236, 240–41, 245, 247, 250, 266
   comparative, 1, 241
Lorenz, Chris, 1, 341
Louvain Method, 200
Lübbe, Hermann, 241–42, 245–46

Magna Carta, 312, 319
Manovich, Lev, 8
maps, 14–15, 110, 164–65, 167–81, 334
Mara, Gerald M., 38
Marek, Tamm, 7, 9
Martin, David, 83

Marx, Karl, 328
   Marxist, 106, 150, 331
   post-Marxist, 331
Matusow, Allen J., 219
McCloskey, Deirdre, 5, 7
mechanicism, 3
media, 2, 6, 8, 15, 16, 63, 78, 84–85, 131, 168, 191–93, 195–99, 203, 209–10, 220, 223–33, 235–37, 242–43, 283, 298–99, 307, 328–31, 339–41
   digital, 242, 329
   new, 8, 192, 213, 237, 297, 329–31
   religious, 85
   traditional, 15, 242
   See also social media
medium, 2, 15, 55, 133, 191–93, 263, 269, 277, 329
   new, 33, 213
Megill, Allan, 5, 7–8, 30, 307
Meinhof, Ulrike, 226–27, 229, 232
Melé, Patrice, 149–50
memory, 1, 16, 37–38, 52, 60–64, 68–73, 75–78, 87, 165, 202–3, 209, 226, 252, 265–70, 277, 287, 298, 312, 330–31, 342n
   'memory boom', 330
   studies, 62–63, 78
memory politics, 52, 62–63, 68–70, 75
Merleau-Ponty, Maurice, 31
Mesopotamia, 124
Metahistory. *See* White, Hayden
metaphorical
   figuration, 77
   progression, 53, 56
   relationship, 57, 219
methods, quantitative, 20
Methodenstreit, 4
Mexico, Mexican, 171–72, 174, 176–80, 184n
   New Spain, 172–75, 177
   Revolution, 176–77
Middle Age, 14, 121, 132, 143, 242, 244, 247, 251, 294, 309, 334
microlevel, macrolevel, 57, 100, 104, 106, 109–12, 338
migration, 152, 157, 177, 269, 274, 285, 290, 311
Mill, John Stuart, 117
Mink, Louis, 1, 3
minorities, 75–76, 143, 169, 181, 328

modernism, 78, 158. *See also*
    postmodernism
modernity, 69, 77, 151–52, 160, 241–42,
    265
modernization, 14, 83, 93, 151, 153, 155,
    157–58, 162n, 261–62, 265, 268, 273,
    282, 331, 336
monarchy, 122, 174, 177–78, 283, 287,
    289, 294, 296
Mongol Empire, 274
monolinear temporal structure, 151, 153,
    160
movements
    '68 protest movement, 231–32
    Black Power Movement, 217
    Civil Rights Movement, 15, 209–20,
        221n, 237
    Dialectical theological movement, 90
    labour movement, 17, 18, 322
    'right identity' movement, 298
    social movement, 18, 226, 328
multiculturallism, 306, 308
multimodality, 192–95, 205
museums, 166–67, 191, 203, 242, 329
Muslims, 14, 132–34, 136–37, 139–40,
    142–43, 157, 167
myth, myths, 29, 61, 89, 91, 125, 133, 162,
    193, 210, 212, 233, 236–37, 269, 283,
    285, 290–91, 319

Narloch, Leandro, 299–301
narration, 12, 16, 17, 30, 51–67, 69, 74, 78,
    132, 134, 141–44, 168, 192, 199, 204,
    213–16, 220, 223, 230, 240–41, 248,
    301, 304, 309, 322
    journalistic, 230
narrative, narrativity
    antagonistic, 64
    fictional, 4, 8, 19n, 101, 335, 341
    historical, 2, 4–11, 15–19, 30, 56, 85,
        164–71, 177, 180–81, 193, 213, 215,
        267, 282, 286, 296–97, 299, 320,
        327–41
    metanarrative, 224, 294, 338
    national, 16–17, 122, 259, 264–66,
        269–70, 276–77, 282, 287
    popular, 340
    techniques, 29, 229, 240, 245, 338
    unprofessional, 329
narrativism, 5–7, 10, 191

narratology, 2, 8, 11, 19n, 31, 54, 85, 210,
    213
narrator, 2, 32– 34, 39, 55–56, 101, 105,
    246, 250, 307, 336, 339, 341
'Nation of Islam', 219
nation
    Chinese, 16 –17, 265, 267
    states, 70, 251
    unitary, 119
national
    consciousness, 264, 266
    culture, 266, 276
    historical narrative, 333–34
    identity, 15, 18, 166, 170, 180, 306, 312,
        342
    master narrative, 17, 164, 166, 170, 181
    question, 58
National Curriculum Standards, the
    (NCS) Japan, 148, 161, 162n
nationalism, 18, 152, 155, 181, 267, 276,
    341
nationalization, 273, 282, 334
'National Socialism', 52, 60–61, 63–71,
    73–74, 76–77, 86, 123, 231, 234, 339
Nazism. *See* 'National Socialism'
neo-Kantian philosophers, 18n
Netherlands, 66, 86, 90–91, 220, 327
    Leiden, 86–87
networks, 56, 89, 106, 109, 112, 117, 191
Neubauer, Friedrich, 118–21
New Zealand, 154
Nietzsche, Friedrich, 251, 338
North Korea, 269
Norway, 66, 260
novel, novelist, 2, 3, 6, 8, 11, 15–16, 19n,
    57, 118, 131–32, 143, 191, 225, 232,
    234, 240, 242–52, 327, 334, 341
    autobiographical, 232
    modernist, 11, 57
    realist, 2, 11, 19n

Oakeshott, Michael, 268
Obama, Barack, 209
Ober, Josiah, 40
objectivity, 2, 4, 7–10, 12, 159, 193, 268,
    334–37
Occident, 137–38, 140
Occidentalism, 160
Ogbar, Jeffery, 218
ontology, ontological, 2, 8

openness, 5–6, 262
Oppenheimer, Klaus, 86–90
oral histories, 329
oral tradition, oral traditionalist, 102, 332
organicism, 3
Orient, 122–23, 137–38, 140, 152, 154, 162, 333
Orientalism, 117–18, 120, 160, 333
Osterhammel, Jürgen, 99

Palestine, 134
Parks, Rosa, 213–14
Parliament, Parliamentary, 17, 84–85, 306, 309, 315, 317, 322
participation, 251, 263, 302n, 306
patriotism, 301, 313, 321
Peloponnesian War, 12, 34–35, 36, 39, 40, 44
Pericles, 35–39
performative dimension, 339
periodization, 87, 150, 152, 162n, 215–16, 218, 309, 336, 343n
Persia, Persians, 117–19, 123, 334
Philainen, Kalle, 8–10
philosophy, philosophical
    narattivism, 1–2, 4, 6, 8, 10, 204, 296, 335
    of history, 1, 7, 52, 57, 160, 300, 335, 340
    of science, 3–4
photography, photographs, 195, 198, 200–4
    amateur, 105, 196
plot, 2–4, 8, 19n, 90n, 99–100, 105, 109, 112, 147, 168–69, 171, 174, 177, 180, 191, 215–16, 229, 232, 248, 250, 293, 300–1, 304, 322, 334, 337–38
Poland, Polish, 52, 64–5, 69, 71–72, 80n, 202, 253n, 294
    Warsaw, 69, 71–72
politics, political
    discourses, 143, 210, 339
    systems, 64, 122, 268, 270
    theorists, 88
    transparency, 68
Portugal, 16–17, 169, 285–86, 290, 293–94, 296, 331
    Coimbra, 283, 285
    Lisbon, 283, 285–86

postcolonial
    history, 112, 322, 332
    theories, 117
postmodern, postmodernist, 14, 149, 159, 163n, 193, 196, 273
post-narrativism, 6
poststructuralism, 52
presentism, 149, 265
privatization, 193
'privileged gaze', 338
progress, progressive, 19n, 53–54, 80n, 90, 122, 150, 153, 158, 160, 179, 210, 216, 220, 251–52, 272, 285–86, 291, 293–94, 331, 337, 338
protagonists, 100–1, 109, 136–37, 141, 224, 226–29, 244–47, 296, 341
Protestantism, Protestants, 86, 90, 151, 151
Psychology, Psychologists, 165–66, 182

Qian, Chengdan, 267– 270
Qichao, Liang, 265, 272

racism, racist, 119–20, 212, 300, 337
RAF, the (Red Army Faction), 224–36
Ranciere, Jacques, 11
Raphael, Lutz, 84
realism, realist, realistic, 2, 5, 11, 16, 19n, 58, 90, 197, 240, 336
reality claim, 4, 334
reformation, 84, 151, 153, 155, 162n
religion, 13–14, 83–88, 91, 121, 143, 153, 157, 269, 274, 287, 290, 294, 301, 311–12, 317, 321, 337
religious fundamentalism, 333
Renaissance, 5, 84, 100, 149, 151, 153, 155, 162n
representation, representational, 2–4, 6–8, 14–15, 30–32, 37, 118–19, 123–24, 165–67, 170–72, 179, 181, 191–99, 203–4, 210, 225–27, 237n, 243, 259, 266, 296–97, 304, 320, 330, 336, 341
    representationalism, 6, 7
    non-representationalism, 6–7
'Rhetoric in Classical Historiography'. *See* Woodman, Anthony
Ricoeur, Paul, 5–6, 8, 340
Riello, Giorgio, 13, 102, 106–12
right-wing politics, 143, 333–34
    histories, 331
Rigney, Ann, 8, 11, 335, 337

Romania, 70
Romans, 285, 308
romanticism, romantic, 210–11, 217, 337
Rood, Tim, 29, 36
Roth, Paul, 2, 7
Rüsen, Jörn, 5, 8, 275, 306
Russia, Russian, 52, 61–62, 66, 71, 122, 168, 253n, 274
   Leningrad, 68, 72

Schleyer, Hanns Martin, 228
scholar, scholarship, 5–6, 11–13, 15, 19n, 30, 52, 54–55, 57, 67, 77, 89, 93, 148, 165, 170, 181, 213, 217, 250, 260, 261, 263, 267, 269, 283, 285–87, 330
schoolbooks, 131–34, 138, 141–44, 171, 328, 334. *See also* textbooks
Schraut, Sylvia, 225–26
Schumacher, Julia, 229
Schütz, Erhard, 331
science
   natural, 1, 140
   social, 1, 4, 16, 84, 165, 181–82, 340
Scotland, 315, 317, 319
Searle, John, 9
secularization, 13, 83–93, 333, 336–37
Sekai no Rekishi (1973), 150
self-determination, 110
semantism, semantic, 8, 54, 58, 60, 67, 80n, 199–200, 202–4, 313, 315
semiotics, semiotic, 2, 15, 192–94, 204, 210, 213, 220
sexuality, sexual, 247, 330
   violence, 73–74, 80n
Shakespeare, 252, 319
Shuppansha, Yamakawa, 150
Sicilian war, 32, 35, 40
Sima Qian, 332
Sitkoff, Harvard, 213–14, 218–19
slave trade – the abolition, 312, 320–21
Smith, Adam, 291
Smith, Carlota, 53–56, 77
Snyder, Timothy, 51, 55, 334
social
   class/group, 44, 168, 171, 181, 300
   Darwinist elements, 300
   identity, 165
social media, 15, 167, 191–93, 196, 204, 297–98

Socialism, 216, 231
sociological
   analysis, 90–91, 231
   theories, 83–84, 89
Soviet Union, Soviet, 52, 60–62, 64–77
space, 13, 41, 43, 69, 149–50, 166–67, 174, 177, 193, 213, 242, 262, 277, 296, 298, 333–34
   historical, 164, 170, 181, 196
   metaphorical, 53
   time and, 55, 148, 156, 159, 264, 270
Spain, 119, 167–70, 172
Spartans, 35
spatial structure, spatial, 13–14, 56, 77, 147–50, 153, 157, 160–61, 164, 166, 170, 178, 249, 262, 276, 317, 332–33, 338
Spielberg, Steven, 197, 341
Srebrenica, 6
Stahl, H.P., 35
Stalin, Joseph, 58–59, 61, 65–68, 71, 75, 335
Steinseifer, Martin, 225
Strauss, Leo, 37
Syria, 134, 140

Tamm, Marek, 7, 9, 10–11
technology, technological, 8, 53, 69, 76, 107, 152, 179, 300, 313, 321, 330
teleology, teleological, 15, 30, 33–34, 44, 142, 149, 168–69, 171, 177, 263, 276, 336, 338
temporality, temporal, 12, 14, 17, 30–34, 36, 39, 41–45, 53–54, 56, 58, 78, 147–48, 150–51, 153, 160–61, 165, 171, 174–75, 177, 180, 215, 217, 245, 262, 265, 276, 282, 294, 330, 334, 336, 338
   structure, 147–48, 150–51, 153, 160–61
   teleological, 33
temporalization, 17, 282
terminology, 3, 17, 56, 77, 90
territorialization, 150
territory, 14, 52, 65, 75, 117–18, 149, 149–50, 164–67, 169, 172, 174, 176–81, 275, 286, 290, 294
'terrorism', 15–16, 223–31, 233–36, 334, 336–37, 340–41
   left-wing, 223–25, 229–30

textbooks, 13–14, 18n, 117–25, 147–51, 155, 160, 164, 167, 168, 170–72, 174, 177–80, 328, 332–34. *See also* schoolbooks
textual features, 8–11, 15, 19n, 54–59, 78, 112, 199, 335
  non-textual, 193
text-immanent, 8, 55–56
theology, 87, 91, 328
theory
  historical, 1, 4, 6, 11, 17–18, 30, 52–53, 55, 57, 78, 93, 112, 150, 271, 273, 334, 341–42
  narrative, 2, 5, 8, 11–12, 29, 165, 191, 194, 335–36, 339–40
Theory of speech acts. *See* Searle, John
Third world, 152, 266, 272–73
Thucydides, 12, 29, 30–45, 338
'Thucydides Mythistoricus'. *See* Cornford, F.M.
tourism, tourist, 73, 191, 198, 200, 203
transnational histories, 332
transitivity, 17, 304, 312–13, 315–19, 322
Trump, Donald, 2
truth, 2, 4, 5, 7–12, 33, 37, 41, 52, 235, 237, 268, 294, 296, 300, 334–36
Turky, Turkish, 134–35, 274
Twitter, 191, 199, 204, 298, 328

Ukraine, 52, 59, 66, 68, 71
United Kingdom, the, 17, 88, 285, 304–5, 307–9, 320–22. *See also* Great Britain
United States, the, 15, 154–55, 158–59, 168, 174, 209, 211, 220, 267
universal history, 299
unity, 143, 153, 156, 277, 290, 304, 306
Urios-Aparisi, Eduardo, 208

Verschaffel, Bart, 5–6
video technology, 192–93, 195
  games, 191, 330
Vietnam, 218
  war, 216

visual
  narrative, 8, 15, 40, 73, 195, 203, 212, 220, 340
  pasts, 330
  representation, 15, 192, 197

Wales, 319–20
  Welsh rebellions, 317
Weber, Alfred, 87–88
Weber, Max, 162n
Weinhauer, Klaus, 225–26
welfare state, 309
Wenzlhuemer, Roland, 102
West Africa. *See* Africa
West Indies, 321
Western-centrism, 262, 267, 271
westernization, 155, 158, 160, 162n
White, Hayden, 1–8, 10–12, 19n, 30, 52, 85, 90, 93, 147, 215, 220, 233, 331, 334, 337, 339
Wickham, Edward Ralph, 88–91
Wikipedia, 191, 242, 328–29
Wilkomirski, Binjamin. *See* Dössekker, Bruno
Wilberforce, William, 321
Wilson, Bryan R., 83–84
Winton, Richard, 35
Woodman, Anthony, 29
working class, 89, 231
World War I, 72, 231, 321
World War II, 60, 73, 93, 123, 148, 231, 344n
world economy, 103
Wright, Donald R., 13, 102–7, 109–12, 113n
'Writing the Nation' project, 11, 161

Yu, Pei, 16, 260, 266–67, 269–71
Yasushi, Yamanouchi, 158
'The Years of Extermination'. *See* Friedländer, Saul

Zelenak, Eugen, 7
Zhaoguang, Ge, 269–70, 274–75

www.ingramcontent.com/pod-product-compliance
Lightning Source LLC
Chambersburg PA
CBHW071331080526
44587CB00017B/2797